Eva-Maria Bruchhaus,
Monika M. Sommer (Eds.)

Hot Spot Horn of Africa Revisited

Hot Spot Horn of Africa Revisited

Approaches to Make Sense of Conflict

edited by

Eva-Maria Bruchhaus
and
Monika M. Sommer

LIT

Cover Picture: Hacky Hagemeyer, Köln

Bibliographic information published by the Deutsche Nationalbibliothek
The Deutsche Nationalbibliothek lists this publication in the Deutsche
Nationalbibliografie; detailed bibliographic data are available in the Internet at
http://dnb.d-nb.de.

ISBN 978-3-03735-905-1 (Schweiz)
ISBN 978-3-8258-1314-7 (Deutschland)

A catalogue record for this book is available from the British Library

© LIT VERLAG Dr. W. Hopf Berlin 2008
Auslieferung/Verlagskontakt:
Fresnostr. 2   48159 Münster
Tel. +49 (0)251–62 03 20   Fax +49 (0)251–23 19 72
e-Mail: lit@lit-verlag.de   http://www.lit-verlag.de

Distributed in the UK by: Global Book Marketing, 99B Wallis Rd, London, E9 5LN
Phone: +44 (0) 20 8533 5800 – Fax: +44 (0) 1600 775 663
http://www.centralbooks.co.uk/acatalog/search.html

Distributed in North America by:

Transaction Publishers
New Brunswick (U.S.A.) and London (U.K.)

Transaction Publishers
Rutgers University
35 Berrue Circle
Piscataway, NJ 08854

Phone: +1 (732) 445 - 2280
Fax: + 1 (732) 445 - 3138
for orders (U. S. only):
toll free (888) 999 - 6778
e-mail:
orders@transactionspub.com

Contents

6   Contents

Preface

The Horn of Africa, both historically and currently, is one of the most conflict prone regions of Africa[1]. The great susceptibility of the region for handling conflict in a violent or warlike way is shown in recent years in the deeply rooted conflict in Somalia, in the Ethiopian military intervention in this conflict, in the unresolved conflict between Ethiopia and Eritrea (following the war from 1998 to 2000) as well as in the diverse local and regional violent conflicts within Ethiopia. The unfortunate tradition of a "culture of violence and of war," authoritarian and repressive regimes as well as a "culture of mutual intervention and interference" contribute to and produce susceptibility to violence in the region. The long-standing and protracted conflicts in the region had and have devastating humanitarian, political and development consequences for the affected people, communities and nations. The Ethiopian political scientist Negussay Ayele rightly criticises this historical legacy, "For centuries the peoples of the Horn have not been celebrating the discoveries of science, the production of material goods, the beauties of art, the edification of philosophy or the triumph of civic culture, but the prowess of individuals, the conquest of subject peoples, the destructive capacities of imported war machines and the subjugation of the vanquished, revelling over 'enemy' dead and dreaming of the 'annihilation of rivals'" [2]. Equally the Horn of Africa has been a geo-political "hot spot" and a zone of international conflicts, in which the impact of foreign powers was felt again and again, and in mostly destructive ways. The most recent example of global political influence on the conflict potential of the region is that of the "war on terror" led by the USA and other countries (including Germany). In view of the lasting violent conflicts in the Horn of Africa it is pertinent to ask, as Negussay Ayele does, "Do we not have enough wars and consequences of centuries of war in the horn? ... Are there no solutions or resolutions to conflicts and problems in the horn other than by 'deadly quarrels'? ...Do we look forward to another generation of warmongers or to a new generation of peacemakers in the Horn?"[3]

The collection of this reader "Hot Spot Horn of Africa Revisited – Approaches to Make Sense of Conflict" addresses these topics that are as much related to academic peace studies as they are to the politics of peace. The emphasis of the contributions is on the analysis of current violent conflicts in and between states and within societies, on all levels, local, regional and international; moreover possible approaches to peaceful conflict transformation and constructive conflict resolution processes are stressed. These central questions and problem formulations are dealt with in specific and differentiated aspects that are thematically grouped around the three large political and territorial units of Somalia/Somaliland, Eritrea and Ethiopia.

With regard to Somalia emphasis is on the current crisis related to the rise of the Sharia-Courts and their destruction by Ethiopian military intervention supported by the USA, with all the related negative humanitarian and political consequences. Annette Weber

---

[1] Volker Matthies, Kriege am Horn von Afrika. Historischer Befund und friedenswissenschaftliche Analyse, Berlin 2005.
[2] Negussay Ayele, A Brief Profile of Wars in the Horn of Africa, in North East African Studies, vol.6, nos 1-2, 1984, p. 6.
[3] Negussay Ayele, A Brief Profile of Wars in the Horn of Africa, p. 10.

systematically analyses the conflict patterns and discusses potentials and perspectives for state-building in Somalia (without Somaliland and Puntland). Medhane Tadesse presents a knowledgeable assessment of the Sharia Courts, in the formation of which "a locally owned, credible, legitimate and sustainable political process" is recognised. In the end he concludes "that the threat of radical Islam in Somalia is probably exaggerated but not totally unjustified." In addition to these differentiated analyses and assessments of events in Somalia, it is also of interest in a theoretical perspective whether the conflicts there can be subsumed under the heading of so-called "new wars." Above all, the crisis in Somalia must be situated in the deeper context of the debate on failed states and state building. In the framework of research on failed states Somalia counts as an extreme example of excessive violence. However the country would equally be an "experimental field", that is to say "laboratory," of new types of indigenous peace and state formation processes with elements of bottom-up peacemaking, state and institution building. This appears above all in the independent reconstruction of democratically legitimatised statehood in the *de facto* independent but internationally unrecognised Somaliland. Several contributions in this collection discuss the conditions for success and the multilayered dimensions of these impressive reconstruction processes. In this context the authors Mohammed Hassan Ibrahim and Ulf Terlinden emphasise that "especially when measured against the countless failures of state-building at the national level of the former Somali state, Somaliland is truly a success story."

With regard to Ethiopia, contributions focus on local and regional violent conflicts (namely in Gambella) as well as the character of the ruling regime and its discourse on terror. One of the most afflicted conflict regions of Ethiopia is the Gambella region bordering Sudan. Several contributions discuss various aspects of the actors, arenas, levels and objectives of these conflicts as well as possibilities to constructively work on conflict towards peaceful conflict transformation. The contributions on Ethiopia's political system emphasise that, especially since the election of May 2005, the country is moving towards a non-democratic, non-legitimised, repressive "ethnocratic state" (Merena Gudina) and suffers under "the curse of a long lasting warrior culture" (Rainer Tetzlaff). The contribution of Wolbert Smidt on "Terrorism and Discourse on Terror in Ethiopia" gives insights on the ways and means the Ethiopian regime instrumentalises the discourse on terrorism with the aim of discriminating its political opponents as well as attracting external resources, thereby also maintaining its own power.

Regarding Eritrea, the formation of a highly repressive and highly effective control and surveillance state, characterised by a high degree of social militarisation is outstanding, especially since the war with Ethiopia. In this context some contributions highlight the problems of Eritrean civil society, of gender based violence in particular in the Eritrean army and of migration of younger and well educated Eritreans abroad. Eritrea's foreign policy is discussed in respect of the changeable relations of this most recent state in the Horn of Africa to Sudan and to the USA in the context of the "War on Terror". The contribution of Nicole Hirt makes clear that parallel to the strategic revaluation of Ethiopia by the USA there was a growing estrangement of the USA with Eritrea.

The authors of the volume, who originate above all from Germany but also from the region and who write from the point of view of various scientific disciplines, contribute an informative, interesting and differentiated picture of the many forms of the current conflictual events in the horn of Africa. This picture is ambivalent indeed. Manifold local and regional forms of violence in and between states and within societies, repression and exclusion continue to be found in the region. Still, quite a few contributions also show that despite these unpleasant findings there are a number of indigenous approaches to constructive conflict resolution, demands for peace and state building which are worthwhile to support. The European Union, in particular, should take the moral and political responsibility to make the region a "test case" of its new European Strategy for Africa, formulated in its concept of a "Regional Partnership for Peace, Security and Development in the Horn of Africa" from October 2006. Thereby, in my opinion, the EU should distance itself far more strongly than before from the problematic US-American policy of counter-terrorism in order to preserve and to strengthen the credibility and thus the acceptance of its peace and development concerns in the region.

This is an excellent volume, which not only enriches the scientific discourse in the horn of Africa but is also equally well suited, through its sound objectivity, to dispel with empirical grounding and analytical focus the widespread distortions and simplifications of external political conceptions of events in the region. This is especially true of the 'War on Terror', which is clearly unhelpful for the politics of peace in the Horn of Africa. Here I must agree with Nicole Hirt when she summarises: "Since September 11, 2001, the American-led 'war on terror' has not significantly contributed toward the stabilisation of the affected regions outside the United States and has been far from successful in extinguishing radical opinions and strategies. It the Horn of Africa, it led to the instrumentalisation of prevailing power struggles in the name of anti-terrorism in order to extract resources from the U.S. budget, thus contributing further to the destabilisation of an already more than unstable region."

I wish a wide distribution for this exceedingly well-conceived volume, for it can make an important contribution to deepening the knowledge of the complex conflict arenas in the Horn of Africa.

Prof. Dr. Volker Matthies   Hamburg, March 2008

Introduction by the Editors

"Horn of Arica – Revisited": The title refers to an earlier collection of studies that was edited by Eva-Maria Bruchhaus in 2003. The reader 'Hot Spot Horn of Africa: Between Integration and Disintegration', which comprised contributions of young (mainly) German scholars working and researching in Ethiopia and Eritrea, was well perceived, and the publisher thought about a new and reviewed edition. It was then that Monika M. Sommer joined the team. The concept of this new publication took shape in discussions among the present editors.

The publication we present here broadens its scope in two ways. First of all in geographic terms: the first thing to adjust was to include Somalia as a core-area of interest. The previous reader eventually contained contributions on Ethiopia and Eritrea only – countries that were broadly accessible since 1991 for researchers. Thus, the book we present here still focuses on the 'smaller' Horn of Africa, paying tribute to Somalia, Eritrea and Ethiopia. Secondly, as we circulated the call for papers in Germany and in the region of the Horn, this publication does not only reflect the work and studies of young German scholars, but includes analyses of authors from the region itself.

In terms of subject areas and content, the book it more focused than the previous one as its attention is centered on conflict and peace in the region. This emphasis has taken shape in the working process. Simultaneously though, it reflects contemporary academic focus as much as a basic calamity of the area. All countries covered are caught in a maze of multilayered and protracted conflicts. Conflicts develop and can be understood as part of the developments that occur in a geopolitically sensitive region, as internal clashes of interest within sovereign states that look back to a belligerent past, as necessary struggles in emerging states, or – in contrast – as an effect of imploding or vanishing state structures as in Somalia. All these conflicts take many-sided forms: internal clashes, rebellions, interstate wars and regional interferences and – not to forget – foreign interventions. In any case the result is increasing instability, and in the worst case imploding or vanishing state structures. But we discover also elaborate traditional practices of conflict resolution on various levels, which often have been the subject of research, but unfortunately have rarely inspired international peace making initiatives. Astonishingly enough, they have been used successfully – without outside assistance – to lay the foundations of the unrecognised state of Somaliland. NGOs as modern actors of civil society are often interacting with these traditional institutions, in a long and often cumbersome process which seems to be appropriate to give peace a chance.

The studies collected here are from a range of disciplines, especially anthropology and political science. The majority of the authors are younger scholars, who embarked on their research in the years after the cold war. Some researches though reflect a long experience in the region. The reader "Hot Spot Horn of Africa Revisited" combines field studies that introduce first-hand knowledge of the area with more general reflections on the geopolitical environment. The latter macro-analytical contributions congenially complement the former ones that focus on the micro-level of conflicts. Both approaches however demonstrate the need for exchange and cooperation between scholars from different disciplines and origins, and some of the contributions clearly show the benefit of such joint efforts. (and that peace will be only achieved in a longer process of interaction that involves all actors from all levels of society).

At this stage we do not want to comment on every single contribution to this reader. Volker Matthies, in his preface, has already highlighted major themes, which seems to be sufficient in guiding the reader through this book. Moreover, it discloses the leitmotif of all articles, which is the commitment to analyse conflict in the search for strategies towards peace. We hope that this attitude will reveal itself to the readers of this book. We would be happy if the book inspired not only further research in the complex area of conflict studies, but also gave some hints for practitioners in the field to better understanding of both local calamities and potentials. When it comes to the question of overcoming conflict, one thing remains clear after reading this book: nothing will change unless the different actors are ready to contribute their part and to use their own assets. The experience of Somaliland that are reflected in two contributions in this volume may serve as an example for the potentials and limitations of purely local initiatives.

We are most grateful to Volker Matthies who wrote a preface for this book that goes far beyond the duties embodied in this task. His knowledgeable reflections gave us reassurance and a sense of accomplishment. Editorial help in fashioning the different chapters into a coherent book was given by Peter Mäkler and native speaker support by Bonnie Keller. Hacky Hagemeyer contributed the picture that not only adorns the front page, but adds a visual contribution to the theme 'approaches to make sense of conflict'. The maps in the beginning of each chapter are courtesy of the Department of Geography, Addis Ababa University.

Last but not least we would like to thank our authors who contributed to this outcome with their work and their shared dedication for the furthering of peace in the countries in the Horn of Africa.

Eva-Maria Bruchhaus
Monika M Sommer   Cologne/Addis Ababa, March 2008

Chapter 1: Somalia

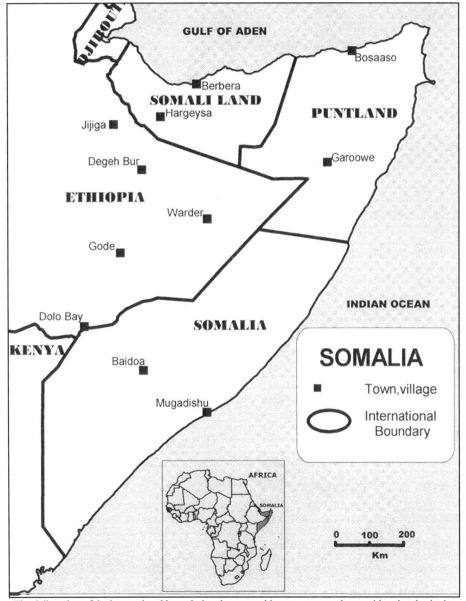

The delineation of the international boundaries shown on this map must not be considered authoritative

State Building in Somalia – Challenges in a Zone of Crisis

Annette Weber

Introduction

Going through any checklist[1] for successful state building, be it normative, realist, institutionalist or constructivist - Somalia[2] appears as the biggest failure. Somalia as a state is neither fragile nor weak - it simply is nonexistent.

There are, however rudimentary state symbolisms such as the seat Somalia keeps in the UN General Assembly. Somalia is a patchwork of warlord oligopolies with clusters of violence spread along clan based fiefdoms. No central authority is in place or functioning since the fall of the last acknowledged President Siad Barre, who fled the country in 1991.

The Ethiopian intervention in Somalia in December 2006 put the country back to horrific violence and turmoil. However, the structural situation: warlord oligopolies run by neopatrimonial[3] leaders distributing goods only through clan-based elites, has not changed entirely.

What does that mean for the possibility to rebuild Somalia as a functioning state? Is the regional setting in favour of a strong and independent Somalia or is the fragile precariousness of the entity that composes Somalia serving a larger purpose in the mutual interventionist[4] agenda on the Horn of Africa?

Somalia now

The conflict in Somalia is multileveled. The domestic causes of conflict lie in the disastrous fragmentation of warlord fiefdoms, the absence of a state, the mushrooming of criminal networks, and repression of the population by warlords, factions of the Islamic Courts movement, and the Transitional Federal Government[5] (TFG). None of the parties, including neither the TFG nor the Union of Islamic Courts (UIC), have presented a political program for creating a functioning government. Beyond Somalia, a main factor in the war is the power

---

[1] Ulrich Schneckener, *International Statebuilding Dilemmas, Strategies and Challenges for German Foreign Policy.* (Berlin: ,[2007]).

[2] For this article Somalia specifies the territory without Somaliland and Puntland.

[3] Further reading on neopatrimonialism see Gero Erdmann and Ulf Engel, *Neopatrimonialism Revisited : Beyond a Catch-all Concept ; GIGA Research Program Legitimacy and Efficiency of Political Systems,* Vol. 16 (Hamburg: Giga, 2006).and Gero Erdmann. *Apokalyptischer Trias: Staatsversagen, Staatsverfall und Staatszerfall – strukturelle Probleme der Demokratie in Afrika.* In: Bendel, Petra / Croissant, Aurel / Rüb, Friedbert (Hrsg.), *Demokratie und Staatlichkeit, Systemwechsel zwischen Staatlichkeit und Staatskollaps,* Opladen: Leske+Budrich 2003, S. 267-292

[4] Lionel Cliffe, "Regional Dimensions of Conflict in the Horn of Africa," *Third World Quarterly* vol. 20, no. No. 1 (1999), 89-89-111.

[5] Also there is some renaming from TFG to TFI Transitional Federal Institutions; I stick to the TFG abbreviation for reasons of continuity. Both however are distinct from the abbreviation TNG, Transitional National Government, referring to the previous attempt to set up a government in Somalia.

struggle between Ethiopia and Eritrea. The absence of a legitimate government in Somalia[6] facilitates this proxy war. Regional interests – economic, political and ideological – are played out in Somalia, relatively unhindered by a functional Somali state. The civil war in Somalia thus increases the existant polarization in the Horn of Africa. This has regional implications far beyond Somalia. The states that identify as Christian majority states in the region, such as Uganda, Kenya, Ethiopia, and Southern Sudan's autonomous government, stand on the side of the TFG and receive support and military backing from the US. In turn, Sudan and Eritrea, along with Egypt and other Muslim majority states in the region, support the UIC.

Although never part of the Ethiopian Empire next door, politics in Somalia always had to take the neighbour into account. If Somalia tried to fight its neighbour it always failed. The most traumatizing example was Siad Barres' defeat in 1977, known as the Ogaden Wars[7]. Almost successful in the beginning of the campaign, the Somali Army and their Ogaden guerrilla allies controlled more than half of the Ogaden territory, inhabited by a Somali origin population, when with the help of the Soviet Union the new leader in Ethiopia, Mengistu Haile Mariam reclaimed the Ogaden by a full victory and defeat for Barre. Nothing in Somalia can be done against the interest of Ethiopia, the leading candidate for hegemonic power in the Horn of Africa. Although the Somali country was in decay for almost two decades, Ethiopia did not show any sign of disturbance by the warlord system in neighbouring Somalia until the UIC started to unite.

Almost at the same time as the build-up of the current transitional government in 2004[8] did some *sharia* courts group themselves under the name of Union of Islamic Courts (UIC)[9]. Mainly supported and financed by the business community in Somalia, tired of loosing profits to the many roadblocks manned by clan militias, the courts started to become a functioning and operational force in 2005. Operating mainly in and out of Mogadishu some of the courts kept their initial function as local *sharia* courts judging in domestic quarrels without a greater political agenda. Some courts however were led by political figures such as Sheikh Aweyes, a man who was in charge of Al Ittihad al Islamiya (AIAI, or Islamic Union) and who had a political, irredentist as well as Islamist agenda for Somalia. Another radical leader of the UIC, the head of the militia, (Shabab), Aden Ayro is an Afghanistan veteran

---

[6] Similar to TFG there is a variety of naming the Union of the Islamic Courts. Some use Islamic Courts Union, others United Islamic Courts. I stick to the early use of the UIC by International Crisis Group in their report: Somalia's Islamists. Africa Report No. 100. 12 December 2005. Nairobi.

[7] On the Ogaden war and its consequences for the relationship between Somalia and Ethiopia see. I. M. Lewis, *A Modern History of the Somali.*, ed. Eastern African Studies (Oxford: James Currey, 2002), 231-247.

[8] There were other attempts before. The last unsuccessful Transitional Government established in 2000 after the Arta conference failed. Some of the members of the TNG (Transitional National Government) are now part of the loose coalition of opposition groups who gathered in Asmara, Eritrea in September 2007. Khartoum took the lead and hosted two peace conferences in 2006 for the TFG and the UIC to negotiate. Although a five step plan was agreed upon, there was neither implementation nor follow up. Yemen (with the Sanaa group) as well as Djibouti (as host of IGAD) played similar roles in negotiation attempts in the region.

[9] International Crisis Group, *Somalia's Islamists* (Nairobi, Bruxelles: ,[2005]).; Roland Marchal, "Islamic Political Dynamics in the Somali Civil War." In *Islamism and its Enemies in the Horn of Africa*, ed. Alexander De Waal (London: Hurst and Company, 2004), 114-146. Kenneth J. Menkhaus, "Somalia and Somaliland: Terrorism, Political Islam, and State Collapse" In *Battling Terrorism in the Horn of Africa*, ed. Robert Rotberg (Baltimore; Washington: Brookings Institution Press, 2005), 23. Andre Le Sage, *African Counterterrorism Cooperation : Assessing Regional and Subregional Initiatives*, 1st ed. (Washington, D.C.: Potomac Books : National Defence University Press, 2007), http://www.loc.gov/catdir/toc/ecip0720/2007022316.html.

with an unmistakable *jihadist* agenda. Although the Shabab became congruent with the *jihadist* military formation of the UIC, the Shabab itself has a longer history, reaching back to the 1980s as the militia of AIAI with Sheikh Aweyes as the military leader.

The current political fragmentation amongst the courts – as it became evident in the Asmara conference in September 2007[10] - is indicative for the current situation in Somalia, and specifically in Mogadishu, where most of the fighting is going on. The Alliance for the Re-Liberation of Somalia (ARLS) headed by former TFG parliamentary speaker Sharif Hassan Sheikh Adan was blamed by Aden Hashi Ayro to push the Shabab even further into jihad, because of the Alliance opportunistic position.

The transitional government seems to be under tighter leadership than the UIC; however there is not less conflict. Many influential politicians left the government since December 2006. The replacement of Prime Minister Mohamed Gedi by Nur Hassan Hussein might be a positive turn. As his predecessor Gedi, Nur Hassan Hussein (Nur Adde) is from a Hawiye subclan. He served as a police trainer as well as a deputy Supreme Court judge and since 1991 he was the head of the Red Crescent International, and therefore a Prime Minister with an understanding of the consequences of the war. In his public announcements the Prime Minister refers to Somalis as citizens, 'whether they support or oppose the government'. This might be a first serious step into reconciliation attempts with an inclusive approach.

State of conflict

Since the fall of Barre, Somalia went militarily from warlord clashes through almost regular warfare between the UIC and the Alliance for Peace and Restoration, and Counter Terrorism (APRCT), and UIC, and TFG troops to a fully fledged insurgency pitting "Shabab" and clan militias against Ethiopian troops, foreign jihadis against TFG and AU forces.

On the side of the TFG, the Ethiopian army remains the strongest fighting force. The TFG army is not yet fully trained nor sufficiently recruited and the trained police force is not strong enough for the duties ahead[11]. From the roughly 18.000 Ethiopian troops during the invasion Ethiopia claims only a few thousand remaining. The exact number of Ethiopian troops is not available[12] because Ethiopian troops were rotated rather than removed from Somalia. What is however apparent is the understaffed Mission by the African Union. Instead of the requested 8.000 troops called for by the AU in February 2007 to be sent to Somalia in a stabilizing mission to support the instalment of the TFG, only 1.600 Ugandan troops really

---

[10] Somalia's opposition alliance elects Islamist as chief. 14 September 2007. Garowe Online.
http://www.garoweonline.com/artman2/publish/Somalia_27/Somalia_s_opposition_alliance_elects_Islamist_as_chief.shtml (Access 2 December 2007).
[11] Training for the Somali police is carried out by the Inter-Governmental Authority on Development (IGAD) Capacity Building Program against Terrorism (ICPAT).
http://www.igad.org/index.php?option=com_content&task=view&id=95&Itemid=62 (access 8 January 2008)
The Police academy in Armo (Puntland) opened on 20 December 2005 and trained more than 3000 police officers. However no current precise actual figures are available.
[12] Ethiopia's foreign minister Seyoum Mesfin in an interview with the BBC on Nov 13th, 2007 stated that the number of troops is rather in the thousands than in the tens of thousands.
http://www.mfa.gov.et/Press_Section/BBCinterviewwithFMSeyoumMesfin.htm (access 4 January 2008)

arrived[13]. According to high-ranking UPDF sources the mission target is to survive rather than to stabilize the country. The AU agreed upon the mission early in 2007 without a full guarantee by the Security Council to replace the mission after six month by an UN mission.

When the Ethiopian forces walked into Somalia in December 2006 the fierce military resistance facing the intervention troops was not expected. Court leaders either merged back into their clan functions or left the country and found exile in Yemen and Eritrea[14]. The era of the rule of the Islamic Courts seemed to be over quickly, since the invaders were hardly met with resistance and took not even a week to get to Mogadishu.

The rule of the courts was perceived ambiguously amongst the Somali society. The courts, for the first time in seventeen years, united and managed to get rid of road blocks and clan-based warlord rule[15]. They gained control over the port in Mogadishu and opened it for business. They arranged road cleaning and garbage collection in Mogadishu and people were able again to walk the streets without the fear of being attacked, shot or robbed. The downside of their rule was their strict moral code and their imposition of Islamic behaviour.[16] Some court leaders alienated the Somali population by enforcing Islamic modes of behavior, e.g. by prohibiting Bollywood movies, public screenings of the World Cup matches, chewing qat and wearing dresses rather than hijabs.[17]

Conflict actors

Historically, Islam did also play a role in the political field. Dervish movements and Sufi brotherhoods were sources of resistance against various colonial regimes. Since the collapse of the state, there has been a massive influx of Wahabi charities[18]. Radical elements in the Islamic Courts have found an interested audience in the otherwise neglected and desperate population. Now there are more and more Quranic recitation schools (madrassas) and public health services provided by religious entities. Yet the warlord system has been based on

---

[13] Although troops pledged by Nigeria and Burundi are expected in due cause. The mission was mandated on 21 February 2007. Further information on the AU Mission in Somalia can be found: AMISOM.
http://www.operationspaix.net/-AMISOM (access 5 January 2008)

[14] On the support for UIC and Shabab by Eritrea see. Sunguta West. *Somalia's ICU and it's roots in al-Ittihad al-Islami*. In: Terrorism Monitor. Vol. 4, Issue 15. July 27, 2006. Ken Menkhaus. In: There and back again in Somalia. MERIP (Middle East Report) 11 February 2007. http://www.merip.org/mero/mero021107.html (access 28 December 2007) Kenneth J. Menkhaus, "The Crisis in Somalia: Tragedy in Five Acts," *African Affairs* 106, no. 204 (2007), 357, http://afraf.oxfordjournals.org/. *UN Monitoring Group on Somalia*. Committee on arms embargo by the SC established pursuant to SC resolution 751 (1992) S/2007/436 und S/2007/154. Both reports list a number of Eritrean supply lines to Shabab and other violations of the arms embargo on Somalia. *Report of the Monitoring Group on Somalia Pursuant to Security Council Resolution 1724 (2006)* United Nations, [2007]), http://www.un.org/Docs/journal/asp/ws.asp?m=S/2007/436 (accessed 30.07.2007).

[15] Further readings on the Islamists in Somalia see ICG 2005 ibid. Roland Marchal. A new front against Terrorism. SSRC, 5.February 2007. and Marchal, *Islamic Political Dynamics in the Somali Civil War.*, 114-146

[16] Somalia: Peace at the Cost of Freedom. East African. December 18, 2006.
http://www.nationmedia.com/eastafrican/18122006/News/News18120610.htm (Access 11 January 2008)

[17] Criticisms against the courts see. Strategic Initiative for Women in the Horn of Africa.
http://www.sihanet.org/Siha_publicationsTM.html

[18] Interviews with western diplomats in Nairobi and Addis Ababa in May 2007. See further: The Rise of the Islamic Charities in Somalia: An Assessment of Impact and Agendas. By Andre Le Sage with Ken Menkhaus. Paper presented at the 45th Annual International Studies Association Convention Montreal 17 20 March 2004.

oligopolies of violence that disregard religion, and Islamist movements have never managed to overrule the tight grasp of the warlords over the past 17 years.

One earlier group with an Islamist agenda, the Al Ittihad al Islamiya (AIAI, or Islamic Union), founded in the mid-1980s, became a strong force with links to Sudan's chief Islamist, Hassan al Turabi, and to the Arab World in general. AIAI was officially defeated in a battle with forces under the command of the current president, Abdullahi Yussuf, in the mid-1990s. But one of the strongmen of AIAI, Sheikh Hassan Dahir Aweys, became a rising star with the Islamic Courts as speaker and leader of its radical wing. Both the organization and its leader Sheikh Aweys appear on the terrorist list of the US State Department.

There is evidence of Al Qaeda members operating in Somalia. Attacks on the US embassies in Nairobi and Dar es Salaam in 1998, and on a hotel and airline frequented by Israeli visitors in Mombasa in 2002, were undertaken after preparation in Somalia. However, there is no evidence of continuously functional Al Qaeda cells and networks. Due to the tightly knit clan network, clandestine operations are almost impossible. Lately, using Ethiopia's occupation as a mobilizing factor, various Al Qaeda members have used websites to rally jihadis to come and fight in Somalia.[19] As the polarization and the abuse of religion by all actors involved in Somalia gains momentum, there is a high possibility that Al Qaeda will take advantage of the *jihadist* agenda of the Shabab, the UIC's zealous armed wing fighting Ethiopian forces.

After the courts fought and won over the CIA sponsored APRCT in the first half of 2006, they settled in Mogadishu without contact to the Baidoa based TFG. The aim for the UIC was to take control over the whole of Somalia and to oust the TFG. The possibility of a UIC rule in Somalia was the main threat to the existence of the TFG; minor hick ups however could be located in the internal quarrel amongst TFG members. As it became apparent after the intervention, some TFG members were sympathetic to the courts and changed sides, such as the former minister of the interior and son of the most well known warlord in Somalia, Hussein Aidid. Neither the TFG nor the international community felt it important to establish sustainable channels of communication to the courts while still in power and while they were still operating under one umbrella. This causes serious problems now, since the courts are fragmented and only a few contacts are responding.

Regional dimension

How does the crisis in Somalia view in its regional dimension? The intervention by Ethiopian troops and subsequent outbreak of violent conflict in Somalia split the region. There are the more western oriented neighbours who are close to the AU and international position that the TFG is the legitimate transitional government of Somalia and should therefore be supported and stabilized in order to be in a position to take over state affairs and to rebuild the state structures in Somalia. Since the TFG originated in various IGAD (Intergovernmental Agency on Development) initiatives, the IGAD countries in the region felt predominantly obliged to accompany the TFG until its functioning as a government in Somalia. In some of these

---

[19] Zawahiri calls for attacks on Ethiopian forces in Somalia.
www.globalsecurity.org/security/profiles/zawahiri_calls_for_attacks_on_ethiopian_forces_in_somalia.htm

countries the threat of an Islamist state in their region might also play an important role why they support the TFG and were not welcoming the Courts rule.

Then there is Sudan, Eritrea and apparently Egypt who supported the Courts.[20] For Sudan, the support however ideologically understandable is nevertheless surprising. It was Sudan hosting the IGAD talks on Somali reconciliation in Khartoum. They were supporting negotiations between the TFG and the courts. However under the regional motto of mutual interventions and neighbourly disturbances the support for the Courts might well be a result of a power competition between Sudan and Ethiopia. Ideologically Sudan would be in favour of an Islamic state in the Horn of Africa. However due to Sudan's aspired role as a number one ally in the war on terror, their involvement in Islamist and *jihadist* activities in the region does not aspire great publicity. What might be frightening to Premier Meles Zenawi in Ethiopia, to be cornered by two Islamic states might be welcomed by President Bashir, who already feels surrounded by Christian majority states in the Horn. The alliance of the precarious Islamic states might well be a motivation for Sudan and even Egypt to support the UIC. Ethiopia itself might become predominantly Muslim[21] but still keeps the national myth as the cradle of Christianity and the Christian Empire in Africa. Even more than for Sudan the alliance with the US administration in the war against terror campaign is a driving force for the regional manoeuvres of the Ethiopian government. One reason for Eritrea to continue its support for all Ethiopian opposition forces, as well as forces fighting against Ethiopia from outside, including the Shabab and courts militias, is the proxy war motive against Ethiopia. Eritrea itself fought against the Sudanese backed "Eritrean Jihad" movement in the 1990s and does not appear ideologically close to the global jihad movement. Even more so because the liberation movement Eritrean Peoples Liberation front EPLF as well as its political follow up PFDJ (Peoples Front for Democracy and Justice) were informed by a Maoist revolutionary ideology[22] of liberation struggle with very few similarities to the *jihadist* ideology.

However, through the support for the UICs militias Eritrea is enabled to engage in a proxy frontline with Ethiopian troops. A war that does not risk loosing neither their own territory nor causing a large number of Eritrean casualties, might be an important factor in domestic politics, given the high number of casualties of 70.000 in the last Eritrean-Ethiopian border war of 1998-2000 and the hundreds of thousands in the Eritrean war of independence. The fight of the Shabab and other militias against the Ethiopian army is almost ideal for Eritrea. Possibly Eritrea hopes to gain new alliances and support from the Arab League as well as from some of the individual countries supplying the UICs. Since Eritrea is sidelined and almost isolated internationally, even more so since the US considers to put Eritrea on the list of state sponsors of terrorists, it might want to orient itself towards more non-western regions. The Arab world might be a viable option for Eritrea.

---

[20] *Report of the Monitoring Group on Somalia Pursuant to Security Council Resolution 1724 (2006)*
[21] Approximately 45% of Ethiopians are Muslims. See U.S. Department of State. International Religious Freedom Report 2004. http://www.state.gov/g/drl/rls/irf/2004/35355.htm (Access 11 January 2008)
[22] Dan Connell, *Against all Odds: A Chronicle of the Eritrean Revolution: With a New Foreword on the Postwar Transition* (Lawrenceville, N.J.: Red Sea Press, 1997).

Statehood in the Horn of Africa

One possible explanation of why the conflict in Somalia is ongoing with different waves of intensification of violence, but hardly any victory in regaining central authority, might be found in the question of state and statehood. States in the Horn of Africa, as mentioned above are ranked in most indices as fragile, precarious or failed. However there are vast differences between an authoritarian predatory elite state as in Sudan and a lack of state but local governance as in Somalia. None of the core functions and tasks of a state, governance, control and legitimacy are provided by the TFG in Somalia.

There is no monopoly on the legitimate use of force as the only functioning force in Somalia is the army of the neighbouring country Ethiopia. Welfare, distribution of public goods, tax revenues, health care and education are subsidised through NGOs and charities. However even the work of humanitarian agencies providing emergency aid for the displaced population in Somalia is hampered by the TFG. The TFG has only weak legitimacy through the parliament but lacks state institutions, mechanisms of participation as well as structures to implement the rule of law or judiciary in general. State or the absence thereof remains the matrix and referential framework of international relations theory, but much more important, international relations in practice cannot work without a state.

Several attempts have been made to create a state in Somalia but there might also be regional and international actors who prefer a failed state in Somalia. Failed attempts as well as possible obstacles for statebuilding in Somali are following.

1   Diaspora government
A state cannot be created outside and imposed on a stateless territory. One consequence of state building processes from outside are the Diaspora governments. Due to the continuous insecurity and the warlords rule it was impossible for any transitional government since 1991 to install itself in Mogadishu.

2   Support for one faction
Another measure used in the case of Somalia is the imposition of a ruling group (warlord or clan based) through one financial sponsor with a very limited chance of sustainability. The Alliance for Peace Restoration and Combat Against Terror (APRCT) is the latest example. The CIA backed alliance which was overturned by the UIC in early 2006 resembles earlier trials by the US in support of one of many warlord militias in the 1990s. The latest two approaches seem straight from the realist school laboratory where security and stability comes first and neither liberalization nor institutionalism nor civil society or participation seem to rank anywhere close to security.

In this unilateral partial support the interest of the warlords is often overlooked. In their neopatrimonial setting of oligopolies of violence controlling fiefdoms but not a state, their interest might be the maximization of short term profit but not the transition into a national government. Deepened by the mistrust of clans and subclans against each other, the possibility to achieve stability and security through the support of one clan against the others cannot turn into a national security strategy for Somalia.

3   Disregard for territorial integrity

Whatever abuses are committed on Somali territory, there seems to be full impunity and no accountability whatsoever for the perpetrators. There is no judiciary, no state to protest, no police to arrest or guarantee the rule of law. This provides space for all kinds of international criminal networks, smuggling, piracy and terrorist groups.

It further encourages other states to act on Somali territory with full impunity and in the logic that there is no international law or human rights law if there is no state. One example would be the three reported direct attacks by the US army on Somali territory, supposedly in order to target Al-Qaida members[23]. These attacks were taken out unilaterally and without further notice or discussion in the Security Council. The US administration decision to attack Somali (and Puntland) territory was not legally challenged. Other examples are the cases of rendition reported in the first half of 2007.[24] Somali nationals living in neighbouring countries were abducted from their homes and taken in planes to Somalia. Reportedly some were interrogated by foreign interrogators and subsequently taken by plane to Ethiopia. For many there are no further traces after they were taken to Ethiopia and are feared of as being disappeared. Among those who were taken from Kenya to Somalia and held without charge or trial and interrogated without access to lawyers were a great number of women and children. Although the cases were documented, no charges however were brought forward.

Neither were the cases of indiscriminate shelling of civilians and direct targeting of civilians by the Ethiopian army as reported by fleeing internally displaced people.[25] Non-state actors such as the Shabab as well as clan militias used civilians as human shields and forced them to provide shelter for their attacks. Both sides are allegedly targeting journalists and aid workers. Both sides commit war crimes on a large scale in Somalia without a legal challenge to their accountability to the Geneva Conventions.

Rule of law and the Justice System

In order to prevent the abuses described above or to stabilize a Somali government, not only security but the rule of law and the end of impunity would be cornerstones. When the new Prime Minister Nur Hassan refers to the Somali population as Somali citizens, this sends a glimpse of hope. It refreshingly distinguishes him from the abuse of justice by the warlord rulers.

As in international relations, human rights also depend on the state as the body guaranteeing the rights for their citizens. This again is not the case in Somalia as a failed state with no judiciary or public administration in place to secure its citizens' rights.

---

[23] US attacks on Jubba river locations took place in January 2007. Seaborn attacks against Puntland were carried out in April. See BBC. US attacks Somali 'militant base'. 2 June 2007.
http://news.bbc.co.uk/2/hi/africa/6714473.stm (access 20 December 2007)
[24] Reprieve and Cageprisoners. Reprieve and Cageprisoners, *Mass Rendition, Incommunicado Detention and Possible Torture of Foreign Nationals in Kenya, Somalia and Ethiopia*, [2007]), www.reprieve.org.uk; www.cageprisoners.com (accessed 21 August 2007).
http://www.reprieve.org.uk/documents/070416ForeignNationalsRenderedinEthiopia.pdf (Access 7.1.2008)
[25] Human Rights Watch, *Shell Shocked: Civilians Under Siege in Mogadishu* (Washington D.C.; New York; London: Human Rights Watch, [2007]).

Since colonization Somalia went through a number of rights-, and states concepts. Other than Somaliland that was under British colonial rule, for what is now Somalia and Puntland under Italian rule the rights system was split in three sectors. Criminal as well as civil law was dealt with on county and state level in a formalized court system. For Muslims *sharia* was the legal body to handle legal family issues.[26] The transformation from a clan based rights structure – where no individual had the legal power over another individual – to a legal system in state formation processes however was highly critical during the colonial era.[27]

Even before the collapse of the state in Somalia, rule of law was not the basis in the state under Siad Barre. Access to lawyers and courts was clan based and required bribes in many cases. When the courts took over control in Mogadishu however the legal system did not improve over night. With the courts it was again the rule of an individual over others without a legal framework, fair trials and proper mechanisms to file objections. Currently the stateless justice system in Somalia is based on four pillars.[28]

- The formal juridical structures in the regional administration. This includes the legal bases of the TFG, the Transitional Charta, as a quasi constitution of growing importance for Somalia.
- The traditional clan based legal system, known as Xeer. This includes custormary law. It is uncanonized law mainly used as a framework for negotiations and conflict settlement mechanisms between clans.
- The *sharia* courts were introduced in the last decade. Islamic law as well as part of *sharia* law is integrated in the Xeer. *Sharia* remained intact during the Italian colonial period as well as during the regime of Siad Barre as a parallel legal system. The *sharia* courts, founded in the 1990s in Somalia were called on when the Xeer-system could not settle a dispute. Or in case the dispute was not of clan specific origin.
- Civil society initiatives and ad-hoc mechanism were introduced in Somalia, partly by warlords.

However, without a reliable body of rules and regulations there is neither accountability nor responsibility in jurisdiction. For the Somali population the parallel existence of jurisdiction meant mainly the power of the most influential clan or individual over the rest. The culture of impunity 0is deeply ingrained in the collective memory.

Statebuilding

At large the main effort by the regional organisations as well as bilateral and multilateral efforts is to restore the state in Somalia. The strategies used so far are dominated by a security first approach and tend to follow a top down rather than a bottom up direction. It is however symptomatic for state building attempts that local authorities and local governance structures are not – or too late – taken into consideration to be included in further institution building

---

[26] Andre Le Sage, *Stateless Justice in Somalia - Formal and Informal Rule of Law Initiatives* (Geneva: Centre for Humanitarian Dialogue, [2005]), www.hdcentre.org.
[27] Somaliawatch, 2000.
[28] Sage, *Stateless Justice in Somalia - Formal and Informal Rule of Law Initiatives*, 14

measures and politics[29]. Comparing the current state building strategies in International Relations theory with the situation and the actors in Somalia might visualise the fractures more clearly. Going through state building strategies[30] in Somalia one could summarize:

Liberalization First: democratisation, economic reforms, liberalization of trade, privatisation, globalisation and integration into world trade.

The main pillar in Somalia's' economy remains to be the high amount of remittance from Diaspora Somalis back to their country. The second pillar was for the livestock exports mainly to the Gulf region. Thirdly the transit of cheap electronic contraband products exported to the East African market[31]. None of this indicates the possibility of a country based on liberal market economy with a rump responsibility of government by guaranteeing a reliable legal framework in which the economy can develop. However the not easy to exploit resource in Somalia, other than in DR Congo or Sierra Leone might turn the interest of business people and warlords themselves into settling for a more stable environment in order to be able to raise, trade as well as export their livestock to their clients.[32]

Another main aspect of the *liberalization first* paradigm would be donor aid and the Millennium Development Goals. As Somalia is without central authority and therefore has no state capacity to absorb donor aid or budget funding, this remains a strategy for the future. Right now not even humanitarian aid can reach those in need. The lack of policing and the obstacles laid out by the TFG itself are not reflective of a government wanting to reach a post-conflict-society with a functioning economy and fairly elected leadership. Besides the privatised warlord economy with roadblock taxation by robbery at least Puntland gains another possible economic pillar by natural gas oil. However resource economy in the context of stateless warlord elite does not provide for any foundation for *liberalization first* strategies as a successful mechanism. As known from other resource rich states, the profit remains in the tight grasp of the ruling elites and is not distributed equally or increases the welfare of its population.

Liberalization first might be a long term strategy privileged by those who believe that trade and the business people's interest will bring stability to Somalia. They have a strong point considering the backbone of the warlord support as well as the support for the UIC. It was the business community interested in less fighting and more security in order to be able to increase their trade volume and profit from the import/export business they are engaged in.[33] This, as seen in eastern DR Congo and other places could change the interest of the warlord to become a landlord or mine owner or other and could therefore transform the manifest conflict.

---

[29] Jutta Bakonyi, Stephan Hensell and Jens Siegelberg, *Gewaltordnungen Bewaffneter Gruppen : Ökonomie Und Herrschaft Nichtstaatlicher Akteure in Den Kriegen Der Gegenwart*, 1. Aufl .ed., Vol. Bd. 181 (Baden-Baden: Nomos, 2006), 38-52.

[30] Schneckener, *International Statebuilding Dilemmas, Strategies and Challenges for German Foreign Policy.*, 16-20

[31] Peter D. Little, *Somalia: Economy without State.* (Oxford: The International African Institute; James Currey, 2003).

[32] On the difference of war economies based on resources and resource exploitation see the discourse on easy to exploit resources such as diamonds, coltan, gold and those not so easy to exploit, such as oil, or livestock. See Globalwitness (ww.globalwitness.org) and other NGOs working on war economies and conflict resources.

[33] Conversation with a high ranking AU diplomat in Addis Ababa, May 2007.

Security First: strengthening of the monopole of violence, the security sector as well as a focus on the security sector reform (SSR). In case of post conflict scenario Demobilization, Demilitarisation and Reintegration DDR module needs to be included.

Security first is the only strategy followed up and supported in Somalia so far. The intervention of Ethiopian troops, on the invitation of the TFG to enhance their military strength to gain the monopole of force over the territory of Somalia could be seen as the starting point. Training of police and army was for the last years one of the main requirements claimed by the TFG from international donors. The TFG as well as the international community has a clear priority in the security first strategy. As strategies in international relations go, they are thought to be complementary and not exclusivist and possibly this is the dilemma of the reaction on the situation in Somalia today. It appears as if the realist school has the upper hand and would not want others to come along. All eyes are on military security, no human security; rule of law, leave alone social interaction and community building is in focus.

But the *security first* strategy came to a halt in its effectiveness at latest when it became clear that the massive Ethiopian force would not be enough to outman the insurgent fighters. The plan was a rapid response by the AU followed by a full-fledged blue helmet mission mandated by the Security Council. Both basic steps of the strategy failed. The AU force with force strength of 8.000 did not come through. The only contribution was realized by Uganda with a force of 1.600. The UN – reassuring in the beginning – postponed the discussion of a mission indefinitely. The General Secretary of the UN, Ban Ki Moon, called upon a 'coalition of the willing' to deploy in Somalia, because no UN mission would be posted, due to security constraints. The classic option of the Security First strategy mainly used in failed states, a UN mission is not feasible for Somalia.

With a set up of desperate warlord militias, clan based fighters, Shabab and other UIC militias mixed with foreign *jihadist* and possible al Qaida offspring a security sector reform might be hard to establish. It might be impossible, if the strategy is not to include the majority of fighters but to fight them. The largest numbers of fighters are urban youth (mooryan) ready to either join their clan militia or to be recruited into the Shabab or other *jihadist* groups. These are the very people who grew up with a warlord war as an income generating survival strategy and they will be the ones that need to go through a demobilisation and demilitarisation mechanism. It is the same youth Somalia has to be rebuild with and for. To fight them with a military aim of eradication is irrational and counterproductive in the long run. Any SSR would now require a proper DDR process and a clan proportional representation including, not excluding the youth of the biggest clan in Mogadishu, the Hawiye as it appears to be the case right now with a majority of Darod being trained for army and police functions.

Institutionalisation First: strengthening of political and administrative institutions, strengthening the rule of law.

To work out a Somali *institutionalisation first* strategy would be a valid step to a road map out of the crisis. A balanced power sharing toolbox usable by a legitimised government would be of enormous help. Institutions therefore need to be reflective of the current governance structure in Somalia. A plain replica of a western style democracy institutional framework will not work. However in the context of Transitional Justice exclusivist justice systems, discriminatory systems or those ad-hoc amnesty mechanisms set up to ensure full impunity will not lead to sustainable peace and a stabilizing state. As Mamdani calls customary law the theory of the decentralized despotism, nothing is won by the exchange of one dominant and exclusive restrictive justice system through another.[34]

Clan elders, shuras, and Islamic courts would need to be involved in an institution building process as well as those organised in civil society. The focus with an *institutionalisation first* framework would be the institutions, which are agreed upon, such as parliament, justice sector, military and policing. The checks and balances and the power sharing system would then need to be fine-tuned to the needs of the Somali society.

In the current situation in Somalia there are a number of entry possibilities to support an *institutionalisation first* strategy. Since Institutions serve any government and help strengthen political mechanisms, they could be helped from outside even before the government went through proper elections and legitimisation. Precisely because these things need to be in place if there ever will be a legitimised government in Somalia it is never too early to start building them. A prime effect of this strategy could be the question of representation. A discourse so fundamentally important in Somalia could be taken out of the sheer clan context and into a larger governance usage.

Civil society first: Focus on the social fabric, improvement of chances of participation, support for NGOs, unions and political parties.

In many conflict as well as post-conflict countries, civil society has taken up the function of a parallel government. In cases where the government in absent, such as in Somalia or in the east of the DRC, civil society groups handle all core functions of a state, from security to the distribution of public goods, education, medical services, even the judiciary. In many cases this leads to a donor impulse that is problematic in two aspects. First, because there are functioning services and because the building of services by a central authority would take much time and might not be effective, civil society is financed and supported to continue being the parallel state. On the other side, through the *institutionalisation first* approach, donors build up institutions and support governments to fulfil their functions. Civil society then should serve as a watchdog and counter balance. To do both, fulfilling quasi state services and being the watchdog simply is impossible. However this is the situation in which many civil society groups find themselves.

Another challenge when faced with civil society groups in Somalia would be their ideological baggage. Whereas western donors and NGOs are used to replicate their value system in funding likeminded local NGOs, there is not much experience when dealing with civil society organisations from an Islamist spectrum, such as wahabi charities or foundations.

This challenge is quite similar to the inclusion of UIC members in the TFG or the *sharia* courts in the institutions. But any strategy not reflective of the reality, the power

---

[34] See debate about Transitional Justice. www.peace-justice-conference.info/documents.asp. On the aspect of customary law as an instrument of power not an authentic remedy see Mahmood Mamdani, *Citizen and Subject: Contemporary Africa and the Legacy of Late Colonialism* (Kampala: Fountain Publishers; Cape Town; London: David Philip; James Currey, 1996), 110.

balance and the values on the ground is bound to fail. However the difference with a bottom up approach – in combination with other strategies – is that the views of many more diverse voices in a society can be included and heard. Enlarging public space for the political engagement of citizens can only be done if institutions of political core functions are in place, people can gather in safety and are free to talk. This requires the work of civil society as well as the institutions.

At the end of the day, if the main aim is stability and a functioning government able to serve its people, their views are important and need to be taken into consideration if any strategy wants to be sustainable.

Conclusion

The crisis in Somalia is multileveled and so be the routes to a calmer future. If however this future lies in a Westphalian[35] type state or in the continuation of warlord oligopolies of violence or in a transformation from warlord to landlord remains to be seen. However the direction in which the country develops will partly depend on the strategies applied to its state building process. A combination of state building strategies would be required, most preferably one that includes civil society as well as the formal political actors.

There is a great risk of arbitrariness in the reliance on local authority mechanism without proper accountability systems, as contained in proper state mechanisms of checks and balances of power. On the other hand there is an ingrained exclusiveness in institutionalisation first state building strategies. Both strategies should be supported on local levels in Somalia. If the priority of efforts continues to be on the security first aspect focused on Mogadishu, a sustainable solution is very unlikely.

Bibliography

Report of the Monitoring Group on Somalia Pursuant to Security Council Resolution 1724 (2006) United Nations, 2007.

Bakonyi, Jutta, Stephan Hensell, and Jens Siegelberg. *Gewaltordnungen Bewaffneter Gruppen : Ökonomie Und Herrschaft Nichtstaatlicher Akteure in Den Kriegen Der Gegenwart.* Demokratie, Sicherheit, Frieden. 1. Aufl ed. Vol. Bd. 181. Baden-Baden: Nomos, 2006.

Buzan, Barry and Richard Little. "Beyond Westphalia? Capitalism After the 'Fall'." *Review of International Studies* 25, no. 5, December (1999): pp 89-104.

Cliffe, Lionel. "Regional Dimensions of Conflict in the Horn of Africa." *Third World Quarterly* vol. 20, no. No. 1 (1999): 89-89-111.

Connell, Dan. *Against all Odds: A Chronicle of the Eritrean Revolution: With a New Foreword on the Postwar Transition.* Lawrenceville, N.J.: Red Sea Press, 1997.

---

[35] Westphalian state model as one based on sovereignty within domestic jurisdictions and non-interference in the internal affairs of other states. Barry Buzan and Richard Little, "Beyond Westphalia? Capitalism after the 'Fall'." *Review of International Studies* 25, no. 5, December (1999), pp 89-104 (accessed 16.07.2007).

Erdmann, Gero and Ulf Engel. *Neopatrimonialism Revisited: Beyond a Catch-all Concept; GIGA Research Program Legitimacy and Efficiency of Political Systems.* GIGA Working Papers. Vol. 16. Hamburg: Giga, 2006.

Human Rights Watch. *Shell Shocked: Civilians Under Siege in Mogadishu.* Washington D.C.; New York; London: Human Rights Watch, 2007.

International Crisis Group. *Somalia's Islamists.* Nairobi, Bruxelles: 2005.

Issa-Salwe, Abdisalam M. *Somalia's Degenerated Authority: Which Way Out?.* Somaliawatch 2000, http://www.somaliawatch.org/archiveoct00/001011202.htm (accessed 25.07.2007).

Lewis, I. M. *A Modern History of the Somali.*, edited by Eastern African Studies. Oxford: James Currey, 2002.

Little, Peter D. *Somalia: Economy without State.* African Issues., edited by The International African Institute, James Currey. Oxford: The International African Institute; James Currey, 2003.

Mamdani, Mahmood. *Citizen and Subject: Contemporary Africa and the Legacy of Late Colonialism.* Princeton Studies in culture/power/history. Kampala. Fountain Publishers; Cape Town; London: David Philip; James Currey, 1996.

Marchal, Roland. "Islamic Political Dynamics in the Somali Civil War." In *Islamism and its Enemies in the Horn of Africa*, edited by Alexander De Waal, 114-146. London: Hurst and Company, 2004.

Menkhaus, Kenneth J. "The Crisis in Somalia: Tragedy in Five Acts." *African Affairs* 106, no. 204 (2007): 357, http://afraf.oxfordjournals.org/.

———. "Somalia and Somaliland: Terrorism, Political Islam, and State Collapse." In *Battling Terrorism in the Horn of Africa*, edited by Robert Rotberg, 23. Baltimore; Washington: Brookings Institution Press, 2005.

Reprieve and Cageprisoners. *Mass Rendition, Incommunicado Detention and Possible Torture of Foreign Nationals in Kenya, Somalia and Ethiopia* 2007, www.reprieve.org.uk; www.cageprisoners.com (accessed 21 August 2007).

Sage, Andre Le. *African Counterterrorism Cooperation : Assessing Regional and Subregional Initiatives.* 1st ed. Washington, D.C.: Potomac Books: National Defense University Press, 2007.

———. *Stateless Justice in Somalia - Formal and Informal Rule of Law Initiatives.* Geneva: Center for Humanitarian Dialogue, 2005.

Schneckener, Ulrich. *International Statebuilding Dilemmas, Strategies and Challenges for German Foreign Policy.* Berlin: 2007.

The Ethiopian Intervention in Somalia: Theoretical Perspectives

Matthias Seifert

1. Introduction

Somalia is usually considered to be the most prominent example of a failed state, a state that has completely lost its governing capacity (Rotberg 2004). Since the violent overthrow of military dictator Siad Barre in 1991, Somalia has not seen any kind of centralized working government. Instead, the territory was ruled by various warlords[1] who mostly represented single (sub-)clans, or did not enjoy any rule at all.

Barre seized power in a bloodless military coup in 1969, following nine years of unsuccessful parliamentary democracy. After coming to power, he introduced what has come to be known as scientific socialism, aligning with the Soviet Union for military aid. Barre followed, among other aims, the policy of a "greater Somalia", which aimed at the reintegration of all five Somali-populated areas in the Horn of Africa.[2] After the overthrow of the Ethiopian Emperor Haile Selassie in 1974 and the ensuing weakness of Ethiopia, Barre invaded Ethiopia in 1977 in order to conquer the Ogaden region which is mostly populated by Ethnic Somalis. The Soviet Union however withdrew its support and started supporting the new Ethiopian regime, which led to the defeat of the Somali army. Barre took this as an incentive to switch alliances and aligned his country with the Western Bloc (Ghebresillasie 1999). During the 1980s however, Barre's rule became increasingly repressive and was based almost exclusively on the support of certain clans.[3] Somalia developed into a full-fledged military dictatorship during this period, especially the clans of the northern part of Somalia suffered from his rule. This led to the formation of various rebel movements, of which the Somali National Movement (SNM) and the United Somali Congress (USC) were the most influential ones (Lewis 2002: 205-262).

In 1988, open civil war broke out. Barre had signed a treaty with Ethiopia, obliging both countries not to tolerate rebel movements against each other's governments any more. This led to the ousting of SNM members from Ethiopia and the first offensive of the SNM against government institutions. The war lasted for three years, in which Barre's regime committed massive violations of human rights by bombing combatants as well as the civilian population (Krech 1996).[4] Barre's forces were defeated in January 1991 and Barre retreated to

---

[1] Warlord configurations are usually distinguished from ‚ordinary' civil war by the „[…] use of violence as a means to regulate markets as well as the transformation of violence to a commodity, respectively a service" (Riekenberg 1999: 200).

[2] These include British and Italian Somalia, North-East Kenya, the Ogaden region in Ethiopia, as well as parts of Djibouti. This is also reflected in the five-pointed star on the Somali flag.

[3] This has become known as the MOD-alliance, the letters referring to the Majerteen (the clan of Barre's father), Ogaden (the clan of his mother) and the Dulbahante, the clan of his son-in-law. For the clan-based structure of Somali society see Lewis (1994).

[4] Especially Hargeisa, the capital of today's Somaliland, was practically razed to the ground. This resulted in a retreat of the civilian population into the rural areas of northern Somalia and massive migration into neighbouring countries.

the South of Somalia. Ali Mahdi Mohamed, a leading member of the USC immediately declared himself interim president, which in turn led to the confrontation with General Mohamed Farah Aideed. Mogadishu was divided between the factions of Mohamed and Aideed and the latent confrontation developed into direct clashes by the end of 1991. These clashes and the rapidly deteriorating situation of the civilian population led to the deployment of UNOSOM I and II (United Nations Missions to Somalia) between 1992 and 1995 (Debiel 2003: 138-161; Lewis/Mayall 1996; Boulden 2001). These missions however failed in their attempt to stabilize the crumbling state and were withdrawn by May 1995.

Since the withdrawal of UNOSOM II in 1995, Somalia has not seen any kind of centralized government. Instead, the country descended into anarchy and warlord rule.[5] A dozen peace conferences have not produced any sustainable results, the first success was the formation of a TNG (Transitional National Government) in 2000 and the installation of a TFG (Transitional Federal Government) in 2004. These governments however remained without power and were not able to raise the level of security for the population. The late 1990s and the early years of the new millennium were thus characterized by statelessness, with various factions competing for power. Since the events of 9/11, Somalia has become one of the fronts of the United States' war on terror, allegedly being a haven state for members of Al'Qaeda.

In June 2006 the UIC (Union of Islamic Courts) took over power in Mogadishu, rapidly extending their influence to the south and central parts of the country.[6] Not enjoying any form of democratic legitimation, the courts nevertheless provided for a relatively high level of security and a modest economic upsurge. Due to repeated accusations of having close links with Al'Qaeda however, the courts were not accepted internationally, the international community kept on supporting the faction-ridden TFG. Ethiopia was not prepared to accept this coup and intervened directly by the end of 2006. The militias of the UIC were quickly defeated and Mogadishu was conquered by the combined forces of the TFG and Ethiopia.

Since then, Somalia has moved back into a questionable state: Ethiopia had intended to return power back to the TFG and pull back its troops as soon as possible. This should have happened with as little external assistance as possible. Still, both the TFG and Ethiopia had to accept that the AU, under the mandate of the UN, sent a peacekeeping force. This force however has proven to be inadequate. Of the intended 8 000 troops, only 1 300 Ugandan soldiers have arrived so far (Africa Confidential, 16.3.2007). These have remained largely ineffective and have even been the aim of direct attacks. The TFG is still unable to exercise any kind of sovereign and effective rule, the security situation of the population remains difficult. In addition, the last months have seen numerous upsurges of violence, of which most have been ascribed to remnant forces of the UIC.[7] Thus the situation has not improved since the Ethiopian intervention, and Somalia seems to have moved from a failed state to a failed state, with a power vacuum that no group is powerful enough to fill.

---

[5] The northern part of Somalia, the former British protectorate Somaliland, took a radically different development and declared itself independent in May 1991. Since then, it has developed into a full-fledged democracy altough it is still not recognised internationally. For the development of Somaliland since 1991 see Prunier (1994); Brons (1994); Bradbury (1997); Bradbury et al. (2003); WSP (2005); Seifert (2007).

[6] Some authors refer to the UIC as Supreme Islamic Courts Council (SICC) or Islamic Courts Union (ICU), but I shall stick to UIC in order to avoid confusion.

[7] It is more probable that the attacks were carried out by both remaining fighters of the UIC and former warlord militias. Still, precise information is almost impossible to obtain.

Both from a theoretical and a practical point of view, the Ethiopian intervention poses a serious problem. It was not a war between two states in the classical sense, since the Somali state ceased to exist in 1991 and has not been resurrected so far. The Ethiopian troops did not fight the army of a representative national government, but invaded the territory of a neighbouring country nevertheless. In addition, the intervention did not enjoy any kind of international legitimation, neither by the UN nor by the AU. This in turn leads to the question if the intervention can be subsumed under what has been called "new", "transnational", or even "postmodern" war (Münkler 2002; Zürn/Zangl 2003; Kaldor 2007). In order to answer this question, I shall first outline the most important features of the new wars (Chapter 2), before turning to the actual intervention and its analysis (Chapter 3). A few tentative conclusions in Chapter 4 will end the article.[8]

2. Theoretical aspects - From old to new wars

Numerous definitions of war and warfare exist. Classical war has been defined, for example, as the „[...] exercise of physical violence by combat units" (Zangl/Zürn 2003: 28).[9] This relatively broad definition includes four different kinds of war: war between states, war between non-state actors within one state (civil war), war between the state and a non-state actor on the territory of said state (anti-regime war), and war between a state and a non-state actor on the territory of another state (ibid.:28). Another possibility is the attempt to categorize wars by a numerical criterion. Chojnacki (2006) argues for at least „[...] 1000 ‚battle deaths' for the whole conflict among military personnel only [...]" (Chojnacki 2006: 17). A different definition is given by Ruloff/Schubiger (2007), who try to categorize warfare and violent conflicts by asking for the categories of conflict (no war, low intensity war, high intensity war) and actor categories (ranging from village societies to military alliances and superpowers). War as a term therefore can be reduced to the „[...] organized and continuous use of considerable violence" (Ruloff/Schubiger 2007: 11). The *Arbeitsgemeinschaft Kriegsursachenforschung* uses the definition of Hungarian peace researcher Istvan Kende: War is "a violent mass conflict, which exhibits all of the following characteristics: (a) at least two or more armed forces have to participate, at least one side has to use regular forces of the government [...], (b) both sides have to have at least a minimal standard of centralized warfare [...], (c) the armed operations need to be carried out with a certain continuity, not just spontaneous clashes [...]" (AKUF/Schreiber 2006: 10). These definitions have in common that they include a relatively broad range of conflicts, not necessarily including a state as participant. Kaldor however focuses on the level of the nation state. She argues that war is „[...] a creature of the centralised, ‚rationalised', hierarchically ordered territorial state" (Kaldor 2007: 35). Thus, she focuses on the nation-state as the main actor in international warfare. The dominance of the nation-state became obvious in the possibility of states to draw certain distinctions in the area of warfare, so for example the distinction between war and peace, combatants and non-combatants, and between enemy or ally (Münkler 2002: 68-70).

---

[8] Due to the security situation in Somalia, field work was impossible. Thus, the article mostly relies on various newsletters and media broadcasts.

[9] All quotes from German are translated by the author.

Turning the above categorization upside down, Tilly (1990) considers wars to be one of the driving forces behind processes of nation-building. Since especially European states were continuously threatened by aggressive neighbours and the possible loss of territory, they were forced to maintain a standing army. This in turn led to the need for an effective system of taxation and administration in order to raise the necessary funds to pay the soldiers. Thus, the administration had to be extended to all of the national territory, bringing all citizens in contact with the state. This again led to an increased identification of the citizens with „their" state, effectively contributing to successful nation-building (Tilly 1990: 54, 63-70, for nation-building in Africa see Herbst 2000).

The above theories share one common feature: Their concepts of war and the execution of organized violence all refer to what has been named the „national constellation" (Habermas 1998). The national constellation is characterised by at least four features that have remained relatively constant since the Treaty of Westphalia and the creation of the modern system of nation states: It encloses *national problems* that could adequately be solved by *national governance*. This was possible because *national resources were bundled*, which in turn was *recognized as legitimate by other states* (Zürn/Zangl 2003: 149-152).

This dominance of the nation state in the international system has been challenged at least since the 1980s and 1990s.[10] In this article however, I shall only deal with one aspect of the changing nature of the international system, namely the transnationalisation of security problems and the changing nature of war.[11] In the national constellation, „[...] only the classical war between - mostly neighbouring - states constituted an international security problem" (Zürn/Zangl 2003: 175). States were the monopolists of violence within their territories and thus the main actors in international warfare. The formerly common exercise of war by big non-state actors such as for example British colonial societies has been reduced since 1648 and the nation state became the main actor of international warfare (Creveld 1998).

The changing nature of the international system has led to the emergence of a new trinity of violence: new civil wars, transnational terrorism and new wars (Zürn/Zangl 2003: 182-197). As admitted by most scholars, the features of the new wars as such are not new, it is rather the combination that qualifies these conflicts for the attribute 'new'. A few recurring features of the new wars shall be outlined in order to provide a more complete understanding of the nature of these conflicts. Münkler (2002: 10-11) names three features of new wars: the *privatization* of violence in wars, an *asymmetry* between the combatants and formerly regulated forms of violence becoming *autonomous*. Kaldor mentions that "the new wars can definitely be distinguished from older ones by their differing *aims*, the *way of warfare* and their *funding*" (Kaldor 2007: 23). For the purposes of this article, I shall summarize these aspects under two headings: the structural aspects (funding, forms of warfare) and ideological aspects (aims, ideology).

---

[10] For further discussion of the nation state in the age of globalization see Beck (1986); Hirst/Thompson (1999); Held/McGrew (2003); Held (2006).

[11] This also excludes other transnational phenomena such as terrorism, organized crime and international environmental problems. The literature on those subjects is diverse to say the least. For an overview see Porter/Brown (1996); Gurr/Cole (2002); Schneckener (2006).

2.1. Structural aspects

War is usually an expensive activity for the participants. Soldiers have to be paid, equipment and arms are necessary, loss of human life causes further costs, international reputation is lost, trade relations are diminished and so on. This used to be the domain of the nation state: "[…] the centralized administration had the task of raising the military capacity and to maximize the incomes to finance the war" (Kaldor 2007: 154). This was usually connected to the combatants being representatives of a government, thereby being identifiable and responsible to an authority. The new wars however are characterized by a privatization of violence and the increasing connection to the inter- and transnational economy. In addition to that, they are relatively cheap, due to the fact that they are mostly fought with light weapons only.

Most of the new wars are carried out under the participation of non-state actors, be they militias, guerrilla fighters or rebel groups. This is often connected to weak statehood and the inability of a state to control its citizens sufficiently. Thus, private militias, mostly under the control of a local strongman or warlord are the main participants in the new wars. These fighters are often poorly equipped and have not had any kind of military training. Closely connected to this aspect is the frequent use of child soldiers who are even cheaper and are often constantly drugged and kept under the influence of alcohol. These militias however need minimal funding as well. This leads to two interrelated problems. On the one hand they have to provide for themselves: "[…] according to the principle that war has to nourish war, they provide for themselves through extortion, pillaging and theft" (Münkler 2002: 132). This of course has devastating effects on the livelihood of the civilian population and the economy of a country. It is especially dangerous if the combatants focus on one group of the population and ruin their income especially. The second problem connected to the funding and the privatization is the connection of these warlords to the international economy. If a local strongman is in control of natural resources that are easy to obtain and that are sought on the international market, a so-called war economy emerges. Illegally obtained resources (be they oil, diamonds, wood or any other kind) are sold on the international black market, thereby keeping the funds flowing into the war (Münkler 2002: 168-170). This makes war profitable once again and is one of the reasons why these conflicts have the potential to continue over long periods of time.

But the illegal trade with obtained natural resources is only one of the possibilities to keep warfare up. Just as important are the different forms of support from outside, which can appear in different forms (for the following paragraph see Kaldor 2007: 173-175). Foreign currency can be transferred to single families or groups, which in turn can be transformed into military resources. The second form is the direct support from the Diaspora communities, for example from Irish Americans for the IRA. The third form is the support of foreign governments as was observable in the support of the Ugandan government for the FPR after the genocide of 1994. The fourth aspect is the plundering of international humanitarian aid. What was intended to support the suffering civilian population is illegally obtained through "taxes" or simple checkpoints: "In fact, […] donors consider a loss of five percent as acceptable" (ibid.: 175). Closely connected is the exploitation of humanitarian aid that is delivered to refugee camps, which often become focal points war economies. This again makes the funding of private militias easier and is often an important aspect in the strategy of warlords (Münkler 2002: 154). This makes the advice of Luttwak to a certain extent obsolete, who argued that these wars should burn out themselves in order to provide for a more inclusive peace afterwards (Luttwak 1999). A further aspect that emanates from the control of resources, militias and violence is the provision of security for certain parts of the population. Illegally obtained or not, if strongmen are able to provide basic services such as security for population segments, this can lead to the emergence of parastatal structures and entities.[12]

The second structural aspect of the new wars that is necessary to mention is the form of warfare, which is usually asymmetric. Classical war between states used to be conducted between the armed forces of the respective states. With the recognition of national sovereignty and at least the formal equality of states, only states had the formal right to fight wars. This in turn became the foundation of the classical European law of war (Münkler 2002: 54, 112-114). This configuration has changed insofar, as the parties of the new wars are often poorly equipped and badly trained militias, with regular armies as their opponents. This might either be the case if rebel movements fight against the army of the country they operate in, or if the international community intervenes in a country to quell unrest. In many cases, guerrilla tactics are employed which are cost-effective and efficient. "Partisans thus do not necessarily have to win militarily, but do only have to keep up an inextinguishable threat potential in order to succeed" (ibid.: 55). In most cases, big direct confrontations are avoided by at least one party, the strategies rather focus on hit-and-run tactics in order to obtain equipment, resources or food.

Due to the unregulated character of these strategies however, they have a tendency to become autonomous. Formerly integrated into overarching strategies and goals defined by a central authority, they often become the only way a war is fought or at least the dominating way (ibid.: 11). A disgusting feature of these strategies is closely connected to the ideological aspects of these wars (see below), namely organized violence against the civilian population, especially against women. The deportation of women, mass rape or rape under the eyes of family members have become a recurrent element of the new wars. On a more abstract level, this can be described as a strategy of ethnic cleansing without full-scale genocide. Violence against women can be instrumentalized to create a climate of fear and terror, thus expelling clearly defined population segments (ibid.: 144-146).

2.2. Ideological aspects

Organized violence against women is only one of the outcomes of the ideological aspects of the new wars. Kaldor has summarized these aspects under the term "policy of identity", which covers different features (for the following see Kaldor 2007: 120-154).

Since former wars were characterized by ideologies as well, a political background seems to be nothing new. In contrast to earlier ideological foundations however "[...] the policy of identity is rather fragmenting, backward-oriented and based on exclusion" (ibid.: 134). These policies often reconstruct (or invent) a heroic past, instrumentalize past (real or unreal) injustices or instrumentalize xenophobia. Examples could be the oppression of a certain ethnic group by a repressive centralized state, massive immigration due to violent conflicts in neighbouring countries or a glorious past of which only the positive sides are

---

[12] This phenomenon however can only be a peripheral part of this article and leads into the realm of democratic theory and the question of statehood. For a fascinating study of the Northern Kivu regions see Tull (2005).

recognized. Two sources for these policies can be distinguished, although they are interrelated and both are connected to the phenomenon of globalization. On the one hand, this strategy can be used by political elites that see their base of legitimacy dwindling. It can thus be a reaction to diminished governing capacities of their state or region, thereby trying to find new legitimacy. These policies can be found either on the national or on the regional level, examples are the former Yugoslavia, the former USSR or Eritrea before its independence. Especially in Africa a development is observable that shows that, directly after independence, national sentiments were the primary source of identification. Following the economic decline, these often reverted to the exclusion of certain parts of the population and the preferential treatment of other groups (ibid.: 134-140). The second source can be found in the growing informal and illegal global economy. Neoliberal SAPs often had devastating effects on developing countries, fostering not 'more market' but networks of clientelism and patronage. These were often justified by exclusionary ideologies based on ethnicity, common heritage or (invented) traditions (ibid.: 142-143). The support for these ideologies is facilitated by the grown communication possibilities with the Diaspora communities. The growth of real-time information flows has contributed to quicker and louder support for the threatened communities in the countries of origin, be the threats real or only perceived. Interestingly enough, Kaldor only glances at the role that religion can play in this respect, although it is one of the factors that can be instrumentalized most easily. Münkler also recognizes some of the abovementioned features, his conclusion however is that the concept of the just war seems to be back. If one side claims to be the sole representative of a certain group or claims the right to war for itself due to religious reasons, then the enemy is automatically the 'essential other' that has no right to war and that is automatically wrong (Münkler 2002: 56-57).

Thus a devastating mix of ideological and structural factors converge that make the new wars even more dangerous than classical war, since the civilian population is among the preferred victims and the difficulties to quell these wars by a simple intervention.

3. The Ethiopian intervention

3.1. The conflict and its outcomes
Having emerged as a serious political actor on the national stage at the beginning of 2006, the militias of the UIC took over power in Mogadishu by June 2006.[13] This was followed by a period of relative peace, stability and a modest economic upsurge. Road blocks in Mogadishu were removed, the airport and the port were opened up again, trade with the neighbouring countries became easier.[14] Due to Somali society being practically 100% Muslim (Brons 2001: 95), the courts enjoyed relatively strong support in the population, although they did not have any kind of democratic legitimacy. The main aim of the courts after coming to power was to provide for law and order and to implement a good deal of Islamic law, including harsh punishments of criminals. For the time they were in power, the UIC considered themselves to be the sole and legitimate representatives of Somalia. This was accompanied by at least the formal rhetoric of further peaceful development. The courts stated that their prime

---

[13] For the history and development of the courts in Somalia see Marchal (2004) and Barnes/Hassan (2007).
[14] On the pastoral base of the Somali economy see Lewis (2002), for the stateless era see Little (2003).

responsibility was to provide basic services as exemplified in a statement by Professor Ibrahim Hassan Adow, then head of the UIC Foreign Affairs department:

> „Our biggest challenge is to go beyond peace and provide social services, to provide the basic needs, whether it is food, medical care, shelter, education, employment. While we do this, we have to simultaneously show the world that we want to pacify Somalia and defend the Somali people, and establish a working relationship [with the international community]." (IRIN: 20.11. 2006)

During their 6 months in power however, they were not able to set up a working government or create sufficient administrative structures to implement the policies they were demanding. Mogadishu remained relatively calm as did most parts of southern and central Somalia, although the administrative structures were mostly limited to single court chapters. No coherent national policies were formulated, neither in the political nor in the economic area. Policies were generally determined by the question of how much of *Shari'a* law was supposed to be implemented, although the split between hard- and softliners remained prevalent throughout their reign (BBC 2006a). To a certain extent, this split did not only complicate decision-making, but also contributed to the negative reactions of the international community. Since especially the more conservative parts of the courts were constantly suspected of having links with Al'Qaeda, international recognition was denied and Somalia once again was suspected of becoming a haven state for terrorists.[15]

The judgements on the Islamic Courts in the scientific literature vary. Some observers argue that „[…] they [the courts, M. S.] quickly switched to a more moderate Islam and a pragmatic policy while mostly trying to establish basic security for the local population" (Heinrich 2007: 2). Others judge them more harshly: „They ruled with an iron fist and imposed their particular conception of morality on the population, at one point even banning the watching of football matches" (Franke/Dehéz 2007: 3).

Ethiopia, Somalia's biggest and most influential neighbour, had been against the Courts since they came to power while keeping good relations with the TFG. Ethiopia did not want to see a strong Islamic state next door and thus kept on supporting the TFG. Fears within Ethiopia were aggravated by some of the Courts' leaders raising the 'greater Somalia' policy again, thereby fuelling Ethiopian fears of the loss of the Ogaden region (Weber 2007: 2).[16] These two factors, the religious and the territorial threat (and probably the encouragement of the US) led to a more active engagement of Ethiopia. Military advisors as well as supporting personnel, technical equipment and weapons seem to have flown into Somalia since July 2006. In September 2006, the AU decided to send a peacekeeping mission to Somalia which should have been conducted under the auspices of IGAD (Intergovernmental Authority on Development). The UN Security Council partly lifted the weapons embargo against Somalia to pave the way for the mission, although no neighbouring state was allowed to participate in the mission. This excluded Ethiopia as well and thus prolonged the deployment of the

---

[15] The question of the alleged links with terrorist organisations can not be solved here. It is however unlikely that Somalia would have become a haven state immediately, since so much of the country has been destroyed during the past decades, and even terrorists need a certain infrastructure. See also Schneckener (2005).

[16] For the development of the „greater Somalia"-policy under Siad Barre and the ensuing Ogaden war see Herrmann (1997); Ghebresillasie (1999).

mission. Following the resolution of the Security Council, the Islamists issued an ultimatum, demanding the withdrawal of all Ethiopian troops from Somali territory, also threatening to extend their fight into the Eastern territory of Ethiopia.

On October 25 2006, the Ethiopian Prime Minister Meles Zenawi officially declared that Ethiopia was „technically at war with the UIC", not yet admitting the ongoing intrusion by military personnel. The UIC countered the declaration of war by declaring a „holy war" against Ethiopians in Somalia (BBC 2007a). The official invasion however did not begin until Christmas Eve, at least this was the date when the "[…] Ethiopian Prime Minister Meles Zenawi officially declared the military intervention of his country in the Somali conflict […]" (Franke/Dehéz 2007: 2). Since the militias of the UIC were relatively weak in military terms, they were not able to fight back the combined forces of Ethiopia and the TFG. This resulted in a quick victory of Ethiopia and the TFG. The capital Mogadishu was captured on December 28, while Kismayo, the last stronghold of the UIC, was conquered on January 1, 2007 (BBC 2007a). The US supported the whole operation and even intervened directly by bombing troops of the UIC in Hayo and Afmadow on January 8 (Africa Confidential, 12.1.2007, p. 16). Following the defeat of the UIC's militias, the prime minister of the TFG asked the Ethiopian troops to remain in Somalia to support the TFG in restoring law and order. Zenawi however, wanted to withdraw his troops as soon as possible, aiming for a period of two weeks' time. This was defied by another statement of his, declaring that Ethiopia would have to stay engaged in order to defeat the remaining islamist fighters and ensure that Somalia would not descend again into chaos and anarchy. In a somewhat contradictory manner, he simultaneously tried to commit the international community for this task as well: „It is up to the international community to deploy a peacekeeping force in Somalia without delay to avoid a vacuum and the resurgence of extremists and terrorists" (BBC 2007b). Difficult negotiations resulted in the deployment of 1. 300 Ugandan troops under the auspices of the AU to provide for security and stability. So far, these troops have not been able to deliver these goods, instead they became targets of direct attacks themselves. In most cases, dispersed fighters of the UIC were blamed for these attacks, some sources speak of up to 3. 000 fighters that might still be active within Mogadishu (Weber 2007: 1). Since January, Somalia has again experienced a vacuum of power, with none of the involved actors being able to fill that vacuum. The UN issued in Security Council Resolution 1744 that

> "[…]there should be a national reconciliation effort led by President Abdullahi Yusuf Ahmed and the "Transitional Federal Institutions" and that the African Union should send in a peacekeeping force to help with this process, with possibly a UN force to take over at a later stage" (BBC 2007c).

So far, this has not happened. The TFG remains split between different factions, the Ugandan peacekeepers remain ineffective, and the remaining troops proposed for by the AU have not been deployed yet. Since January, violence in Somalia is on the rise again, despite an offered amnesty for former UIC fighters that was proposed by Somali President Abdullahi Yusuf (BBC 2007d). At the beginning of July 2007, violence upsurged again, forcing many families again out of Mogadishu who had returned between February and May (IRIN 2007a). Most attacks are blamed on Islamist insurgents and remnants of the UIC, who might have gone into hiding and are now conducting a Partisan war against the Ethiopian-backed TFG. Excluding the peaceful area of Somaliland, the security situation in Somalia is deteriorating again, showing most features of a low-intensity-conflict.

3.2. Analysis

his brief glance at the events in Somalia from June 2006 to mid-2007 allows some illuminating insights. I shall try to connect the aforementioned theoretical aspects to the actual events, highlighting the most important features that characterize the Ethiopian intervention and its aftermath.

Having a longer history in Somalia than is usually expected, the courts had close connections to the business area from the beginning (Barnes/Hassan 2007: 4). Some observers even argue that they were only set up in order to provide for safe trade again and were thus only an instrument for the business community (BBC 2006a). If the courts had established an exploitative system and established a monopoly on certain economic areas remains unclear, since they were ousted so quickly. It remains true however that they were able to provide for a secure enough environment that trade could be resumed and at least a modest economic upsurge could be achieved. How much funding the courts received from the business community, private donors or regional allies remains unclear. It is suspected that Eritrea played a large part in financing and equipping the UIC, at least according to a UN report (Mail & Guardian 2006a). Thus it seems that the influence of foreign powers (Eritrea, US in the case of Ethiopia) seems to have played the dominant economic role in the intervention, with only very limited influence of the international community.

The Courts and their militias emerged as private actors on the political stage nevertheless and only claimed to be official national representatives after defeating the warlord militias. To a certain extent, the privatization of violence is observable in this case - although the classification is difficult due to the absence of any kind of centralized government over the past 15 years. The Courts claimed to possess more legitimacy than the faction-ridden TFG, which can even considered to be true. The civilian population accepted their rule for the most part, although critical voices were heard on the more drastic punishments. What keeps the courts from being classified as simple warlords however is their mostly positive impact on Somalia. Surely it is not justified to speak of the Courts' rule as a 'Golden Age' (Barnes/Hassan 2007: 6), but it can not be denied that Somalia experienced one of its calmest periods under the rule of the Courts. If the Courts had been able to develop coherent and progressive national (economic) policies and support further development must of course remain an open question.

As already mentioned, the use of Islamic law greatly enhanced the legitimacy of the Courts. Nevertheless it has also to be mentioned that Islam was also instrumentalized against Christian Ethiopia when, for example, Sheik Hassan Aweys called for a *jihad*, a holy war, against Ethiopia. In combination with the recurring rhetoric of 'greater Somalia', this developed into an intense mixture of nationalism and religious ideology. It still remains open if the hard- or the softliners within the Courts would have won in the long run, what can be said however, is, that the intense focus on religion contributed to the negative reactions of the international community and the actual Ethiopian intervention. It was thus a double-edged sword, strengthening internal support and effectively cutting most of the possible support from outside the country. Nevertheless, Islam as a unifying factor was no simple top-down ideological construct, but has long and deep roots in Somali society, therefore appealing to all sections of society. It is difficult to decide if the focus on Islam had developed into an exclusive ideology against certain parts of the population later on, or if the cleavages between the clans would have developed dividing capacity as well. What can be observed however, is, that Islam was used as an exclusive ideology against Ethiopians in the calls for the holy war.

With regard to the asymmetry of new wars, the Ethiopian intervention is an almost perfect example. The highly trained Ethiopian army first supported the troops of the TFG through military advisors and intervened directly afterwards. Enthusiastic though they were, the militias of the UIC were no match for the Ethiopian troops, resulting in their quick defeat within a few weeks. They were aware that they could not win a direct confrontation with the Ethiopians and went quickly into hiding. If the remnants of the militias of the UIC are responsible for the repeated attacks on government officials and institutions or if former warlord militias are to blame is an open question at the moment. It might also be possible that it is a mixture of both, maybe with a few clan militias trying to secure more influence. At present, a Partisan war against the TFG, the Ethiopian troops as well as the Ugandan peacekeepers is going on, resulting in large losses of civilian lives and property. Since the conflicts that led to the coup of the UIC in the first place remain unresolved, it is improbable that the security situation is going to improve in the near future.

4. Tentative Conclusions

The aim of the article was to analyze the Ethiopian intervention in Somalia under the theoretical perspective of new forms of warfare. Several tentative conclusions can be drawn. On the theoretical level, more work is necessary. The existing literature on the new wars does not provide for a coherent theoretical framework, but can only highlight a few recurring aspects and their changed combination. This however does not allow the construction of causal relationships, nor does it sufficiently answer the question as to why this transformation has occurred in the past few years. The crumbling of the Eastern Bloc, accelerating processes of economic and political globalization offer hindsights, but remain insufficiently theorized. These theoretical problems reflect back on the level of analysis: Is the numerical criterion now excluded, or is it necessary to develop a more inclusive definition of 'battle deaths'? When can a new war be labelled as finished if there has never been an official declaration of war? How much 'low-scale-violence' justifies calling a conflict a war? And not least of all, how is the international community supposed to react? What could be promising strategies against 'smouldering wars'? How much can traditional mechanisms of conflict resolution contribute to a lasting peace settlement? These questions remain unresolved so far.

With respect to the practical level, a few conclusions can be drawn as well. The Ethiopian intervention exhibits aspects of old as well as of new wars. First, there even was a classical declaration of war (quite late in the conflict, but nevertheless) and the official Ethiopian army was one of the main actors in the defeat of the militias of the UIC. Second, they did not fight the national army of a representative Somali government. It is difficult to decide on the status of the UIC for the time they were in power. They can neither be categorized as a legitimate government since there never were any elections, but they also defy the classical definition of warlord configurations, since they used violence to come to power but tried immediately afterwards to regulate violence and to return to an at least moderately stable state. It would be too confusing to subsume them simply as a non-state actor, because this would lead to a huge residual category in which charity NGOs, guerrillas and churches would be found side by side. I thus want to call them for the time being a hybrid actor, exhibiting features of more than one category.

The strong influence of Islam surely qualifies the conflict for the label new war, since the explicit use of religion had a significant impact on the actual outcomes of the conflict. As mentioned above, this case is quite unusual, since religion is accepted as important force in everyday life by the elites as well as by the civilian population. Nevertheless, the use of religion as an exclusive ideology against Ethiopia definitely counts in favour of the label new war. If, in Kaldor's terms, there would have been the possibility to use Islam as a progressive ideology, promoting Somalia's development under the rule of the Courts can only be guessed at.

With regard to the way of warfare, a mixed picture emerges. During the actual intervention, the Ethiopian troops and the troops of the TFG used 'normal' strategies, with the militias of the UIC already resorting to Partisan tactics. This seems to continue up to today, when most attacks are carried out as hit-and-run, with violence suddenly emerging and then subsiding again. Mogadishu, mid- and central Somalia seems to slide back into a low-intensity-conflict, with sudden upsurges of violence, carried out by a plethora of groups.

Thus it seems to be reasonable to draw the overall conclusion that the Ethiopian intervention can be subsumed under the heading 'new war', with the devastating function of triggering the next new war, namely the fight against the Ethiopian troops on Somali soil and the TFG by various groups. Depressingly, Somalia seems to be moving from failed state to failed state.

Bibliography

Africa Confidential, Vol. 48(6), 16. 3. 2007, p. 4.

Africa Confidential, Vol. 48(1), 12. 1. 2007, pp. 15-16.

Arbeitsgemeinschaft Kriegsursachenforschung/Schreiber, Wolfgang (Eds.), 2006, *Das Kriegsgeschehen 2005*, Wiesbaden: Verlag für Sozialwissenschaften.

Barnes, Cedric/Hassan, Harun, 2007, 'The Rise and Fall of Mogadishu's Islamic Courts.' Chatham House Briefing Paper, April 2007.

Beck, Ulrich, 1986, *Risikogesellschaft. Auf dem Weg in eine andere Moderne*, Frankfurt a Main: Suhrkamp.

Boulden, Jane, 2001, *Peace Enforcement. The United Nations Experience in Congo, Somalia, and Bosnia*, Westport/London: Praeger.

Bradbury, Mark, 1997, *Somaliland*, Totton: Hobbs the Printer.

Bradbury, Mark/Abokor, Adan/Yusuf, Haroon, 2003, 'Somaliland: Choosing Politics over Violence.' In: *Review of African Political Economy*, Vol. 30(97), p. 455-478.

Brons, Maria, 1994, *Somaliland zwei Jahre nach der Unabhängigkeitserklärung*, Hambg. Lit

Chojnacki, Sven, 2006, 'Democratic Wars and Military Interventions, 1946-2002: the Monadic Level Reconsidered.' In: Geis, Anna et al. (eds.), *Democratic Wars. Looking at the Dark Side of Democratic Peace*, Basingstoke: MacMillan, p. 13-41.

Creveld, Martin Van, 1998, *Die Zukunft des Krieges*, München: Gerling.

Debiel, Tobias, 2003, *UN-Friedensoperationen in Afrika*, Bonn: Dietz.

Franke, Benedikt/Dehez, Dustin, 2007, 'Somalia Reloaded. Risks and Chances of a New Beginning.' http://www.worldsecuritynetwork.com/ showArticle3. cfm?Article_ID= 13905, as on 11.6.2007.

Ghebresillasie, Girma, 1999, *Kalter Krieg am Horn von Afrika. Regional-Konflikte: Äthiopien und Somalia im Spannungsfeld der Supermächte 1945-1991*, Baden-Baden: Nomos.

Gurr, Nadine/Cole, Benjamin, 2002, *The new face of terrorism. Threats from Weapons of Mass Destruction*. London/New York: Tauris.

Habermas, Jürgen, 1998, *Die postnationale Konstellation. Politische Essays*, Frankfurt am Main: Suhrkamp.

Heinrich, Wolfgang (Interview), 2007, 'Gegen die Islamisten gibt es keinen Frieden in Somalia.' In: *E+Z*, Vol. 48(2), pp. 2-3.

Held, David (Ed.), 2006, *The global transformations reader: an introduction to the globalization debate*, Cambridge: Polity Press.

Held, David/McGrew, Anthony, 2003, *Globalization, anti-globalization*, Cambridge: Polity Press.

Herbst, Jeffrey, 2000, *States and Power in Africa: Comparative Lessons in Authority and Control*, Princeton: Princeton University Press.

Herrmann, Ron H., 1997, *Der kriegerische Konflikt in Somalia und die internationale Intervention 1992 bis 1995: eine entwicklungsgenetische und multidimensionale Analyse*, Frankfurt: Lang.

Hirst, Paul/Thompson, Grahame, 1999, *Globalization in question: the international economy and the possibilities of governance*, Cambridge: Polity Press.

Irinnews, 2006, Newsletter 20.11.2006.

Irinnews, 2007a, Newsletter 5.7.2007.

Kaldor, Mary, 2007, *Neue und alte Kriege. Organisierte Gewalt im Zeitalter der Globalisierung*, Frankfurt am Main: Suhrkamp.

Krech, Hans, 1996, *Der Bürgerkrieg in Somalia (1988-1996)*, Berlin: Köster.

Lewis, Ion Myrdal, 1994, *Blood and Bone. The Call of Kinship in Somali Society*, Lawrenceville: Red Sea Press.

Lewis, Ion Myrdal/Mayall, James, 1996, 'Somalia.' In: Mayall, James (Ed.), *The new Interventionism 1991-1994. United Nations Experience in Cambodia, former Yugoslavia and Somalia*, Cambridge: Cambridge University Press, pp. 94-127.

Lewis, Ion Myrdal, [4]2002, *A Modern History of the Somali. Nation and State in the Horn of Africa*, Oxford: Oxford University Press.

Little, Peter, 2003, *Somalia: Economy without state*, Oxford: Currey.

Luttwak, Edward, 1999, 'Give War a Chance.' In: *Foreign Affairs*, Vol. 4(78), pp. 36-44.

Marchal, Roland, 2004, 'Islamic Political Dynamics in the Somali Civil War.' In: de Waal, Alex (ed.), *Islamism and its Enemies in the Horn of Africa*, London: Hurst, pp. 114-146.

Münkler, Herfried, 2002, *Die neuen Kriege*, Bonn: Bundeszentrale für Politische Bildung.

Porter, Gareth/Brown, Janet, 1996, *Global Environmental Politics*, Boulder: Westview Press.

Prunier, Gerard, 1994, 'Somaliland: Birth of a new Country?' In: Gurdon, Charles (Ed.), *The Horn of Africa*, London: UCL Press.

Riekenberg, Michael, 1999, 'Warlords. Eine Problemskizze.' In: *Comparativ*, No. 5/6, 1999, pp. 187-205.

Rotberg, Robert (Ed.), 2004, *When States fail. Causes and Consequences*, Princeton: Princeton University Press.

Ruloff, Dieter/Schubiger, Livia, 2007, 'Kriegerische Konflikte: eine Übersicht.' In: *ApuZ*, 16-17/2007, 16. April 2007, pp. 10-16.

Schneckener, Ulrich, 2005, 'Fragile Staatlichkeit als globales Sicherheitsrisiko.' In: *APUZ* 28/29 2005, 11. July, pp. 26-31.

Schneckener, Ulrich, 2006, *Transnationaler Terrorismus. Charakter und Hintergründe des „neuen" Terrorismus*, Frankfurt am Main: Suhrkamp.

Seifert, Matthias, 2007, 'Die Neugründung von Somaliland – Ein endogener Staatsbildungsprozess am Horn von Afrika.' In: Seifert, Marc et al. (eds.) (2007): *Beiträge zur 1. Kölner Afrikawissenschaftlichen Nachwuchstagung (KANT I)*. http://www.uni-koeln.de/phil-fak/afrikanistik/kant/data/SM3_kant1.pdf, abgerufen am 1.6.2007.

Tilly, Charles, 1990, *Coercion, Capital, and European States: AD 990 - 1990*, Cambridge: Blackwell.

Tull, Denis M., 2005, *The Reconfiguration of Political Order in Africa: A Case Study of North Kivu (DR Congo)*. Hamburg: Institut für Afrika-Kunde.

Wartorn Societies Project (WSP), 2005, *Rebuilding Somaliland. Issues and Possibilities*. Asmara: Red Sea Press.

Weber, Annette, 2007, 'Alte Karten neu gemischt.' SWP aktuell, January 2007, http://www.swp-berlin.org/ de/common/get_document.php ?asset_id=3633, as on 12. 6. 2007.

Zangl, Bernhard/Zürn, Michael, 2003, *Frieden und Krieg*, Frankfurt am Main: Suhrkamp.

Sharia Courts and Military Politics in Stateless Somalia

Medhane Tadesse[1]

Overview

The emergence of a radical Islamist[2] movement in Somalia becomes real, manifest in the leading roles played by the Union of Islamic Courts/UIC/[3] and its supporters within the Transitional Federal Parliament in the recent conflicts in Somalia. In this situation the full engagement of scholars and policy makers in understanding and engaging in Somalia, one way or the other, becomes ever more pivotal. Some say that the Islamist constituency in Somalia is very narrow, that the UIC is a Hawiya dominated movement and that it is unable to expand much beyond Hawiya territory. These dominant arguments, echoed mainly by the anti-TFG forces are unfortunately shared by many academic specialists on Somalia giving a lot of emphasis to the clan aspect of the conflict (Menkhaus, 2003:37; Bryden, 2002:28; DeWaal, 1999:8). These are powerful, but misleading arguments. The truth is that the UIC was about to expand beyond the clan boundaries, but that time was too short to become manifest.[4] Therefore, any conclusion that relegates the Islamist factor of the conflict into the sideshow should be received with a great deal of caution.

This paper argues that the threat of radical Islam in Somalia is probably exaggerated but not totally unjustified. It is a great misconception to call the Somali conflict a clan conflict. Clan identity didn't prevent war between the same clan members with opposing business and political interests.[5] The growing influence of Islamist (political and military) actors in Somalia has little or nothing to do with the clan aspect of the conflict. The strength of political Islam lies in its ability to address the needs of certain groups that have been affected by the absence of law and order and basic services. Somali Islamists seek credibility and command popular support due to other legitimate roles. Understanding the Somali crisis requires scholars to concentrate on the intractable heart of the Islamist constituency in a failed state. Such basic argument and analysis, which I hope this paper may provide, is essential in formulating realistic assessments of the radicalization of Islam in Somalia.

This paper is a brief analysis of the role of Islamists in a collapsed state. It is completely outside the scope of this contribution to discuss the regional dimension of radical Islam or the nature of the crisis in Somalia. The following analysis attempts to construct an analytical framework for understanding the reasons behind the rise and expansion of radical Islam in

---

[1] Center for Policy Research and Dialogue (CPRD), Addis Ababa, Ethiopia
[2] The name Islamist implies political and military Islam.
[3] I am hesitant to include the name Consultative Council, as the UIC has never been consultative in the true sense of the term.
[4] Discussions with Somali informants: Sheik Dolal, Haji Ibrahim Mukhtar. Around half of al-Shabab fighters were from Darod and Isaq clans. The expansion of the UIC in southern Somalia and activities of their supporters in Puntland and Somaliland is a clear sign. However, most of the leaders of the UIC came from the Haber-Gidir Ayr sub-clan, and within it, the Ayaanle lineage. This is partly associated with the history and formative stage of the *Sharia* courts in early 1990's.
[5] Infact, the recent war in Mogadishu which led to the rise of the Union of Islamic Courts was triggered by a clash between the business tycoon Abubakar Adani and Bashir Reaghe who belong to the Abgal clan family.

Somalia today. It puts into perspective some of the otherwise puzzling elements behind the growing importance and influence of Islamic armed groups in a failed state. In doing this it seeks to discuss the historical background to the rise and spread of radical Islam. It also describes the context in which radical Islam continues to appeal to some sections of the population.

Political Islam in Somalia: Rise and expansion

The Horn of African region is one of the footholds of early Islam. In short, Islam is, like Christianity, deeply rooted in many countries of the Horn of Africa. Unlike in other parts of North Africa and the Middle East, in the Horn Islam entered by peaceful means such as trade and not through the *jihad* (Ethiopia & the Horn,1995:6). Of equal importance to its depth is its application. Apart from the brief Gragn Wars (1527-1543) the Sufis, who evangelized Islam were accommodating the native culture and customs. On the other hand, Islamism as a political movement in Somalia and the rest of the region traces its origins only to the 1980s. The Somali fundamentalist movement was reinforced by state collapse in 1991 and the resultant civil war, international intervention, external influence, and the subsequent efforts made by the Somalis themselves towards new patterns of political reconstruction in a bid to shape their own destiny (Medhane, 1999:4; Erlich, 2003:3) In the absence of such a sequence of events, Islamic fundamentalism would have remained a politically marginal force in Somali politics.

The rise and development of the Islamist movement in Somalia, like in many other countries of the Horn is the result of over 20 years of meticulous and deliberate policy of creating an Islamist constituency in the country. What is unique about Somalia though is the absence of a government, which made it easier than in neighboring countries for the Islamists to be visible and project political power.[6] Mainly, over the past two decades Somalis have become accustomed to political Islam and a significant part of them are attracted by its message. To a great extent this is not unique to Somalia. Religious approaches to intractable social and economic ills are being phrased anew throughout the Horn of African region. Among others, this tendency can be traced to the widespread poverty, which lies at the heart of militancy, the rapid change in religious equilibrium and the growing influence of religion stimulated by the economic weakness (or total absence) of the state, and the apparent bankruptcy of secular ideologies (Samatar, 2006:9; Medhane 2003:132). The post-colonial African state (which doesn't exist in Somalia at all) is widely seen as having failed to provide the basic social services in terms of education, health, security and economic freedoms. But, I think, the crisis is not one of economics only, or of security only: it is a crisis of hope, one of the soul, one that reflects the lack of believing into a model for the future[7] (Prunier, 2002:2.).

In Somalia the deconstruction of the Somali state created an ideological vacuum that religious institutions have been competing to occupy, at least in part. In fact, the increasing bankruptcy of secular ideologies, the defeat of Somali nationalism, as well as the failure of clan alliance to save Somalia from perpetual chaos have contributed to the steady expansion

---

[6] By comparison Islamists don't have similar visibility in Eritrea and Ethiopia.

[7] Increasing desperation and hopelessness pushes many people to believe more and more in religion and rest their hopes on the next life and for many this means that the hour of the miracle worker (religion) has finally come.

of Islam as the preferred ideology. This is probably due to shifting primary identities: once people no longer find hope and are alienated from one of their identities, they react by adopting and emphasizing another identity—particularly if the exponents of that view are heavily-funded and committed to their task. And this is exactly the case with Somali Islamists who have been more organized and enjoy external financial support and patronage. Many Somalis argue that pan-Somali nationalism and its irredentist agenda led to the destruction of the Somali state and the misery that followed; hence that clan as an organizing principle failed to deliver in terms of peace and stability or economic survival.[8] For many people Islam has given the answer. Consequently, one possible explanation will be that Islamists are trying to elevate one form of identity (Islam) by destroying the other (clan identity.) Later on the Islamic courts would say they want to promote Islamic law rather than clan allegiance, which has divided Somalis over the past 15 years. It is like an attempt to subdue one form of identity to another.

Facing Ethiopian forces, the UIC in the recent conflict played the nationalist card and gained some sympathy as a result, but it did not command sufficient inter-clan consensus for this to translate into national mobilization. For them the only effective way to destroy clan loyalty and devotion was to channel their loyalty towards religion. This is not limited to Islam. All variations of fundamentalism tend to do this. But practically it was a return to the slogan of 'Greater Somalia.' This has always been a popular crowd-pleasing slogan and source of legitimacy in Mogadishu for successive Somali governments, but was forcefully rejected by the neighboring states (Samatar, 2006:13).

Somalia's combination of institutional collapse, conflict and poverty has led to hopelessness, abject poverty, desperation and criminality which served as a potent recipe for extremism and a fertile ground for Islamists. This, in many ways is a reaction to the wider socio-economic and political crisis. Civil war and state collapse have rendered Somali society susceptible to external extremist influences. This largely explains the rise and expansion of militant Islamic groups in Somalia. Even in other countries of the Horn, such movements are displacing the state by deploying large amount of resources, manpower and organizational skill. The one common element of these apparently emerging religious phenomena is the attempt to address what was formerly addressed by politics and the state. Another trend is evident too. Throughout northeast Africa, societies are accustomed to a certain level of violence, ranging from organized armed clashes to inter-communal raids and disputes. Militarisation in Somalia, as in most countries of the sub-region, is a product of structural conditions that constitute a crisis for human security and the state. These conditions include a history of civil wars and authoritarian rule; the exclusion of minorities from governance; socio-economic inequity and deprivation; last but not least weak states are to mention that are unable to manage normal societal conflict in a stable and consensual fashion. These conditions create a security vacuum that non-state groups and individuals seek to fill through the use of violence, sometimes in an organized and sustained fashion and at other times in a spontaneous and sporadic manner. Indeed, the provision of security matters in poor communities, especially in (the Horn of) Africa, which has a particularly high concentration of impoverished people. Although there is little hard evidence to suggest that effective delivery of security or policing necessarily reduces poverty, crime is undoubtedly 'expensive'

---

[8] Discussions with Somali intellectuals, Hargeisa 2000.

for poor people in terms of their ability to protect themselves, or recover from victimization (Hills, 2000:3; Carothers, 2006:56; Baker,2005:36). Security is not available or affordable or both. Perhaps in response to the lack or poor governance record of African states, communities have resorted to other ways of protecting themselves and providing security.

The need for Sharia courts

Not only are most of the states in the sub-region unable to provide security, attempts to make them effective have been compromised by structural deficiencies. This gave way to the emergence of non-statutory armed groups and policing agencies. Efforts at modernizing and reforming them have largely been frustrated, and not only have decades of aid and assistance failed to establish Western styles of policing, but also state policing remains poorly resourced, trained, and managed; it is often ineffective and sometimes blatantly corrupt and violent (DFID, 2002:17; Hills, 200:4).The reality in Somalia is that state security agencies are non-existent. The resultant security vacuum attracts an array of alternative policing and/or security agencies. It is in this context that the emergence of *Sharia* courts and their militias need to be partly understood. Non-state security agencies and armed groups are invariably dismissed as 'vigilantism', or as 'customary' or unwanted even though research shows that community-based groups are popular, provide security to most people, and are potentially valuable assets for advancing safety and security (Baker, 2004:39). Yet little is known about their nature, conduct of operations, their impact and how they might be integrated into security analysis, political transition, crime prevention strategies or security governance. An examination of non-statutory armed groups, their nature and components, and the levels of security they offer or deny is therefore needed.

   Sharia courts became a feature in Mogadishu in the mid 1990's and slowly and steadily increased their resources, territorial coverage and organization. After the collapse of the Somali government in 1991, a system of *Sharia*-based Islamic courts became the main judicial system funded through fees paid by litigants. Over time the courts began to offer other services such as education and health care. The courts also acted as local police forces, being paid by local businesses to reduce crime. At first they concentrated on petty crime but by the mid 1990s they had progressed to dealing with major crimes in north Mogadishu.[9] They soon saw the sense in working together through a joint committee to promote security. This move was initiated by four of the courts - *Ifka Halan*, *Circolo*, *Warshadda* and *Hararyaale* - who formed a committee to co-ordinate their affairs, to exchange criminals from different clans and to integrate security forces. In 1999 the group began to assert its authority.[10] Due to the unique situation of Mogadishu the UIC as an organization remained firmly established in the *Hawiye* clan.

   As the courts began to assert themselves as the dispensers of justice they came into conflict with the secular warlords who controlled most of the city. In April 2006 they took control of the main market in Mogadishu and, in July, captured the road from Mogadishu to Afgoi. They had reached out to military politics by then. Originally, the Islamic Courts were

---

[9] Discussions with former al-Ittihad members, June 1998.
[10] Informants: Sheikh Daqane Sherif, Sheik Ali Bayr.

basically the creation of businessmen, clan elders and community and religious leaders within specific sub-clans and their authority came from the clan leaders.[11] Their initial aim was to provide security through the use of Sharia law, prevent local clan/sub-clan lineage conflict and provide a more secure environment for business. Hence, it could be argued that the Court's movement was a logical response to the condition of Somali society, and the complete absence of any law enforcement whatsoever. In reality, most of the businessmen involved in supporting the *Sharia* court's militia are pragmatists, seeking to harness the courts to provide better security and a safer environment in which to conduct commerce. Many also saw in the Islamists a potential to arrest the progressive fragmentation of Somali politics along clan lines. An Islamic Courts' movement, it was believed, sprang up to impose some sort of cohesion on a rapidly disintegrating social order. Slowly the business community and public opinion rallied behind these courts. But the most determining factor was the support given by clan leaders. Thus, Islamist groups were poised to fill the vacuum created by lawlessness and anarchy, and found acceptance as providers of security from many Somalis, notably the clan leadership and business class.

Other trends are noteworthy. Most of the business and socio-economic infrastructure in post-1991 Somalia was built through the Islamist agenda. As much as there has been an internal fertile ground for extremism, the ideological roots and financial backing of militant Islamic groups lie outside Somalia. Thus international connectedness has been key to political Islam in Somalia (Medhane, 2002:89); DeWaal, 1999:8-9). It has facilitated the operation of financial services and has enabled access to Islamic philanthropic resources. Trust networks established on common commitments to political Islamist agenda gained Somali businessmen easy access to capital through connections to Islamist counterparts in Dubai and Saudi Arabia (LeSage, 2001:3-6). This explains the recent advances made by the *Wahabi* movement in Somalia. Either due to expediency, security or access to financial resources (such as credit), or to tap into the network of business contacts and information that it provides, the big business in Somalia is almost exclusively associated with Islamist finances (Menkhaus, 2003:18. Political Islam had for long remained pervasive among the small, middle-class elite, before it slowly spread to other sections of the population, mainly the youth. Mainly the business class of Mogadishu found the Islamists a useful mechanism for providing law and order, through Islamic courts, which in turn provided an opportunity for the Islamists' re-entry into military politics, through court militia.

Even if some of these business ties are claimed to be defined by expediency and self-interest, its actors cannot escape from involving (or cooperating) in activities to promote and defend the Islamic project and cause. The fact is that Western aid is virtually non-existent, whereas Islamic aid agencies are providing free or subsidized schooling, running health posts and community outreach services, supporting Mosques, and offering scholarships for study in the Middle East.[12] This means that Islamists have some influence among all major players. In this regard a major shortcoming of scholarly pieces on Somalia is that the number of *madrassas*, mosques controlled by radical clerics,[13] nature and size of Islamist business class is underreported, and that many of their activities are not included in the analysis of the

---

[11] Ibid.

[12] Field Notes (March, 2001).

[13] The biggest Mosques in Mogadishu are now controlled by radical clerics. This includes the Solidarity Mosque, which draws over 40,000 prayers at a time.

political situation in Somalia. The usual suspect is, however, Islamic philantropism. Although some of these Islamic aid agencies are relatively apolitical, seeking only to deepen the Islamic faith in Somalia, the majority of them promote ideas that could produce a new generation of young Somalis who are much more receptive to radical Islamic agendas.[14] Thus, Islamist groups in Somalia are both products of a domestic social and political trend and an essentially extraterritorial phenomenon sustained by donors in Saudi Arabia and the Gulf states. A web of interrelated internal and external factors facilitated the Islamists steady penetration of the Somali society.

Entry to national politics

In the year 2000,[15] the courts formed a union of Islamic courts, partly to consolidate resources and power and partly to aid in handing down decisions across, rather than within, clan lines which culminated in the formation, on October 5, 2006 , of the Supreme Islamic Sharia Court of Banadir province.[16] That announcement from the central Islamic Court was destined to end all tribal Islamic Courts in the capital.[17] The UIC did not exist for long enough for the intended transformation into a multi-clan national movement to become fully realised. The Islamic Courts' original mission was to improve security, bring social justice and combat iniquity. In this regard they have achieved a lot. They also represented a genuine, grassroot-based and legitimate process of peace and state building in Somalia. The UIC represented a step towards resolving Somalia's problems. Hence, it had every reason to prevail until the time it was hijacked by extremist elements with disastrous results for the movement and its followers. On December 24, 2006 Ethiopia reacted with strikes against the movement.[18]

Somali Islamists have relied heavily on external support and ideology which made them hostage to a wider agenda of confronting Ethiopia. When the Ethiopian army decisively intervened and overrun their bases all over Somalia, it dealt a severe blow to their self-immage of military invincibility, to their popularity, credibility and legitimacy. The Sharia courts and their militia have been largely disbanded, and organized military presence has greatly diminished since. Whether due to the Somali social fabric, extraordinary pragmatism, military blunder or lack of an ideology of self-sacrifice essential for the continuity of a committed fighting force, the Islamist militia was unable to face up to the combined attack of the Transitional Federal Government/TFG/ of Somalia and their Ethiopian allies.[19]

Somalia has always been a candidate for a resurgent militant Islam. The question has been to which extent the militant Islam would be able to cause real political harm in Somalia?

---

[14]The Somali branch of the al-Haramain Islamic Foundation, a large Saudi charity closely linked with the Saudi government; Mercy International, a worldwide Islamic relief agency registered in Switzerland; the International Islamic Relief Organization/IIRO/.

[15] Informant: Ahmed Shide, Abdisalam, Gush

[16] UIC press release by Ibrahim Adow

[17] The announcement ceremony was attended by all Islamic officials; both consultative and executive councils, intellectuals and civil society members and took place in the former Somalian presidential palace in central Mogadishu.

[18] Following UIC claims of attacks by its militia on the Ethiopian troops sent to train the forces of the TFG, Ethiopia reacted with hard and fast military offensive. This sentence is unclear!

[19] It is worth mentioning here the argument that the Somali pragmatic desert worldview militates against the growth of organized, Islamic militancy or, for that matter large-scale movement of any sort.

However, the actions of the UIC during their brief occupation of central and southern Somalia proves the extent to which radical Islam spread in Somalia, for several reasons:

The attempt by the UIC to institute the strict Sharia Law of *Wahabism* as the only form of Islam to be practiced in the country, seen also as a means to achieve their political power, has revealed the intent and ambition of the Islamist movement. It also revealed the degree of association of the militant leaders of the UIC with global Islamic movements, and the way they positioned themselves globally. Indeed, the UIC leadership had thoroughly alienated most of the population by its erratic behavior, and attempts to impose an extremist version of Islam, previously unknown in Somalia (Milas, 2007:13-15).[20]

Another event shows a related strategy: talking as a Somali nationalist but acting as a global *Jihadist*. This was the case, when the blue colored Somali flag was publicly burned,[21] and replaced by a black flag, probably symbolizing the close association with *al-Qaeda*. As it turned out, the frequent mentioning about Somali nationalism was clearly rhetoric. It served some few radical Islamists recruiting young fighters for an alleged Islamic revolution devoid of national boundaries.

The *Salafi* leadership brilliantly used Somali irredentism as a political factor in its bid for power. In actual fact, however, Somali nationalism was subservient to international Jihadism. Particularly, the use of the black flag, instead of the blue-white colored Somali flag, by the UIC - mainly the *Hizb al-Shabaab* - is telling that Somali Islamists are not inspired by what happened inside Somalia.The often ruthless way the *al-Shabaab (*the UIC's Youth League*)* have imposed themselves on Mogadishu, and the indiscriminate (in terms of clan) history of assassination and murder of opponents is prove that they weren't motivated by clan agendas. The commander of the Youth League, Sheikh Ayro, and his followers are credited with more than two hundred killings, mainly targeting Europeans and Somalis, human rights and democracy activists, even before the Courts took control in June 2006. The killing of westerners has nothing to do with a clan (Hawiya) or Somali nationalist agenda.

The ban imposed by the UIC on less radical Islamic groups such as the *al-Islah* is another indication of their radical and violent character. The ban took not the clan nature but rather the theology of *al-Islah* into consideration.[22].

The UIC leadership quite deliberately associated itself with the international confrontation between Islam and non-believers. Its repeated call for *jihad* and appeal to Muslims all over the world is an indication that it considered itself as a group fighting for the cause of Islam.

A quite extraordinary development in the Somali context relates to the recent use of Arabic names and Arabic language by the leadership of the Somali Islamist movement.[23]

Using a combination of international connections and finance, and appealing to the majority of Somalis, Somali Islamists have carved a significant constituency for themselves, threatening their internal and external enemies. Probably, an additional factor is the recent development in the Middle East, the Israeli-Palestinian conflict, and of course the war in Iraq.

---

[20] Conversations in Gedo with acquaintances from Somalia, December 2006.For instance in Bulobarde, Hiran Region, a UIC cleric had ordered that anyone who did not pray five times would be executed.

[21] This happened in many towns, particularly Kismayo.

[22] Conversely this could lead us to assume that Sufi traditionalists and moderate Islamic groups like al-Islah still have considerably more popular support than the Jihadists elements of al-Ittihad and al-Shabaab, as demonstrated by the UIC need to ban al-Islah meetings

[23] For the first time in modern history leaders who claim to represent Somali refused to use the Somali language, instead requested Arabic as a medium of communication in a dialogue with a foreign power in another country.

Globalization and more access to communications and the media, seem to have attracted the attention of many Muslims in the Horn, including those in Somalia, to events in that part of the world; in the process new alliances were shaped, and many have come to associate themselves along the new lines. This is not unique to Somalia, and is an evolving phenomenon in the broader radicalization of Islam in the sub-region, a neglected but crucially important issue.

Conclusion

The above analysis attempts to locate the origin and status of military Islam in Somalia, including its successes, the recent military setbacks it has suffered as well as the crisis that has unfolded itself only recently. The way in which the Union of Islamic Courts consolidated its power was a genuine political process in which the Somali business class entered into a pact with the political elite (in this case the Islamists), forging the first political contract in southern Somalia. This alliance was not built on aid resources and sovereign rents, as it was the case with other political formations. It therefore could be argued that it was a locally owned, credible, legitimate and sustainable political process. However, there have always been those actors, who aimed at developing the courts as a vehicle for the creation of an Islamic Emirate, encompassing large areas outside Somalia. Extremist elements with these broader ambitions easily hijacked the Courts movement for political ends with disastrous effects. This revealed an inconvenient truth about the Somali Islamist constituency: that the Islamists are the best organized group that can easily control the flow of armaments and external resources. At the same time the real importance of Somali Islamists lies in the fact that they successfully targeted the unmet needs of urban society, notably in providing security and social services, as much as assistance in the field of education, health and financial and credit needs. In this scheme Islamic philanthropic organizations have played a key role. The business class of Mogadishu found the Islamists a useful mechanism for providing law and order, through Islamic courts, which in turn provided an opportunity for the Islamists' re-entry into military politics, through court militia. Therefore, though external factors and purely ideological motives do play an important role in consolidating the position of the Islamists, it cannot be separated from the broader security role of non-statutory groups in fragile and failed states. Indeed, it is among these variables that the deeper and enduring appeal of militant Islamic groups in Somalia can be located.

Bibliography

Bruce, Baker, 2005. *Multi Choice Policing in Uganda: In Policing and Society. Volume 15, n.1.,* London, Routledge

Bryden, Matt, 2002. *Security Challenges and the International Dimension of the Somal Crisis.* Washington D.C.

Carothers, 2006, *Promoting the Rule of Law Abroad: In Search of Knowledge Carnegie Endowment.* Washington, DC: Carnegie Endowment for International Peace

DeWaal, Alex, 2004, *Class and power in a Stateless Somalia.* Discussion paper, Addis Ababa
    Department for International development/DFID/, 2002, Safety, *Security and
    Accessible Justice: Putting Policy into Practice*
    http/www.dfid.gov.uk/pubs/files/safesecureaccjustice.pdf

Erlich, Haggai, 2003, *Arabia and Ethiopia – Muslims and Christians Across a Sea,
    Conference of Ethiopian Studies,* Hamburg 2003

Ethiopia and the Horn, Teaching Material on Ethiopian History. Department of History,
    Addis Ababa University, 1995

Hills, Alice, 2000, *Policing Africa's poor. Leeds, UK*

Hills, Alice, 2005, Business as Usual: Police, Conflict Prevention and Development. Cotonou,
    Benin.

LeSage, Andre, 2001. *Prospects for al-Ittihad and Islamist Radicalism in Somalia.
    Unpublished Article, Nairobi, Kenya.*.Medhane Tadesse, 1999, *Islamic
    Fundamentalism in Somalia: History, Nature and Implications.* Paper presented to the
    Conference on Islamic Radicalism, Hargeissa, Somaliland

Medhane Tadesse, 2002, a*l -Ittihad:Political Islam and Black Economy in Somalia.* Addis
    Ababa

Medhane Tadesse, 2003, *Religions, Peace and the Future* of Ethiopia. Conference on
    Federalism. Addis Ababa, Ethiopia

Menkhaus, Ken. 2003. Somalia: A Situation Analysis and Trend Assessment. UHNCR.
    Nairobi Milas , Seifulaziz. 2007. Flawed Sheikhs and Failed Strategies: Lessons of the
    Jihadist Debacle in Somalia..Addis Ababa,Ethiopia

Prunier, Gerard, 2002. *The Far Edge of Religion: Religions and Quasi Religious Answers to
    the Crisis of the State in Eastern Africa. Unpublished Memo.*Addis Ababa, Ethiopia.

Samatar, Said, 2006, *Unhappy Masses and the Challenge of Radical Islam in the Horn of
    Africa.* Minneapolis, USA

Emerging Governance in Somaliland:
A Perspective from Below

Ulf Terlinden

Authorities taking over when states fail, and ultimately collapse, include the actors of war, such as military faction leaders; but they also include remnants of the former state administration, revitalised traditional authorities, religious courts, local businessmen, etc., who continue or begin to exercise authority as "functional equivalents" of the state. These actors differ widely in their influence, in their sources of legitimacy, the degree and modes of their accountability vis-à-vis respective communities, etc. Partly determined by these features, there are also great differences in how actors within emerging governance structures relate to each other, what kind of actors gain the upper hand, what degree of stability these structures develop, and ultimately, whether they can lay the foundations to ending civil war, re-establishing a political entity and fostering democratic practices of governance.

Founded in 1991, Somaliland has become prominently known as a non-recognised de-facto state in the North-western part of the collapsed Somali Republic. In striking contrast to much of the rest of Somalia, and with few exceptions, it has maintained a considerable degree of political stability since then. Drawing heavily from the traditional elders' system, public security and order have been restored, local, presidential and parliamentary elections have been held, administrative structures have been established, and a good deal of economic reconstruction has been achieved.[1]

Based on these observations, this article identifies explanations as to why and how Somaliland's governance structure emerged. Contrary to much of the existing literature, which tends to focus on the national level of state formation, the re-establishment of governance structures will be considered from the perspective of two of the country's six regions here. Awdal Region in Western Somaliland, and Sanaag in the East, are two of three regions that are not or only partly inhabited by the majority Issaq clan of Somaliland, therefore posing particular challenges to the re-establishment of a unified system of governance.

The processual examination of emerging governance structures in the two regions and their comparison is intended to distil some of the variations of sub-national constellations that led to Somaliland's current form of governance. Particular emphasis is placed on relations between the regional and the national level.

Theoretical approach

There is no firmly established standard definition of *governance* (Hyden et al 2004: 12; Weiss 2000: 796/797). Since none of the existing approaches (UNDP, World Governance Survey,

---

[1] For a detailed review of Somaliland's peace-making, state-building and democratisation processes, see my joint article with Mohammed Hassan Ibrahim in this volume.

Commission on Global Governance, World Bank) fully fits with the direction of this research, applicable elements of the different definitions are combined here:

Governance for the purpose of this research is defined as the exercise of authority to address public affairs at any level of social aggregation. It involves formal institutions and regimes empowered to enforce compliance, as well as informal arrangements that people and

institutions have either agreed to or perceive to be in their interest. Governance thus includes both the establishment of "rules of the game" for social actors (North 1993: 2), as well as specific mechanisms and processes through which citizens and groups of citizens articulate their interests, exercise their rights, fulfil their obligations or resolve their conflicts.

This research focuses on deliberate and targeted actions intended to address challenges in the area of governance (see also Hein 2003: 395).

The process of governance establishment is studied through a prism combining *actors, institutions and shared mental models*. Strong emphasis is placed on *actors'* behaviour, assuming that the development paths of governance structures are eventually a result of the "contextual, continuous redefinition of perceived preferences, strategies and opportunities for action of the relevant actors" (Merkel & Puhle 1999: 48/49, tba).

However, adopting a descriptive-empirical actor-orientated (rather than actor-centred) approach, due consideration is given to the other two "corners" of the theoretical triangle, too. *Institutions* will be considered as "humanly devised constraints that structure human interaction. They are made up of formal constraints (rules, laws, constitutions), informal constraints (norms of behaviour, conventions, and self imposed codes of conduct), and their enforcement characteristics" (North 1993: 2). Institutions reduce insecurity and are intended to order and steer human behaviour (Croissant et al 2003: 191-192). Following rational institutional theory, they define the incentive structure of societies.

The term *Shared Mental Models (SMM)* captures the continuum of "myths, dogmas, ideologies and half-baked theories" (Denzau & North 1994: 1) that actors hold and act on. Individuals construct these mental models "to make sense out of the world around them" (Denzau & North 1994: 3). SMM such as perception patterns, collective memories, assumptions and identities are tracked because of the way they inform the decision-making process of individual and collective actors.

Governance, the clan system and the state

Political developments in Somaliland since 1991 can be characterised as a continuing, endogenous process of political reconstruction, for which the clan system provides the main basis. This process relies strongly on consensus building and cooptation strategies, which mainly crystallised in the framework of peace conferences during the 1990s (see e.g. Bradbury et al 2003; Brons 2001: 247-253; Cabdiraxmaan Jimcaale 2005: 60-86). The form and focus of these processes has gradually changed during the democratisation process since 2001. However, until today, the central government (including the regional governments it controls) as the main entity of the new state commands relatively modest capability to assert itself or to project power against resistance. The clan system remains highly relevant.

Decisively, the clan system does not present itself as an order alternative to the state. Instead, on the one hand, it undertakes classical state functions such as security and penal action in a complementary way. On the other hand, it penetrates state-based institutions such as elections, decision-making mechanisms and administrative bodies where necessary[2]. As a result, clan-based "rules of the game" are often applied behind the scenes of the state. Meanwhile, the new state as the nominal umbrella organisation remains unquestioned, even in places where it does not possess general acceptance (see e.g.Ciabarri: 8).

Yet manipulation and adaptation are not at all unilateral. Resulting from the availability of state resources, state-based interventions and the formation of new government bodies, the institutions and agents of the clan system undergo a transformation which by tendency affects their modes of legitimacy. For example, as one effect, it can occasionally be observed that the traditional authority of clan elders is substituted with allegiance based on patronage[3]. In view of the mutual reconfiguration of "the state" and "the clan system" in Somaliland, they are not considered as strictly dichotomous categories here, but as overlapping and partly integrated structures. This forms a central point of departure of the research on the webs of local actors and institutions to be summarised here.

Despite having had principally similar clan-based institutional settings at the outset, the new order develops neither linearly nor homogeneously in the different parts of Somaliland. This applies although the nominal existence of state structures such as regional administrations, representative organs and electoral processes in most parts of the country may generate a different impression. Governance after state collapse is shaped by a variety of influences and determinants in different historical periods and in the various parts of the country. As of today, the resulting local realities behind the scenes of the state are not at all uniform. It is against this background that the genesis and key characteristics of the governance structures in Awdal and Sanaag will be elaborated in short case studies below.

A commonality of both areas is that core functions of local violence control, penal action, security and conflict resolution are largely guaranteed by recourse to traditional institutions of the clan system – i.e. mainly through traditional law based on clan-treaties (*xeer*) and implemented by ad-hoc councils of elders. In practice, a legal pluralism between traditional and state systems of order has primarily developed in urban spaces, though in case of conflict, clan-based rules would likely retain superiority (Battera & Campo 2001; APD 2002). State authorities rarely intervene in rural areas, but when they do, it is in highly-escalated conflicts, and usually in conjunction with the traditional elders. This reality appears to be quite disconnected from the state building process; it does not seem to have questioned the acceptance of the state (where it has been achieved). And yet it fails to generate performance-based "everyday legitimacy"[4] for the state.

By contrast, the course of local pacification after the state's collapse, and the transformation processes of structures of violence display fundamental differences. Partly as a consequence of these features, the development of supra-local forms of governance as well as the establishment, acceptance and practical meaning of the state's administrative structures

---

[2] The nomination process for the parliamentary candidates in 2005 and the electorate's voting patterns provide illustrative examples for this. See APD/Interpeace 2006: 36/37.

[3] See e.g. APD / WSP 1999: 25/26. "Clan elders" here refers to *Suldaanno, Ugaasyo, Garaaddo, Cuqaal,* thus titled and non-titled traditional authorities in Somali society.

[4] The state remains unable to accumulate any of the "basic legitimacies" ("Basislegitimität" according to Trotha 1995: 8-11) of either a) superior force, b) organisational power or c) security of order.

vary considerably in the two regions. This will be considered here as part of the institutionalisation process of new forms of power and control.

Furthermore, the two areas have noticeable differences in their relationships with the national level and in the institutional transformation of their governance structures. These aspects are both positioned in the context of the central government's efforts to consolidate power and in the framework of the democratisation process. All these questions are at the interface of security and political governance.

The case of Awdal: Self-governance under the Somaliland umbrella

After the collapse of the state, the relatively homogeneous Awdal Region in Western Somaliland was facing primarily external rather than internal challenges. Next to the three sub-clans of the Gadabursi, a small minority of Ciisse inhabits Awdal, whose main clan territory is located in Djibouti and Ethiopia[5]. After the overthrow of Siad Barre's regime in 1991, the elders of the Gadabursi quickly installed an "administrative committee" in order to pacify the local situation. The elders also organised the continuation of the local and regional administration in the regional capital Boroma under the auspices of the committee. The process was further supported by civil society initiatives and the Diaspora. The main challenge lay in the precarious relationship with Somaliland's new rulers, since most of the Gadabursi clan had sided with the Somali regime during the war (Prunier 1994: 2) until the *Somali National Movement*, which was dominated by the Issaq clan, ousted the government army from Somaliland in 1991.

However, the difficult situation of the Gadabursi further united the clan, which anyhow had been relatively cohesive throughout history (Menkhaus 1997: 9). Its bargaining position strongly benefited from the emerging rift among the Issaq-based SNM and its ambitions to achieve international recognition for Somaliland. The latter required a consensual, negotiated resolution of outstanding issues, and brought the need to obtain at least minimal endorsement of independence by all clans of the territory (see e.g. Prunier 1994: 3/4). What could be described as negotiation process of several years resulted in a setting where Awdal was largely "self-administered" – thus, Gadabursi were ruling Gadabursi affairs. In return for this relative autonomy, the clan accepted that the administrative structures of Awdal and Boroma were brought under the roof of the new state, and since, at least ostensible backing is given to the notion of Somaliland's independence.

This mutual understanding facilitated the early integration of Awdal's militia into Somaliland's police, army and custodial corps. However, in situations of internal conflict, the soldiers' loyalty is likely to remain primarily with their own clan or clan segment. Following the new arrangement, the administration on the local and regional level – now officially part of the state framework – was also able to establish itself more firmly (Menkhaus 1997: 35/36). The role and influence of clan elders in everyday politics shrank, with other clan agents[6] gaining weight.

---

[5] There are a few other minorities, such as the Gaboye, but discussing their role would go beyond the scope of this chapter.

[6] These are not limited to members of the administration, but also include a variety of private actors, such as influential business men, religious authorities, intellectuals, etc.

Among the existing institutions, those related to the clan system decisively shape the development and functioning of Awdal's current governance structure. While the *xeer* – the traditional law applied by councils of elders – is of central importance, it is by far not the only relevant clan-based institution in this context. These regulatory mechanisms only stand a chance to work because the clan system itself represents an accepted "rule of the game". It forms a social matrix that structures society into segments between and within which institutions such as the *xeer* can function. This social setup corresponds with the nested identities of the clan system, which provide an inter-subjective framework of orientation and can best be captured as a shared mental model.

Gadabursi traditional institutions in particular survived the colonial period as well as Somali statehood in good shape. While they certainly underwent change, by and large, most of the basic rules remain functionally intact and highly relevant. The range and assertion capabilities of the elders in Awdal strongly benefit from the relative homogeneity and cohesion of the clan structure. Applying traditional law within a clan (the Gadabursi) is usually more smooth and effective than across clan lines, particularly if these lines run parallel to other cleavages. Furthermore, the social fabric of the Gadabursi was hardly disrupted by the war.

The importance of the *xeer* in the area of public security, the most important aspect of governance in day to day life, has already been mentioned. The traditional system has earned an enormous degree of "basic legitimacy" (see footnote 79) of organisational power and security of order from its remarkably effective performance throughout the decades and under various regimes. The fact that these functions rested on actors outside of the state apparatus meant that public order remained comparatively unaffected by the collapse of the state, and has been maintained quite continuously until today. The general public experienced relatively little change in terms of everyday security.

But the security role of the elders' councils (as institutions) is not limited to law enforcement under the *xeer*. They are also instrumental in organising security against external threats, in particular by forming and controlling the clan militia. Among the Gadabursi, the mobilisation of clan militia under the auspices of the elders primarily took place after the Qulujeed Conference in 1988 (Gilkes 1993: 7). It must be recalled that, at the time, the Somali government even supplied weapons and ammunition for this very purpose. While Siad Barre's regime urgently needed the military support of the Gadabursi, it unwittingly undermined its own position in two ways: It shored up the formation of armed units outside of state control, actively surrendering the claim to a monopoly of force, and simultaneously supported the traditional institutions' open resumption of the external security function for the Gadabursi clan. In fact, as a consequence of these developments, the clan was identified even more closely with the government in Mogadishu, but the actual influence of state institutions in Awdal dwindled further.

These developments ultimately resulted in the formation of the Gadabursi council of 21 elders (*guurti*) which took over in July 1991 to lead the clan's affairs after the collapse of the Somali regime earlier that year (Gilkes 1993: 39-41). The fact that the elders had maintained control over most of the clan militias in the region throughout the war and beyond was of fundamental importance for the further development of the governance structure of

Awdal. Looting and the setting up of uncontrolled road blocks could largely be prevented. The autonomy of action of emerging commanders remained very limited. Apart from the authority that the elders drew from their wide recognition among the population and the other violence control functions mentioned above, their ability to control the militia arose from their continued interface role in the funding of the armed force. The elders were the ones to demand and collect the resources from the community which fed the militia. In the near absence of "predatory resources", Awdal offered very little alternative to these community resources.

Yet the functional efficiency of the traditional structures extends far beyond security governance. Partly based on these functions, the clan system forms a "fall back position" of political governance. It can step into the breach with broadly accepted governance institutions where other structures, such as those of the state, prove to be unable or unwilling to cater for the interests of the clan. The elders' continuing ability to mobilise the clan members – including their privately-owned small arms – is a further safeguard to this function. Even more important than the elders' actions in such highly escalated crisis scenarios is their capability as agents of these institutions (and sometimes with other accepted leaders of the clan) to effectively claim that they represent and assert the interest of the clan as a collective actor.

The degree and kind of the state's acceptance within the clan largely determines exactly how this parallel structure relates to it. The clan's enduring autonomy and its effective chances of participation on the different levels are important factors in this relationship. From a clan perspective, the experiment of Somaliland's new statehood must feel like walking a tightrope. Yet knowing the strong networks of Awdal's traditional institutions below them, the Gadabursi may walk quite comfortably.

The existence of this safety net has also marked the long "negotiation process" for the emerging web of state entities. The close connection between the traditional system and the formal government bodies on the local and regional level (especially during the initial years), as well as the successful self-organisation of the administration also determined the development of relations between Awdal (or the Gadabursi) and the new state apparatus at the national level. Put simply, the elders of the Gadabursi Guurti brought "their administration" from below and introduced it to the national framework. This marks a significant difference to so many state and government formation processes where it is usually the central government that forms local and regional administrations from above. This happened primarily as a result of the understanding reached between the agents of the region's traditional institutions – primarily the elders – and the central government. The essence of this was whether and on what conditions the Gadabursi would accept the central government as the political roof for its region and its administration. There was no debate on whether the central government should be allowed to install itself institutionally in the region from the top down.

On balance, by 1996/97, when the overall focus of Somaliland's reconstruction shifted from mainly peace-making to mainly state-building, the national level of the state had gained something of an "entry ticket" to Awdal region. But by and large, its manoeuvres remained limited to consensus-based action. The functioning of this connection between the centre and Awdal region continues to rest primarily on factors outside of the immediate relationship, chief among which is the existing actors' constellation. As a consequence, the link – although comparatively well-developed – lacks institutionalised reliability. Major shifts in the context may still have the potential to dislodge the relationship.

In the course of the state center's efforts to consolidate power (from 1996) and the subsequent democratisation process (from 2001), the Gadabursi managed to develop a significant degree of political participation and shareholding at the national level, which culminated in Dahir Ra'yale Kahin's ascent to the vice presidency in 1997 and to the presidency in 2002 (see Bradbury 2007: 243). The rise of a Gadabursi to the top post of the country has also had an effect on the equilibrium between the centre and the region. Under the earlier President Egal, the Issaq-dominated centre of power used to serve as a uniting factor for the Gadabursi. Within the nominal framework of the state, his "subsidiarity approach"[7] to Awdal supported a local legitimisation of governance. It also provided space for mostly endogenous processes to strengthen structures which formed part of this state.

These dynamics have changed since the President of Somaliland hails from Awdal. A national counterpart from one's own ranks does not have the uniting effect on the region that the national government headed by a member of the majority clan of Somaliland used to have. Furthermore, the centre of power now maintains direct, vertical networks in the region. This has opened up channels through which the national level may involve itself with the regional political process, changing the previously quite autonomous governance reality of the region.

In addition, these interactions primarily utilise one of the three sub-clans of the Gadabursi. As a consequence, the elders of the other two sub-clans have increased their involvement with politics again, holding regular meetings to safeguard their collective interests. Thus, the changes to the equilibria between the centre and the region, and between the sub-clans of Awdal, have shifted some of the collective decision-making back to a lower level of aggregation and outside the formal arena of the state.

The case of Sanaag: Keeping the peace in an environment of shifting sand

Sanaag in Eastern Somaliland, including its capital Erigavo, is inhabited rather heterogeneously by four different sub-clans. Among these, the Habr Jeclo and the Habr Yonis in the West belong to the Issaq, whereas the Dhulbahante and Warsangeli in the East belong to the Harti group of the Darod clan.

The region's pacification was presented with primarily internal challenges after the state's collapse in 1991: Issaq militia under the SNM banner[8] and government-supporting Dhulbahante and Warsangeli had fought each other in Sanaag since 1989. The region's losses in the civil war reportedly amounted to nearly 3.000 dead, 7.000 wounded and 2.000 houses destroyed (SDRA/MCC 1994: 4). The victory of the SNM displaced many Dhulbahante and Warsangeli, especially from Erigavo and its surroundings. Furthermore, in parallel with Somaliland's first internal conflict in 1991/92, local tensions arose between the Habr Yonis

---

[7] "The principle that a central authority should have a subsidiary function, performing only those tasks which cannot be performed at a more local level." (Concise Oxford Dictionary).

[8] It has to be noted that the SNM group in Sanaag had fallen out with the SNM headquarter and command structure in 1989. Since then, it was organised quite independently from positions in the Daallo mountains (APD 2008: 5). The relevance of this split cannot be discussed in detail here.

and Habr Jeclo sub-clans, too.[9] Thus the communities emerged divided from the war, with the collective memory of neighbours killing each other, while imminently having to face new disputes among the victorious forces (Höhne 2005: 12).

It took a series of 16 peace conferences within the region to incrementally improve local relations between the sub-clans. These meetings took place on the level of sub-clans, applying (notwithstanding adaptations) the well-developed and widely practiced institution of traditional conflict resolution, embedded in the clan system. Eventually, a regional charter signed at the Erigavo Conference in November 1993 formally re-established peace. Above all, it opened up the desperately needed common grazing land, which is often described as the decisive incentive for the four sub-clans to come to terms with each other (Renders 2006: 223). The fact that the meetings were not conducted in a political format (SNM vs. former Barre-supporters) and that future power relations were not discussed is also seen to have facilitated reconciliation. It reportedly helped to avoid perceptions of "winners and losers" and furthered the view that the "arrangements served the interests of all"(Renders 2006: 241).

However, the conference's decision to return all immovable assets (especially privately-owned land) could not be implemented because the Habr Yonis were reluctant to give up these "spoils of war" (Haroon Ahmed Yusuf [n.a.]: 5). So although the clan-based Sanaag peace process set the stage for a normalisation of inter-clan relations and re-established basic stability by the end of 1993, it failed to fully address the remaining conflicts and to provide sufficient basis for political reconstruction.

Partly as a reflection of these circumstances, governance in Sanaag remained minimal and highly segmented. During the war, the local and regional administration had collapsed completely. Authority rested with the local elders of the individual sub-clans, as well as the sub-clan commanders of the relevant armed groupings. In 1991, initial attempts by the dominant Habr Yonis commanders in Erigavo to start up their own regional administration did not gain recognition from the other sub-clans and collapsed immediately. Early in 1992, talks between Habr Yonis and Habr Jeclo led to the temporary formation of a 43-member Issaq Guurti. However, although it had been assigned to appoint a regional administration, the authority of this council remained more or less limited to conflicts resolution and the maintenance of stability. This Guurti did not have influence beyond the two Issaq sub-clans and the immediate environments of Erigavo (Renders 2006: 222). It could not take decisions on behalf of other parts of the region. An aid worker observed at the time that "[a]greements needed to be reached with elders at all levels in each community" (Bradbury 1994: 5). Meanwhile, the self-declared regional governor maintained his claim to power and disregarded the elders. The ensuing power struggle between the Guurti and the governor created a temporary security vacuum in the regional capital.

Although the Erigavo Conference in 1993 finally decided to establish a new regional administration, including a security force and courts, these agreements were not implemented.

---

[9] The shape and extent of these tensions is disputed. Some argue that the majority of the Habr Jeclo population already "retreated from Erigavo to their home territories" after June 1991 (APD 2008: 18), and that "it has been the Habr Yonis (HY) which has captured the town" (Haroon Ahmed Yusuf [n.a.]: 5). Other sources say that the Habr Yonis militia drove the Habr Jeclo militia out of Erigavo when fighting started between Habr Yonis and Ciisse Muuse militia Berbera and Burco (central Somaliland) in 1992 (Renders 2006: 224). On balance, Gilkes reports that "[e]nough tension became apparent between the Habr [Jeclo] and Habr [Yonis] in mid 1992 to make the need for a reconciliation committee obvious" (Gilkes 1993: 45).

Meanwhile, the sub-clans and their traditional institutions remained exclusively responsible for the maintenance of peace in their respective local contexts (Actionaid Somaliland 1998: 5). Apart from the incomplete peace process mentioned above, this deadlock was largely due to circumstances outside the region (Haroon Ahmed Yusuf [n.a.]: 5), which stalled further progress in the area of governance till 1997.

The first external factor was Sanaag's precarious relationship with the central government. Early in 1993, when Somaliland's first President, Cabdiraxmaan Tuur, who hailed from the Habr Yonis, was replaced by President Egal at the Boroma conference, the Habr Yonis fell out with the center of power. Having lost the presidency and following the allocation of what was seen as a disproportionately small number of seats in the new chambers of parliament, the Habr Yonis strictly opposed Egal's rule (Gilkes 1995: 11/12). Combined with their dominant position in Erigavo, this effectively blocked government access to Sanaag for years. As just one indication of this, the elders in Sanaag strongly opposed Egal's efforts to establish a regional administration and to appoint a governor in late 1993 (Gilkes 1995: 22).

The relationship with the national level was further complicated during Somaliland's second internal conflict (from late 1994 till mid-1996), which among other battles involved heavy fighting between government-allied Habr Jeclo and opposing Habr Yonis in Sanaag's neighbouring Togdheer region. Not only did the war with the Habr Yonis undermine relations between Sanaag and the central government further, it also threatened the "fragile peace" (Peace Committee for Somaliland 1997: 6) achieved in Sanaag. Through hard efforts the elders as the agents of the clan institutions effectively prevented the establishment of local 'warlords' and stopped the Togdheer violence from spreading eastwards (Actionaid Somaliland 1998: 5). However, the war still overshadowed the achievements of local reconciliation: It preoccupied people with maintaining the peace rather than building shared institutions.

The second external factor has a much longer-term effect on governance in Sanaag: Emerging entities to the east of the area present competing "political bidders" for Eastern Sanaag and Sool region, both in terms of identity and statehood. Even when no such entity existed during most of the 1990s, reminiscence of the former Somalia was still an important concept appealing to many people in these areas. But a real player entered the scene when the neighbouring regional autonomous state of Puntland was declared in 1998. The participation of Warsangeli and Dhulbahante in the inception of "Puntland" at the Garowe conference turned eastern Sanaag and Sool "into disputed territory" between Somaliland and Puntland (Renders 2006: 362). Puntland claims Eastern Sanaag because the Warsangeli and Dhulbahante in this area belong to the Darod (Harti) clan that dominates Puntland. Somaliland claims the territory on the basis of the boundaries which separated the British protectorate Somaliland from the Italian colony Somalia.[10] I will come back to the impact of this second external factor later.

Meanwhile, by demonstrating the risk of renewed conflict, Togdheer's bloody conflict between 1994 and 1996 ironically facilitated the finalisation of Sanaag's peace process. The

---

[10] The establishment of the Transitional Federal Government for Somalia in 2004 added a further dimension to this conflict, but this aspect shall not be discussed here.

Garaad of the Dhulbahante also pressed the Habr Yonis to comply with the 1993 agreement. As a result, by early 1996, 600 families had been resettled peacefully, reportedly transferring ninety percent of the assets in three locations to the returning Dhulbahante clan members. Thus, when the second internal war of Somaliland ended in mid-1996, the local inter-community relations had improved significantly and favoured a fresh attempt at setting up an administration. Also, at Erigavo level, a structure referred to as the "NGO Co-ordinating Committee" (NGOCC) had emerged as a relatively stable inter-clan body. Appointed by the elders, and relying heavily on the traditional authority of some of its members, it "was increasingly seen as the effective regional structure" by 1997 (Haroon Ahmed Yusuf [n.a.]: 5/6; 10). Thus inter-clan governance had undergone some practice.

The end of the war in 1996 finally paved the way to overcome the distance between the central government and the Habr Yonis of Sanaag, too. To a large extent, this was achieved through the cooptation of members of the local Habr Yonis elite. During the Hargeisa Conference at the end of 1996 / early 1997, Egal brought several of the former Habr Yonis adversaries into the central government. Following Egal's re-election, the conference mandated the government to attempt to appoint district and regional authorities throughout the country (Actionaid Somaliland 1998: 6).

For five months in 1998, the President dispatched a high-level delegation of ministers under the leadership of the Vice-President to the Eastern regions. It certainly was not by chance that this effort coincided with the Garowe conference which founded Puntland. The ministers hailed from the relevant sub-clans in Sanaag and many of them entertained direct family ties to influential key figures in the local context, often from other sub-clans. This strongly supported their position and trust in the negotiations to establish an administration. The elders cooperated with the ministerial delegation - partly to retain a role in their region's governance, partly to be relieved of some of the burdens they had carried all along. As a result of the top-down efforts of the central government, an administration was established. The President also furthered this success by accommodating the former self-declared Governor of Sanaag at a vice-ministerial position in Hargeisa.

In the course of the overall rapprochement between Egal and the Habr Yonis, the latter turned from opposing the central government to representing it: Despite the heterogeneous clan composition of the region, the strong influence of the Habr Yonis received a further boost. While this continues to be a cause of some discontent by the other three sub-clans, at the time, it paved the way to a decisive and fundamental transformation of Sanaag's structures of violence. Most of the militia, especially of the Issaq, were now demobilised or integrated into the "umbrella organisation" of the national army (with similar limitations as in the case of Awdal). This is particularly remarkable in view of the significant degree of autonomy that some of these units had developed, including vis à vis the elders. One important incentive to strike this deal with "Hargeisa" lay in the fact that the central government was going to foot the bill for the demobilisation and reintegration of the militia. The prospect of a continuous, reliable supply of rations or cash not only attracted the militia, but also relieved the elders and the local communities of the pressing burden to feed them.

The working foundation especially of the existing regional government (and to a lesser extent the municipality of Erigavo) is the general consensus to maintain peace above all, which is the fundamental lesson of the havoc caused by the previous conflict (Höhne 2005:

12). What may appear as a tediously unoriginal observation is in fact fundamental to the region's relative stability in spite of the difficult political environment. The experience of the war from 1989 onwards is deeply engraved in the shared mental models of the Sanaag population, and not only because of the numbers of dead and wounded. Given the economic dependence on shared grazing in the remote pastoral setting of Sanaag, the impact of conflict on people's livelihoods is potentially catastrophic in Sanaag. The development of reciprocal relations between neighbouring communities of whatever sub-clan is inevitable. This is also reflected in the enormous degree of intermarriage between the clan segments of the region[11]. "[P]eople have to make a common living as residents in the same places and as relatives on the mother's side" (Höhne 2005: 15). Thus the commitment to maintain peace is firm and remarkably effective.

And yet, this consensus does not provide sufficient basis to develop truly shared, collective institutions in the given constellation in and around Sanaag. Until today, supra-clan governance could barely be developed, neither in the clan system nor in the state arena. The regional administration hardly commands capacity to assert itself. In every dispute and on every matter, its role and authority is limited to the facilitation of ad hoc consensus-building, with frequent references to the need for peace. Although the local administration of Erigavo has greater operational capacity, it is perceived to be primarily under Habr Yonis' influence. The other sub-clans therefore focus primarily on their own clan representatives, who are mostly found outside the government framework of the state.

To a large extent, these limitations derive from the undecided status of Eastern Sanaag between Puntland and Somaliland. From the internal perspective of the Warsangeli and Dhulbahante, opting for one side would seem very risky and is unlikely to happen as long as the long-term future of both political entities remains undefined. Meanwhile, local leaders take advantage of the continuing canvassing by competing emissaries from both sides, be it for their constituencies or for their personal gain. The announcement of the (rather unpromising) independent "Makhir State" in Eastern Sanaag in August 2007 is sometimes described as a political project solely designed to this end.

But the undecided status of the area should not only be considered as a matter of divided allegiance within Eastern Sanaag, but also as a continuing dispute over it from the outside. In other words, even if the large majority of the Warsangeli and Dhulbahante were to choose one side of the divide, tensions with the other political entity would emerge immediately. The most likely price of such a decision would be further internal division[12] and conflict. Apart from Somaliland's and Puntland's interests to maintain their claim over the territory as such, the feud is also linked to Somaliland's status. From a Harti, Darod or wider Somali perspective, sabotaging the full integration of eastern Sanaag (and Sool) into Somaliland appears to be a suitable means of undermining its chances of international

---

[11] See Höhne 2005: 13. On intermarriage between Habr Yonis and Dhulbahante, see Haroon Ahmed Yusuf [n.a.]: 6.
[12] For example, Markus Höhne describes the coronation of competing traditional elders as a result of the divided allegiance of the Dhulbahante (Höhne 2005: 14).

recognition[13]. Since 2004, there have even been several violent confrontations between armed forces of or loyal to Somaliland and Puntland.

This limbo means that governance in Sanaag is operating in shifting sand. Apart from other relevant effects, it does not provide a secured framework to build shared institutions and to grow a supra-clan regional polity. The development and transformation of post-war governance in this region seems to be stuck somewhere between peace-making and state-building.

On balance, the government bodies in Erigavo, primarily exist as a skeleton. Within these structures, not much more than a passable form of security cooperation between the clan segments has been institutionalised. Governance in general and collective decision-making in particular remain highly segmented. In contrast to Awdal, this form of "subsidiarity" does not converge on the level of a relatively homogenous clan which encompasses almost an entire region. In Sanaag, effective governance is localised primarily within each of the four different sub-clans. Especially among the Dhulbahante and Warsangeli, legitimised governance processes are limited to the lowest local level, strongly constraining their ability to address larger, more comprehensive governance matters. Naturally, in the absence of state structures, mainly traditional and other non-state authorities prevail as the agents of governance.

Despite a widespread sense of pragmatism in the area, Eastern Sanaag's state of abeyance continues to affect its relations with the national level of Somaliland. While the Somaliland government considers Sanaag to be under its "umbrella" since the arrangement with the Habr Yonis and the establishment of the regional government in 1997/98, it has not gained reliable, practical access to Eastern Sanaag. Over the years, the range and influence of Somaliland government officials appears fluid. For a long time, representatives of the Somaliland administration (of all levels) could not reach much more east than the regional capital Erigavo. In 2007/08, as Puntland sinks ever deeper into crisis, Somaliland has made successful efforts to increase its clout in the Warsangeli and Dhulbahante land. However, a sustainable resolution of the issue is yet to be developed.

These circumstances also lead to Sanaag's somewhat contradictory political participation and shareholding at the national level: While elections could not be held, and Somaliland lacks acceptance and tangible presence in most of Eastern Sanaag, the Dhulbahante and Warsangeli from the area are represented by a number of quite respected, nominated clan members in both houses of parliament and in the national cabinet.

Comparative summary

In both case studies, pacification and violence control after the state's collapse succeeded primarily through traditional governance by councils of elders, applying the institutions of the *xeer* (the traditional law) and *shir* (inter-clan reconciliation conferences). Together with the structuring clan system, this local set of rules forms the decisive backbone of society and principally exists in similar forms in both regions. Yet the development paths of governance show major differences in the two regions discussed here.

---

[13] The flip side of this is of course that Somaliland's efforts to take full control of the area are partly driven by its quest for recognition.

	Awdal	Sanaag
Remaining level of violence	Minimal	Sporadic resource conflicts, armed conflict over the disputed boundary
Demobilisation	Locally owned	Initiated by the central government
Establishment of the Administration	Locally owned continuation of the previous administration	Fresh start, initiated by the central government, following complete collapse in 1991
Development of a supra-local polity and supra-clan governance	Succeeded (despite limitations)	Largely failed Governance primarily limited to very local level and inter-clan mechanisms
Transfer of authority into state-based bodies	Part of the clan agency shifted into the state apparatus, gradual retreat of the elders	Little authority transferred to the regional administration Transfer of authority to the local administration largely concentrated on one sub-clan
Mandate of state bodies within the region	Administration possesses some autonomy of action in the region	Any autonomy of action limited to regional capital
Relationship with the national level	Negotiated acceptance of the Somaliland umbrella, consensual subsidiarity	Partial, negotiated acceptance / partial abeyance Dissensual subsidiarity in Eastern Sanaag
Political participation / shareholding on the national level	Strong	Existent in the West, nominal or sporadic in the East of the region

Within the theoretical prism of actors, institutions and shared mental models, much of the strikingly deviating development paths of the two regions' governance structures must be attributed to the differences in the actors' constellation and the corresponding shared mental models. Together, they decisively configure the framework conditions in which principally similar institutions achieve different outcomes. The relatively high internal homogeneity of Awdal strongly favours the performance of traditional institutions such as the collective decision-making in councils and the traditional law. This was further enhanced by the cohesion induced by the Gadabursi's shared predicament vis-à-vis the Issaq majority clan at the center (as part of the region's external actors' constellation). This process was also supported by the emergence of a new shared mental model, under which the Gadabursi ascribe to themselves a pioneering role in Somaliland's reconciliation struggle, based on their mediation role between the warring Issaq factions in the 1990s.

By contrast, Sanaag's traditional institutions are not only confronted with the heterogeneity of four sub-clans (of two clans), but also with the collective memory of a divisive war experience. Furthermore, the region's remoteness, resource scarcity and vast distances place far greater demands on the performance and efficiency of traditional institutions, whose range – in the absence of strong uniting factors – tends to be limited to local contexts. These deviating paths of political reconstruction go some way to explaining the differences in the level of violence, in the demobilisation process, and in the establishment of the administration.

At the same time, although Sanaag's achievements in the area of governance remain limited to peace-making and rudimentary state-building, it must not be overlooked that, in view of the challenges present in Sanaag and the heterogeneity of the clan composition, the clan-based institutions did remarkably well. This is owed to a large extent to the developed cross-clan links, of which the high degree of intermarriage is most important. The livelihood system clearly contains particular incentives supporting this degree of cohesion, even in the face of grave conflict.

More significant still is the role of Puntland as a competing political bidder. Particularly in the precarious context of the unresolved international status of Somaliland, it appears to be in the rational interest of the Dhulbahante and Warsangeli to keep all their political options open. From this perspective, a combination of maintained "connectivity" and the denial of a clear-cut association with either Somaliland or Puntland seems only logical. The resulting ambivalence effectively blocks the region from developing a shared polity and largely constrains the central government's efforts to establish administrative bodies to the Western half of Sanaag.

Another interesting observation from the case studies is how the establishment of state structures may change dynamics in the development paths of governance. As stated earlier, the institutions of the clan system and the elders as their primary agents indeed remain highly relevant, whether in parallel to or within the state's structures. However, once the state takes root and develops practical relevance, it may gradually become the "central arena" for governance. When governance shifts primarily to a state arena, the elders increasingly retreat to a role complementary to the state, solely taking care of local conflict resolution and violence control under normal circumstances. In Awdal, the elders only interfere with day to day politics when vital stakes of the clan are affected, and the new agents within the structures of the state either violate these interests or fail to secure them on their own. Contrary to this, governance in Sanaag routinely takes place outside the government arena, and especially among the Warsangeli and Dhulbahante, the sub-clans with their respective elders continue to present the main locus of governance.

Furthermore, the change of dynamics comes along with a creeping transformation of governance on the local and regional level. Following the establishment of state bodies, the gradual retreat of the elders is not only accompanied by a step by step transfer of authority to alternative clan-agents within the state apparatus, it also affects the practical application of different institutions. On the one hand, it principally opens the possibility that state-based "rules of the game" gain relevance in parallel to the strengthening of administrative capacities. On the other hand, by tendency, the growing autonomy of action of the local and regional administrations threatens to disconnect these bodies from their legitimizing roots. E.g. the further they deviate from the careful balancing of clan interests, the greater gets the pressure to substitute the legitimizing effect of the "basic consensus" reached at the inception of the administration.

In view of their very limited capacity to gain support through output-legitimacy (which is performance-based), state officials show a marked propensity to patronage. Instead of generating legitimacy through traditional means of consultation and representation, patronage aims to shore up support by strategically co-opting selected members of local elites. It is precisely the short-sightedness of this strategy that – despite all the changes – serves to perpetuate a significant role for the elders outside the domain of the state. If nothing else, they remain on stand-by to be remobilised to safeguard the interests of a clan or clan segment. The "creeping transformation", therefore, is not at all irreversible.

The two regions' relations with the national level further illustrate the potential of consensual versus cooptative approaches in transforming governance. Clan-based, traditionally-consensual efforts primarily driven by traditional leaders opened the door to the Gadabursi's effective political participation at the national level, and a degree of acceptance of Somaliland's independence. To the contrary, in Sanaag, where elite cooptation played a far greater role, regional-national relations remain shallow, and so far, the central government can do little but watch the localised governance reality in Eastern Sanaag.

On a wider perspective, despite the variations, both cases demonstrate that bottom-up peace-making, state and institution building can be relatively successful compared to the countless failures of top-down approaches. At the same time, the differences observed between Sanaag and Awdal underline the importance of specific aspects of the social and political context which are required to support and sustain such bottom-up efforts. The experiences in these two regions do not reveal a "magic bullet" for overcoming state collapse, but they offer valuable approaches to be adopted and adapted where conditions appear to be conducive. In any case, they call for a differentiating revision of widespread views that locally-grown institutions per se present an obstacle to state formation.

Bibliography

Actionaid Somaliland, 1998, Pastoralism and Peace-building in the Sanaag and Tughdeer Regions of Somaliland. An Application to the Joint Funding Scheme of the Department for International Development. Application, November 1998.

APD, 2002, The Judicial System in Somaliland. April 2002. Hargeisa: Academy for Peace and Development, <http://www.apd1996.org/docs/Judiciary_Report.PDF> (Accessed 14.03.2005).

APD, 2008, Sanaag Peace Process and the Lead-up to the Erigavo Conference (June 1991 - November 1993). Draft. Peace Mapping Project, 16.02.2008, Academy for Peace and Development, Hargeisa.

APD / WSP, 1999, A Self-Portrait of Somaliland: Rebuilding from the Ruins. December 1999. Hargeisa: Academy for Peace and Development/War-torn Societies Project, <http://www.apd-somaliland.org/docs/Self_Portrait.PDF> (Accessed 16.12.2006).

APD/Interpeace, 2006, A Vote for Peace. How Somaliland successfully hosted its first Parliamentary Elections in 35 years. Dialogue for Peace, September 2006. Hargeisa: Academy for Peace and Development/Interpeace, <http://www.apd-somaliland.org/docs/apd2006electionspluserrata.pdf> (Accessed 01.03.2007).

Battera, Federico/Alessandro Campo, 2001, 'The evolution and integration of different legal systems in the horn of Africa: the Case of Somaliland', in: Global Jurist Topics, 1 (2001) 1, p. Article 4.

Bradbury, Mark, 1994, 'The Case of the Yellow Settee - Experiences of Doing Development in Postwar Somaliland', in: Community Development Journal, 29 (APR 1994) 2, pp. 113-122.

Bradbury, Mark, 2007, Becoming Somaliland (Draft).

Bradbury, Mark/Adan Yusuf Abokor/Haroon Ahmed Yusuf, 2003, 'Somaliland: Choosing
     Politics over Violence', in: Review of African Political Economy, No. 97 (2003), pp.
     455 - 478.

Brons, Maria, 2001, *Society, security, sovereignty, and the state in Somalia: from
     statelessness to statelessness?* Utrecht: International Books.

Cabdiraxmaan Jimcaale, 2005, 'Consolidation and Decentralization of Government
     Institutions', in: Programme, WSP Somali (Ed.), 2005:Rebuilding Somaliland: Issues
     and possibilities. Lawrenceville, N.J.: Red Sea Press, pp. 49-122.

Ciabarri, Luca, (forthcoming), 'No representation without redistribution: Somaliland plural
     authorities, the search for a State and the 2005 parliamentary elections', in:
     Bellagamba, A./G. Klute (Ed.), Beside the State. Emerging forms of power in
     Contemporary Africa. Leiden: Brill, p. 19.

Croissant, Aurel/Wolfgang Merkel/Hans-Jürgen Puhle/Claudia Eicher/Peter Thiery, 2003,
     Defekte Demokratien Band I: Theorien und Konzepte. Opladen: Leske+Budrich.

Denzau, Arthur T./Douglass C. North, 1994, 'Shared mental models: ideologies and
     institutions', in: Kyklos, 47 (1994) 1, pp. 3-31.

Gilkes, Patrick S., 1993, *Two Wasted Years. The Republic of Somaliland 1991-1993,
     24.06.1993,* Biggleswade.

Gilkes, Patrick S., 1995, *Acceptance but not Recognition: The Republic of Somaliland 1993-
     95, 20.04.1995,* Biggleswade.

Haroon Ahmed Yusuf, [n.a.], *The Role of the Traditional Authority in Conflict Resolution and
     Peace-Building in Somaliland,* Hargeisa.

Hein, Wolfgang, 2003, '"Governance" und gesellschaftliche Entwicklung', in: Nord-Süd
     aktuell, (3.Quartal 2003), pp. 394-410.

Höhne, Markus V., 2005, Political identity and the state in Northern Somalia. Between
     Somaliland, Puntland and Somalia. Draft, May 2005, Max Planck Institute for Social
     Anthropology, Halle/ Saale.

Hyden, Goran/Julius Court/Kenneth Mease, 2004, *Making Sense of Governance: Empirical
     Evidence from Sixteen Developing Countries.* Boulder/London: Lynne Rienner.

Menkhaus, Kenneth, 1997, *Awdal Region. Studies on governance,* December 1997. Nairobi:
     UNDOS.

Merkel, Wolfgang/Hans-Jürgen Puhle, 1999, *Von der Diktatur zur Demokratie.
     Transformationen, Erfolgsbedingungen, Entwicklungspfade.* Opladen/Wiesbaden:
     Westdeutscher Verlag.

North, Douglass C., 1993, Economic Performance through Time. Prize Lecture to the
     memory of Alfred Nobel, December 9, 1993,
     <http://www.nobel.se/economics/laureates/1993/north-lecture.html > (Accessed
     02.06.2004).

Peace Committee for Somaliland, 1997, The Peace Committee for Somaliland. 27.01.1997.

Prunier, Gerard, 1994, Somaliland: Birth of a Nation? Pre-publication manuscript (August
     1993), in: Gurdon, Charles (Ed.), 1994:The Horn of Africa, pp. 61-75.

Renders, Marleen, 2006, *"Traditional" leaders and institutions in the building of the Muslim
     republic of Somaliland. Gent:* Universiteit Gent, Faculteit Politieke en Sociale
     Wetenschappen.

SDRA/MCC, 1994, Proceedings of the Erigavo Peace Conference, Sanaag Region, Somalia. May 1994. Djibouti: Somali Development and Relief Agency (SDRA) / Mennonite Central Committee (MCC).

Trotha, Trutz von, 1995, ,Gewalt, Staat und Basislegitimität. Notizen zum Problem der Macht in Afrika (und anderswo)'. in: Willer, Heidi/Till Förster/Claudia Ortner-Buchberger (Ed.), 1995:Macht der Identität - Identität der Macht. Politische Prozesse und kultureller Wandel in Afrika. Beiträge zur Afrikaforschung. No. 5. Münster: Lit-Verlag, pp. 1-16.

Weiss, Thomas George, 2000, 'Governance, Good Governance and Global Governance', in: Third World Quarterly, 21 (October 2000) 5, pp. 795-814.

Somaliland – a Success Story of Peace-Making, State-Building and Democratisation?

Ulf Terlinden / Mohammed Hassan Ibrahim

Having overcome bouts of internal conflict, Somaliland has established key state institutions and in 2005 held its first round of parliamentary elections. While Somaliland is not recognised by any other government, and the eastern regions of Sool and Sanaag are disputed with Puntland, its territory has been largely stable for the past twelve years.

This chapter elucidates the question whether Somaliland can, in various ways, be regarded as a success story in terms of fostering peace and reconciliation, building a state and developing democratic forms of governance – all in the absence of international recognition. The first part of this paper outlines the historical background of Somaliland, and the next three sections deal with the processes of peace-making, state-building and democratisation respectively, taking stock of both the challenges and achievements since the country declared independence in 1991. Following this, we review the role of external assistance in and the "unfinished business" of these processes and provide a future outlook.

Historical Background

The Somali people traditionally live in an area in the Horn of Africa that stretches from the far north east corner of the Republic of Somalia (now Puntland) into modern day Djibouti, the Ogaden Region of Ethiopia and northern Kenya, united by the Somali language, Sunni Islam and a clan-based form of socio-political organisation. Thus Somalis have been described as 'an ethnic nation but not a single polity' (Lewis 1994: 17). Following a devastating conflict, the northwest Somali region seceded in 1991 as the Republic of Somaliland, claiming the boundaries of the former colonial British protectorate. Today, Somaliland consists of an estimated two million people[1] living in a territory of 137,600 square kilometres. Stretching from the shores of the Gulf of Aden, Somaliland extends southwards to Ethiopia, westwards to Djibouti and eastwards to the regional administration of Puntland.

During the pre-colonial period, Somali society was predominantly nomadic, stateless, and organised on the basis of kinship, with social and political relations structured around clans, sub-clans and families. Ad hoc assemblies of elders (*shir*) managed the internal and external affairs of the respective groups, drawing on customary law (*xeer*) as well as the Islamic Sharia (Lewis 1982: 196-201). The British signed various protection treaties with Ciisse, Gadabursi and Issaq clan elders in the north west, establishing the Protectorate of British Somaliland in 1887 (Brons 2001). A centralized administration was introduced with some elders incorporated as salaried chiefs (*aqils*) and judges (*qaadiyo*). But even in coastal and Western Somaliland, clan-based arrangements were still widely used, particularly to resolve inter-group conflicts. In the East, the colonizers faced stiff resistance from Dhulbahante, Warsangeli and other Darod (Drysdale 2000: 6/7).

---

[1] Population estimates vary significantly between one and three million (Bradbury 2007: 161), while the official figure from the Ministry of National Planning and Co-ordination is three million.

An independent Republic of Somalia was created in 1960 from the union of the former Italian colony to the south and Somaliland to the north. The post-independence period was characterised by a mushrooming of clan-based political parties, heavy reliance on budgetary support from other countries, and growing public discontent, particularly in the northwest, at visible corruption and the over-centralisation of power in the southern capital, Mogadishu (Lewis 1994).

Following a military coup in 1969, General Siyad Barre launched on a path of 'scientific socialism', supported by Soviet military and development aid. Following Somalia's defeat in the Ogaden War with Ethiopia in 1978, and a subsequent coup attempt, the regime became increasingly repressive. While anti-tribalist laws formally banned manifestations of clan organization including compensation payments (blood money), Barre was in many respects a 'master tribalist' (Lewis 1994). Deserted by the Soviets, Somalia experienced a huge influx of Western development and humanitarian aid, fostering domestic clientelism (UNDP 2001). Moreover, where the state failed to establish responsive and broad-based formal institutions, the clans offered viable alternative frameworks, and continued to provide (some) security and justice, particularly in the North. Over time, the Issaq majority in the north west region was gradually marginalised in the regime's manipulation of clan politics. Increasing state intervention in the economy was seen as interference by many business-minded northerners, compounded by growing extortion and corruption by state officials. Dissatisfaction with the regime led to the establishment of the mainly Issaq-based Somali National Movement in 1981 (Jimcaale 2005). After Somalia's defeat in 1978, a large portion of the estimated 1.5 million Ogadeni refugees had arrived in the North and posed a threat to the Issaq's lands. Most of the refugees politically supported the Barre regime, and were later armed by the government to fight the SNM.

The government responded to the SNM's attacks inside the north west in 1988 with savage reprisals against Issaq civilians, killing more than 50,000 people, generating massive displacement (APD/WSP 1999: 19). But other rebel movements were also growing and the regime was sinking into crisis. In January 1991, the United Somali Congress ousted Barre and appointed an acting President and interim government. While the SNM had originally intended to maintain the union with the South, this unilateral announcement and other signs of southern domination were rejected by the SNM, as by some southern factions.

Despite the political cleavages between their clans, the people of present day Somaliland had shared a distinct colonial history, resentment against the post-independence concentration of power and resources in the South, and grievances against Barre's military rule, too. More specifically, the joint experience of persecution, rebellion, and flight was etched in the collective memory of the Issaq clans (Bradbury 1997: 11). Yet at the same time, the military regime and the civil war had fostered divisions between the Issaq on the one hand and the Gadabursi (Awdal), Warsangeli and Dhulbahante (Sanaag, Sool) on the other, who largely supported the Barre regime till the end. From this complex political context, Somaliland emerged. Clearly the peace-making, state-building and democratisation processes in Somaliland are intricately related, but can be discussed separately in three broad and overlapping historical phases.

The Peace-Making Process

After the collapse of Siyad Barre's regime in 1991, efforts to consolidate peace and security in Somaliland took a very different path from that of the South. Following their take-over of most of the former North-West Somalia, the victorious Issaq-led SNM opted for reconciliation and a cessation of hostilities with the non-Issaq clans, rather than engaging in retribution and the settling of old scores. Above all, the Issaq sought to consolidate political control over the territory. For their part, the non-Issaq (Dhulbahante, Warsangeli and Gadabursi), who had been associated with the previous regime, more than anything needed peaceful relations with the predominant SNM force, particularly in the absence of any viable alternatives.

Thus both sides were committed to bring an end to the hostilities. A strategic decision was reached to base the reconciliation process on the indigenous system of conflict resolution, putting the peace-making capacity of traditional elders of the various clans to a serious test. Albeit transformed, these traditional institutions had survived British colonial rule and Somali statehood functionally intact, while they had been broken up more actively in the Italian settlement colony and Barre's regime in the South (Reno 2003).

Peace and stability were achieved through a series of no less than 38 clan-based peace and reconciliation conferences and meetings between 1990 and 1997 (APD/Interpeace 2008). But the foundations of peace-making in the North had been laid well before the collapse of the regime: For instance, a key figure of the Dhulbahante clan, Garaad Abdiqani Garaad Jamac, and Jaamac Rabileh of the Gadabursi, already held dialogue to mend fences with the SNM leadership in 1990. After 1991, these relationships with the SNM facilitated an immediate ceasefire between the Issaq and Dhulbahante (Bradbury 2007: 84/85). Similar efforts to reconcile the Issaq with their western neighbours of the Gadabursi in 1991 strongly benefited from the bridge building role of Abdirahman Aw Ali Farah, a Gadabursi who had played a key role in the Issaq-led SNM struggle.

Early in February 1991, the Berbera Meeting organised by the SNM brought delegations from all Issaq and non-Issaq clans of Somaliland together. The gathering agreed on a formal cessation of hostilities and set the date for the "Grand Conference of the Northern Peoples", the first inter-clan conference held in Burco in May 1991 (Drysdale 1992). At Burco, the elders made seven proposals, which were then endorsed by the Central Committee of the SNM. These brought about a basic reconciliation of the warring parties to the conflict, the declaration of the Somaliland Republic on 18 May 1991, and the initiation of a separate reconciliation process for Sanaag Region (APD/WSP 1999).

On balance, the Burco conference succeeded in defusing the potential for violent conflict between the Issaq and their non-Issaq neighbours to a certain extent, and chartered a course of action for the pending issues of Sanaag. But it did little to address the pre-existing tensions within the SNM itself, which had previously been suppressed for sake of the struggle against the regime. Less than a year after the Burco meeting, the SNM found itself immersed in factional fighting. Early in 1992, government attempts to initialize the disarmament and reintegration of the up to 50.000 irregular militias and to form a national army triggered violent clashes between the forces of the Habr Yonis (pro-government) and Habr Jeclo (now termed "opposition") sub-clans in Burco (Jimcaale 2005: 61/62). Government-associated troops unsuccessfully tried to capture the strategic port town of Berbera for about six months, and the fighting ultimately spread to the capital Hargeisa.

The traditional elders once again stepped in. Hostilities were ended by another (more local) peace conference in the town of Sheikh late in 1992, which in turn sparked the national reconciliation meeting known as the Boroma Conference. Held between January and May 1993, this meeting represents a turning point in Somaliland's peace and reconciliation process. The 150-member *Guurti* (council of elders), together with hundreds of delegates and observers from across Somaliland, adopted a Peace Charter as the basis for efforts towards longer-term peace building, to be implemented during a further transitional period of two years. Much of the success of the conference is attributed to the fact that based on the traditional leaders' direct involvement it was a genuinely locally-owned process. In the absence of any meaningful external support or interference, the burden for hosting the meeting was mainly shouldered by the Boroma community, inducing a strong sense of ownership.

The Boroma conference also paved the way for an initial round of reintegration and demobilisation. In particular, it effectively brought the port of Berbera under government control, making crucial revenues available for the stabilisation of the country. Furthermore, many of the former SNM commanders were appointed into the new cabinet, thus neutralizing much of their potential to undermine the government. All this allowed the government to complement the clearing of roadblocks, which had started after the Sheikh conference, with the formal integration of some of the militia into a "national army", leading to their encampment and preparing for demobilisation. However, the integration process could not be accomplished on full scale, especially as clans in the Eastern regions were reluctant to cooperate and dependence on the government rations remained high. Only little assistance was provided for the reintegration of ex-fighters into civilian life, the bulk of which took the form of "self-demobilsation". The oversized security apparatus henceforth consumed a huge share of the national budget, seriously constraining state expenditures in other sectors.

Hostilities between government forces and clan-based opposition troops erupted once more in 1994 in Hargeisa and then in Burco in 1995, and continued until early 1996. These hostilities arose mainly from the discontent of some sub-clans over their political representation after the Boroma conference. In particular, the Habr Yonis sub-clan of the Issaq – who held the presidency from 1991 to 1993 – had immediately voiced dissatisfaction with the removal of "their" president from power. They were further angered by the number of parliamentary seats and cabinet positions allocated to the sub-clan. This combined with the government's efforts to have power over revenue-generating facilities, like the capital's airport, thus far controlled by militia of the Eidagalle, close brethren of the Habr Yonis (Jimcaale 2005). Despite numerous efforts both from within Somaliland, as well as from the diaspora, peace talks made little progress until 1996 (Bryden & Ahmed Yusuf Farah 1996). Eventually, a peace settlement was instituted at the subsequent national conference held in Hargeisa in 1996/7, addressing some of the grievances of the opposition by increasing their share in the two Houses of Parliament (Bradbury 1997). General stability returned in 1997.

In parallel to these different conflicts, meetings and conferences, a peace and reconciliation process took place in Sanaag region, where lineages of the Issaq (Habr Yonis and Habr Jeclo) and Harti (Warsangeli and Dhulbahante) reside side by side, have intermarried and maintain long-established social and economic ties. During the Somali civil war until 1991, the Harti had been broadly supportive of Siyad Barre's regime, while the Issaq had backed the SNM. While the peace-building efforts of the Burco and Boroma Conferences had focused on the macro-level and national political power-sharing, another kind of locally-driven peacemaking initiatives was needed to re-establish broken relationships. This was necessary to share grazing lands, return agricultural land and looted property in exchange for access to trade and movement. A total of twelve local meetings culminated in a grand conference in Ceerigaabo between August and October, 1993 (APD/Interpeace 2008).

Despite these achievements, political instability continues in Sool and eastern Sanaag regions, which are claimed by both Somaliland and neighbouring Puntland.

The State-Building Process

The starting point for every successful state building effort is the facilitation of basic security and the establishment of an acceptable framework of governance. Tackling other political, social and economic challenges of post-war reconstruction must fail without these underlying conditions. As Somaliland lacks international recognition, and external assistance thus remains limited, it had to enhance security and rebuild political structures on its own. To a large extent, this meant starting the post-authoritarian transition process from scratch.

Beyond a cessation of hostilities and initiating reconciliation, the Burco Conference had also achieved the formation of the first post-war government. As part of the new arrangement, Abdulrahman Ahmed Ali Tuur became Somaliland's first interim President, and the Somali National Movement (SNM)'s Central Committee, broadened by the inclusion of members from non-Issaq clans, was to serve as a provisional national council (Brons 2001: 247/248). The SNM Transitional Government consisted of nineteen ministries, a civil service, a high court, security branches and a central bank. In an attempt to establish a broad-based government, six cabinet seats were allocated to non-Issaqs (two Dhulbahante, two Gadabursi, one Warsangeli and one Ciisse) (Drysdale 1992: 8). The Tuur administration served from 1991 to 1993 and assumed the task of forming a functioning government. However, due to factional fighting, the condition of the territory and the people, and the lack of resources, it was hard to attain concrete progress during Tuur's term.

In the absence of local administrative structures, ad hoc councils of elders (*guurtiida*) were formed to take on the role of quasi administrations, managing militias, mediating disputes, administering justice, interacting with international agencies and raising local revenue (Bradbury 1994: 75). These different councils of elders (at regional level and district level) were established from 1991 to 1993 in Awdal, Togdheer, Sanaag, and Sool regions.

The Boroma Conference became a defining moment in terms of state building, too. The Transitional National Charter produced during the conference foresaw the drafting and ratification of a constitution within a two-year period. In order to accommodate and balance clan interests in terms of political representation and power-sharing, the *beel* system of government was adopted: It incorporated the clans and their leaderships within a formal framework of governance (Bradbury 2007: 102/103). *Beel* refers to a temporary settlement of nomadic pastoralists, a community and "clan family". The *beel* clan- or community-based system has been debated as a "dynamic hybrid of western form and traditional substance"

(Jimcaale 2005: 81). It institutionalised the participation of Somaliland's traditional elders in the further political reconstruction process – a role they had assumed as a result of the paralysis of the SNM and the need for reconciliation.

The Transitional National Charter defined the executive (President, Vice-President and Council of Ministers), the legislative (bicameral Parliament with an upper House of Elders – the Guurti – and a lower House of Representatives) and an independent judiciary. The Charter further prescribed that the Auditor General, the Head of the Central Bank, and the regional governors and mayors were to be appointed by the central government (Bradbury 2007: 103).

At Boroma, Mohammed Haji Ibrahim Egal, a veteran politician, was selected as Somaliland's new President, with Abdirahman Aw Ali Farah as his Vice-President, to lead the two year transitional administration. Within this period, the government was to re-establish functional government institutions and move the country towards a western style multi-party system of governance. This ambitious political programme proved to be a formidable challenge. Until 1997, Egal, who enjoyed considerable public trust, was able to make significant progress in establishing the institutions of government, in demobilisation, creating a revenue system, and providing a secure environment for economic recovery (Bradbury 2007) – but not sufficient for political reforms to allow elections. However, based on his leadership qualities and legitimizing support from the Guurti, President Egal was able to consolidate the power of the state and to pave the way towards a democratisation of the country.

During the first two years of his administration, the government was able to provide security and revive a basic rule of law. Ministries were reinstituted, offices were refurbished, and a new Civil Service Commission was installed. Government staff began to receive regular salaries. The police was re-organised and equipped in Hargeisa, Boroma and Berbera. Regional and district courts, utilising the 1960 penal code, were re-established.

Significant progress was made on the economic front, too: Customs offices were established and revenue collection restarted. A government-controlled Central Bank was created and the Somaliland Shilling was introduced as a new currency in 1994, which contributed heavily to the country's economic and political stabilisation (War-torn Societies Project 2005: 64). In November 1994, Somaliland's first annual budget was agreed, almost half of which went to the security services. Education and health together received 17% of the total (Gilkes 1995: 29). Regular coordination meetings were established between the Ministry of Planning and international NGOs and UN agencies (Bradbury 2007: 113).

Meanwhile, political reconstruction was slower than expected. In April 1995, when Egal's two year mandate ended, his tenure and that of the legislature were extended by the House of Elders for a further eighteen months. This was meant to provide time for him to end the war, finalise a constitution and prepare the country for elections. Yet disagreement between the President and the House of Representatives over the drafting of the new constitution hampered the development of a single document. A draft constitution was eventually adopted and ratified at the Hargeisa Conference early in 1997 to set the stage for multiparty elections within five years (till February 2002).

As far as decentralization and the extension of the administration are concerned, the government began to develop functional relationships with the regions. However, the rebuilding process remained uneven across the country. Until the Hargeisa Conference in 1996/7, it was largely confined to Hargeisa, Berbera, Boroma and to some degree Burco, which fell under the government's writ. The central government authorised regional health and education plans and started to pay incentives to health workers and some education officials, although often funded by international agencies. Supported by UN-Habitat, Hargeisa municipality embarked on initial stages of town planning and civil engineering, including the rehabilitation of government offices and the reconstruction of basic infrastructure (Bradbury 2007: 114).

Following the Hargeisa Conference and the government's realignment especially with the Habr Yonis, political reconstruction gradually extended to the East. However, it remains less successful around Burco (Togdheer). In Ceerigaabo (Sanaag), only a skeleton of the government's structures has been established to date, while Eastern Sanaag remains outside of its control. Efforts to establish the Somaliland administration in Sool only started after the take-over of Las Anod in October 2007.

The Democratisation Process

A decade after Somaliland embarked on an ostensible two-year political transition period in May 1991, the country was still in transition and ruled by a government based on the clan system. Most troubling, as the government's 1997-2001 term drew to a close, Somaliland's political future was up in the air. Although the draft constitution adopted at the Hargeisa conference in 1997 foresaw multiparty elections, the public was unaware of the course of action that the government would take.

A vigorous public discussion on the future political direction of the country ensued. As indicated in public debates, people held diverse opinions on this matter (Jimcaale 2005). Some advocated for a continuation of the existing clan-based system of governance, with gradual changes and improvements. Others stressed the importance of holding the elections, despite risks, as it was time to move forward. However, the majority of the population supported neither the holding of another Grand Clan Conference *(shir-beeleed)*, nor western-style multiparty elections, and instead proposed something in between. They considered a *shir-beeleed* as regressive and multipartyism as impractical. To all intents and purposes, no one was able to come up with a workable compromise formula.

The entire country, particularly the political opposition and critics of the government, was taken by surprise when President Egal suddenly announced the schedule for a referendum on the constitution. In March 2001, the Parliament adopted a Provisional Constitution, including some amendments proposed by the government, and passed a law scheduling a referendum on the constitution for May 31, 2001. Passage of this law was the first and crucial step in the long overdue process of political transition (Ibrahim 2004).

During the preparations for the scheduled referendum, the opposition became more vociferous in its criticism. The government ignored this. A veiled threat of armed response from the opposition pushed the political temperature up. The public, which had previously paid little attention to the debate on constitutional reform, began to fear that a veritable crisis was in the making. By publicly engaging both the government and the opposition, a forum debate on the referendum, hosted and organized by the Academy for Peace and Development, helped diffuse the tensions (Ibrahim 2004).

According to the Somaliland government, about 1.18 million people voted in the constitutional referendum of May 31, 2001, with an overwhelming 97.7 % approving it.[2] However, voter turnout in Eastern Sanaag and Sool Region was limited, reflecting the fact that many in the area opposed the political system of Somaliland. Nevertheless, outside observers concluded that the process adhered to internationally accepted standards and estimated that approximately 66% of Somaliland's eligible voters had endorsed the new constitution (Initiative and Referendum Institute 2001).

The approval of the constitution was to finally set in motion the implementation of the electoral process. On August 6, 2001, Law No 14 was passed, legalizing the formation of political organizations. Only a month after the referendum and already two months before the legalization of political organizations, President Egal had launched his political organization UDUB at a grand conference in Hargeisa. Another seven political organizations had been announced by the end of September 2001. An electoral law was passed in November 2001, and the National Electoral Commission (NEC) was formed in February 2002 (Bradbury et al 2003).

During the second half of 2001, people started to doubt the possibility of free and fair elections under Egal, and the opposition was able to galvanize support from some members of Parliament and clan leaders. In August 2001, President Egal survived an attempted parliamentary impeachment by just one vote. The same month, a group of sultans (traditional clan leaders) challenged the President's authority, calling for UDUB to be dismantled within 45 days and for a national conference to chart the country's political future. When the government arrested several sultans of the group in Hargeisa, the country was taken to the brink of another civil conflict, which could only be avoided through mediation by religious leaders, businessmen, and civil society groups (Bradbury et al 2003). Egal's second term eventually expired without elections being held. On January 12, 2002, the *Guurti* invoked Article 83 of the constitution, and extended the term of the government (which was to expire on February 22, 2002) by one more year – within which it should complete the transition. This move eased the political tensions that had embroiled the country towards the end of 2001.

While visiting South Africa, Egal died unexpectedly in May 2002. The Vice-President, Dahir Rayaale Kahin, was swiftly sworn in as his successor, ensuring continuity. The death of Egal allowed a more level political playing field, and it encouraged some groups who had previously opposed the political process to participate more fully.

The new President continued the transitional process. On December 15, Somalilanders went to the polls for the first time in more than thirty years. The electoral cycle started with the local council elections because the result of this contest between the six political organizations (ASAD, Hormood, Kulmiye, Sahan, UDUB and UCID) was to determine who would be eligible to form the three political parties to stand in the presidential and parliamentary elections. On December 23, 2002, the National Electoral Commission (NEC) declared that UDUB, Kulmiye and UCID would contest in the following polls (Ibrahim 2004).

---

[2] The vote did not involve control mechanisms to avoid double-voting. However, it is not disputed that the great majority of the people endorsed the constitution (Bradbury et al 2003: 463).

According to the constitution, the presidential elections had to be held before February 2003 and parliamentary polls before May 2003 – thus a month prior to the end of either term. However, it was neither technically, financially nor politically feasible to have back-to-back elections within these two months. Furthermore, the electoral law pertaining to the parliamentary elections remained controversial and potentially divisive. Disagreement on such issues as the allocation of parliamentary seats by region and the demarcation of electoral districts remained unresolved.

But without extending the mandate of the government, it would have been unconstitutional to postpone the elections. The government insisted on holding the presidential election as scheduled, while the two opposition parties (Kulmiye and UCID) wanted them on May 30. After consulting all sides, the electoral commission finally scheduled the presidential election for March 31, citing technical and financial issues. The *Guurti* saw the move as a violation of the constitution, as it claims the sole constitutional right to extend the government's mandate. In the end the commission backed down and the *Guurti* extended the mandate of the government by three months to allow the holding of presidential elections. In April, the *Guurti* extended the tenure of the House of Representative by one year, which also added two years for the *Guurti*, whose term always ends one the year after the one of the House of Representatives (Bradbury et al 2003).

On April 14, 2003, nearly half a million Somalilanders finally went to the polls to select a new President. Voting was peaceful, orderly, and without notable security incidents. International and domestic observers confirmed the free and transparent way in which polling was conducted (Bradbury et al 2003: 468/9).

Political observers and pundits in Somaliland predicted a very close contest, and were proven right. The preliminary results, announced by the National Electoral Commission on April 19, gave the ruling UDUB a narrow victory over Kulmiye, by a margin of 80 votes. Kulmiye contested the results and presented evidence of a tabulation error by NEC in the final tally. UDUB also contested the election results, hoping to increase its margin of victory. The NEC refused to review either side's complaints and referred the matter to the Supreme Court. On May 11, 2003, after listening to the arguments of both sides as well as the NEC, the Supreme Court ruled in UDUB's favour. Kulmiye rejected the verdict and questioned the competence of the court, but Dahir Rayaale Kahin was sworn in on May 16, 2003 as Somaliland's President. Shortly after, Kulmiye's leadership bowed to increasing public pressure and conceded Rayaale's victory (International Crisis Group 2003).

After the presidential elections, it took almost two and a half years to hold the first elections for the legislative – the House of Representatives. On 29 September 2005, the people could finally elect the 82 MPs for the new lower House of Parliament. In the run up to the polls, political tensions between the government and the opposition parties, Kulmiye and UCID, cast doubts over the electoral process. Occasional autocratic and undemocratic practices to stymie the freedom of speech and expression threatened to derail the campaigning process (Kibble & Abokor 2004). With 33 seats, the final result gave the ruling UDUB Party the largest single share, but 28 Kulmiye MPs and 21 of UCID provide the combined opposition with an almost 60% majority in parliament.

The upper chamber of the Parliament, the Guurti, remains unelected. The Guurti was supposed to be freshly constituted in September 2006, but while the House of Representatives was still debating an applicable law for the election or new selection of Guurti members, the latter extended its own term of office by four additional years. The House of Representatives, the political opposition parties and large segments of Somaliland's society denounced the move and continue to challenge its constitutionality (APD/Interpeace 2006b).

External Interventions

The involvement of the outside world, whether at multi- and bilateral level of the international community or through civil society activities, business relations and the exposure of the media may have a critical influence on processes of political reconstruction. In the case of Somaliland, external engagement gradually changed both in terms of intensity and form, as well as in the role it played for the internal processes.

The near absence of external support to Somaliland's peace-making is often depicted as a major factor in its success (APD/WSP, 1999: 84). Apart from minor material inputs by some NGOs, all peace conferences in Somaliland were funded from internal sources. None of the UNOSOM blue helmets ever set foot into Somaliland, and international attention was limited to short observer visits. These circumstances provided the space for serious local ownership, while the parallel deployment of UNOSOM in Somalia created additional incentives for home-grown solutions. Both the Sheikh and the Boroma conference were marked by a considerable desire to avoid an extension of the peacekeeping mission into Somaliland.

In contrast to this, the state-building process showed significant discrepancies between internal needs and external offers of support. In fact, especially during the early years after the end of Somaliland's internal conflicts in 1996, international involvement with the building of the unrecognized state was uneasy. When initial caution after the war began to fade, assistance gradually moved from token to strategic engagement, in parallel with the growing absorption capacity of the administration. For example, UNDP supported the Ministries of Finance and Planning with international consultants, and a major "Somali Civil Protection Programme" benefited the Ministry of Justice, the courts, and the police. Yet the lack of international recognition continues to limit the scope of foreign assistance, denies the government access to international financial instruments, and discourages major foreign direct investment. While the factors limiting state-building are certainly not only external, the restrictions associated with non-recognition tend to hinder effective assistance at least in the more sensitive areas of state building.

Over the years, external engagement with the democratization process has witnessed a complete and decisive "change of heart". Modest international support was provided for voter education and training before the local elections in 2002. Only few donors were ready to support the presidential elections in 2003 by funding technical assistance and voter education (Bradbury et al 2003: 466-468). The parliamentary elections in September 2005 marked a breakthrough, when donors came in in full force. The success of these polls not only boosted Somaliland's international reputation, but won it enormous donor confidence in terms of assisting the further democratization process in spite of non-recognition. Donor governments have meanwhile pledged strong support for the costly voter registration exercise and the local and presidential elections due in 2008. By providing funds, technical expertise and close political monitoring, international assistance in this field not only had a decisive role in

Somaliland's democratization process, but also demonstrates the enormous potential of concerted international engagement with the political reconstruction of the country.

Peace, State, Democracy – Unfinished business?

Peace-Making: External and Internal Challenges

The major challenge in the area of peace and reconciliation for Somaliland is not primarily an internal affair: The settlement of the country's longstanding dispute with neighbouring Puntland (Somalia) over the Sool and Eastern Sanaag is pending. Somaliland's claims are rooted in the history of its colonial boundary with Somalia, while the neighbouring region bases its position on the fact that the Dhulbahante and Warsangeli inhabiting the area are part of the Harti clan that controls Puntland. The conflict between the two entities remained a 'Cold War' during the Egal administration (1993-2002), but it erupted in bloody confrontations after President Rayaale assumed the Presidency in 2002 and paid a visit to Sool Region. Since late 2002, forces of Somaliland and Puntland have been locked in a standoff, resulting in several rounds of fighting, especially in 2004. Following clashes in Dhahar (Eastern Sanaag) in March/April 2007, the year saw a considerable change of landscape when shifting alliances and further fighting resulted in the eventual capture of Sool's capital Las Anod by Somaliland forces in October 2007. The situation remains very tense, and observers expect a series of recurrent clashes so long as the underlying conflict remains unaddressed.

Internally, Somaliland looks back at well over a decade of tranquillity. Peace-making within the country must therefore be recognized as remarkably successful, especially when measured against the context of the former Somalia and the conflict-ridden environment of the entire Horn of Africa Region.

However, some concerns remain as to whether the reconciliation process is complete, and to what extent the institutionalized forms of conflict resolution can maintain the still fragile peace when it comes under stress (APD/WSP 1999: 84). This sentiment could clearly be felt when, early in 2007, fighting raged between rival members of the Habr Yonis and Eidagalle sub-clans in Daroor, in Ethiopia's Somali Region near the border with Somaliland. 43 people were reportedly killed, 50 wounded, and scores of others fled. Though this conflict took place inside Ethiopia, Somaliland bore the brunt of the conflict, because the communities of these sub-clans (of the Issaq-Garxajis) live on both sides of the border. Hospitals in Hargeisa and Burco received dozens of wounded, and many worried that the conflict could spread into these major urban centres of Somaliland (APD 2007).

There is no shortage of potential for future conflict: From the recurrence of local confrontations over natural resources (land, water, etc.), revenge and counter-revenge killings, a number of unsettled scores on the local level (especially in the east), and the risk of a derailed political process spiralling out of control and escalating into wider violent conflict. Undoubtedly, there is a universal commitment to maintaining the peace, and Somalilanders have more than once demonstrated their dedication to compromise for the sake of this greater good. But this provides no guarantee that, if parties are deliberately mobilized for individual or political aims, the usually ad hoc, often improvised and localised mechanisms of conflict resolution will be sufficient to guard against renewed internal violence. To consolidate stability, Somaliland still needs to move from improvised regulation and peaceful coexistence to the institutionalization of peace and an amalgamation of society. In particular, this involves the building of truly crosscutting rather than just inter-clan institutions of conflict resolution and conflict management, as well as a long-term structural transformation of conflict.

The Struggle of Consolidating the State's Institutions

With the three branches of government in place, a civil service, army and police forces established, and local and regional administrations existing in almost every part, Somaliland has certainly succeeded in reorganizing the nominal structures of the state. While – particularly in the absence of strong and direct international assistance – these achievements must not be underestimated, the new state in many ways continues to resemble a skeleton rather than a fully-fledged body with functioning organs and lively structures. "A state is always 'work in progress'", Mark Bradbury concludes[3]. The capacity and effectiveness of the state, the separation and balance of power, the degree of centralization, and the lack of international recognition remain important "construction sites" in Somaliland's state-building efforts.

Of all issues, turning the existing administration into an effective, stable, formalised, and professional bureaucracy presents an uphill struggle. The limited **capacity and effectiveness** of the state's institutions is rooted in a combination of factors, including the striking lack of financial and human resources at government disposal, but also resistance to reforms and mismanagement, both of which are closely tied to the role that the current state plays within Somaliland society.

Not only does the state survive on little more than twenty million US Dollars per year, government bodies are also staffed with largely unqualified personnel, much of which has been recruited due to clan identity and proportions, rather than merit. Likewise, the ministers are as much government officials as they are clan representatives. The need for clan-balancing at this level has bloated the number of portfolios, while the ministries underneath continue to lack effective "bodies" to deliver services. Moreover, in these one-man ministries, all decisions rest with the minister; in his/her absence, everything stands still. As another result, the national budget is largely consumed by the basic running costs of this huge skeleton, leaving hardly anything for an operational budget and thus seriously limiting the scope to implement government programmes.

Though some bureaucratic procedures have been put in place, much of the business of administration is still conducted through personal contacts rather than a formal system for all. A deficit in transparency, accountability, professionalism, and sense of civic duty is manifest, and has encouraged corruption.

Though the **balance and separation of powers** between the three branches of government is clearly stipulated in the constitution, in practice, the executive is overwhelmingly stronger than the other two branches. With no effective clout in the process of government, the judiciary and the legislative are unable to provide tangible checks and balances within the new political system.

The **Parliament** with its two chambers must ratify all legislation. The elected lower house may also initiate bills, and most importantly has the constitutional privilege to amend

---

[3] See Bradbury 2007:248, paraphrasing Milliken and Krause 2003:1.

and approve the national budget of the country. However, the Parliament has not been able to exercise these rights effectively: Of the bills passed since the September 2005 parliamentary elections, only four have been accepted by the Guurti and signed into law by the President. Parliamentary initiatives to develop legislation independently from the executive have been greeted with hostility and in fact have been very limited. Since 2002, only the annual accounts of 2005 were presented to Parliament in 2007, and the parliament's changes to the 2007 budget were rejected. Calls for members of the cabinet to report to Parliament have regularly been ignored, and ministers and other officials have remained in office over extended periods of time even though they had not been confirmed by the house. In a nutshell, the elected Parliament has got very little in its hands to exercise effective oversight.

Yet, to be fair, the limitations of the Parliament are not only external. Half way into its first elected term, the legislature still lacks a good understanding of both its role and functional capacity. There is a continuing disagreement between the ruling and the opposition parties over the role of the house leadership, which has affected the ability of the House of Representatives to function as a single, collective institution. The house leadership also stands accused of acting independently of the assembly. Overall, the legal expertise of the parliament to draft laws is inadequate, parliamentary procedures are poorly defined and understood, and initiative is limited. To hold the executive branch accountable, the further development of these seemingly technical aspects will also be crucial.

The **House of Elders** (Guurti, the upper chamber of Parliament) is a particular case. Historically, it played a crucial role in making peace and laying the foundations for the new state, and as such was an innovation in its time. However, unlike many other parts of the state apparatus, the further development and adaptation of this fundamental institution to the increasingly complex political challenges has stagnated. Although Somaliland's second electoral cycle is imminent in 2008, legislation governing the future nomination (if not election) to the House of Elders has not yet been developed. Meanwhile, many members of the Guurti have become urbanised and somewhat disconnected from their largely rural constituencies. These issues concern the Guurti's legitimacy and raise an increasing number of questions, especially in the context of its comprehensive powers to rule on matters that are judged to threaten the peace. This is particularly sensitive because these are no longer clan conflicts alone: The Guurti tends to be drawn into constitutional disputes beyond its original capacity and role.

The **judiciary** of Somaliland by and large lacks the capacity and professionalism to enforce the rule of law (APD 2002). Civil and criminal codes date back to the immediate post-independence era and there have not been major reforms after the war. There is a legal pluralism of Somali, Italian, and British statutory law, customary law (*xeer*) and Sharia law – all of which are marked by serious contradictions. With a fundamental lack of professional judges, and in the absence of a functional regulatory body, the judicial system remains weak. Most courts do not have the resources to function adequately, and corruption is endemic. Moreover, the judiciary does not have the independence to provide effective checks and balances for the new political system: The Chief Justice is appointed and removed freely, and efforts by Parliament to vet candidates for the post have largely failed. There is no courts administration independent of the Ministry of Justice, which controls all relevant funds with the exception of the Supreme Court. The lack of safeguards for the judiciary's independence is particularly critical with regard to the Supreme Court, which has repeatedly had to rule on crucial legal disputes between government and opposition since the beginning of the democratisation process.

Intending to prevent a return to authoritarian rule and to strengthen participation in governance, Somaliland's constitution provides for a **decentralized system** of government (Jimcaale 2005; APD/Interpeace 2006a) But despite the establishment of local administrations and the introduction of local council elections, realizing this goal is a continuing challenge. Not only has the development of the local administrations been uneven, most local councils have so far failed to take on their roles effectively. The defined roles of the councils (as decision-makers) and the mayor (as the executive) are not followed, and mayors have frequently been threatened with impeachment if they failed to meet the expectations of the council members. Furthermore, the system has failed to provide better access for the public. Revenue collection remains mostly centralized, providing little power to the councils.

Last but not least, another key aspect of Somaliland's unfinished state-building is obviously the lack of **international recognition** and the unresolved relationship with Somalia. In material ways, this can be felt in its implications for international assistance, which can hardly flow through government channels as long as Somaliland has not been recognised. This status has also barred the country from establishing links with international financial institutions (Bradbury 2007: 247). As another effect and an area of growing concern, the lack of international sovereignty minimizes the extent of protection Somaliland would receive in a case of external aggression. While these aspects clearly constrain the continuing state-building efforts, observers have also pointed out that non-recognition has simultaneously provided the space and freedom to develop genuinely home-grown institutions and to experiment without unhelpful international pressure for conformity.

Democratisation: From Formal Democracy to Democratic Transformation?

With a constitutional referendum and the full cycle of local, presidential and parliamentary elections having been held, Somaliland has come a long way in its democratisation process. As far as the credentials of formal democratisation are concerned, the key challenge is when and at what quality this process will be continued. There are growing concerns over the electoral timetable, which foresees a voter registration process to be followed by the second round of local and presidential elections in 2008. Implementing the first and complex voter registration is a tough call, particularly under serious time pressure combined with the risk of inherent tensions of any further delay. In addition, a legal dispute over the eligibility of new political associations to contest the local elections continues to simmer unresolved.

Meanwhile, despite the achievements in the formal democratisation process, Somaliland's democracy so far remains somewhat "narrowly legal" and at a fragile and formative stage. A deep democratic transformation, embracing society and delivering a sustainable and *functional* democracy, is still pending. More than legal aspects, "the reformation of government and the state and the development of other elements that foster a democratic culture" will be critical (Carothers 2003). Many of the unfinished aspects of state-building, in particular a greater separation and balance of powers, the strengthening of the rule of law and a continuation of the decentralisation process are key elements to this. From a functional perspective, the development of effective channels of popular participation is central to this transformation. This includes in particular:

- The democratisation and opening up of internal structures of political parties, providing equal access to engaged citizens and guaranteeing opportunities for participation within the framework of the restrained three-party system.
- Political space for the active involvement of civil society organisations and marginalised political interest groups. This includes in particular the development of advocacy platforms and dialogue interfaces with Parliament and the executive.
- The strengthening of the parliament, inter alia through internal capacity building and the bolstering of constituency relations.
- Free political competition including the right to peaceful political association and expression.
- The liberalisation of the media sector, combined with the development of a greater sense of responsibility among journalists (including editorial boards and self-regulation mechanisms).
- Respect for human and civil rights as safeguards to unrestricted participation.

In the longer run, these issues are also closely connected with the development of a stronger domestic constituency to promote and safeguard a continuation and deepening of the democratisation process. So far, Somaliland lacks a critical mass that could clearly be identified as the popular driving force of democratisation. In the absence of experience of participation in a system of liberal democracy, there is a tendency to look up and wait for concepts to come from above. Although there is a broad perception that democracy is beneficial to the populace, there is no urge or disposition to fight for it. Democracy has very little active lobby, despite its general approval.

Few individuals are reform-minded in the true sense and have the horizon of experience to understand the concepts and complexities of this. Those who do find it difficult to connect to each other and to create a common platform, particularly due to clan divisions, economic competition including in the civil society, and the (partly experience-based) perception that there is no political space for an organised civic movement taking on a political and advocacy role in the young state.

Ironically, it is equally difficult to identify clearly "anti-democratic forces". It often seems that the question of democratic orientation depends very much on where in the system actors stand at a particular moment. Throughout the different periods of Somaliland's development, those in power tended to object reform in order to maintain the status quo, whilst the powerless called for democratisation in order to gather clout and gain access to power. This image was further reinforced by the legacy of long dictatorial rule: In the eyes of the public, those in power seek to consolidate their position and centralise everything in their hands.

Overall, the main cleavages of society continue to be along clan lines and alliances. Cross-sectional and "horizontal" forms of civic association and organisation remain very limited, strongly contributing to the absence of a culture of broad-based movements. As a consequence, organisational capacity focuses on the representation of the interests of sub-sections of society, rather than on issues and particular policies. This creates a tendency to wash out formal democracy, reducing it to a regulatory arena for segmented interests instead of an engine of comprehensive social change.

The Way Forward

On balance, Somaliland has an outstanding record of peace-making, laid all the basic foundations of statehood, and demonstrated remarkable commitment to the development of a formal democracy. A key lesson to be learnt from this experience is that international recognition is not a prerequisite to the re-establishment of functional structures of governance. Such efforts can go very far even when embarked upon in a functional entity that once formed only a part of a collapsed state. Especially when measured against the countless failures of state-building at the national level of the former Somali state, Somaliland is truly a success story.

In some ways it may have been a blessing that this was achieved with relatively little international assistance as it increased local ownership and provided incentives for consensus building and good governance in the country. Yet this constellation has its limits, and it would be foolish for the outside world to just take a continuation of the country's successes for granted. The grudge against the international community is already growing because recognition and strong development cooperation were expected to provide a "peace dividend" that largely failed to arrive. Securing Somaliland's accomplishments, including against external threats, and deepening state-building and democratisation requires increased assistance and international engagement. It also goes without saying that the potential for external leverage in such matters – if and when it may be needed – is obviously tied to the level of involvement one has with a given country.

Meanwhile, Somaliland remains interested in and in fact eager for increased international cooperation. As long as the country has not been recognised, the international community remains challenged to creatively craft forms of support that can nevertheless help tackle bottlenecks in the state-building and democratisation process. The international donor investment in Somaliland's 2005 parliamentary elections presented a formidable example for the effective and valuable support that can be provided even below the threshold of international recognition, but beyond "classical" forms of foreign governance support to a non-recognised country. Another illustration of such efforts is assistance through the World Bank to develop Somaliland's Public Finance Management, which involves serious incentives for good governance.

These initiatives underscore that the world is abandoning the principle of "good enough by comparison with Southern Somalia" and considers Somaliland's achievements and needs in their own right. This signals readiness for increased engagement as much as it forbids any potential sense of complacency.

Bibliography

APD, 2002: The Judicial System in Somaliland. April 2002. Hargeisa: Academy for Peace and Development, <http://www.apd1996.org/docs/Judiciary_Report.PDF> (accessed 14.03.2005).

APD, 2007: The Burco Dilemma - Striking a Balance between Troubleshooting and Peace Building, in: The Academy Today, 1 (April 2007) 1, pp. 7-8.

APD/WSP, 1999: A Self-Portrait of Somaliland: Rebuilding from the Ruins. December 1999. Hargeisa: Academy for Peace and Development/War-torn Societies Project, <http://www.apd-somaliland.org/docs/Self_Portrait.PDF> (<ccessed 16.12.2006).

APD/Interpeace, 2006a: Local Solutions: Creating an Enabling Environment for Decentralisation in Somaliland. Dialogue for Peace, October 2006. Hargeisa: Academy for Peace and Development/Interpeace, <http://www.apd-somaliland.org/docs/apd2006decentralisation.pdf> (<ccessed 01.03.2007).

APD/Interpeace, 2006b: A Vote for Peace. How Somaliland successfully hosted its first Parliamentary Elections in 35 years. Dialogue for Peace, September 2006. Hargeisa: Academy for Peace and Development/Interpeace, <http://www.apd-somaliland.org/docs/apd2006electionspluserrata.pdf> (accessed 01.03.2007).

APD/Interpeace, 2008 (forthcoming): Somaliland Peace Mapping. Draft. Academy for Peace and Development, Interpeace.

Bradbury, M./Adan Yusuf Abokor/Haroon Ahmed Yusuf, 2003: Somaliland: Choosing Politics over Violence, in: Review of African Political Economy, No. 97 (2003), pp. 455 - 478.

Bradbury, Mark, 1994: The Somali conflict: prospects for peace. Oxford [England]: Oxfam.

Bradbury, Mark, 1997: Somaliland. CIIR country report. London: Catholic Institute for International Relations.

Bradbury, Mark, 2007: Becoming Somaliland (Draft).

Brons, Maria, 2001: Society, security, sovereignty, and the state in Somalia: from statelessness to statelessness? Utrecht: International Books.

Bryden, Matt/Ahmed Yusuf Farah, 1996: The Somaliland Peace Committee: Case Study of a Grassroots Peace-Making Initiative. Addis Ababa: UNDP/EUE.

Drysdale, John, 1992: Somaliland: The Anatomy of Secession. Hove, UK.

Drysdale, John, 2000: Stoics without pillows: A way forward for the Somalilands. London: HAAN Associates.

Gilkes, Patrick S., 1995: Acceptance but not Recognition: The Republic of Somaliland 1993-95, 20.04.1995, Biggleswade.

Initiative and Referendum Institute, 2001: Somaliland National Referendum, May 31, 2001. Final Report of the Initiative & Referendum Institute's Election Monitoring Team. Washington, D.C.

International Crisis Group, 2003: Somaliland: Democratisation and its Discontents. Nairobi/ Brussels, <http://www.icg.org//library/documents/report_archive/A401067_28072003.pdf> (accessed 29.07.2003).

Jimcaale, Cabdiraxmaan, 2005: Consolidation and Decentralization of Government Institutions, in: Programme, WSP Somali (Ed.), 2005:Rebuilding Somaliland: Issues and possibilities. Lawrenceville, N.J.: Red Sea Press, pp. 49-122.

Kibble, Steve/Adan Abokor, 2004: Somaliland - CIIR Draft Pre-election Assessment for the 2005 Parliamentary Elections (Third Draft). 22.12.2004. London/Hargeisa.

Lewis, I. M., 1982: A pastoral democracy: a study of pastoralism and politics among the northern Somali of the Horn of Africa. New York, N.Y.: Africana Pub. Co. for the International African Institute.

Ibrahim, Mohammed Hassan, 2004: Somaliland's Election: Transition without Transformation. Draft Paper prepared for Somali Studies Conference, Denmark.

Milliken, J./K. Krause, 2003: State Failure, State Collapse, and State Reconstruction: Concepts, Lessons and Strategies, in: Milliken, J. (Ed.), 2003:State Failure, State Collapse, and State Reconstruction. Oxford: Blackwell Publishing, pp. 1-21.

Reno, William, 2003: Somalia and Survival. In the Shadow of the Global Economy. QEH Working Paper Series 100. Northwestern University, <http://www2.qeh.ox.ac.uk/pdf/qehwp/qehwps100.pdf> (accessed 20.06.2003).

UNDP, 2001: Human Development Report 2001, Somalia. Nairobi, Kenya: UNDP.

War-torn Societies Project, 2005: Rebuilding Somaliland: Issues and possibilities. Lawrenceville, N.J.: Red Sea Press.

The European Commission in Somaliland: Development Assistance in an Unrecognised State

Christina Rosendahl

In recent years, the emergence of 'fragile', 'failing' or 'failed states' has prompted an intense debate in academics as well as among practitioners of foreign and security policy and development policy.[1] Somalia[2] is the prototype of the 'failed state', as government institutions are not only unable to deliver essential functions, but have ceased to exist. Therefore, Somalia is often perceived as an anarchic, institutional vacuum in which religious and tribal conflicts merge with organised crime. The rapid expulsion of the Union of Islamic Courts by Ethiopian forces in December 2006 and the consequent installation of the Somali Transitional Federal Government (TFG) in Mogadishu has raised new hopes that peace and stability would finally emerge. However, until today, these hopes have failed to materialise: In April 2007 the UN Humanitarian Coordinator for Somalia stated that "[t]he scale of the fighting during recent weeks has been the worst residents of Mogadishu have experienced in the last sixteen years"[3].

Those who turn to the North-west of Somalia will find an entirely different picture from the one prevailing in south-central Somalia and from that one suggested by the 'failed state'-lens. After Somalia's former dictator Siad Barre had ordered the bombing of the north-western towns Hargeisa and Burao in the former British protectorate Somaliland in 1988, the Somali National Movement (SNM), dominated by the north-western Issaq-clan, together with various other Somali movements from other regions succeeded in overthrowing Barre.[4] But whereas the south-central regions were to remain contested regions in the hands of warlords and militias, on 18 May 1991 the SNM declared Somaliland an independent republic. Since then, Somaliland has realised an internally initiated and steered peace building and democratisation process.[5] After the Constitutional referendum in May 2001, Somaliland entered the last stage of the transformation process to a democratic multiparty system. Between 2002 and 2005 Somaliland successively held local-, presidential and parliamentary elections which were judged as sufficiently free and fair by international observers. Although several challenges remain[6] – for example, reconciling the multiparty system with the effective dominance of the clan factor, the question of how to elect the *Guurti* (the Upper House), the

---

[1] See, for example, the Political Instability Task Force (formerly: State Failure Task Force) at the University of Maryland, http://globalpolicy.gmu.edu/pitf/, last access: 25.06.2007, Countries At Risk of Instability Project of the British Prime Minister's Strategy Unit,
http://www.cabinetoffice.gov.uk/strategy/work_areas/countries_at_risk/index.asp, last access: 01.08.2007, OECD/DAC Fragile States Group, http://www.oecd.org/dac/fragilestates, last access: 01.08.2007.

[2] In this article the term „Somalia" refers to the entity of Somalia as defined by international law, covering the south-central regions as well as the self-declared autonomous Republic of Puntland in the North-East and the self-declared independent Republic of Somaliland in the North-West. The terms "South-Central Somalia" and "Somaliland" refer to the specific entities. This terminology does not indicate any political position of the author.

[3] United Nations Office of the Humanitarian Coordinator for Somalia (2007: 1).

[4] Bakonyi (2001: 85).

[5] For the following paragraph see: Bradbury/Abokor/Ahmed (2003), Cabdiraxmaan Jimcaale (2005), ICG (2003b).

[6] See article by Terlinden/Mohammed Hassan Ibrahim in this book.

question of a national census, voter registration and demarcation of regional and district boundaries within a nomadic society marked by historic displacement, as well as the status of the regions Sool and Sanaag on the eastern border with Puntland[7] – Somaliland is an outstanding example for internal peace-building and democratisation in the Horn of Africa.

Since the early to mid-1990s, the European Commission (EC) has been the largest donor in Somalia and played a key role in shaping international policies towards the country.[8] Given the disparate developments in South-Central Somalia and Somaliland since 1991, and the heightened interest in 'failed states', the present article explores how the EC has reacted to the specific developments in Somaliland. The article argues that due to Somalilands non-recognised status as well as some other factors, the effectiveness of EC aid to Somaliland has initially been suboptimal. During the past years there have been positive changes. The article will attempt to provide some explanations for these changes and point to some remaining challenges.

During the 1990s, the increased number of violent internal conflicts in Sub-Saharan Africa as well as the 'failure' of states such as Somalia, Liberia and Sierra Leone led to a recognition by the European Union (EU) of the need to prevent conflict and 'state failure'.[9] This new policy focus was reinforced by the establishment of the European Common Foreign and Security Policy (CFSP) and the events of September 11, 2001. The 2003 *European Security Strategy* describes 'state failure' as one of the principal threats for *European* security, as state failure causes regional instability, organised crime and terrorism.

At the same time, donors also started to perceive 'state failure' as a developmental problem to which development policy had to react. Whereas during the 1990s development aid was concentrated on so-called 'good performers', donors realised that the Millenium Development Goals (MDGs) could not be achieved without dealing with 'poor' or 'bad' performers'. Futhermore, allowing for 'pockets of exclusion' would stimulate the 'vicious cycle' of underdevelopment, conflict and 'state failure'. Therefore, at the Senior Level Forum on Development Effectiveness in Fragile States held in London in January 2005, it was agreed that a short list of *Principles for Good International Engagement in Fragile States* be drafted. The *Principles* were then piloted in nine countries and adopted by the OECD/DAC High Level Meeting in April 2007.[10] The 2005 *European Consensus on Development* furthermore committed to implement the *Principles* in all its programming.[11]

The *Principles* contain, among others, the following elements:
- "focus on state-building as the central objective", namely, on building capable, legitimate and accountable state structures;
- "align with local priorities", avoiding activities "which undermine national institution-building, such as developing parallel systems without thought to transition mechanisms and long term capacity development.", and

---

[7] In contrast to Somaliland, Puntland is fully committed to a united Somalia. In 1998 Abdullahi Yusuf, today's President of the TFG, became elected President of Puntland but declined to resign after the expiry of his three-year term of office. In 2001, he played a lead role in an Ethiopian-backed effort to unseat the Transitional National Government formed in Arta, Djibouti, in 2000.
[8] Bayne (2001: 1), von Hippel/Yannis (1999: 74).
[9] Rye Olsen (2005: 137).
[10] OECD/DAC (2007)
[11] European Council (2005: 26)

- "avoid pockets of exclusion".

Principles aim to complement the partnership commitments set out in the *Paris Declaration on Aid Effectiveness.*[12] In the *Paris Declaration*, member countries and organisations commit themselves to, among others, 'ownership' by partner countries, 'harmonisation' among donors and 'alignment' with partner countries.

Whether or not the EC respects these principles in its dealings with Somaliland is part of the present analysis.

Background: The European response to the collapse of Somalia

After the overthrow of the Barre regime and the following descent of Somalia into civil war it became obvious that in the long run, humanitarian aid as provided by the European Commission Humanitarian Office (ECHO) would not be sufficient to respond to the manifold needs of the war-torn Somali population. However, Somalia under Siad Barre had not signed the 1990 Lomé IV Agreement and therefore was not allocated any development aid from the European Development Fund (EDF). At the same time, without any internationally recognised government Somalia would not be able to join later Lomé Agreements, which are periodically revised by EU member states and ACP[13] states.[14] In order to solve this problem the ACP-EC Council of Ministers in November 1992 decided to allocate unspent money from the preceding 5th and 6th EDF to Somalia. The EU Commissioner for Development was to perform the functions of the National Authorising Officer (NAO), which are usually carried out by the Planning Minister of the ACP-state.[15] Thus Somalia became the first country worldwide to receive EDF-money without having an internationally recognised government.[16]

This provisional arrangement for Somalia was replaced by a general, long-term solution to the problem of aid financing in 'failed states' in 2001: The Cotonou Agreement, the successor of Lomé IV *bis*, stipulated that EDF-funds from then on may be allocated to ACP-states, which, „in the absence of normally established government institutions, have not been able to sign or ratify this Agreement."[17] Since December 2001 Somalia has benefitted from this regulation.[18] As of mid-2007, Somalia has still not joined the Cotonou Agreement, even though Somalia now possesses an internationally recognised government, the TFG.

These legal modifications for financing aid to Somalia were accompanied by organisational and strategic adaptations. After the EC Delegation had closed its office in

---

[12] OECD/DAC (2007: 1)

[13] African, Caribbean and Pacific states, signatories to the ACP-EC-Partnership Agreements as first signed in 1975 in Lomé, Togo

[14] Bayne (2001: 1)

[15] Illing (1997). Today the function of the NAO is performed by the Delegation of the European Commission.

[16] Visman (1998: 2)

[17] Cotonou Agreement, Article 93 (6). The case of Somalia may have led to the addition of this Article into the new Agreement, as the funds from previous EDFs to be allocated to Somalia were constantly shrinking, Bayne (2001: 1).

[18] After the Cotonou Agreement entered into force in 2003, Somalia was allocated €149 million from the 9th EDF. In 2007, it was allocated another €36 million, Delegation of the European Commission (2004: 26). In comparison, the post-conflict countries Rwanda and Burundi whose population and per capita income is largely comparable with that of Somalia were allocated €186 and 172€ repsectively. In 2007, Somalia was allocated an additional €36,1, Rwanda an additional €19 (no information on Burundi available), http://ec.europa.eu/development/geographical/regionscountries_en.cfm.

Mogadishu in 1991, in 1994 the Commission opened the so-called *EC Somalia Unit* in Nairobi. Its head was Sigurd Illing, the EC Special Envoy for Somalia. In addition, the EC opened Liaison Bureaus in Mogadishu, Bossasso (Puntland) and Hargeisa (Somaliland). Sector-related Technical Assistants have regularly travelled to Somalia since then and have supported the EC in aspects of strategy development and identification as well as monitoring of programmes.[19] Due to the fact that there is no public legal system in Somalia, the implementation of projects is assigned to international NGOs (non-governmental organisations) or UN agencies.

In 1994, Illing took a leading role in establishing the *Somalia Aid Coordination Body* (SACB), consisting of donors, UN agencies, international and Somali NGOs. In formulating common criteria for the allocation of aid and progressively devising sector strategies, the SACB has served to enhance harmonisation of donor activities. Since 1998, when Illing's mandate was discontinued, the EC has taken a somewhat less prominent stance in donor coordination. After the establishment of the TFG in October 2004, the SACB was transformed into the *Coordination of International Support to Somalis* (CISS). At the same time, the international community and the TFG established the *Coordination and Monitoring Committee* (CMC) in order to facilitate coordination between the international community and the TFG in political as well as in aid matters.[20] Until today the CMC has not been able to work properly according to its mandate. As a result co-ordination seems to shift back to inter-donor co-ordination within the CISS/SACB. The appointment of Georges-Marc André as new EC Special Envoy to Somalia in June 2007 signals the EC's renewed effort to play a more active role in Somalia.

On the level of strategy, the EC and the SACB adopted the concept of Linking Relief, Rehabilitation and Development as well as the so-called *Peace Dividend-Approach*. This was a reaction to the need to proceed from emergency aid to developmental aid in the long run. The *Peace Dividend-Approach*, as the Commission states,

> "has three main components: first there is the 'enabling environment', a specific responsibility
> for the beneficiary community to provide the basic security conditions for aid to be delivered;
> secondly, communities/areas which are able to assure such conditions, are supported by new
> or increased development funding, a factor which in turn further enhances this enabling
> environment; finally, the success of those areas in securing stability and the development
> activities that were delivered, should work as an incentive for other, conflict-stricken areas to
> try and achieve indigenous peace too."[21]

At the end of the 1990s the *Peace Dividend-Approach* was complemented by the *Building Block-Approach*, which was strongly promoted by Ethiopia through IGAD and lateron Puntland. Without further specifications, the approach proposes that „'local administrative structures could constitute building blocks' in the restoration of peace and statehood to Somalia'"[22].

---

[19] Bayne (2001: 20).
[20] Coordination and Monitoring Committee, 2005.
[21] Delegation of the European Commission (2004: 8).
[22] Bryden (1999: 134)

On the basis of this approach, the 2002 *IGAD-Peace Process*, jointly managed by Kenya, Ethiopia and Djibouti, consented on a federal governance structure for the intended future Somali state. This decision was one of the main reasons for European support to the *IGAD-process*. Despite this general consensus, there are still many questions which have remained unanswered up to today: the number of federal states to build, the criteria of setting the state boundaries, the relation between federal states and central government and other relevant questions. It was clear from the outset, however, that the *IGAD-process* would lead to a *united* Somali state, of which Somaliland would form part[23] - notwithstanding the fact that the government of Somaliland refused to participate in the process.

EC aid to Somaliland – the early years

Although Somaliland has been seeking international recognition for 16 years, it has not been recognised by any country in the world. European diplomats insist on the right of *all* Somalis to have their say in a decision on a separation of Somaliland. This was impossible in the past 16 years because a government representing Southern Somalis did not exist. European diplomats also stress the leadership role of the African Union (AU) in this respect maintaining that recognition by European states is dependent on prior recognition by African states.[24] They fear that contravening the OAU-principle of the inviolability of postcolonial borders might stimulate an all-African domino-effect.[25] Furthermore, there is a scepticism as to whether Somaliland is merely a project of the region's dominant Isaaq-clan.

On the other hand, some diplomats quietly acknowledge a number of arguments in favour of a recognition of Somaliland. These include rewarding Somaliland for its peace- and democracy building process, supporting it against quarrels in the south, and freeing it from the numerous financial and political disadvantages of its non-recognised status.[26]

Because Somaliland is not recognised as an independent state, European aid to Somaliland follows the same pattern as European aid to Somalia: Humanitarian and developmental projects are financed by ECHO, the European budget and the EDF, administered by the EC Somalia Unit in Nairobi, coordinated by the SACB/CISS, and implemented by UN agencies and international NGOs, sometimes together with local NGOs. Somaliland, however, differs considerably from South-Central Somalia with respect to security and development. Therefore, the *Peace Dividend-Approach* can be regarded as an

---

[23] The Declaration on Cessation of Hostilities, Structures and Principles of the Somalia National Reconciliation Process of October 2002 refers to the "sovereignty, territorial integrity, political independence and unity of Somalia", Somalia National Reconciliation Process (2002: 1).

[24] ICG (2006a: 13), based on personal interviews with European diplomats. Despite these common principles, there are certain differences in attitude towards Somaliland's bid for independence: Whereas the United Kingdom has always shown a certain degree of sympathy for its former colony's request, Italy, the former colonial power of today's South-Central Somalia and Puntland, is taking a staunchly pro-unity posture, ICG (2006a: 13), Huliaras (2002: 171).

[25] Countering this argument, some scholars have pointed out that Somaliland not only fulfils the Montevideo criteria for statehood, see Schoiswohl (2004: 183). Gilkes (1995: 39) and Huliaras (2002: 165) contend that independence is also in accordance with the OAU-principle: After gaining independence from Britain in June 1960 Somaliland had been recognised as a state on its own. The Union with the former Italian-administered trusteeship territory of Somalia was formed only five days later.

[26] Gilkes (1995: 39), Huliaras (2002: 165).

appropriate instrument to accomodate the resulting different needs in Somaliland:[27] In 2001, Somaliland received €29,68 million from the EDF, whereas South-Central Somalia received only €10,50 million.[28] Long-term infrastructural projects, such as the rehabilitation of port facilities, mainly exist in Somaliland. Nonetheless, European aid to Somaliland has been far from ideal in its early years; on the contrary there were several shortcomings.

The following paragraphs briefly describe and analyse these shortcomings as well as progress made in the last years.

Deficiencies have been caused by the fact that about 50% of the funding is spent on overhead, Nairobi offices or international personnel.[29] More importantly, there has been limited co-operation between donors and the Somaliland government. In contrast to this, the *OECD Principles* state that lack of co-operation with an existing government structure often results in inefficient development strategies, deprives existing but weak institutions of capacity building,[30] and may even undermine legitimate authorities.[31]

The reasons for this lack of co-operation lie, above all, in Somaliland's non-recognised status, due to which it cannot participate as a 'partner' in intergovernmental aid relations. In practical terms, this structural problem was reinforced by the non-co-operative attitudes of both the Somaliland authorities and the EC: On the one hand, in Nairobi diplomats occasionally had the impression that Somaliland authorities gambled away opportunities for co-operation by insisting on being treated as a sovereign country.[32] On the other hand, the EC made little effort to acknowledge and to cope with the specific situation in Somaliland in a pragmatical way. Rather, the EC was more worried that co-operation might imply recognition of independence.

Changes in EC aid to Somaliland

Recent developments show that this fear was not justified.[33] Since the end of the 1990s there has been a reversal of trend in EC aid to Somaliland and the EC's interaction with the Somaliland authorities. In this regard five aspects will be outlined briefly:

First, in contrast to former times, the EC has started to discuss the process of project planning and implementation with the Somaliland government. In 1998, Somaliland's Minister of Planning observed a willingness of aid agencies and NGOs "never seen before, to cooperate directly with the central government and its departments"[34] – even though this was still no generally practiced procedure. Since then, there has been further progress: Today,

---

[27] This is explicitly stated by the European Strategy for the Implementation of Special Aid to Somalia (SISAS), European Commission (2002: 18).

[28] Further €18 million were spent countrywide, €6,16 million in Somaliland and Puntland together, European Commission (2002: 2). In 2003 relations have changed slightly to the disadvantage of Somaliland and Puntland, probably due to the financing of the *IGAD-process*, Somalia Aid Coordination Body (2003).

[29] ICG (2003b: 7).

[30] Bayne (1999: 34), taken from Menkhaus, Good Governance and Foreign Assistance, Horn of Africa Bulletin No. 9, 1997.

[31] See also Visman (1998: 13).

[32] For instance, the Somaliland authorities refused to take part in a Somalia-wide strategy for the control of epidemics, since it was published and signed by "WHO *Somalia* Office", personal interview with the SACB, 04.03.2007, italics added by the author.

[33] Gilkes (1995: 61) has made this argument very early.

[34] Ministry of National Planning and Coordination, Republic of Somaliland (1998: 14).

each proposal for EC-financed projects has to be coordinated to the central government in Hargeisa as well as to local government structures at the respective location of the project. After project approval has been given, the Ministry of Planning and the Line Ministers sign a Memorandum of Understanding in which all project activities are written down, possibly including activities of certain Ministries. Furthermore, the project budget and quarterly reports are submitted to the Ministers.[35]

A *second* development relates to efforts of capacity building directed at Somaliland government institutions. In 2000 the EC sponsored a capacity building project to the National Demobilisation Commission. Other projects included capacity building of public veterinary agencies and the Ministry of Livestock as well as drafting a veterinary code.[36] Since the end of 2006, the EC has increasingly financed capacity building projects to Ministries. Somaliland's Minister of Health and Labour described this development as the beginning of a "new era", reflecting Somaliland's real needs.

A *third* development in EC aid to Somaliland started with drafting the *Somali Reconstruction and Development Framework* (RDF)[37] and the *Somali Country Strategy Paper* (CSP)[38] in 2006. During this process, the EC and other donors strongly consulted and co-operated with Somaliland authorities. This may have two positive effects in the future: On the one hand, 'governmentally-owned' international aid strategies may enhance the legitimacy, impact and efficiency of donor activities. At the same time, they may serve the Somaliland government as a basis for its own development strategy. In this vein, the Minister of National Planning and Coordination stated that his forthcoming Five-Year Development Plan will integrate RDF-/CSP-priorities.[39]

Fourthly and importantly, the EC has started to actively support Somaliland's democratisation process.[40] With the legalisation of political parties in May 2001, Somaliland has laid the ground for a transformation from clan-based power-sharing to a democratic multi-party system. This process started with the local elections in December 2002. In the run-up to these elections it became clear that the independent National Electoral Commission (NEC), responsible for the implementation of the elections, lacked experience and financial resources to fulfil its tasks. In response to NEC's request, the EC therefore supplied technical support through consultants from the GTZ (German Enterprise for Technical Cooperation) and allowed for awareness campaigns and training of over 3000 electoral officials. After the elections had taken place, the International Crisis Group (ICG) emphasised that EC-support not only had made the elections possible in technical and financial terms, but had also raised public confidence in the NEC.[41]

---

[35] Personal interview with the EC Liaison Officer in Hargeisa, Somaliland, 18.02.2007.

[36] An early example of this was a capacity building project with the Ministry of Livestock in 1995. However, at that time the project represented a rare exception, personal interview with Vittorio Cagnolati, 05.03.2007.

[37] The RDF is based on the Joint Needs Assessment, which was undertaken by the United Nations Development Group (UNDG) and the World Bank in 2005. It includes three geographic Volumes (South-Central Somalia, Puntland and Somaliland) that can be widely used for programming assistance to these regions, see: United Nations, World Bank (2006: iii-iv).

[38] The CSP is the European Commission's instrument for programming development assistance in partner countries. It is prepared for planning periods of 5 to 6 years. The Somali CSP 2007 – 2013, which is not yet finalised, is based on the RDF, European Commission et al. (2006).

[39] Personal interview with the Minister, 17.02.2007

[40] For a detailed description of this process see article by Terlinden/ Mohammed Hassan Ibrahim in this book.

[41] ICG (2003b: 15)

In April 2003 Somaliland elected a new President. The EC was unable to support the election of the head of the executive of an internationally non-recognised state. This would have been even more contradictory as the *IGAD-process* took place at the same time, aiming at the establishment of a transitional government for *all* Somali regions including Somaliland. Therefore, only a last-minute payment to the NEC of about €300.000 from the United Kingdom (U.K.), Denmark and Switzerland financially saved the elections.[42]

During the preparation of the 2005 parliamentary elections the EC became active again. After the British Embassy in Addis Ababa had made the first step,[43] the EC and DfID (U.K.), Denmark, Norway, Switzerland and USAID established a 'Democratisation Programme Steering Committee', which coordinated donor support to the elections and which has remained active up to now.[44] Targeting a programme explicitly at the democratisation of a non-recognised state could have been misconceived by both the Somaliland government and the TFG. Therefore, the Committee classified support to Somaliland's parliamentary elections as 'first phase' of a *Somalia-wide* democratisation programme.[45]

Once again, the existence of an independent Electoral Commission was instrumental in facilitating donor support to the elections. It permitted the EC to fully support the NEC and achieve maximum impact without having to cooperate with the Somaliland government on this sensitive issue.[46] The EC negotiated directly with NEC on the modes of EC-support. Again, the EC did not disburse funds immediately to NEC but channelled approximately US$ 2 million through an international NGO, which was chosen by NEC and to which NEC was responsible.[47] Apart from technical and financial assistance, the EC also supported the elections politically. European diplomats from Nairobi and Addis Ababa travelled to Hargeisa and discussed controversial topics with the government and opposition parties. Nevertheless, despite this increased political involvement European member states strongly rejected the U.K.'s proposal to issue a CFSP-declaration taking note of the elections in positive terms.[48]

Today, promotion of Somaliland's democratisation process has started to go beyond electoral support and includes training programmes for parliamentarians and the judiciary system. With regard to future external support to Somaliland's democratisation process, the International Republican Institute noted:

> "There is not yet a general consensus as to what "Phase Two" will entail, but some of the following objectives are now being widely discussed: Developing expertise in legislative policy-making and agenda building among Somaliland's new parliamentarians, (...); Institutionalizing parliament as an effective check on the executive while maintaining political stability; Democratizing and decentralizing political parties' decision-making processes; Maintaining party unity and discipline in parliament, (...); Implementing a continuous

---

[42] Ibid., Bradbury/Abokor/Ahmed (2003: 468).
[43] The Embassy financed consultants, who advised the Somaliland parliament on the drafting of an electoral law, APD/Interpeace (2006: 17). The Embassy administers a budget for projects in the area of human rights, civil society and democracy support, of which 40% is spent in Somaliland, personal interview with the Embassy, 27.04.2007.
[44] APD/Interpeace (2006: 17)
[45] International Republican Institute (2005: 12)
[46] Personal interview with an external consultant to the NEC, 20.02.2007
[47] ICG (2006a: 6), personal interview with an external consultant to the NEC, 20.02.2007
[48] Huliaras (2002: 171)

program of voter education; Further engaging women, minorities, and other marginalized groups in politics (...)."[49]

Recently there have been steps towards a more political European presence in Somaliland, which is not restricted to the timetable of elections. For instance, in March 2007 a European delegation lead by the head of the EC Delegation in Nairobi travelled to Somaliland and visited journalists held in Mandera prison, whom Amnesty International classified as "prisoners of conscience". Only hours after the visit the journalists were released by a presidential decree. It must be stated, however, that such political involvement does not and cannot take place within a regular diplomatic framework but always requires exceptional procedures.[50]

Some civil society activists in Somaliland would welcome an enhanced European involvement in Somaliland's internal politics, in order to foster democratic principles and to strengthen respect for human rights. In that case, involvement should be based on agreed criteria and bind both sides, Somaliland as well as the EC/EU. Europe would then be free to criticise any conflicting development, but also be obliged to reward positive developments. However, recognition by European states as an ultimate consequence for abiding by such criteria is highly unlikely – as prior recognition by African states is a European *sine qua non*.[51]

The changes in EC aid to Somaliland during the past decade mentioned above show a positive tendency: Eventually the EC seems to introduce the principles of 'partnership' and 'alignment', as confirmed in the *OECD Principles* and the *Paris Declaration*, into its relations with the Somaliland government.

Explaining the changes in EC aid

The reasons for this can be attributed to several developments, some of which shall be pointed out briefly.

The more Somaliland government institutions consolidated, the less was the EC able to turn a blind eye to them. Furthermore, after September 11, 2001, acting like this would have appeared rather careless: Due to the rise of the Union of Islamic Courts and their suspected ties to Al-Qaeda, South-Central Somalia came under the suspicion of being a breeding ground for terrorists. In this context, it appeared quite sensible for the EC to assist weak but stable Somaliland and to prevent the rise of Islamist tendencies and its slide back into the *de facto*-statelessness of the south.

Along with this, the EC came to realise that the benefits of co-operation were bigger than the risk of implicit recognition. This recognition is shown by the Conclusions of the EU's General Affairs and External Relations Council (GAERC) of July 2002. The Ministers proposed to complement the *Peace Dividend-Approach* with a so-called *Peace Building-Approach*, "focussing on the early establishment of effective administration including an

---

[49] International Republican Institute (2005: 33)

[50] Art. 8 of the Cotonou Agreement calls for regular political dialogue between the EC and the respective ACP state, including on the human rights situation, democratic principles, the rule of law and good governance.

[51] This was the case outside of Africa, when, in 1991, European foreign ministers set up guidelines for the recognition of emerging states in Eastern Europe and the former Soviet Union, demanding, amongst others, respect for the rule of law, democracy and human rights.

allinclusive, broad-based administration and, in parallel, the consolidation of provisional regional administration representing components of Somali society"[52]. Applying this approach, the EU could support such administrations that display,

> "a commitment to peace and to restoring credible governance and democracy; an effective collaboration with the international community in the fight against terrorism; an effective control of the main population centres and economic infrastructures; (...) the launching of effective reconciliation programmes including clanic and political special conferences; conditions for the return and reintegration of Somali refugees (...); willingness to participate in functional co-operation programmes that will lead to collaboration with other regional entities", and, "at a pace that respects the specific developments of the different regions of Somalia since 1991, participation in an open agenda dialogue with a provisional broad-based administration and other regional administrations with the genuine aim of re-establishing definitive institutions in Somalia."[53]

The timing of this proposal is remarkable: It is directly connected to the *IGAD-process* and its efforts of building a new central government for a – federally organised - united Somali state. Although it seems paradoxical, enhanced co-operation with and support for the Somaliland government were made possible in the very moment when a central government was established whose territorial claims included Somaliland. The international community does not regard this as a contradiction in itself because it has not recognised Somaliland's claims to independent statehood. Understandibly, the Somaliland government cannot easily accept co-operation under these prefixes, as it does not see itself as a regional state within a united Somalia. Under these circumstances it is striking that Somaliland authorities seem to be becoming more pragmatic: As long as the authorities can draw benefits from co-operation and the TFG does not lay a foot on Somaliland soil, Somaliland seems to be willing to co-operate.[54]

Remaining Challenges

At the moment, this strategy seems to pay off: Almost three years after its election the TFG is still too weak to even control Mogadishu. Nonetheless, these current positive effects of the *IGAD-process* on EC co-operation with Somaliland must not be taken for granted. The problem of the future relationship between Somalia and Somaliland remains unsolved. Its solution only has been postponed due to the TFG's weakness. Although a military invasion by the TFG into Somaliland is highly unlikely due to its military engagement in the south, the continued in limbo-status of Somaliland harbours two potential threats to the *de facto* independence and stability of Somaliland:

---

[52] European Council (2002: IX)

[53] Ibid.

[54] An example of this is the drafting-process of the CSP: Whereas the Somaliland government initially refused a single strategy paper for the whole of Somalia, which would have included separate chapters for the different "regions" South-Central Somalia, Somaliland and Puntland, the TFG rejected Somaliland's request for a separate strategy paper. However, Somaliland did not jump off the process but got back to negotiating the substance. A diplomat from Nairobi commented: "It seems as if the programmes are more important to the Somaliland government than their name.", personal interview, 07.03.2007.

First, there is a risk that Somaliland will be drawn "into the tangled web of conflicts in Somalia's south and central region"[55]. This risk has been sharply demonstrated by Somaliland's move into Las Anod on October 15, 2007, the capital of the disputed Sool region, and subsequent exchanges of artillery, riots and the displacement of scores of families. Somaliland seems to fear that Puntland unites with South-Central Somalia under a Darod-dominated government led by president Yusuf, shifting the power balance to its own disadvantage and impairing its territorial claims.[56] Taking control of Las Anod and 'closing its borders'[57] might lead to further conflict in the region.

Second, the unsettled status of Somaliland and the international recognition of the TFG as the transitional government of Somalia entails a risk that the TFG will try to exert political influence over Somaliland.[58] To preclude this, in 2004 the TFG had to agree to "avoid actions which undermine existing areas of tranquility"[59]. At the same time European foreign ministers further stated that "the EU will continue to provide direct assistance to existing areas of tranquility."[60] Especially due to its increased involvement in Somaliland's democratisation process, it is highly improbable that Europe would accept attempts by the TFG to undermine positive developments in Somaliland. Irrespective of this, a scenario in which the TFG will fail to master the transition period expiring in 2009 is currently much more likely. In that case, the EC will stay involved in Somaliland as much as it has been in recent years and possibly even enhance its activities. Should African states then make a move to recognise Somaliland,[61] European states would probably follow.

Somalilanders, on their part, need to be aware that gaining international recognition cannot be a goal in itself. Even though it is true that Somaliland for the past 16 years has done a great deal of work in terms of peace and democracy building and that it is now time for the EC to move – Somalilanders and the Somaliland government should refrain from becoming complacent. Improving respect for human rights and democratic governance will stay on Somaliland's agenda for quite a while. Therefore, international recognition and the ensuing increase in development aid should be regarded as an instrument which might further help Somaliland reach these goals. One should not forget that recognition would acknowledge democratic achievements, but it cannot dismiss any country from proving its constant commitment to increased democratic governance.

---

[55] Weinstein (2007: 1)

[56] This has been suggested by the merger of Puntland's security forces with the TFG's forces, Weinstein (2007: 2)

[57] Weinstein (2007: 1)

[58] Bryden (2004: 11). In some regions of Somalia there has already been opposition against attempts by the TFG to control local ressources and appointments of top political posts.

[59] Coodination and Monitoring Committee, 2005

[60] European Council (2004: 23)

[61] A move that cannot be taken for granted, as African states generally fear the opening of a 'pandora's box'. For example, Egypt is interested in an allied, strong and united Somalia due to its latent conflict with Ethiopia over access to the Nile.

Bibliography:

Academy for Peace and Development (APD), Interpeace, 2006, *A Vote for Peace. How Somaliland Successfully Hosted its First Parliamentary Elections in 35 years*, Nairobi: Interpeace Regional Office for Eastern and Central Africa.

Bakonyi, Jutta, 2001, *Instabile Staatlichkeit. Zur Transformation politischer Herrschaft in Somalia*, Hamburg: Universität Hamburg IPW.

Bayne, Sarah, 1999, The European Union's Response to State Collapse in Africa: The Case of Somalia, Edinburgh: University of Edinburgh.

Bayne, Sarah, 2001, *The European Union's Political and Development Response to Somalia*, Maastricht: ECDPM.

Bradbury, Mark; Abokor, Adan Yusuf; Yusuf; Haroon Ahmed, 2003, 'Somaliland: choosing politics over violence.' In: *Review of African Political Economy*, Vol. 30 (97), pp. 455–478.

Bryden, Matt, 1999, 'New Hope for Somalia? The Building Block Approach.' In: *Review of African Political Economy*, Vol. 26 (79), pp. 134–140.

Bryden, Matt, 2004, 'Somalia and Somaliland. Envisioning a dialogue on the question of Somali unity.' In: *African Security Review*, Vol. 13 (2), http://www.iss.co.za/ASR/13No2/F2.htm, last access: 21.11.2007.

Coordination and Monitoring Committee Somalia (CMC), 2005, *Declaration of Principles*.

Delegation of the European Commission in Kenya, 2004, *2002 Annual Report. Cooperation between The People of Somalia and The European Community. Final Report*, Nairobi.

European Commission, 2002, *European Commission Strategy for the Implementation of Special Aid to Somalia (SISAS)*. DEV/027/2002-EN.

European Commission, Denmark, Finland, Italy, Sweden, United Kingdom, Norway, 2006, *Country Strategy Paper 2007 - 2013. A Response to the Reconstruction and Development Framework. Draft 1*.

European Council, General Affairs and External Relations (GAERC), 22.07.2002, *Somalia - Council Conclusions*. 2447th Council Meeting, 10945/02 (Press 210), Brussels.

European Council, General Affairs and External Relations (GAERC), 22.-23.11.2004, *Somalia - Council Conclusions*. 2622th Council Meeting, 14724/04 (Press 325), Brussels.

European Council, Representatives of the Governments of the Member States, European Parliament, European Commission, 13.07.2005, *The European Consensus on Development. Joint Statement*, COM(2005) 311 final, Brussels.

Gilkes, Patrick, 1995, *Acceptance But Not Recognition. Draft*, Bedfordshire.

Hippel, Karin von; Yannis, Alexandros, 1997, 'The European Response to State Collapse in Somalia.' In: K. E. Jørgensen (ed.): *European approaches to crisis management*, The Hague; Boston: Kluwer Law International, pp. 65–81.

Huliaras, Asteris, 2002, 'The Viability of Somaliland: Internal Constraints and Regional Geopolitics.' In: *Journal of Contemporary African Studies*, Vol. 20 (2), pp. 157–182.

Illing, Sigurd, 1997, 'Somalia-EU cooperation. Helping the people in their time of greatest need.' In: *The Courier ACP-EU*, No. 162.

International Crisis Group, 2003b, *Somaliland: Democratisation And Its Discontents*, Nairobi/Brussels.

International Crisis Group, 2006a, *Somaliland: Time For African Union Leadership*, Nairobi/Addis Ababa/Brussels.

International Republican Institute, 2005, *Somaliland September 29, 2005 Parliamentary Elections Assessment Report*, Washington D.C.

Cabdiraxmaan Jimcaale, 2005, 'Consolidation and Decentralization of Government Institutions.' In: War-torn Societies Project (WSP) International Somali Programme (ed.): *Rebuilding Somaliland. Issues and Responsibilities*, Asmara, Eritrea: The Red Sea Press, Inc., pp. 49–121.

Ministry of National Planning and Coordination, Republic of Somaliland, 1998, *Two-Year Operational Plan for Economic Development 1998-1999, Volume Two*, Hargeisa.

Organisation for Economic Co-operation and Development/Development Assistance Committee (OECD/DAC), 2007, *Principles for Good International Engagement in Fragile States and Situations*, Paris.

Rye Olsen, Gorm, 2005, 'The European Union. 'European interests', bureaucratic interests and international options.' In: U. Engel, G. Rye Olsen (eds.): *Africa and the North: between globalization and marginalization*, London; New York: Routledge.

Schoiswohl, Michael, 2004, *Status and (Human Rights) Obligations of Non-Recognized de Facto Regimes in International Law: The Case of Somaliland*, Leiden (u.a.): Nijhoff.

Somalia Aid Coordination Body (SACB), 2003, *Donor Report*, Nairobi.

Somalia National Reconciliation Process, 2002, *Declaration on Cessation of Hostilities, Structures and Principles of the Somalia National Reconciliation Process*, Nairobi.

United Nations, World Bank, 2006, *Somali Reconstruction and Development Framework, Deepening Peace and Reducing Poverty, Volume I, Draft*.

United Nations Office of the Humanitarian Coordinator for Somalia, 2007, *Somalia: Open Letter to Leaders, Military Commanders, Elders And Community – Representatives*, http://allafrica.com/stories/200704301660.html, last access: 30.04.2007.

Visman, Emma, 1998, *Cooperation with Politically Fragile Countries: Lessons from EU Support to Somalia*. ECDPM.

Chapter 2:   Ethiopia

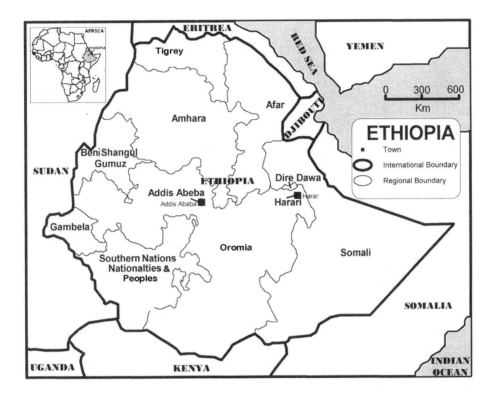

The delineation of the international boundaries shown on this map must not be considered authoritative

Committed political leadership matters! Ethiopia under Prime Minister Meles Zenawi and the question of continuity of political leadership

Rainer Tetzlaff

Introduction: three categories of African countries with regard to different natural (and political) endowments and prospects for democratic rule - a framework for analysis

With a population of some 80 million people, its long history as a sovereign Christian state and a relatively strong government, Ethiopia remains for Western governments one of Africa's most attractive countries. This is affirmed by the fact that that it also hosts the seat of the African Union in the capital. When the present Ethiopian Peoples Revolutionary Democratic Force (EPRDF) led government under Prime Minister Meles Zenawi came into power in 1991, a federal constitution was established successively. The government under the leadership of the Tigrayan People's Liberation Front (TPLF) "was aware of the need to build up trust among the citizens who had fought against the Dergue often in military groups that were comprised along ethnic lines. The necessity of decentralisation of state power therefore was apparent; the call could not be ignored" (Sommer 2006: 1). Since the new constitution based on ethnic federalism came into effect, three parliamentary elections have taken place so far, (in the years 1995, 2000 and 2005), and became the formal base of political legitimacy of the new established republic. Its fragile internal condition however causes questions on the duration and sustainability of social progress in regard to nation-building and democratisation.

Until now the institution of the state continued to be weak due to permanent ethno-political conflicts, chronic food insecurity, massive poverty, lack of productive capacity beyond agriculture and a high degree of political repression. On the other hand Ethiopia under Prime Minister Meles Zenawi is not a stagnant society, in the contrary. Some remarkable developments as far as social and economic innovations are concerned, are under way, which might change the country' s character in a long run (Bertelsmann Transformation Index 2008). The following article will deal with some aspects that have a propensity to limit chances for political change..

Under the current conditions of globalisation Third World countries are increasingly divided by the dichotomy into two broad categories, namely into those who know and those who own. It was the Kenyan political scientist *Ali Masrui* who made the point that in the 21st century, societies that *own* resources but without the requisite know-how to maximise them are likely to lose out to societies that *know*, irrespective of whether or not these societies own resources. While Taiwan, South Korea and Mauritius, for example, belong to the latter group, Africa's large area states like Nigeria, DR Kongo (= Zaire), Angola and Sudan belong to the group of 'owners': they are rich on natural resources like oil, gas and copper, but they all rank under the poorest countries of the world. Obviously these societies have not acquired the necessary knowledge to transform natural richness of the state in societal wellbeing for the people. Meanwhile an impressive amount of scientific publications exists which try to explain the "*paradox of plenty*" (see for ex. Basedau/Mehler 2005).

But obviously the African continent contains a *third category* of countries: those which do have neither considerable amounts of natural resources nor the societal knowledge to make use of the existing scarce potential, including *"human capital"* and *"institutional capital"*. In contrast to *physical capital* which means manmade production facilities and funds (available through services, revenues, taxes and loans), *human capital* refers to education and skills of people which may be considered as essential in order to improve one's living conditions. In addition, both formal and informal political institutions, which include legal systems and property rights, can be described by the notion of *"institutional capital"*. A country might have considerable amounts of "human capital" as a result of its well-equipped education system, as long as there are no appropriate legal procedures and institutional settings in place that guarantee the rule of law and a basic reliability, development will be blocked (Boeckh/Sevilla 2007). The best and the brightest might be forced by circumstances to leave the country as migrants to higher developed countries in Europe, North America and elsewhere. This unwilling *brain drain* – one could also call it migration with reluctance – happens today in too many African countries, causing an immense developmental damage. Actual examples of this grievance are Sudan and Zimbabwe – potentially rich countries in which "bad governance" (used as a short form for undemocratic, authoritarian or repressive governments) have destroyed the hopes and perspectives of development.

These countries with weak natural endowment, as far as mineral and other resources are concerned, often face enormous difficulties in launching and consolidating stable and efficient *state institutions*. These are regarded as integral parts of *good governance*, which is considered as a condition for all strategies to accelerate social progress and economic development. From a comparative point of view, difficulties and failures in achieving democratic objectives should not take us by surprise, because history tells us that the establishment of democracy is not a political agenda without *cultural preconditions*. These conditions relate to the perceptions, values and world-views of political elites as the dominant social groups in any country that has embarked on its path to modernity. The twentieth century was a time of extraordinary democratic success; one speaks of a "third wave of democratisation" (Samuel Huntington), but at the same time it was a time of frequent democratic failure. Until the end of the 20th century, in more than seventy occasions democracy collapsed and gave way to authoritarian regimes (according to Robert Dahl 1998: 145). Therefore, the conclusion may be justified that not all modernising societies in Africa South of the Sahara are a stage of development to accept the inherent rules of the democratic game, which mainly consist of two rules: the right of the majority of an electorate to govern the country and the rule of the limited use of power following the rules and regulations set up in the country's constitution. The political decline of *Kenya* under Prime Minister Mwai Kibaki (who is accused to have manipulated the parliamentary elections in December 2007 – a fraud which caused lasting violence against the Kikuyu – and retaliations against the Luo - with more than thousand casualties) is due to the practice of irresponsible political leadership which has refused to accept democratic rules of the game.

A social scientist with a non-African background (as the author) is well advised to keep in mind that for an African citizen the motion of *democracy* often means more than free elections; it is more encompassing than merely drawing up a new constitution and launching a multi-party system. Democracy is perceived by Africans often "as a way of life. It is a long-term process of reorganising the institutions of a civil society. Many of the struggles are more than struggles for access to political power. They are for access to the ordinary opportunities of life – land, water, living space and basic social services" (according to a definition by the Human Development Report 1993, quoted in Adewoye 2000: 44). Democratization in this sense may mean a peaceful struggle for improved living conditions of the society, even when the question of changing the power structure at the top of the state is not at the focus of interest of the political agenda. Therefore the famous radical thinker *Issa Shivji* from the University of Dar Es Salaam substitutes liberal democracy by popular democracy and popular power:

> "Popular power tries to address both the limits of parliamentary democracy and party politics while at the same time positing a new mode of politics... [It] is meant to draw attention to the issue of political legitimacy and institutional organisation of state power" and to focus on "the right to self-determination" whose essentials are: "the right to livelihood, right to food, shelter, education – in short, the *right to be human*" (Shivji 2000: 34).

In the spirit of the late president of Tanzania *Julius Nyerere* , Malimu (the "teacher") who as a rare exceptional leader of the African continent had proclaimed a far-reaching ethical *"code of conduct"* for popular leaders" (the Arusha Declaration from 1967, which emphasised the political ideas of Self-reliance and self-determination) Issa Shivji advocates a popular democracy in the sense of self-determination of people who determine its own policies "according to the requirements of its own historic experience, culture, and circumstances" (Shivji 2000: 34).

Therefore it is worthwhile to have a closer look at the circumstances and background conditions of *democratic governance* in East Africa. By doing so, I will use *Robert Dahls five conditions for democracy* as a framework of reference. Dahl distinguishes three "essential conditions for democracy" and two "favourable conditions for democracy". The three *essential* conditions for democracy are (Dahl 1998: 147):

- control of military and police by elected officials;
- democratic beliefs and political culture;
- no strong foreign control hostile to democracy.

The two *favourable* conditions for democracy are:

- a modern market economy and society;
- weak sub-cultural pluralism.

African attempts to democratic transition reach from outright disaster (Somalia, Congo-Brazzaville, Rwanda) to relative success (South Africa, Namibia, Benin, Mali, Ghana), with stalemate being a frequent outcome (as in Nigeria, Zaire, Togo, Kenya and Cameroon). Even the few successful cases of transition were essentially grappling with what turned out to be

> "the must intractable political problem facing the region: that of crafting representative public institutions on a social foundation of deep-seated ethnic rivalries and economic inequalities" (Chege 1995: 44).

Key to the outcome of democratic transition in all cases was the *quality of political leadership*, whether in government or in opposition, and its capacity to steer hitherto hostile constituencies toward mutual accommodation.

In the following chapters I will deal mainly with the two first named "essential conditions for democracy", while assuming that nowadays there does (with the exception of China!) not exist any great power that can be regarded as "hostile to democracy" in principle. That does not imply the assumption that great powers will not pursue own interests in Africa, which consequently will not favour democratic change. For example, the interests of the administration of the USA under the presidency of George W. Bush concerning the horn of Africa seem to be guided not by exporting *universal* democratic values but rather by *national* security considerations in order to gain regional allies in the international "war on terror". Here the moral quality of leadership does not rank high on the political agenda of values, as the support of regimes like those in Sudan and Ethiopia by Washington may indicate.

China off course is another case! I hope that it is not unfair to state that Beijing's foreign policy towards African countries behaves more or less unconcerned with or indifferent to issues of democracy or dictatorship. The government of China imposes no conditionality on the recipient country, regarding criteria such as good governance, democratic participation or social and environmental standards. With this policy China supports authoritarian regimes in Sudan, Angola, Zimbabwe and Congo-Brazzaville, which are sanctioned by the international community. According to the "five principles of peaceful coexistence", drawn up by China's Communist Party early in the 1950s, it pursues *"mutual non-interference"* in so-called "internal affairs", in which principle human rights violations and ethnic cleansing operations are included. It is needless to underline the fact that African governments very much welcome this easy and pragmatic approach when doing business. Tired of the 'Big Brother' behaviour of the West, that emplies demanding the acceptance of developmental and political conditions before receiving loans and technical assistance, African politicians praise the new comfortable and lucrative partnership with the Asian giant (Tull 2005). For Africa's identity and politics, this new partnership, which rhetorically emphasizes friendship, respect, and equal rights,

> "represents an enormous increase in self-esteem. The fact that Africa is no longer treated as a group of needy recipient countries but rather courted as a trade and investment partner contributes significantly to this" (Hofmann et al 2007: p.88).

1   *Ethiopia's thorny path to modernisation: the emergence of repressive but strong power regimes as an unfavourable historic heritage*

Where then, should *Ethiopia* be placed within the above-mentioned analytical framework? The Federal Republic Ethiopia is a large country with limited natural resources (according to our present knowledge, but with promising oil deposits in Ogaden and Gambella). It has with great agricultural potential (for coffee, vegetable, fruits etc.) and with still underused human and institutional capital. Obviously Ethiopia with its large population of estimated 83 million people (2007) belongs to the *poorest* countries of the world, with a GDP (Gross Domestic Product) per head of 149 US $ in 2006 or 834 US $ (GDP at PPP, Purchasing Power Parities). Compared with the economic indicators of neighbouring African countries it lacks far behind

Tanzania with 299 US $ GDP per head (resp. 1241 US $ GDP at PPP) and Kenya with 661 US $ GDP per head (resp. 1504 US $ GDP at PPP). As far as democratic achievements are concerned, Ethiopia belongs to the *non-free* countries, according to the Freedom House assessment (Freedom House 2006: Freedom in the World 2007).

Ethiopia's performance in 2005-2007 was characterised by a contradiction of the politics of the ruling elite: While the autocratic political leadership under Prime Minister Meles Zenawi showed some flexibility and learning capability in market reforms, it refrained from implementing democratic reforms. His behaviour in the aftermath of the elections May 2005 questioned the legitimacy of his rule fundamentally. Turnout was high for parliamentary elections. Voters returned the ruling party, the Ethiopian People's Revolutionary Democratic Front (EPRDF) to power, albeit with a much-reduced majority. Opposition parties went from 12 seats in the parliament up to 176 and won every constituency in the capital, Addis Ababa. Announcement of the election results was delayed for eight weeks owing to complaints of irregularities from more than half of the country's electoral constituencies. The elections themselves were delayed for over two months in the Somali region due to security concerns. European election observers noted that the polling was marked by irregularities (for details see the report of the by the report of the European Union Election Observers Mission, EU-EOM, 2005 and Merera, in this volume). The outcome of the elections and accusations of fraud led to massive protests in Addis Ababa. As a result of clashes between protesters and security forces, 38 people were confirmed dead, hundreds injured, and 3,000 arrested. Further riots in early November over alleged election fraud left at least 23 more people dead. The United Kingdom temporarily froze aid to Ethiopia in protest against the violent crackdown.

In September, 43 members of the opposition political party, the Coalition for Unity and Democracy (CUD), were arrested in the Amhara region for "violent activities aimed at subverting the constitutional order." Some of the elected opposition candidates consciously did not join the parliament at the start of the session, in protest against alleged vote-rigging and other manipulations during the elections. Clashes between Oromo and Somali groups continued throughout 2005 in the Oromiya region and led to the deaths of more than 70 people and the internal displacement of thousands.

The respect for civil human rights and political rights even has diminished since May 2005. An official report for the parliament on post-election violence in 2006 concluded that "excessive force" had been used by government, 199 people were killed, mainly as result of gunfire, and that about 30.000 people were arrested. Three judges who were responsible for the inquiry report preferred to flee to the UK, after they received death threats. The aftermath of the third parliamentary elections must be regarded as a *regress in institution building*.

A culture of state-ownership and management still dominates government thinking that still has to embrace fully free-market reforms in many areas of the economy. At the same time though, the government is eager to attract foreign investment and has encouraged public-private-partnership-activities in various fields. In November 2006, the *World Bank's Africa Development Indicators 2006* praised Ethiopia in key areas and gave it a high rating in areas such as annual GDP growth, "structural policies", "economic management", "public sector management and institutions". How can these salient *differences in public performance* be explained?

An answer to the question of Ethiopian singularity lies certainly to a large extent in its history as a unique society with a long established *culture of despotic governance and civil war*. There is no reason to put into question the fact that the generation-long struggle for centralisation and consolidation of political power in the highlands absorbed much of the societal energies and national resources, which got lost for more *productive* purposes. In modern history, the largest country at the Horn of Africa suffered from the war against the liberation movement of Eritrea for thirty years. After Eritrea became independent, the war between Ethiopia and Eritrea again cost the life of approximately two million people and paralysed considerable economic and social activities of the whole country – thereby blocking all civil innovations and institutional capital formation. Thus, the present situation of underdevelopment, poverty and dependency in Ethiopia can be regarded as a mixture of different *external and internal causes and circumstances*, under which two factors rank foremost: Italian colonialism and continued political hegemony of the "highlanders", together forming a continuity of paternalistic governance, that starts with Emperor Menelik, through Emperor Haile Selassie, military president Mengistu Haile Mariam up to the present Prime Minister Meles Zenawi. The argument of this article though refers to *latest changes in the overall continuity* of paternalistic rule.

To proof this argument we will have a look at some hallmarks of Ethiopian history. The modern Ethiopian state was created by highland rulers in the latter half of the 19th century. Emperor Menelik founded the modern Ethiopia. In 1916 a noble man from the province, *Ras Tafari Mekonnen* seized power and became the effective ruler as crown prince in 1916, established ascendancy over regional feudal lords and was enthroned as *Emperor Haile Selassie* in 1930, with the program of modernising the feudal nature of the society. But his modernising ambitions were brought to a halt and he was driven into exile when the army of fascist *Italy* invaded and occupied Ethiopia between 1936 and 1941. Italy had tried to capture the country in the 19th century, but had been defeated by Ethiopian forces in a famous victory at Adowa in 1986. Italy nevertheless consolidated its holdings on the Muslim coast and the highland plateau, creating the colony of Eritrea. Following Ethiopia's liberation by allied forces in 1941, Haile Selassie returned from Britain, and hence tried to establish more firmly his power.

The present conditions of Ethiopia as a country which faces periodically famines and has to ask for foreign development assistance permanently is also due to the fatal mistake of Emperor Haile Selassie in the 1960ies to abrogated the federation between Ethiopia and Eritrea. Unilaterally he annexed the territory, provoking Eritrean separatists to launch a protracted guerrilla war. One year later, Ethiopia became embroiled in a war with newly independent Somalia over the eastern region of Ogaden. Domestic discontent was further fuelled by corruption among feudal officials, and by rampant inflation and high unemployment. Even in his late seventies Haile Selassie showed neither willingness to loosen his grip on power, nor would he discuss the issue of his succession. Everything depended on the emperor's decision. He alone was the arbiter between competing factions and individuals. He alone decided on appointments, promotions and demotions. He in person redressed grievances, received petitions, granted pardons, distributed largesse, cancelled debts and overturned court decisions. He also authorised each trip abroad of his officials. "No minister would dare to take any decision of consequence without having first obtained the *fakad* – his approval" (Meredith 2005: 210).

This type of governance can best be named a *singular personal rule-system*; its lifetime was restricted to the physical ability of the ruler to work up information to useful political decisions. To keep himself informed, Haile Selassie relied on a constant stream of secret intelligence and gossip. In private audiences, ministers were encouraged to report on the activities of their colleagues. The key to all advancement lay in loyalty and service to the emperor, which he was careful to reward. The largesse he distributed came not just in form of appointments, titles, land grants and salary increases but in gifts of money, houses, cars and other luxury items. Officials competed to provide him with choice titbits of information, what can be regarded as a typical method of totalitarian rule in a feudal costume. "Officials who served him well he rewarded with scholarships, free medical treatment and foreign holidays. Those who plotted against him or earned disfavour faced expropriation and ruin" (Meredith 2005: 211).

Under these conditions no civil society with young elites having acquired modern education could emerge, and no split in the upper classes between traditional elites and modern educated Africans, striving for reforms, could develop, as it happened in Ghana, Kenya, Uganda and in other countries. In colonial and post-colonial societies, such *social and cultural contradictions* as an unintended result of European rule used to stimulate political modernisation. That was the case in Tanzania as well as in Kenya, Sudan and Uganda (although not always with peaceful consequences!).

2   Political stabilisation by force: a long continuity in Ethiopian's governance culture

The unique and extreme kind of *personal rule* in imperial Ethiopia without any institutional checks and balances (which was described by the Polish Africa correspondent Ryszard Kapuściński in a wonderful novel called "The emperor: Downfall of an autocrat") could not last for ever; it was unable to cope with external challenges. Public discontent was brought to head by revelations of government indifference towards the 1972-74 famine, which cost an estimated 200.000 lives. Peasant revolts followed, underlining the need for land reform. In January 1974 a series of strikes and mutinies in the armed forces prompted the resignation of the prime minister of the previous 13 years. The event marked the beginning of what evolved into a coup by army officers in 1974. Then, in early 1974, a few small and random incidents occurred that were eventually to culminate into a revolution. At different places in the country, in Asmara as well as, for example, at an army outpost in Neghelle in southern Ethiopia mutinies occurred, accompanied by a series of spontaneous civilian protests erupted on the streets of mayor towns. In the capital students demonstrated over plans for educational reforms; teachers went on strike demanding higher pay; taxi drivers struck in protest against fuel price increases; labour unions took to the streets to voice grievances over pay, food price rises and union rights. A national revolution took place, and people urgently wanted a new system of government with a committed and responsive leadership (Meredith 2005).

Within the armed forces, a group of radical junior officers conspired to take control; they formed a military committee or *"Derg"* (or *"Dergue"*), comprising 108 representatives chosen by units of the armed forces, to run the country. Stage by stage, growing in confidence, the Derg began to dismantle the whole imperial structure. In the government press, on radio and television, the ancient régime was accused for corruption and exploitation. Haile Selassie, being over eighty-two years of age himself was accused of squandering the country's meagre resources on expensive trips abroad and of being wilfully negligent over the *Wollo famine*. At a four-day secret meeting in early September 1974, the Derg voted to dethrone Selassie, and in November the Derg, under the command of a young ordnance officer, Major Mengistu Haile Mariam, ordered the execution of some sixty prominent prisoners. Among them there were mostly high officials associated with Haile Selassie's regime, including two former prime ministers and the emperor's grandson.

What followed can be characterised as a period of *military dictatorship under a Marxist-Leninist ideology* to legitimise the usurpation of power and the brutal eradication of opposition supporters. In a conservative estimate, 100.000 people were killed and several hundred thousands fled to the United States and Western Europe, establishing a trend of youth emigration. The brutal repression of the civil society as well as of the peasants and workers who were forced in a network of rural and urban dweller associations, known as *kebeles*, provoked political resistance. In Eritrea and the northern province of *Tigray*, the nucleus of the military movement that was to win power in 1991 emerged, and eventually overthrew the Mengistu regime.

The new government, led by a Tigrayan, the EPRDF chairman Meles Zenawi, claimed that it would democratize Ethiopia through recognition of the country's ethnic heterogeneity. No longer would the Ethiopian union be maintained by force; rather, it would be a voluntary federation of its many peoples. To this end the EPRDF and other political groups agreed to the creation of a transitional government that would engineer a new constitution and elections; to a national charter that recognized an ethnic division of political power; and to the right of nationalities to secede from Ethiopia (thus paving the way for Eritrea's legal independence).

Soon the government declared that it intended to strengthen ethnically based regional governments whose ruling parties were affiliated politically and ideologically with the EPRDF. A new regional map reflecting the changes was issued in 1992. Some Ethiopians criticized the new ethnic units as similar to an antinational reorganization of Ethiopia drawn up by the Italians in 1936. The Amhara, identified by the EPRDF as colonizers, were particularly affronted by the apparent disunification of the country. The government fought back by denouncing Amhara leaders as antidemocratic chauvinists and by muzzling the press through application of a new law that theoretically guaranteed its freedom. In the provinces, the government did not bother to maintain even the guise of freedom: there, the suppression of anti-EPRDF forces, especially the Oromo Liberation Front, was so blatant as to be noticed by the members of an international team sent to observe regional elections in June 1992 (following Marcus 2007).

To conclude this short review of the violent history of modern Ethiopia, it can be said that the strained *stabilisation by force phase* that began more than sixty years ago, is still casting its shadows on the present time. Even after the creation of an independent state of Eritrea violence between both states did not come to a halt, and in 1998 even a new (interstate) war broke out (on the ridicules pretext of the question of the "true" territorial belonging of the small area of *Badme)*. Therefore the *regional circumstances* and historic *conditions* for establishing democratic rule in an ethnically extremely heterogeneous country were not very favourable, when the society began to breathe freely after the collapse of the brutal Mengistu dictatorship which had forced many young and well-educated citizens to leave the country.

In the aftermath of the civil war people could not fall back onto a tradition of political participation. The knowledge of free discussions on public matters and the practice of common *political rules of the game* were not existent which would have been necessary to match social coexistence of different people and cultures peacefully. As *Robert Dahl* stated, "democratic political institutions are more likely to develop and endure in a country that is culturally fairly homogenous and less likely in a country with sharply differentiated and conflicting subcultures" (Dahl 1998: 149-150). The explanation Dahl offers seems rather plausible: "Distinctive cultures are often formed around differences in language, religion, race, ethnic identity, region, and sometimes ideology. Members share a common identity and emotional ties; they sharply distinguish "us" from "them"…As a consequence, they consider their demands too crucial to allow for compromise. They are nonnegotiable. Yet under a peaceful democratic process, settling political conflicts generally requires negotiation, conciliation, compromise" (Dahl 1998: 150).

It is obvious that the multi-ethnic and multi-cultural society of Ethiopia with its decades of power struggles since the conquest of the southern "tribes" by Emperor Menelik – the biggest group being the Oromo (then called Galla) among other southern peoples – lacked all preconditions for a peaceful coexistence in a unified nation-state. Up to now, Ethiopia is a vertically stratified society with various regions and cultures which never have been ruled by an overriding consensus instead of force and discrimination from above. There are 64 major ethnic groups in Ethiopia, although academics have identified more than 80 distinct languages in Ethiopia. Despite the state's traditional association with Orthodox Christianity (the church of Coptes), the Ethiopian population is split fairly evenly between Christians and Muslims. By constitution (from 1995), which guarantees *"ethnic federalisms"* and regional autonomy, each "nation" of Ethiopia has the right of independence and secession; but in reality the capital has a firm control over all regional governments and their revenues (Nugent 2004: 487). Therefore it can be duly asked whether a sane political development towards democracy and social progress is probable or possible at all, taking the unfavorable historic heritage into account.

3   *The supremacy of power maintenance, ethnic federalism and the policy of decentralisation*

As already mentioned, Ethiopia's political performance in recent years was characterised by a contradiction of the politics of the ruling elite: While the autocratic political leadership under Prime Minister Meles Zenawi showed some flexibility and learning capability in market reforms, it refrained from implementing democratic reforms as well as from respecting civil rights. When it comes to the crucial question of control of state power the incumbents behave merciless and without compromise. From the point of view of civil society members his behaviour in the aftermath of the elections May 2005 questioned the legitimacy of his rule fundamentally. Since then the situation of civil human rights and political rights has worsened. An official report for the parliament on post-election violence in 2006 concluded that "excessive force" had been used by government.

Faced with the possibility of loosing control of power relations, the government periodically falls back to a culture of state ownership and central power management which still dominates the attitude and reflexes of the power elite. The unconditioned maintenance of state power is obviously regarded as a supreme value in the basic perception of governance (cf. also Ayittey 2005: 57f.). The People's Republic of China since the successful reforms of Party leader Deng Xiaoping (1904-1997) may function as a shining example of governance because of its guarantees of political stability. Like Beijing the government of Meles Zenawi has not only to embrace fully free-market reforms in many areas of the economy, but also in the area of political freedom and democracy. Moreover, both governments are eager to attract foreign investment. In addition to that both have encouraged some public-private-partnership-activities in various fields.

This economic reform course shows first signals of success. In November 2006, the *World Bank's Africa Development Indicators 2006* singled out Ethiopia for praise in key areas and gave it a high rating in areas such as annual GDP growth, "structural policies", "economic management", "public sector management and institutions". Ethiopia posted an estimated growth rate of 7.3% and had an excellent harvest. However, food aid was still needed for the acutely undernourished, however. Historically, most of Ethiopia's GDP revenue came from agriculture, the primary export crop being coffee. Low world coffee prices over the past five years prompted a diversification into the production of flowers, vegetables, and khat for the export market. Ethiopia was one of 18 countries that benefited from 100% multilateral debt relief of loans from the International Monetary Fund, the World Bank, and the African Development Bank in a deal agreed to by the Group of Eight finance ministers in June 2005. All these benevolent gestures by international actors indicate their conviction that Ethiopia is of great importance for the stability of the region. Political stability seems to be much more appreciated than human rights and liberal and human right's standards of "good governance".

Civil liberties for the citizens have improved to a limited extend, but Ethiopia is still regarded as one of the slower *transformation countries* with severe shortcomings and deficits by social scientists. Ethiopia has never been able to change the government democratically (although the 2005 elections made a potential step forward in the development of the country's political culture, concerning the emergence of conflict-prepared opposition forces). In addition to a widespread internal dissent, the European Union and other observers state that these elections did not meet international standards. This verdict triggered a rude verbal reaction of Prime Minister Meles who blamed the observers of the EU as incompetent and racist. In reaction to international pressure on the government, in July 2007 the government of Prime Minister Meles Zenawi granted amnesty to leaders of the opposition Coalition for Unity and Democracy (CUD). Thereafter the EPRDF appointed an interim administration for the capital because too few of those elected were willing to take up their seats. The government has declared the freed CUD politician's seats in parliament vacant and plans to hold by-elections in 2008, which will give the CUD leaders a chance to win their seats back (EIU Nov. 2007: 3). The present government in Addis Ababa wants to underline its belief that the purpose of political elections is the confirmation of the acting government rather than its removal.

Ethiopia applied for membership of the WTO, but her negotiations with the WTO is threatened by its reluctance to open the economy to foreign competition in the central areas of banking and telecommunications. Another issue of concern is the governments unchanged *land policy*: As all land is owned by the state, the lack of private property denies businesses access to much-needed credit, as well as it prevents banks from the collateral necessary to encourage lending. Thus the authoritarian government is part of Ethiopia's problem, not its solution. Here we face the well-known dilemma of dictatorial rule: The political leaders, who are mainly concerned with their own survival at the top of the state, do not trust their own people thus paralyzing the energies of the peasants, workers, market women and traders, businesspeople and professionals. It will take a long time until the various fractions of a national civil society will be strong and courageous enough to challenge the ethnically dominated rule of the present government.

The future of Ethiopia may be severely damaged by her imprudent *foreign policy*. The border dispute resulting from the 1998–2000 war with Eritrea has been continuing without resolution. Ethiopia rejected the 2002 ruling of the *Eritrea-Ethiopia Boundary Commission*, which was created by the 2000 Algiers Peace Agreement. The UN Mission in Ethiopia and Eritrea *(UNMEE)* noted continued violence along the border. The UN Security Council extended the mandate of UNMEE until March 2006 and called upon Ethiopia to fully accept the ruling of the boundary commission. Meanwhile, UNMEE is about to leave the country, and Mr. Zenawi in a recent speech to Parliament said: his country did not seek war, but if Eritrea launched a "suicidal attack, it would be driven into the sea" (The Economist, November 2007: 44).

If it was the aim that Ethiopia tried to achieve 1998-2000, the war with Eritrea can be considered as a failure. Relations with other bordering countries can be described as tactical: Ethiopia gave political and military support to Somali's President in exile, Abdullahi Yusuf Ahmed. Ethiopia benefited from an economic relationship with the self-declared republic of Somaliland that included access to the port of Berbera for exports. Ethiopia welcomed the peace agreement between northern and southern Sudan, anticipating that it would help to end ethnic violence along the Sudanese border with Ethiopia and increase trade between the two countries.

5   Conclusion and outlook: Political leadership matters! Civil society's strength is crucial

Referring to the criteria of *Bertelsmann Transformation Index* (BTI), the reform process in Ethiopia is complex and contradictory. The biannual BTI measures the performance of some 130 developing countries with regard to market economy and political democracy in a Western sense. According to BTI 2006, the treatment of women for example, is still a "national disgrace". Further, despite economic liberalization, television and radio remain under government control. As part of its policy of devolution, the government is encouraging broadcasting in local languages and the formation of regional radio stations. Ethiopia's record on press freedom is relatively poor, and the government has harassed and imprisoned scores of independent journalists and editors in recent years.

Among social scientists today there exist a wide consensus concerning the crucial importance of *enlightened responsible political leadership* for postcolonial African states, especially in those countries in which stable public institutions, rule of law and a strong network of checks and balances could not yet be developed. In his brilliant book "The Fate of Africa. The history of 50 years of Independence" *Martin Meredith* characterized the first post-colonial generation of political leaders as economically ignorant and *ethnicity-centered* leaders who failed to set in motion economic and social institutional reforms. "The political arena became a contest for scarce resources. In a continent where class formation had hardly begun to alter loyalties, ethnicity provided the strongest political base. Politicians and voters alike came to rely on ethnic solidarity...primary loyalty remained rooted in tribal identity. Kinship, clan and ethnic consideration of African politics became, in essence, kinship corporations" (Meredith 2005: 156).

In a symposium on "Reflections on Leadership in Africa" held in 1997 in Dar Es Salaam, Tanzania, on the occasion of "Forty years after independence", *Omonyi Adewoye* (vice-chancellor of the University of Ibadan, Nigeria) deplored "the lack of honest, upright and people-friendly leadership" in post-colonial Africa. "In other words, whilst the African predicament is often expressed in economic terms, it is really little more than a "superstructural" problem, grave as it has been. Africa's crisis lies mainly in the political domain, in the 'structural sector from where poor or bad leadership often reflects adversely in all other sectors and facets of the political system and society" (Adewoye 2000: 39). Therefore the solution to Africa's crisis "lies not so much in the economic as in the political domain" (ibd.), and in the political culture of its society. Without a courageous national civil society who dares to challenge the political class, the progressive development of Ethiopia may be severely blocked. Africa, like the rest of the world, will need *skilful and intelligent policy makers*, "that is, men and women capable of 'deliberately forging and regularly fortifying links between economic growth and human development, she will require more the services of intellectuals. Yet, the latter have virtually become an endangered specie. A large chunk of them are living in Western Europe or North America on account of an unwholesome and disenabling intellectual and economic environment at home. For those resident at home, perennial official assaults on their human dignity and fundamental liberties are added onto economic and material disempowerment that virtually make the work place and life one big bore" (Adewoye 2000: 46).

This point of view of a high caliber African intellectual stressing the importance of democratic values and pluralistic institutions is most sympathetic and may represent the sentiments and hopes of many citizens in African states. They are the first victims of irresponsible selfish governance, the "governance of the belly" (Bayart). As a consequence of these circumstances in African countries many otherwise brilliant and talented academics opt for "exit" (in the sense of Hirschman's terminology), i.e. migration to a neighboring country or to a "western" liberal democratic country. At presence we witness of the thousands of children from Zimbabwe, fleeing the misery of their home-country in search of new lives in South Africa. "Even for those who make it, it is a perilous business. Many of those who have fled have fallen victim to sexual predators and abusive employers. Many are used to as slave labor (Basildon Peta "Flight of the Young Ones. Thousands of children are fleeing the misery of Zimbabwe", in: The Independent, London, 11 December 2007, p. 23). Besides Eritrea, Zimbabwe represents today the most detrimental example of self-destruction of a potentially rich and flourishing African country by irresponsible leadership. And it is not a bare accident that dictator Mengistu after his defeat 1991 fled to his spiritual brother Mugabe of Zimbabwe where he lives in exile, sentenced to death *in absentia*.

The growing political tensions in the region thus give both countries an excuse to spend more on guns and spies, some to be turned on domestic enemies. Prime Minister Zenawi has announced to put his defence budget up by 17 % to 390 million $ in order to equip the 100.000 men under arms along the borders with adequate weapons. With the increasing tendencies to *militarization* the prospects in the Horn of Africa to cope successfully with the challenges of mass poverty and structural dependence. Ethiopia is not a country suffering from the "curse of minerals", but rather from "the curse of a long lasting warrior culture". If a new generation of political leaders in Ethiopia really would want to get rid of Ethiopia's reputation as being a permanent looser of modernisation than it should brake with this fatal tradition of being a people with a belligerent identity. Whether cultural identities of people change is a question of a courageous political leadership.

Bibliography:

Adewoye, Omonyi, 2000, *Leadership and the Dynamics of reform in Africa*, in: Haroub Othman (ed), "Reflections On Leadership in Africa. Forty Years After Independence", Dar Es Salaam and Brussels

Ayittey, George B. N., 2005, *Africa Unchained. The blueprint for Africa's Future*, Houndsmill/Basingstoke and New York

Basedau, Matthias/Mehler, Andreas (eds.), 2005, *Resource Politics in Sub-Saharan Africa*, Hamburg

Boeckh, Andreas/Sevilla, Rafael (eds.), 2007, *Kultur und Entwicklung. Vier Weltregionen im Vergleich*, Baden-Baden

Chege, Michael, 1995, *Democracy's Future. Between Africa's extremes*, in: Journal of Democracy, Vol.6, Number 1, January 1995, pp. 44-51

Dahl, Robert A., 1998, *On Democracy*. New Haven and London

Hirth, Nicole, 2002, 'Eritrea', in Hofmeier, Rolf; Jakobeit, Cord (eds): *Afrika Jahrbuch 2002*, Opladen

Hofman, Katharina, Jürgen Kretz, Michael Kroll and Sebastian Sperlin, 2007: *Contrasting Perceptions: Chinese, African, and European Perspectives on the China-Africa Summit*, in: Friedrich-Ebert-Stiftung (ed), "Internationale Politik und Gesellschaft", Nr. 2/2007, pp. 75-90

Marcus, Harold, 2007, in *Encyclopaedia Britannica 2007* (Ultimate Reference Suite DVD)

Meredith, Martin, 2005, *The Fate of Africa. A History of Fifty Years of Independence*, New York

Nugent, Paul, 2004, *Africa Since Independence*, New York

Othman, Haroub (Ed.), 2000, *Reflections On Leadership in Africa: Forty Years After Independence. Essays in Honour of Mwalimu Julius K. Nyerere, on the Occasion of his 75th Birthday*. Institute of Development Studies. University of Dar es Salaam

Sommer, Monika, upcoming: *Ethiopian Federalism Seen from the perspective of the Regional State of Gambella: cause of conflict and fierce competition or access to resources and democratic participation?*, in: Grawert, Elke (ed)

Medhane Tadesse, 1999, *The Eritrean-Ethiopian War: Reprospect and Prospects. Reflections on the Making of Conflicts in the Horn of Africa*, 1991-1998, Addis Ababa

Tetzlaff, Rainer, 2006, *Afrika in der Armutsfalle: Big Push als Antwort auf Afrikas „big problems"?* in: Michael Take (ed), „Politik als Wissenschaft". Festschrift für Wilfried Röhrich zum 70. Geburtstag, Berlin, p.617-634

Tetzlaff, Rainer, 2007, *Afrika in der Globalisierungsfalle*, Wiesbaden (in print)

Tetzlaff, Rainer (ed), 2000, *Weltkulturen unter Globalisierungsdruck*, Bonn

Tetzlaff, Rainer/Jakobeit, Cord, 2005, *Das nachkoloniale Afrika.* Politik- Wirtschaft, Gesellschaft, Wiesbaden

Tetzlaff, Rainer, *Ethiopia. Country Report in Bertelsman's Transformation Index (BTI)* 2006 and 2008, Gütersloh

Electoral Politics and Regime Changes in Africa: The Ethiopian Experience

Merera Gudina

1   Introduction

Since the change of regime in 1991, Ethiopia has been undergoing a major political metamorphosis which has promised a dual transition, i.e. a transition 'from an ethnically-dominated empire state of un-equals to an ethnically egalitarian nation-state of equals, and from authoritarian rule to democracy'[1]. Elections have been expected to play a role of a midwife in the dual transition to multi-party democracy while the decentralization of governance is expected to end centuries of ethnic domination[2]. Accordingly, four major elections were held - the most critical one being the May 2005 one - which put to a severe test the political engineering premised on the fundamentals of 'revolutionary democracy'.

The May 2005 elections, which can go down as the first competitive multi-party elections in the country's long recorded history, came as a political earth quake for the regime that has been badly seeking to transform the legitimacy earned through the barrel of the gun to that of the ballot box. When contrary to the expectations of the leaders of the ruling-party, the opposition had the poise to make a dramatic showing at the polls, the Ethiopian People's Revolutionary Democratic Front (EPRDF) leaders have quickly turned to their natural constituency – the army of the revolutionary democracy that brutally suppressed the citizens in what can be termed a post-election systematic state repression. Consequently, the rising expectations created as the result of the popular expression allowed to millions of people across the country during the May elections, turned into rising frustration - following the herding of thousands of opposition members and supporters to prisons, which at times included extra-judicial killings.

To be sure, at the centre of frustrated hope for an Ethiopian democratic transition was electoral authoritarianism, which raises both theoretical and practical questions such as: are there universally accepted standards for "free and fair" elections? Can elections by themselves guarantee successful democratic transitions? In the Ethiopian and/or African context, can elections lead to regime changes? Do multi-party elections lead to further political polarization or national consensus? Is multi-party democracy a product of national consensus or vice versa? Given the existing Ethiopian situation, and the political trajectory of the ruling party, is there a future for electoral politics and/or multi-party democracy in the country?

---

[1] Even if the main stream Ethiopian historians trace back the origin of the Ethiopian state to 10th century B.C., Ethiopia took its present shape in the second half of the 19th century under what can be termed the "making" of Ethiopia. Hence, the post-1991 radical reordering of the Ethiopian state can be characterized as the "remaking of Ethiopia" a century later.

[2] The claim of the present Ethiopian regime is both to end the domination of one ethnic group over the others and democratize the Ethiopian state. But in reality what is emerging is "an ethnocratic state".

By the way of answering the above mentioned questions, this paper discusses the nature of electoral authoritarianism and the future of democracy and/or democratic governance in Ethiopia within the wider African context.

2 Theoretical framework: elections and regime changes in Africa

Following the end of the Cold-War, which Fukuyama (1992) dubbed as the 'end of history', in what initially hoped to end the chapter of authoritarian rules in Africa, the entrenched leaders of the continent – some of them presidents for life - were forced to leave office either through the barrel of the gun or the ballot box. Consequently, some of the most brutal African dictators such as Siad Barre of Somalia, Mengistu of Ethiopia, Mobutu of Zaire and Doe of Liberia were removed from power through successful popular insurgences, while milder authoritarian leaders such as Kaunda of Zambia submitted to the verdict of the ballot box. And, in both cases donors' conditionality and internal pressure combined to produce positive results in the initial democratization drive across the continent. But, as the wind of change started to subside, instead of out-rightly opposing elections authoritarian leaders have started to cleverly embrace multi-party democracy and the game of 'free and fair 'elections thereof in theory to legitimize themselves - but have been busy in fixing election results, which have resulted in what Jean-Francois Bayart, *et al* (1999: 107) call '*The great deception'*.

True to Bayart, *et al's* characterization, by the turn of the 21st century, the hopes for democratization of states and society in the continent have failed to produce the desired results, and there have been few real regime changes across the continent. Much talked about democratic transitions elsewhere in Africa are failing to pass the acid test for multiparty democracy as the so-called "free and fair" elections have been reduced to instruments of legitimization of regimes, rather than effecting regime changes. In this connection, some years back Felix K.G. Anebo, in his summary of the post-independence African political trajectory, has noted that: "Of the 190 African heads of state since independence only 20 relinquished power voluntarily and less than 10 stepped down in a democratic transition: the bulk simply retired after long years in office" (p. 41). The main reasons are, as Anebo himself correctly observed:

Another intriguing characteristic of electoral politics in Africa is that the incumbents, however, bad tend to win elections. It is not uncommon for ruling parties and their leaders to manipulate the vote with ease. Most African heads of state see nothing in using the trappings of office to campaign for re-election. Some presidents also appoint those who run the election. And, when all else fails, they can loot the treasury to buy votes. Furthermore, with only a small middle class, many of whose members owe to the government, opposition parties are poor and fractious, and defections to a cosy official job are not uncommon (p.70).

Consequently, the universally accepted role of elections, which is to bring about regime change and/or change of policies whenever the electorate so decides, is distorted in Africa by the majority vote with the effect of creating political apathies and disillusionment among the peoples of the continent. And, as indicated above, generally elections in the continent are designed not for regime changes, but to legitimize and retain incumbents in office by any means necessary that run from political manipulation and maneuvering to constitutional engineering and technical fixes of election results. This is what has led Bangura to make the following pertinent remark by way of drawing a balance sheet between what has been achieved to date and what remains to be done in Africa's disillusioned hope for democratic transitions:

> "There is still much arbitrary rule in many parts of Africa, including in countries that have made significant progress in instituting the rule of law as a cardinal principle of statecraft ... Much remains to be done in the crucial area of separating ruling parties from the institutions of the state, the organization of free and fair elections, and the alternation of governmental power by the political parties." (1998: 23).

In the same vein, Bratton and Van de Walle advise that 'a transition to democracy can be said to have occurred only when a regime has been installed on the basis of a competitive election, freely and fairly conducted within a matrix of civil liberties, with results accepted by all participants' (1997: 194). But, contrary to similar advice by many, as well as the promises made by African leaders at such meetings as New Partnership for Africa's Development (NEPAD)[3] for many African leaders it is business as usual and regime change through 'free and fair' elections have remained exceptions to the rule.

At a more global level, a very recent work edited by Schedler (2006) has introduced a very useful concept in the study of elections, which the authors have termed *Electoral Authoritarianism* ... In introducing their work, Schedler himself - who incidentally includes Ethiopia in his classification of 'electoral authoritarianism' regimes - noted that:

> "A specter is haunting the developing world – the specter of electoral authoritarianism. ... A large number of political regimes in the contemporary world, ranging from Azerbaijan to Zimbabwe, from Russia to Singapore, from Belarus to Cameroon, from Egypt to Malaysia, have established the institutional facades of democracy, including regular multiparty elections for the chief executive, in order to conceal (and reproduce) harsh realities of authoritarian governance. Although in historical perspective the authoritarian use of elections is nothing new, contemporary electoral authoritarianism regimes take the time-honored practice of electoral manipulation to new heights". (2006: 1)

By partly quoting Powell (2000), he further argued:

> "Electoral regimes play the game of multi-party elections by holding regular elections for the chief executive and national legislative assembly. Yet they violate the liberal democratic principles of freedom and fairness so proudly and systematically as to render elections instruments of authoritarian rule rather than 'instruments of democracy' ... Under electoral authoritarianism rule, elections are broadly inclusive (they are held under universal suffrage) as well as minimally pluralistic (opposition parties are allowed to run) minimally competitive (opposition parties, while denied victory, are allowed to win votes and seats), and minimally open (opposition parties are not subject to massive repression, although they experience repressive treatment in selective and intermittent ways). Overall, however, electoral contests are subject to state manipulation so severe, widespread, and systematic that they do not qualify as democratic."

---

[3] Academic cynics have started to describe the much talked about NEPAD as "Never Expect Popular African Democracy".

Identifying the different mechanisms that are widely used by authoritarian regimes in their attempt to hold on to power by using any means necessary, he notes:

> "Authoritarian manipulation may come under many guises, all serving the purpose of containing the troubling uncertainty of electoral outcomes. Rulers may devise discriminatory electoral rules, exclude opposition parties and candidates from entering electoral arena, infringe upon their political rights and civil liberties, restrict their access to mass media and campaign finance, impose formal or informal suffrage restrictions on their supporters, coerce or corrupt them into deserting the opposition camp, or simply redistribute votes and seats through electoral fraud." (ibid.).

Interestingly enough, as we shall see further down, Schedler's observation equally apply to the Ethiopian situation both to the letter and the spirit - where elections have been held for legitimating authoritarian rule, rather than regime change or empowerment of ordinary citizens. In summary, much of the talk about elections across the continent, except in few areas, such as South Africa, Ghana, etc.; are largely fixed, most of the governments in power lack both popular mandates and democratic legitimacy. Hence, elections do not aim at regime changes, but are show cases for the donors. As such the Ethiopian case, which is one of the classic examples where elections are conducted to legitimate the regime, can be explained in light of the above discussed global context and the specific African environment.

Yet another important dimension of Ethiopia's experiment in multi-party democracy is the ruling party's introduction of its own version of democracy as the ideological cover-up for its hegemonic project. This refers to the ruling party's concept of 'revolutionary democracy'. It is borrowed from Mao's 'new democracy', at the time designed to prepare the pre-capitalist society of China for a socialist revolution. The EPRDF leadership though has twisted Mao's original idea, which aimed at a socialist transformation, to serve its agenda of a 'capitalist revolution'. Two useful concepts in this Marxist tradition of the EPRDF project are the idea of the vanguard party and the principle of democratic centralism, both of which are instrumental mechanisms for central control. As fully demonstrated by the experiences of the socialist states, both are negations of the practice of liberal democracy, whose basic tenets are *'regular free and fair elections, universal suffrage, accountability of the state's administrative organs to the elected representatives, and effective guarantees for freedom of expression and association as well as protection against arbitrary state action'* (see Vanhanen, 1997: 323). Needless to add, in liberal democracies elections serve as key instruments to change governments.

After the May 2005 elections, which came as a shock to the Ethiopian regime and weakened the hegemony of the ruling party, the EPRDF leadership had to come out more openly both in rationalizing the departure from basic tenets of liberal democracy and in giving their new version of democracy a new ideological cover. Consequently, of late South Korea, Taiwan, and other Asian 'tigers' have suddenly become models to be emulated where a recycled idea of a 'developmental state' is presented as a better way out of 'Ethiopia's dead ends'. To this end, two guidelines for training of party members were issued in November 2006, which have been further strengthened by the country's Prime-Minister's book (see the EPRDF Guide-lines, November 2006; excerpts from Prime-Minister Meles' book, January 2007). In both cases liberal democracy is presented in a negative light – as the 'democracy of the rent seekers and anti-development' while 'revolutionary democracy' is presented as a system that better serves as engine for quick economic development. In the Ethiopian context, liberal democracy is presented as a system supported by beneficiaries of the old order and hence, could retard both the democratic transformation of the Ethiopian state and economic development. It appears, according to many critics, the South Korean and the Taiwanese models are chosen not so much for being 'developmentalist states, but for being models for 'a dominant party rule' over a period of more than one generation. This is what has inspired a critic to the newspaper headline, *'Meles' thesis: EPRDF must rule for the next 50 years'* (Addis Tribune January 26, 2007).

At any rate, as we shall see below, true to the Leninist tradition, there is a strong fusion between party and state in the Ethiopian experiment. The *modus operandi* of the party, the state as well as the emerging institutions under its control are accordingly essential for democratic centralism. In fact, the Ethiopian regime's conception of the state as an instrument of class rule stands in the Marxist tradition. As such the institutions under the command of the state are used by the ruling party overtly and covertly to implement its narrow interests, rather than delivering the public good to the larger society (see Aalen, 2002; Ottoway 1995, Harbeson, 1998). Above all else, unlike the rules of the game in liberal democracies, elections are allowed only to the extent that they do not challenge the hegemony of 'revolutionary democracy', which now began to be rationalized as the ideology of the 'developmental state' – a political façade to legitimate the hegemony of a minority.

3   Constitutional engineering and the early non-competitive elections

From 1991 to 1995, the EPRDF was busy in consolidating power by reordering the Ethiopian state through the Charter it initiated immediately after capturing the state power. To ensure the permanency of the new political order, created according to their own image, the EPRDF leaders had undertaken a constitutional engineering in 1994, where the ethnic-based federal structure, first-past-the-post[4] electoral system, a bicameral parliament and above all a parliamentary system of government were introduced. Arguably, the authors of the Ethiopian constitution had consciously designed the new structures to ensure their own hegemonic aspiration instead of building democratic institutions for the country as a whole. For instance, the ethnic-based federal formula, which has served as the basis for the decentralization of power, was implemented in a top-down manner and consistently used for 'divide and rule'-politics rather than for the empowerment of the various ethnic groups of the country. In fact, in much of the country it was exactly this policy, which made possible the pitting of one ethnic group against the other (Merera 2002; Aalen 2002). Furthermore, the first-past-the-post electoral system made it easier to manipulate votes and to facilitate the 'winners takes all' policy, which favours the incumbent - especially when the playing field has not been leveled. The odd bicameral parliament is neither bicameral in real terms: The Upper House, the House of Federation, has little law-making power and is not composed of democratically elected members. More specifically, Ethiopia's Upper House of parliament is constituted by indirect representation from the regional councils which - according to the current practice - send

---

[4]   The so-called Westminster majority electoral system

members from the party that won a given region[5]. Consequently, the process has fully blocked the opposition from representation in the House of Federation until now – which appears to be likely to continue.

Another immediate outcome of the 1994 constitution-making was to serve as a legal basis for the 1995 elections, which formally closed the transitional chapter (Lyons 1996). Simultaneously, it became the legal basis for the EPRDF coalition to establish itself as the permanent government of Ethiopia. At any rate, the 1995 elections were generally judged neither "free nor fair" by both Ethiopian and non-Ethiopian academics alike (Ottaway 1995; Harbeson 1998; Yacob 1997). In fact, in the absence of any independent opposition group, the EPRDF and its affiliates won nearly hundred per cent, which allowed the control of both, the federal and regional governments.

The 2000 national and regional elections once again were conducted under political conditions, where civil liberties were severely curtailed and the playing field was far from leveled. As the result, the oppressed opposition was allowed to win only 13 seats in the national parliament of 547 seats - more as a show case for the donors' needs than for the cause of a multi-party democracy.

To be precise: even the 13 seats were divided among six political groups: Council of Alternative Forces for Peace and Democracy in Ethiopia (CAFPDE), Oromo National Congress (ONC), All Amhara People's Organization (AAPO) and Ethiopian Democratic Party (EDP), Southern Ethiopian People's Democratic Coalition (SEPDC) and Hadiya National Democratic Organization (HNDO). Under this lopsided political landscape, the opposition was too small and fragmented to make any meaningful political move. This is what led the Norwegian observers group to comment:

Beneath democratic institutions, TPLF has established an administration and a power structure that perpetuate its rule. This structure also prevents democratic change, at least in the short and medium terms. The formal structures have allowed some free space in Addis Ababa, and the party has tolerated the capital to develop into a kind of democratic show case, within strict limits, until it disturbed the central hierarchy. But TPLF has set clear limits on activities that might be considered to threaten its rule. (Pausewang, Tronvoll & Aalen: 242 – 243).

What appears to be a fulfillment of a prophecy of the Norwegian Group, came into being five years later. With the May 2005 elections the ruling party's hold on the populace through an intricate system of control was shaken from its foundation. In a nutshell, up to the eve of the May 2005 elections, the fortune of the opposition changed very little - although the political landscape in the country has somewhat changed following a serious spilt within the ruling party itself. The institutionalization of the *de facto* one-party state had continued as planned until the May 2005 elections: the elections then severly challenged both, the hegemony of the EPRDF and its elaborate system of state control over the citizenry.

---

[5] The House of Federation, seemingly the country's Upper House Parliament has little power to legislate laws, and generally designed to help the institutionalization of the emerging *de facto* one-party state.

4   The May 2005 elections as a political earth-quake for the EPRDF regime

After several years of non-competitive elections Ethiopia made a great leap forward in the direction of "free and fair" elections with the May 2005 national and regional elections[6]. The leap was possible as a result of a combined national and international pressure, which forced the EPRDF regime to open up the political space in a manner unknown in the country's long recorded history. As we shall see below, the EPRDF-regime was only able to hold on to power through massive manipulations of election results that has provoked a serious post-election confrontation between the regime and its opponents. This in consequence left deep cracks in the authoritarian regime structures of control, as well as the running out of steam by the EPRDF leaders. It appears that the country's political landscape will never be the same again[7].

4.1   Major challenges in the run-up to the elections

*Voters' and Candidates' Registration***:** Once the decision was made to participate in the elections, the next political business was voters' as well as candidates' registration, which were immediately followed by election campaigns. Here it is important to note that in a lot of areas, especially in areas where the opposition appeared to have strong support, serious attempts were made by the regime's controlled *Kebele* associations either to selectively register or discourage registration of voters. In these deliberate schemes, the youths who were generally known for their opposition to the regime were specifically targeted for exclusion[8]. Furthermore, some eligible voters did not bother much to register because of the widespread political apathy and little faith in the ballot box inherited from Ethiopia's past political legacy, which appeared to have lowered the number of registered voters to 26 million from about 39 million eligible voters.

The voters' registration was followed by the candidates' registration, which invited even more troubles from the incumbent party, which had never faced real challenge from opposition parties before. As a result, both voters' and candidates' registration turned into a fierce struggle, almost into a war against the opposition. Hundreds of candidates were intimidated and forced to withdraw while hundreds of opposition members and supporters – including potential candidates - were detained and some were even killed. Both stick and carrot were used to reduce the number of candidates. For instance the United Ethiopian Democratic Forces (UEDF), one of the two major coalitions, did not know how many of its candidates were still on board until the election day[9].

The Campaigns: Campaigning was restricted at the beginning, public media was closed and the local government cadres were hostile to the opposition and active in blocking the movement of the opposition members and supporters. Despite the establishment of two

---

[6] Since 1957 Ethiopia had several elections under the three successive regimes including the imperial regime. But it is only the May 2005 elections, which can resemble competitive, "free and fair" elections in the country's long recorded history.

[7] Many Ethiopians believe that the May 2005 elections have changed the country's political landscape, and that there is no point of return.

[8] The EPRDF targeted young members of the opposition parties, as the youth was particularly active within the opposition.

[9] The EPRDF forced the opposition candidates out of the game until the last day of the May 2005 elections; strategies included the use of the devote NEB.

major coalitions, the opposition camp was also not solid and there was little coordination between them. The existence of several dozen smaller parties, which were operating in the name of the opposition, further complicated the political landscape. Some of them were openly used by the ruling party to undermine the unity of the opposition.

As the election day approached, and with the arrival of the international observers, the situation rapidly changed for the better. Critical aspects of the new situation were the national debates and the mass rallies, which were positively unique and new in the country's long recorded history. Albeit late, the unprecedented national debate over key election issues between the ruling party and the opposition, the massive mass rallies across the country held by the opposition parties, and other public campaigns, moved millions towards the history-making event. Television programs were eagerly watched and radios were listened to by the public while the turn-out for opposition rallies was astonishingly high. As a result, the country's hitherto repressed opposition as a whole was able to break its isolation and galvanized the support of millions. With this, a genuine rise of expectations that engulfed the nation, could be sensed. Consequently, despite alarmingly high harassment at the last minute, people came out in might to vote for the candidates of their choice, where in most places voters waited for several hours to cast their votes. In fact, the turn-out of 26 millions was a record high in the country's history of elections (see EU-EOM, 2005).

4.2   The election day and after: From rising expectation to rising frustration

Despite mass arrests and harassment of opposition members and supporters at the eve of the May 2005 elections, despite the exclusion of oppostion party poll watchers to open the way for fraud, the elections day passed relatively peacefully. But already during the evening of the Election Day, the Prime Minister, who had a better grasp of the overall situation and expected trouble, declared a semi-state of emergency in Addis Ababa, which was practically applied throughout the country by the zealot cadres[10].

To be sure, until the May 2005 elections, the EPRDF leaders were using the Peoples' Democratic Organizations (PDOs) to win elections[11]. The little opening before and during the May 2005 elections exposed the limited capability of the PDOs. With the shock of losing nearly 100% in Addis Ababa, the ruling party declared its victory in the major regions of the country and claimed to have won enough seats to form the next government (see EU-EOM, *ibid.*)[12]. Arguably, while there was an element of surprise in the opposition camp for its excellent showing at the polls, the election results were a shock to the ruling party and its new strategy was both to pacify its bewildered cadres on the one hand, and to prepare the ground for the intended massive rigging during the vote counting - without which it became impossible to win elections - on the other. Surprisingly, the declaration of victory by the

---

[10] Among others, public meetings (more than 5 persons) were restricted and popular signs of the opposition parties banned.

[11] In addition to using the principles of revolutionary democracy for central control, the EPRDF regime has also been using the PDOs, which are peoples' democratic organizations created by the TPLF for the multitude of the country's ethnic groups to facilitate them for central control. To put differently, generally the function of PDOs are translators of official orders to the local communities.

[12] If the game was fair from the fielding of candidates to vote counting, it appears that EPRDF could have lost the last elections. Many Ethiopians believe that the two major coalitions (UEDF and CUD) won and that the government only remained in power, because the barrel of the gun controlled the ballot box.

incumbent was made even before 50% of the votes were counted. In response, the two major coalitions, the UEDF and the Coalition for Unity and Democracy (CUD) countered the move of the ruling party by declaring their own election victory. At any rate, using the hand-picked partisan election executives throughout the country, massive tampering with vote-counting took place in many constituencies, which led to 299 cases of complaints of irregularities, which is more than 50% of the total seats for the whole country (see *ibid.*).

The central problem here is that the ruling party leaders thought it was business as usual and were not prepared either to give up power or share power in the event of electoral defeat, while they had little preparation to deal with the situation. And, as the results of the declaration of the incumbent victory continued to trickle in even after weeks of the Election Day, the opposition continued to challenge the results while the frustrated populace   started to react. Consequently, in the chain of events, from June 5 – 8, 2005, first the university students of Addis Ababa, and then the larger populace of Addis Ababa came out in thousands, demanding an independent   investigation into the election fraud. The EPRDF leaders, as noted earlier, who neither prepared to share power nor to give up power, responded with a massive show of their military muscle. And, in what can be termed a post-election systematic state repression, tens of people were killed; thousands were wounded while several thousands herded to prison houses (see *ibid.*).

The diplomatic community moved fast to defuse the confrontation between the government and the opposition. But, the donors' intervention helped very little as the Americans and the EU diplomats gave different signals to different groups. It appears that the Americans bent on working to salvage a friendly regime, while the EU leaned towards the cause of the visibly repressed opposition that – most obviously - enjoyed popular support. As a result, the agreement brokered by the diplomatic community between the government and the two main opposition coalitions on how to address the more serious irregularities following the June incidents did help very little to narrow the rift between the contending parties. The attempt of the opposition to avert the alarmingly tense situation that followed the May 2005 elections by proposing a broad-based National Unity Government - was also frustrated by the outright rejection of the EPRDF before it took off the ground[13]. No less serious, the EPRDF used the agreement to regain lost ground in the first round of the elections by bringing in - through the back door - the defeated big fish from the government in the rerun largely boycotted by the opposition. These include the leading party members like the Ministers of Information and National Defense as well as the President of Oromia - by far the country's largest region. Consequently, when the final result was declared by the National Election Board (NEB), the EPRDF said to have won 327 seats, far more than the 274 seats needed to form a government (see the table below).

---

[13] The National Unity Government was proposed by the opposition as the best solution to resolve the controversy over the results of the May 2005 elections. It was meant to include the major opposition parties and the incumbent party, based on the officially declared seats won by each political group

Table 1: Seat Distribution of 2005 Elections

Name of the Political Parties	Seats won
Ethiopian Peoples' Revolutionary Democratic Forces (EPRDF)	327
Coalition for Unity and Democracy (CUD)	109
United Ethiopian Democratic Forces (UEDF)	52
Oromo Federal Democratic Movement (OFDM)	11
Benishangul – Gumuz Peoples' Democratic Front (BGPDUF)	8
Afar National Democratic Party (ANDP)	8
Gambella People's Democratic Movement (GPDM)	3
Shako-Majangar People's Democratic Unity Organization (SMPDUO)	1
Somali People's Democratic Party (SPDP)	24
Harari National League (HNL)	1
Alaba National Democratic Organization (ANDO)	1
Independent	1
Total Seats	**546**

Source: Ethiopian National Electoral Board Report

Declaration of these final results had further increased the tension between the government and the opposition. Consequently, as a last attempt before the opening of the parliament, the opposition called a mass rally in the capital for October 2, 2005 to exert pressure on the government to change course. The key demands of the opposition were: restructuring of the NEB, freedom of movement by opposition party leaders and members; strict neutrality of the government security personnel in election affairs, especially stopping of harassment of members and supporters of political parties; reasonable access to public media by the opposition and presence of international observers.

Although the opposition intended a peaceful demonstration, the call for the mass rally alone alarmed the government, which started to accuse the opposition of intending to organize a Ukrainian' type of 'orange revolution'. To defuse the tense situation, the diplomatic community made another attempt to bring the government and the two main opposition groups to a negotiating table at the eve of the opening of the parliament. This attempt failed again, as the EPRDF leaders refused to include the main agenda item proposed by the opposition, i.e. the issue of restructuring of the National Election Board (NEB) in the discussion[14].

In the meantime, the opposition's position that the EPRDF regime had stolen the opposition victory was further strengthened by the report of the European Union Election Observers Mission (EU-EOM) which deployed by far the largest number of foreign observers. To the anger of the EPRDF leaders, the EU-EOM stated that there were major irregularities at the counting stage and that the Ethiopian election was short of meeting international standards. For instance, in what appears to be a balance sheet of its overall assessment of the May 2005 elections, in its executive summary, the EU-EOM unambiguously noted that:

---

[14] The National Election Board (NEB) is still a point of controversy yet to be resolved. In fact, it is one of the main agenda items which have continued to polarize the country's body politic.

The 2005 parliamentary elections were the most competitive elections Ethiopia has experienced, with an unprecedented high voter turnout. However, while the pre-election period saw a number of positive developments and voting on 15 May was conducted in a peaceful and largely orderly manner, the counting and aggregation processes were marred *by* irregular practices, confusion and a lack of transparency. Subsequent complaints and appeals mechanisms did not provide an effective remedy. The human rights situation rapidly deteriorated in the post-election day period when dozens of citizens were killed by the police and thousands were arrested. Overall, therefore, the elections fell short of international principles for genuine democratic elections (EU-EOM 2005: 1).

The anger from the EPRDF side was not hidden. The Prime-Minister himself broke with diplomatic niceties and wrote a lengthy open letter accusing the head of the EU-EOM for being biased toward the opposition[15].

The Report of the Carter Center, which deployed only few observers and covered a much less number of constituencies, put the government in a positive light, but it too has identified some of the major irregularities, especially during the investigation and rerun periods. The stolen election thesis though stuck in the minds of the people and became a rallying point for the anti-government forces at home and abroad. This in turn further undermined the legitimacy of the regime both in the eyes of the Ethiopian people and that of the international community.

4.3   Joining the parliament became a divisive issue

With the dead-lock on one side and the continued repression of the government on the other, the question of joining or not joining the parliament became a very critical and divisive issue that led the two major opposition parties to take different options. Consequently, the CUD decided not to join the parliament before its preconditions such as access to media, restructuring of the National Election Board, respect for the rule of law, etc. were met. The UEDF, even if it shared the position of the former, opted to join the parliament in order to remain within the legal framework. Consequently, the UEDF was roughly split between its external wing and its internal wing while the CUD experienced internal tensions and betrayals when its key leaders were arrested and put behind bars.

As the gaps widened between the protagonists, the country's capital city was once again rocked by the anti-government protesters. Consequently, because of the heavy handed manner of the government in suppressing any public protest, once again several people were killed; thousands were wounded while tens of thousands were herded to prisons and detention camps. This time, the confrontation between the regime and its opponents spread to the regions, especially Oromia and the Amhara areas, where support for the opposition was high.

The repeated and excessive use of force by the government in order to suppress peaceful protesters alarmed the donor community including the World Bank. Some eventually stopped direct budgetary support to the Ethiopian Government and devised a new system of channeling foreign aid to the country under what is called Protection of Basic Services (PBS). Moreover, the chairman and vice-chairman of the commission of inquiry, established by the government itself to investigate the June and the November 2005 incidents, fled abroad. They took with them the original report which accused the government for excessive use of force.

---

[15] The Ethiopian Prime Minister accused the chief of the EU-EOM by saying that she has supported the opposition and meddled in Ethiopian affairs. The letter was published for several continuous days on the government controlled daily, The Ethiopian Herald.

The report set the number of civilian deaths at 193, three times higher than what the government admitted. Thus, the image of the ruling party got further damaged[16].

5   The state of Ethiopian politics two years after the historic May 2005 elections

About 90% of the elected members took up their seats in parliament, partly in the hope that the political landscape improved for the better and partly because of the government's reaction against those who refused to join. Conspicuously, despite the increase in their number of seats from 13 in the last parliament to 173 in the current parliament (see table above), the fortune of the Ethiopian opposition has not been improved much as the result of the introduction of new parliamentary rules of procedure, which totally hampers the opposition from tabling any agenda item for debate by its own. For instance, the new set of rules of procedure raised the number of members required to propose an agenda item for debate from 20 to 183 members. Even worse, because of these new rules of procedure, the role of the parliament could not even develop to a level of a talking-shop, as the ability of the members to engage in a parliamentary debate is seriously undermined through a system of time-budgeting fully dictated by the ruling-party. No less disturbing, the extensive powers given to the speaker of the parliament undermine any effective debate. In fact, the speaker acts as a chief minister and holds the power to stop members even at the middle of their speech, can give orders to the police to drag a member out from sessions, as well as take punitive administrative actions against members he thinks have violated the new procedures (see the HPR Rules of Procedures and Members Code of Conduct Regulation No. 3/2006). The measures taken are likely to have a debilitating effect on the workings of the country's parliament as an independent law-making institution that can ensure checks and balances – a critical factors in modern representative democracies.

The major political groups, which have joined the parliament, started to engage the government in what has been termed as inter-party dialogue in the hope to bring the democratization process back to track. As such, with the help of the diplomatic community the opposition and the government agreed on six major agenda items at the beginning of 2006, the main ones being: respect for the rule of law by both groups, which includes opening of closed opposition party offices; restructuring of the Election Board of Ethiopia, which has been the source of much controversy; a new media law and freedom of the press, as well as government support to political parties.

Surprisingly, even after two years passed - out of the six agenda items only the first three were discussed; and out of these three - there was no consensus over the two. Out of the two, the most serious one is the failure to reach a consensus on the composition of the Election Board to which the future of electoral politics in the country is tied. No less disturbing is the lack of interest of the ruling-party in the inter-party dialogue. Judged by its record so far, much of what the government is doing can be dubbed as public relations exercise, mainly for the consumption of the donors. Hence, the one step forward and two steps back policy of the ruling party pushed the initial hope for an Ethiopian democratic

---

[16] The Ethiopian government created an Inquiry Commission after both national and international pressure was exerted. Surprisingly, some of the handpicked members run away from the country and exposed the government, which shocked the regime.

transition to a dead-end. Consequently, the country's political crisis has continued to deepen – with low intensity conflicts in the Ogaden, Oromia and the Afar regions, and a politically tense situation in the rest of the country.

The emerging academic consensus regarding the crisis of the Ethiopian state after the May 2005 elections also points towards the intransigence of the EPRDF regime for peaceful transformation. Both Ethiopian and non-Ethiopian academics have already converged in depicting the EPRDF as a road block to Ethiopia's hoped for democratic transition. For instance, Clapham (2005), one of a keen observer of Ethiopian politics since the last days of Emperor Haile Selassie in the 1960s has underlined that

> "the EPRDF has now reached a state at which it is almost impossible to imagine it winning a remotely fair election against any reasonable plausible and effective opposition". He has further argued that "It [EPRDF] has lost 'the mandate of heaven' and has envisaged three possible scenarios, i.e. that "The EPRDF government might leave power peacefully ---; The government might leave power violently;--- [and that] The government might succeed in retaining its hold on power, in the process converting itself into an overtly repressive regime ".

Clapham's conclusion raises two important theoretical questions: (1) can a minority regime with little political support base sponsor a successful democratic transition without committing - what I call for want of a better term - political suicide – similar to "the Marxian class suicide" in history; (2) is it democracy which allows "free and fair" elections, or 'free and fair' elections which lead to democracy? A Somali academic, Abdi Ismail Samatar has also arrived at similar conclusion regarding the Ethiopian reality after the post-May 2005 elections. He has written among others:

> TPLF's instrumentalist political agenda and practice contradicted the rhetoric of liberation and regional development. The PDOs which the Tigray party spawned won provincial elections in 1992 and dominated federal parliament ever since. Two subsequent elections reconfirmed a new pattern of supremacy in which TPLF held all organs of political and military power. Such manufacture of puppet parties beholden to federal authorities and pseudo-elections doubly undermined regional autonomy from the center and accountability of leaders to their communities. TPLF's practice to unseat and appoint any regional authority at will has completely alienated the public from the system of governance, and has turned local authorities into sycophants who serve their masters and themselves. The dominant federal party's obsession with retaining power in spite of its narrow popular base has deprived the country of an opportunity to gain a civic footing, and has unnecessarily heightened ethnic political identity (p. 5).

Two American academics, who largely share the same opinion with Clapham and Samatar describe the situation as "troubled transitions" (Lyons, 2006) and "democratic uncertainty" (Smith, 2007).

6 *Summary*

If we have to sum up the discussion with a clear picture of the reality on the ground, the country's political impasse is approaching a dead-end, and as the result, the birth pang of Ethiopian democracy appears to be long as the ruling-party is still speaking about "a developmental state" where its hegemony is ensured by all means under the command of the state[17]. As such, our discussion can be summarized around six major road-blocks to the country's hoped for democratic transition, with their implications for the future of electoral politics as well as for democratic governance in Ethiopia.

Major Road-Block 1: Democratization without national consensus. What I can call, for want of a better term, a 'bad beginning' is that, following its impressive military victory in 1991, the EPRDF quickly moved to the "remaking "of Ethiopia without creating a national and/or a democratic consensus over the basics of state transformation. A process of consensus building though would have been badly needed in a   country like Ethiopia where contradictory perspectives regarding the interpretation of the past, the understanding of the present and the vision about the future prevail. Moreover, contrary to the expectation of many at the time, the EPRDF set the rules of the game and invited others to accept the rules fixed by only one of the players[18] .

Major Road-Block 2: Perception of the EPRDF leaders towards the opposition. Judged by its actions, the EPRDF leaders appear to have never envisioned a role for opposition parties. If at all, it appears that they have envisioned one that was not expected to win elections. Opposition parties have never been considered as partners in the building of a democratic Ethiopia. Even more disturbing is the ease with which the EPRDF leaders characterize major opposition parties with significant followings by giving them tags such as chauvinists, narrow nationalists, or servants of the n*eftegnas*[19], and its determination to divide and weaken them by all means, including by using naked force. In a nutshell, it has continued to criminalize opposition politics.

Major Road-Block 3: The determination of the ruling-party to use emerging institutions to promote its partisan interests. Major institutions, which are supposed to act impartially and promote democratic governance, such as the election board, the parliament, the judiciary, the police, the army and the civil administration as a whole are not fulfilling and not allowed to fulfill their duties impartially as per the provisions of the country's constitution. The end result is no separation of power between the three branches of government, but a strong fusion between party and state, comparable only to the old socialist days. Consequently, what is being institutionalized is what can be termed a "shadow state"[20], i.e privatization of the state and its institutions - so as to make them work mainly for the survival of the leaders, rather than delivering the public goods for the citizens fairly and equitably.

---

[17] In October 2006, the EPRDF distributed two guide lines written in Amharic for training of its cadres. The two guide lines clearly state that the hegemony of their "revolutionary democracy" must be protected at any cost. This is the most serious road-block to Ethiopia's hoped for democratic transition.

[18] The EPRDF imposed its own rules of the game from above without any negotiation with stake holders both from political society and civil society organizations. Far worse it kept on changing the rules of the game as they fit it.

[19] In the Ethiopian language "*neftagna*" literary means gun holder. Later the system introduced through the intermediary of the gun started to be known as the "*neftegna*" system.

[20] The concept of the "shadow state" was developed by William Reno. This concept is used to explain the use of the state as a private property to ensure ones own survival. For a detailed discussion see Clapham (2000: 249 - 266).

Major Road-Block 4: Fixing Elections: The EPRDF leaders apparently do not regard electoral politics as a positive-sum-game and have developed a culture of fixing elections, which includes outright harassment as well as manipulation of election results by using such mechanisms as massive tampering with vote counting, manipulation of numbers, damping or burning of votes for opposition candidates, etc. In fact, the importance of the May 2005 elections is partly its role in exposing such frauds of the EPRDF regime both in the eyes of the citizens and the international community.

Major Road-block 5: The use of federalism and decentralization of power as instrument of 'Divide and Rule'. The Ethiopian federalism has never achieved its historic mission of creating shared-rule and self-rule by being broadly inclusive, a promise of real federalism. Contrary to the claims of the ruling party, what has been achieved is facilitating the divide and rule policy of the regime by pitting one ethnic group against the other. Ironically, the EPRDF and the PDOs have little interest in respecting the rule of law, while demanding from others to respect it. Far worse, there is a fusion of party and state sustained by an omnipotent executive branch that has blurred the separation of powers and the check and balances thereof – central elements in the functioning of modern representative democracies.

Major Road-block 6: The lust for hegemony. The mother of all problems is the hegemonic aspiration of the ruling party, which has not only blurred the vision of the EPRDF leaders, but also made them think that "we know what is good for the people" and labelling diverse opinions as 'anti-people' as well as 'anti-development'. Ironically, the EPRDF leaders novelty of "I know what is good for you" includes fabrication of fake leadership for the opposition parties and telling members that this is the leadership that best represents their interest. In the meantime institutions such as the NEB, the court and the governments' security personnel ensure any desired result. That is what happened to both CUD and ONC – the latter now renamed OPC - which emerged as the largest parliamentary opposition groups. One resulting problem with such type of thinking is the refusal to allow the people to judge independently on what is good for them. The government arrogates itself to the role of an omnipotent entity that knows and decides what is good for the people.

7   *Quo Vadis* Ethiopia?

Close to three years after May 2005, the sequel of the event elections is still rocking the regime. Still there is no workable *modus vivendi* between the opposition groups in the parliament and the ruling-party while the CUD leaders, who appear to have been released through a deal after 20 months of confinement. They are obstructed to assume the leadership of their party because of a legal game fabricated by the Election Board. Still worse, the more militant opposition groups that work outside the legal framework, appear to have stepped up their anti-government pressures, while the confrontations with Eritrea and the Somali Islamic Courts Union are likely to lead to an all out war with devastating consequences for the country and its people.

The crack created as the result of the May 2005 elections is also creating more visible cracks within the politico-security structure of the regime. Loyal army officers, senior judges, diplomats, parliamentarians, etc. have been defecting at an alarming rate. Journalists, civic society leaders, youth, opposition members and supporters alike have been running away. All are accusing the government for serious human rights violations, thus further damaging the image of the EPRDF regime. Yet, the response of the regime is business as usual. And, the strategy of manufacturing fake opposition parties, and/or capturing those already existing to marginalize the major opposition parties, could in the long run have detrimental effects on the hoped for democratization drive - have continued unabated. In fact, the ruling party is about to set the country on war footing, targets being Eritrea, the Somali Islamic Courts and the internal armed opposition. Hence, it is not difficult to conclude that with the sequel of the May 2005 elections still rocking the country and the EPRDF regime continuing to defend its authority with the barrel of the gun, the country's political impasse is approaching a dead-end. To bring back to track the democratization process and make the coming elections more open and inclusive, the creation of a national consensus on the basics of state transformation appears to be central in shortening the birth pang of Ethiopian democracy.

Bibliography

Aalen, Lovise, 2002, *Ethnic Federalism in a Dominant Party State: The Ethiopian Experience, 1991 – 2000*, Chr. Michelsen Institute, Development Studies and Human Rights Report.

Addis Hiwot, 1975, *Ethiopia: From Autocracy to Revolution*, Occasional Publication No.1 of *Review of African Political Economy*, London.

Addis Tribune, 2007, Meles's Thesis: EPRDF Must Rule for the Next 50 Years, Addis Tribune January 26, 2007.

Anebo, K.G., 2001, *The Ghana 2000 Elections: Voter Choice and Electoral Decisions*, in *African Journal of Political Science (AJPS)*, Vol. 6, 1 June 2001 (2001: 69 – 88).

Barkan, Joel D, 1993, *Kenya: Lessons from A Flawed Election*, in *Journal of Democracy* Vol. 4; No. 3 July 1993.

Bratton, Michael & Nicolas v. de Walle, 1997, *Democratic Experiments in Africa: Regime Transformation in Comparative Perspective*. Cambridge: Cambridge University Press.

Clapham, Christopher, 2005, *Comments on the Ethiopian Crisis*, http://www.african.cam.ac.uk/people/registry/subjectlist/clapham.html *12/28/2005*.

Clapham, Christopher, 2000, *Africa and the International System*. (Reprint) Cambridge: Cambridge University Press.

EHRCO, 2000, *The May 2000 General Election: A Report*, Addis Ababa.

EPRDF, 2006, *Yeabiyotawi Demokrasi Estrategi, Taktikina Yeamarar Tiyake* (in Amharic), Addis Ababa.

EPRDF, 2006, *Limat, Demokrasina abiyotawi Demokraci* (in Amharic), Addis Ababa.

European Union – Election Observation Mission (EU-EOM), 2005, *EU Election Observation Mission Ethiopia 2005, Final Report on the Legislative Elections*.

Federal Democratic Republic of Ethiopia (FDRE), 1995, *The Constitution of the Federal Democratic Republic Of Ethiopia*, Federal *Negarit Gazeta* 1st Year No. 1, 21st August 1995 (Addis Ababa).

Harbeson, J., 1998, *Is Ethiopia Democratic? A Bureaucratic Authoritarian Regime*, in *Journal of Democracy*, Vol. 9, No. 4 (October 1998): 62 - 69.

Huntington, Samuel P., 1993, *The Third Wave: Democratization in the Late Twentieth Century*. Norman & London: University of Oklahoma Press.

Lyons, Terrence, 1996, *Closing the Transition: The May 1995 Elections in Ethiopia, the Journal of Modern African Studies*, Vol. 34, No. 1 (March 1996): 121-142.

Lyons, Terrence, 2006, *Avoiding Conflict in the Horn of Africa: U.S. Policy and Eritrea*, CSR No. 21, December 2006, Center for Preventive Action, Council on Foreign Relations.

Mazrui, Ali A. , 2001, *Who killed Democracy in Africa? Clues of the Past, Concerns of the Future*, A Key Note Address to a DPMF *Conference on Democracy, Sustainable Development and Poverty: Are They Compatible?* 4 – 6 December, United Nations Conference Center, Addis Ababa.

Merera Gudina, 2002, *Ethiopia: Competing Ethnic Nationalisms and the Quest for Democracy, 1960 – 2000*. The Hague, the Netherlands: Shaker Publishing.

Merera Gudina, 2000, *The Contradictory Perspectives on Ethiopian Politics and their Implications for the country's Quest for Democracy*, a paper presented to *the 14th International Conference of Ethiopian Studies*, November 2000, Addis Ababa.

Merera Gudina, 1997, *Party Politics and Elections in Ethiopia: 1991 - 1995*, in 'The May 1995 Elections in Ethiopia: The Quest for Democratic Governance in a Multi-ethnic Society', DPSIR, Addis Ababa University (unpublished report).

National Democratic Institute and the African - American Institute (NDI – AAI), 1992, *An Evaluation of the June 1992 Elections in Ethiopia*, June 25, 1992.

Negasso Gidada, 2005, *We are now living under Dictatorship*, Interview in *Der Spiegel* November 23, 2005.

Ottaway, M., 1995, *The Ethiopian Transition: Democratization or New Authoritarianism?*, in *Northeast African Studies*, Vol. 2, No. 3 (New Series) (1995): 67 - 84.

Pausewang, Siegfried, Kjetil Tronvoll &Lovise Aalen (eds.), 2002, *Ethiopia since the Derg: A Decade of Democratic and Pretension and Performance*, London & New York: Zed Books.

Samatar, Abdi Ismail, 2005, *The Ethiopian Election of 2005: A Bombshell & Turning Point?*, in *Review of African Political Economy*, Nos. 104/4, 2005.

Schedler, Andreas (ed.), 2006, *Electoral Authoritarianism: The Dynamics of Unfree Competition*. Boulder & London: Lynne Reinner Publishers.

Smith, Lahra, 2007, *Political Violence and Democratic Uncertainty in Ethiopia*, Special Report, United States Institute of Peace.

The Carter Center, 2005, *Final Statement on The Carter Center Observation of the Ethiopia 2005 National Elections* (September 2005).

Transitional Government of Ethiopia, 1991, *The Transitional Charter of Ethiopia*, in *Negarit Gazeta*, 22nd of July 1991 (Addis Ababa).

Vestal, Theodore M., 1999, *Ethiopia: A Post-Cold War African State*. Westport, Connecticut & London: Praeger.

Yacob Arsano, 1997, *People's Choice and Political Power in Ethiopia: The Politics of Elections and Representation, 1932 - 1995*, in *The May 1995 Elections in Ethiopia: The Quest for Democratic Governance in a Multi-ethnic Society*, DPSIR, Addis Ababa University (unpublished report), Addis Ababa

Terrorism and Discourses on Terror in Ethiopia

Wolbert G.C. Smidt

Introduction

Immediately after September 11[1], 2001 the Federal Republic of Ethiopia declared her alliance with the United States of America in the newly proclaimed "War on Terror". As George Bush had declared: "Who is not with us, is against us", it would be better to be with him, and enjoy (and continue to enjoy) all the positive aspects of friendship with the United States. Ethiopia underlined that it had itself been the victim of terrorism: "The Ethiopian government has over the past 10 years been at the forefront in the fight against terrorism, and it will therefore continue to fully support any and all struggle against terrorism in Ethiopia, the sub-region and the world as a whole, it stressed."[2]

Already before the shocking events of September 11 the Ethiopian government had entertained good relations with the US and used these in the realisation of their aims in regional and internal politics: The financial support for the government budget was important, and the military aid could not be underestimated, even after the devastating war against Eritrea of 1998 to 2000. Ethiopia had successfully established itself as a reliable ally to counter the Sudan with its diverse Islamist governments and as a potential hegemonic regional power, which could help that the permanent Somali crisis would not become a threat to "world security" as it was defined by the US (and in this case: also by Ethiopia); the formerly very active Islamist organisation *al-Ittihad al-Islamiyya* in Somalia claimed to have been behind several bomb attacks of 1995/96 in Ethiopia, Ethiopia could therefore be seen as a victim of Somali warlordism and terrorism. It was most important for Ethiopia to enjoy the backing of the US, as the war with Eritrea was over, but the conflict not. Ethiopia could be sure: Winning the US on their side would mean a greater margin of action in their dealing with that unsolved conflict – and not only that: It would also mean a greater liberty in their dealings with internal problems. The "War on Terror" provided the necessary arguments and instruments to justify oppression (at least a "slight" one), where it seemed necessary to the Ethiopian government.

It is not uninteresting that Eritrea, Ethiopia's new archenemy, also immediately joined the "Coalition of the Willing". But hopes cherished by some Western observers that this Coalition could mean more than just a strategic alliance with the US and could instigate some new processes of negotiations and initiatives of reconciliation within that Coalition were without substance. The "Coalition of the Willing" seems more a specific form of US

---

[1] In Ethiopian discussions this date played a quite specific role; by chance, September 11 is the New Year according to the Christian Ethiopian Calendar (September 11, 2001 was the first day of the first month of the year 1994 A.M.). There were questions in Ethiopia if the Arab attack on the World Trade Centre was not also an attack on Christian Ethiopia, using the ancient Christian calendar of Ethiopia as a symbol. But these discussions did not reach far, as this coincidence did not explain anything of what happened then and later, even for paranoid minds.

[2] Declaration of the Ethiopian government of 29 September 2001, see for example:
http://english.people.com.cn/english/200109/29/eng20010929_81360.html

unilateralism than a real coalition. No process started, which brought the two neighbours closer together. Both were mainly interested to use the US for their own local strategic interests, and no greater initiative was started by the US – too much occupied by their own problems – to establish some sort of reconciliation processes. The New World Order was more based on alliance with the US than on the strengthening of initiatives of peace and collaboration within the very heterogeneous Coalition: In fact, they were rather part of a new system of vassalage than a new system of international collaboration. We witnessed the establishment of a shadow network of states, within which the rules of international law and international organisations were slowly redefined. It did not replace the United Nations, which are, together with the International Court of Justice, the only recognized institutional source of international law and order (even if extremely weak) – but it established a parallel system, where a permanent re-interpretation of international law outside the UN system was backed by the US. This re-interpretation occasionally included the open breaking of that law. Ethiopia was happy to be part of that new system.

> "In conclusion, my Delegation would like to re-iterate two points. Firstly, the urgent need for an agreement on a comprehensive convention in fighting international terrorism. While it is important to have a precise legal definition of terrorism[3], I agree with Mr. Kofi Annan when he says, quote 'There can be no acceptance of those who would seek to justify the deliberate taking of innocent civilian life, regardless of cause or grievance.' unquote. Surely, the peoples of the world whom we represent here will not understand nor forgive us if we fail to quickly arrive at an agreed comprehensive convention because some of us may descend to being pedantic. I hope that will not happen. Secondly, it is important and fitting that the United Nations should act as the focal forum for combating international terrorism.

> However, it must not also be forgotten that if and when terrorists do attack a country, such as happened on September 11, then that country has the legitimate right to defend itself. Not only this, it has an obligation to its people to seek out those who planned, funded, encouraged and harbored the terrorist and hold them accountable." (Ambassador Abdulmejid Hussein[4])

These concluding words by the Ethiopian representative were read on the crucial UN General Assembly meeting, which inaugurated the War on Terror. They were certainly marked by the then very widespread feeling of shock and of international solidarity with the American victims of that horrifying terror attack. However, a closer look into the words used shows well the agenda, which was important for the Ethiopian government. Ethiopia wanted to use this chance: We should not be "pedantic" (in choosing the weapons in the War on Terror); there should be politics of "no acceptance ... regardless of cause"; the country attacked "has the legitimate right to defend itself". A reinterpretation of the understanding of civil rights (internally) and of international law (externally) is prepared: It would be a great mistake not to take any measures *possible*, and it would also be a mistake to follow existing regulations and restrictions of state power too "pedantically" and by doing so allowing terrorists to find

---

[3]   The most widely accepted definition of terrorism is found in the UN General Assembly Resolution 54/109 of 9 December 1999; see also Münkler 2002.
[4]   Quoted from the text of the statement of Ambassador Abdulmejid Hussein, Permanent Representative of Ethiopia to the UN, at the 56th UN General Assembly on Agenda Item 166 Measures to Eliminate International Terrorism, October 3, 2001 (http://www.un.org/terrorism/statements/ethiopiaE.html).

save harbours. The message is clear: The supreme law is not international law; the supreme law is the *right* for self-defence and the *duty* to combat terrorists. The rhetoric figure on the legal definition of terrorism is interesting: It shows that the focus should certainly not lie on a legal definition, but on combat; terrorists might even have a "cause or grievance", but this should not be looked at or should not be the priority at least. The new conflict situation gave Ethiopia a chance for redefining its position within the existing conflict systems.

This article looks into specific developments and detail examples, to investigate to which degree terrorist activities (and militant movements defined as "terrorism") in Ethiopia are related to *international* terror networks or rather to *local* and *interregional* developments. The question is: Is the terror, which Ethiopia combats, really the same as the one the US administration has in mind? And in which way this combat is related to the officially declared "War on Terror"? My hypothesis is, that the threats are real, but not in the sense as defined by the US and her allies. The problem would rather be militant politics, which is practised by all the *governments* of the region, internally as externally, and by *militant movements*, who want to be the future governments and reproduce long-established rules of militant politics.

Terror is not only a problem for the victims, but also for international stability. It is therefore a key question to inquire where terror comes from. Only if terror is understood in its manifold causes, policy measures can be undertaken to eliminate these causes. A side-question, which, however, becomes a central one when looked at more thoroughly, is if the "War on Terror" itself provides new grievances, and thus, provides a breeding ground for terror.

Islamist networks in Ethiopia: After the attempt on the life of Mubarak

The Horn of Africa was always interesting for Islamist networks. It even became the stage for Islamist terrorism activities quite early. Ethiopia, where state control is rather weak, could be a place in which Islamist networks find a secure haven. And in fact, Ethiopia did become a victim of terrorist networks, both international and national. When Egyptian President Mubarak visited Ethiopia on 26 June 1995, an attempt on his life failed. It was quickly discovered, that Islamists from the extremist Muslim Brotherhood of Egypt had built up networks in Addis Ababa; later reports confirmed that these circles also had contact with al-Qa'ida[5]. The Ethiopian security – known to be quite effective – quickly managed to arrest anyone who was part of the clandestine Islamist networks. After that, it does not seem that Islamist terrorist activities could rely on networks in Ethiopia. The Ethiopian state, in collaboration with the United States, continued to strictly monitor Islamist activities.

Requested by the West, Ethiopia closed down the informal Somali Barakat banking system (and the informal *hawalas* banking system in general[6]), the only financial system which allowed Somalis in the Diaspora to send money to Somalia and other regions, as no official banking system had survived the collapse of the Somali state. While the closing of this system could be presented as a good example of effective Ethiopian action and

---

[5] Cp. Thamm, Berndt Georg, 'Al-Qa'ida – Hydra des islamistischen Terrorismus', in *Deutsche Polizei* 9/2003, p. 14.

[6] immediately following 9/11, 2001, s. *Country Reports on Terrorism 2005*, ed. by the US Department of State (Washington, 2006), Ch. five: http://www.state.gov/documents/organization/65468.pdf

collaboration with the West, it also meant that individual Somalis lost one of the last opportunities of supporting their families back home. There is today no visible Islamist scene in Ethiopia. But Muslim communities enjoy economic growth and unheard opportunities for their cultural and religious activities. Solidarity with the international Islamist "struggle" remains low (except isolated, individual cases like the London Ethiopian bomber arrested in 2005, who seems rather a product of the London Islamist scene than of the Ethiopian one). Traditionally Yemenites are quite present in Ethiopia, mainly as merchants, which led to fears of some Western analysts that Ethiopia might be or become a haven for Yemenite Islamist networks[7]. A problem for future developments might be the steadily rising presence of Wahhabite "missionary" activities from Saudi Arabia, which is seen by some analysts the breeding ground for Islamist fundamentalism. Never in Ethiopian history so many mosques had been built, a great number of them with the help of Saudi (Wahhabite) charity organisations. The Wahhabiyya ideology will have a certain influence on the development of a new, "modern" (in the sense of more integrated in a world-wide, partially Saudi-led) Islam also among Ethiopian Muslim communities. Ethiopian Islam, however, is marked by a history of its own tracing itself back to prophet Muhammad's days and firmly established in the Ethiopian highlands since about the 9th century (s. Trimingham 1952), it is therefore highly improbable that Ethiopian Islam will fundamentally change – except in a situation of heavy and continuous local conflict, and also, to some degree, in the urban context. Reports on conflicts with traditional Muslim communities, related to returnees educated in Saudi Arabia, are still quite isolated and will in all probability stay isolated[8].

Ethiopia and the US-led War on Terror

Ethiopia is a member of the US-led Trans-Saharan Counterterrorism Initiative, which comprises around 10 countries, a multimillion-dollar partnership between the U.S. Defense Department (DOD) and Sahelian nations. The "IGAD sub-region in particular have become an integral part of the global coalition against terrorism ..."[9] A US government information page on Security Assistance, set up by the Bureau of Political-Military Affairs of the US Department of State, underlines: "Ethiopia is an African front-line state in the war on terrorism, supporting efforts to apprehend terrorists in Ethiopia and beyond. (...) A long-term U.S. goal is to eradicate sources of terrorism in the region in order to protect U.S. national security. Ethiopia has provided outstanding cooperation in the war on terrorism. Ethiopia enhanced security for the U.S. Embassy, shut down avenues of terrorist funding, and is cooperating in the effort to counter terrorism in and emanating from Somalia. Ethiopia has a large and professional military that has provided support for the war on terrorism (including an offer of troops for the US-led effort in Afghanistan). (...) FY 2007 International Military

---

[7] Cp. West, Deborah L, *Combating Terrorism in the Horn of Africa and Yemen,* Wold Peace Foundation, Belfer Center for Science and International Affairs and John F. Kennedy School of Governance (Cambridge: World Peace Foundation, 2005).

[8] David H Shinn, 'Ethiopia: Governance and Terrorism', in Robert I Rotberg (ed.), *Battling Terrorism in the Horn of Africa (*Washington, D.C., 2005) p. 97.

[9] *Kinfe Abraham, 'Combating Terrorism in the Horn of Africa, Legislative and other Responses of IGAD Countries', Paper read at the Conference on Combating and Preventing Terrorism, Addis Ababa, June 25 – 27, 2003.*

Education and Training (IMET) funds will be used for training that will further increase the professionalism of the Ethiopian military, focusing on senior level professional military education courses (War College and Command and General Staff level schools) and instructor training to assist in the development of Ethiopia's own military training institutions. FY 2007 Foreign Military Financing (FMF) will be used to provide Ethiopia with additional equipment and spare parts to increase its counter-terrorism and peacekeeping abilities, including enhancing Ethiopia's own training capabilities, and to finance the existing vehicle and C-130 aircraft maintenance contracts."[10]

According to the same source, in the year 2005 the Foreign Military Financing (FMF) funds provided 7,050,000 USD to Ethiopia (ca. 2,000,000 in the years 2006 and 2007 each), in addition to 572,000 USD (and slightly more in the coming two years) for the International Military Education and Training (IMET). The involvement of US military in Ethiopia is important, not only through financial means: "US Army Special Forces and the Combined Joint Task Force-Horn of Africa 'continued to provide training to enhance Ethiopian border patrol and security skills' while the Ethiopian government 'enhanced physical security, conducted investigations and provided protective surveillance in response to threat information directed at U.S. citizens'."[11] The Country Report of the State Department[12] describes the activities of the Ethiopian government as follows:

"Ethiopia devoted high-level attention to the fight against terrorism and continued its counterterrorism cooperation with the United States. As evidence of its political will to fight terrorism, the Government of Ethiopia agreed to a number of new initiatives and continued to cooperate in efforts to collect and share intelligence on terrorist groups. As a developing nation with constrained resources in a volatile region, Ethiopia has limited, but increasing, capabilities to address terrorism threats. Draft counterterrorism legislation is currently before Parliament for approval.

Ethiopia did not provide sanctuary or offer political or financial support to any terrorist groups, and there were no significant terrorist incidents directed against U.S. citizens in Ethiopia. Ethiopia made a concerted effort to eliminate the ability of any terrorist groups to operate in the country. (...)

Ethiopia's recently renamed National Intelligence and Security Service (NISS, formerly known as SIRA) combined the duties of counterparts to the CIA, FBI, DHS, BICE, State/Consular Affairs, and the Secret Service. NISS was responsible for overall counterterrorism management. Federal and local police counterterrorism capabilities were primarily focused on response to terrorist incidents.

Ethiopia actively participated in African Union (AU) counterterrorism efforts, nominated a focal point for the AU's Center for Study and Research on Terrorism[13], and participated in meetings of the new Committee of Intelligence and Security Services of Africa. Ethiopia

---

[10] http://www.state.gov/t/pm/64657.htm, September 2006.
[11] Jim Fisher-Thompson, African Cooperation Growing on Anti-Terrorism, U.S. Report Says, April 29, 2006 (http://www.kinijit.org/content.asp?contentid=1571), quoting from the US government *Country Reports on Terrorism 2005*. Cp. also Peter Woodward, *US foreign policy and the Horn of Africa* (London, 2006).
[12] *Country Reports on Terrorism 2005*, ed. by the US Department of State (Washington, 2006), Ch. five: http://www.state.gov/documents/organization/65468.pdf
[13] AU counterterrorism websites are www.africa-union.org/terrorism/terrorism2.html and www.caert.org.dz.

ratified AU counterterrorism conventions and protocols. In addition, Ethiopia was active in Intergovernmental Authority on Development (IGAD) counterterrorism efforts".

Debates on the *causes* of terrorism are also part of the Ethiopian discourse on terror. The War on Terror in this sense plays an important side role as a guaranty that the fight against poverty will not be forgotten: "... terrorism is deeply rooted in poverty and apathy which result from the widening wealth gap between rich and poor countries ..."[14] Other reasons for terrorism will be discussed below. But it is certainly directly linked to the cleavage between the rich (arrogant, culturally over-dominating) North (i.e. the so-called "Western countries") and the poor (culturally disillusioned, humiliated, uprooted) South. As Kinfe Abraham (ibid.) pointed out on a 2003 Ethiopian Conference on Terrorism: "A strategy for narrowing the wealth gap and improving the dialogue between civilizations is, therefore, of cardinal importance for seeking durable medium-and long-term solutions to the problem of terrorism..."

Among all third-world countries Ethiopia is – and has been most of the time since the mid-1980s – receiving the greatest amount of aid, both in kind and in cash, by governments, international organisations and NGOs. During the severe drought year 2003, the U.S. provided a record $553.1 million in assistance, of which $471.7 million was food aid.[15] Ethiopia is vitally interested to keep this machine going – the main state institutions and an important percentage of the population depending on these networks of international aid. The War on Terror has the side-effect to guarantee the prolongation of aid. Poverty is, indeed, a factor, which can disturb the stability of society and erode it from within, making it vulnerable to extremism. There are, however, also other causes.

The Oromo Liberation Front (OLF): Oromo "terrorists"?

In 1991 the Tigray People's Liberation Front (TPLF) and allied liberation fronts – forming the Ethiopian Peoples' Revolutionary Democratic front (EPRDF) – overthrew the bloody dictatorship of Colonel Mengistu Haile Mariam. Thus a civil war, which had marked Ethiopia since more than two decades, came to an end. The Provisional Government of Ethiopia comprised all important liberation fronts, including the Oromo Liberation Front (OLF). This organisation, however, soon declared their disappointment with the leadership, which disregarded the interests of the Oromo, the most numerous ethnic group of Ethiopia. Therefore, the OLF left the government and declared to boycott the first elections – against the advise of all concerned international organisations and foreign diplomats. Soon thereafter the OLF was declared an illegal organisation. During the years, numerous Oromo were arrested, if they were suspected of membership in the OLF. Anyone suspected to have links to this organisation, which mainly operated from exile (often militantly), had to fear arrest or at least to loose his/her job. At the beginning of the War on Terror Ethiopia referred to their fight against the OLF as an integral part of the international fight against terrorism. Reportedly, the Ethiopian government had repeatedly crossed the borders of neighbouring

---

[14] *Kinfe Abraham, 'Combating Terrorism in the Horn of Africa, Legislative and other Responses of IGAD Countries', Paper read at the Conference on Combating and Preventing Terrorism, Addis Ababa, June 25 – 27, 2003.*
[15] US Department of State Background Notes, Ethiopia (http://www.state.gov/r/pa/ei/bgn/2859.htm).

states in order to attack OLF camps, but faced no criticism by the international community. The conflict with the OLF, however, has no relation with any international networks of terror, but is an integral part of a complex system of local alliances and conflicts. In 1999 eyewitnesses reported from Mogadishu port that they had seen Eritrean ships delivering weapons to Oromo, who were receiving the weapons there: The OLF then had become an attractive partner for Eritrea during the Ethio-Eritrean war, fuelling Eritrean hopes that Ethiopia might break into pieces one day, due to internal turmoil and tension[16]. The OLF, however, in fact militarily played a rather marginal role, as until recently they never managed to control substantial parts of the territory. Another result of the unsolved conflict was the fact, that Oromo in general were continuously seen as potential suspects.

An exemplary case study: The events of April 2004[17]

In April 2004 a new Oromo crisis marked the disturbed relationship between the EPRDF leadership of the government and state and a great part of the Ethiopian population, especially those living in the Regional State of Oromiyaa – the largest Regional State, by surface and number of population. In this case the responsible persons, one is tempted to say, did everything "necessary" in order to create unrest among the Oromo. It started all with a group of students who wished to organize a party. In early 2004 an Oromo students' group at Addis Ababa University planned to invite an Oromo cultural group and asked the University administration for permission. They were promised that permission would be granted after some preliminary procedures. They were waiting quite a while and asking repeatedly for permission. Then the University announced an Oromo cultural festival for students, while the request of the independent Oromo students' group remained still unanswered. This made a great impression on the concerned students: When the Oromo festival started, an Oromo student declared loudly not to accept that the state takes the initiative, and asked for boycott. He left the hall, followed by a number of other students. This first step of the conflict followed an undeclared principle in Ethiopia: independent initiatives are often countered by initiatives of state or party officials with similar shape and content, in order to keep control. The concerned Oromo students who had declared their boycott were soon arrested. This in turn resulted in a declaration of solidarity of about 300 Oromo students. The University leadership in reaction relegated them from Addis Ababa University.

---

[16] This issue is highly complex, however. Even if after the 1998 outbreak of the war one could occasionally hear hopes of Eritreans close to the government, that Ethiopia - hold together only by suppression, in their perspective - might dissolve itself, this hope was not the official policy of the Eritrean government. It was rather hoped that the establishment of a new, friendly government through alliances with opposition movements within Ethiopia would become possible. The Eritrean government was well aware that turmoils in Ethiopia might also strongly affect Eritrea's stability and damage it economically. After Ethiopia had refused the implementation of the 2002 decision of the international Ethiopia-Eritrea Boundary Commission (EEBC) in The Hague, however, this policy changed. It was now about five years that Eritrea and Ethiopia had been economically strictly separated from each other, which did not only mean that Eritrea suffered from the economic isolation, but also that its economic links with Ethiopia were gradually replaced by alternative connections to the Arab world. The new analysis in 2003 was, that the potential threat which consisted in the breaking-apart of Ethiopia was less serious than in a continued existence of Ethiopia, Ethiopia having "always tried to destroy and suppress Eritrea".

[17] This and the following sub-chapters are based on my field research in Ethiopia (Addis Ababa and Tigray), which started in April 2004 and ended in January 2006. I thank the German Research Foundation (DFG) very warmly for generously supporting my research within the research project "Friedensräume in Eritrea und Tigray unter Druck" under the direction of Rainer Tetzlaff.

The necessary conditions for the outbreak of a real crisis were now set. A student in Ethiopia lives in the University compound, he sleeps in the dormitory, he eats in the cafeteria and studies in the library and follows the courses – his entire day is centred around University life, and he lives from it; his studies are fully state-sponsored. Many students come from far (especially many Oromo, the most important ethnic group of Ethiopia), as they are selected from among the best secondary school students from over the whole country, and have no other home to stay. The decision of relegating these students did therefore not only mean to deprive them from further studies, but they even lost the basis for their daily living. Having no accommodation any more, some started to sleep in the streets near the University compounds. In this situation an Oromo self-help organisation, the Macaa-Tuulama-Organisation, started to act: In newspaper advertisements this organisation asked Addis Ababa inhabitants to spend money in order to accommodate and feed these students. With the help of this solidarity campaign it was possible to feed these students and provide them places to sleep. Tension among students at Addis Ababa University was high at that moment. Tigrayan students (from the ethnic group of the TPLF-leaders who dominate the Ethiopian government) were aggressed by other students. Many Oromo students were still continuing their studies; opinions among them were very divided; a number of those who were relegated were pardoned later and re-admitted to the University. Finally, in April, a bomb exploded within the University compound. Very quickly the government announced through radio and newspapers, that they had caught the suspects, who were Oromo students. Rumours said that the bomb was in reality the work of others, namely government agents; but the partially radicalised atmosphere preceding the bomb explosion makes it highly plausible that it was really the (individual!) work of one or more University students[18]. Generally students (including Oromo) agreed that this action was counterproductive, but it was too late.

Within a few days the Macaa-Tuulama-Organisation was accused of entertaining terrorist networks and instigating the bomb attack, their office closed down and several leading members arrested. The most important independent Oromo organisation thus suddenly disappeared from the public scene. This, in turn, led to continuous demonstrations by secondary school students and University students in different regions in Oromiyaa. The unrest continued well into summer 2004 and was strongly countered by Federal Police action. From several cities far from the capital it was reported, that demonstrations were brutally oppressed. The "initiators" of these protests were arrested; in some cases (reported, among others, from Wallagaa in Western Ethiopia) such Oromo students were found dead (at least one case had been confirmed by independent observers; others speak of more). This again led

---

[18] There are indications, however, that the radicalisation of individual students were linked with attempts from outside to gradually destabilize the situation in Ethiopia. Concretely, there is evidence, from interviews with Oromo outside Ethiopia, that several OLF cadres trained in Asmara had started activities in Ethiopia since 2002 with the aim to help to stage Oromo students protests, using whatever local grievance could be exploited. Local discussions on measures of the Ethiopian government or government agents perceived as suppression were fueled by a number of "recruits", who were said to have received money to organize protests. This strategy was adopted by several important OLF leaders, in an attempt to counterbalance the serious military defeats the OLF suffered from Ethiopian government troops in western Ethiopia and the Somali border region. However, not all did agree on that; some OLF leaders tried to use their contacts to Oromo communities to keep their children away from the protests. Interviews with Oromo students involved in the 2004 clashes who had left Ethiopia, confirm that (a) the students were largely unaware of an influence coming from outside, and (b) that there were indeed student activists which acted following the advise of OLF cadres.

to more demonstrations. One factor, fundamental for modern Oromo identity, plays an important role in the quick reaction of Oromo students all over Oromiyaa: Oromo have developed a strong common feeling of victimisation and of identification with an imagined common culture and nation; any new act of suppression will be perceived by many as directed against all Oromo. This in turn causes a strong feeling of solidarity and identification with the victim.

The state had acted quickly: Local reports especially from Western Ethiopia suggested, that the multi-ethnic Federal Police (controlled by the central government, not the regional state!) was reorganized in regions of crisis, as several Oromo policemen were accused of freeing several of the arrested students prematurely. They were replaced by Tigrayan policemen, most of them ex-fighters of the former armed forces of the Tigrayan People's Liberation Front (who had toppled the government in Mai 1991). Finding themselves in "enemy territory" and used to quick and martial solutions outside legal procedures, these experienced policemen in some cases have evidently used their gun to solve the problem. The government, consulted behind the scenes by diplomats of different countries, declared, that such extra-judiciary action was not tolerated by the government. However, the reshuffle of the Federal Police created all what was necessary for this kind of "solution". It is therefore hard to believe that the results of it were not foreseen.

In this context it is interesting to note that government officials, during discussions in absence of cameras, admit the existence of problems with their police staff, but underline that they cannot get rid of them due to the great group solidarity, which results from the war of liberation fought together. A Tigrayan policeman, however, interviewed by me in June 2004 in Meqele / Tigray, openly and proudly assured me that he and his fellow policemen were extremely proud of their profession, as people fear them and they are the only ones who can guarantee order – through quick action without asking any judge. These people, he added with contempt, just consume time, and the effects are not sure; "we, however, quickly identify a problem and eliminate it using our own methods". They can do this, he said, because "the state leadership is with us".[19]

A turn in the discourse on terrorism: The CUD opposition

In summer 2005 the National Election Board published the election results of the national May elections, followed by great unrest in Ethiopian cities. Until the day of elections, discourses fundamentally denying the legitimacy of the respective "other" marked the political scene. The main opposition party, the Coalition for Unity and Democracy (CUD, Amharic short form: Qinijit), had declared that if it will not win, it would be only possible due to election fraud. The CUD and its adherents in their turn were called "street boys" and remnants of the former dictatorial regime. From the day of the elections on tension rose

---

[19] The above résumé of events is based on interviews with Oromo teachers, among others from Wallagaa and Addis Ababa, Tigrayan, Amhara and Oromo students of Addis Ababa University, University teachers (who largely confirmed the stories told by the students), discussions with foreign diplomats and other observers, and even acting and former government officials, from April to July 2004. For understandable reasons it is not possible for me to quote any names. The interviews were carried out in the framework of the above-mentioned DFG-sponsored fieldwork focused on Tigrayan conflict resolution systems, traditional social cohesion and local history, in relation to the modern state.

quickly; both sides declared victory before any results were known; reports on fraud and irregularities quickly led to demonstrations and bloody clashes in Ethiopian cities. In June Police was shooting at demonstrators only armed with stones, which resulted in heavy casualties[20]. Tension rose even more when in October most elected CUD-Members of Parliament (but not all), and some members of the smaller UEDF (Amharic short form: Hibret), boycotted the first session of the new parliament. The November clashes in Addis Ababa again led to bloodshed and this time tens of thousands of youngsters were arrested. ETV regularly showed scenes of street violence (see picture below!). The CUD was publicly accused to have tried to instigate a coup d'état in order to topple the government; the most important CUD leaders were arrested and charged with high treason. In the rhetoric of government officials the legally elected opposition quickly turned into "terrorists": They were warned that they would be treated as other terrorist organisations if they would not be ready to integrate into the institutions of the state.[21]

Simultaneously the OLF was re-discovered as a potential partner. "In October 2005, the Ethiopian government, through Norwegian intermediaries, offered to the OLF to negotiate its reintegration into the legal political process in Ethiopia."[22] After first indications that talks could start, the OLF, however, already in November called upon its followers "to rise up against EPRDF-rule" – evidently in a hope, that the time to put an end to the EPRDF-led government had come, in the framework of the violent clashes between the government and demonstrators in the streets of Addis ababa and other cities. This was followed by renewed armed clashes in Western Wallagaa (Oromiyaa) and arrests, especially of secondary school students in Oromiyaa. There are indications that again the choice of conflict rather than of resuming cooperation was linked with the still close contacts with the Asmara government; on the other hand, there was also still a great reluctance among the EPRDF leadership to give up enmity towards the OLF, which had turned out to be a useful scapegoat.

Present developments

The 2005 June and November clashes in the streets of Addis Ababa were followed by peaceful demonstrations of secondary school students in December 2005 to January 2006, which were also immediately suppressed. In early 2006 a series of bomb explosions in Addis Ababa, Jigjiga (Amharic: Jijiga) and Gedo (with about 100 people injured) indicated a further aggravation of the situation. The bomb attacks in Addis Ababa were declared by the government to have been instigated by the CUD, while "Somali Muslim extremists", allied with Eritrea, had operated in Jigjiga (but, contrary to that, local rumours maintained that the bomb attacks were organised by government agents in order to justify oppressive measures; there are, however, indications that there had really been an involvement of militant members of the CUD). So-called "terrorist cells" were discovered in February 2006: "The National Intelligence and Security Service and the Federal Police Anti-Terrorism Task Force claimed

---

[20] Cp. Smidt, Wolbert G.C.: Parlamentswahlen in Äthiopien, in *Afrika Spectrum* 2/2005, 319-330
[21] Cp. Smidt, Wolbert G.C., Ein demokratischer Versuch zuviel – zurück zur bewährten Diktatur? Äthiopien ein Jahr nach den Parlamentswahlen, in *Afrika Spectrum* 2/2006.
[22] swisspeace / FAST International Early Warning Program (ed.), *Ethiopia, Special Update January to June 2006*, Bern 2006 (FAST Update), p. 7.

to have dismantled and arrested 'the leadership and executers of a clandestine group linked to the Coalition for Unity and Democracy (CUD) and undertaking preparations over the past few months to launch an armed urban terror'."[23]

The level of confrontation remains high, even if it is the first time in Ethiopian history, that there is an active opposition even in the Parliament itself. The remaining parts of the legal opposition within Ethiopia try to use state institutions to initiate change and reform from within; however, the now Diaspora-led CUDP (former CUD) and UEDF have declared the local CUD- and UEDF-members of Parliament "traitors". The hardline members of the CUDP diaspora opposition have reached an important success: In May 2006 the diaspora CUDP has joined a militant coalition, the Alliance for Democracy and Freedom (ADF, of which also the OLF and other militant organisations are members), which aims at the removal of the EPRDF government. The highly *exclusive* way of dealing with dissent continues on both sides. Even if there are signs that also exiled opposition leaders try to find ways for peaceful civil disobedience, the risk for further clashes remains high. These, however, are not part of the international problem of terrorism. They are mainly a further example of an old Ethiopian problem: The political history of Ethiopia is deeply marked by ideological (and often militant, as a result) exclusion of dissent.

During the last year Ethiopia has strongly engaged itself in Somalia. When in 2006 the Islamic Courts quickly took control of Mogadishu and most of its surrounding regions (but not of Puntland, however, and of de-facto-independent Somaliland) the Ethiopian army sent troops to Baidoa in Somalia. This was reliably reported by eyewitnesses, but denied over a long time by the Ethiopian government; the task of the troops was the protection of the internationally-sponsored, but weak government of Somalia, which, however, had failed to appease Somalia. Even if internationally recognized, they had de facto ceased to be the government, being replaced by the Islamic Courts. By December 2006 Ethiopia was involved in an open full-scale war against the Islamic Courts, repelling it quickly from the capital city and other key-positions - but finally being caught in a durable guerilla war.

This was again more part of a regional power play than a question related to international terrorism. From the Ethiopian point of view the Islamic Courts were a danger, because they seem to provide a promise of stability and justice to the Somalis, which, however, excludes reconciliation with Ethiopia: The Islamic Courts maintain Somali claims on the Somali-regions of Ethiopia, namely the Ogaden. By consequence, again, Eritrea is openly supporting the Islamic Courts. The danger is evident, that both adversaries use Somalia as a playground for their conflicting views on how the Horn of Africa should be shaped and re-ordered. The unresolved Ethio-Eritrean conflict – and, more hidden, the open "Somali" question – remain a key-factor for a possible future destabilisation of the whole Horn. It is this instability, which can give rise to future growth of extremism and terror networks, not the Islamic Courts, not the Ethiopian opposition or others. Islam is, both in Ethiopia and Somalia, deeply marked by local cultural traditions and does not tend to harbour ideas of international Islamist extremism or Holy War. Conflicts are rather about leadership, control of territory and populations, not about religion. The continuation of conflict, however, might create new chances for Islamist "missionary" activities. Also fifteen years of instability

---

[23] swisspeace / FAST International Early Warning Program (ed.), *Ethiopia, Special Update January to June 2006*, Bern 2006 (FAST Update), p. 9.

and warfare have greatly contributed to the attractivity of radical Islamism as an alternative response to modern problems. Traditional Islam has already started to erode. The Islamic Courts have accepted foreign fighters in their ranks. Several djihadists with experience in the Afghanistan war live today in Sub-Saharan Africa and may once use their chance to gather followers.[24]

Terror is not popular in Ethiopia. But Figures who dare to challenge the Western super-power are. It is therefore no wonder that young street merchants in some Ethiopian cities offer a number of (China-produced) watches with the portrait of Osama Bin-Laden (see the photo of a watch purchased in summer 2005 in Meqele/Tigray, fig. 3). Such artefacts are interesting indicators for specific local developments. Only at the first sight it seems surprising and paradoxical that such watches are sold in the Christian-dominated highlands – would these Christians have hidden pro-Islamist feelings? Is it a sign for a mental preparation for terrorist ideology? Or a strange form of third-world-solidarity? The explanation is simple: People like to possess things related to great figures, regardless if they are considered "evil" or "good". They are great, that makes their photo popular. And they are even greater because they challenge a far-away, but too dominating friend, the United States: the country where everyone wants to go, but also a country, whose culture is regarded at least sceptically, or even seen as culturally "degenerated" – and cynical in its politics. However, if people would be forced to choose: They will choose the US for living, but might be hanging pictures of Osama (or Saddam) on their walls.

Conclusion

Terror threats in Ethiopia are real. This is at large based on *local* militant movements and groups, and partially linked with neighbouring states, who are using these groups for their own aims in the *regional* framework of unsolved conflicts. *International* terror threats are virtually non-existing. Internationally agitating terror networks could try to get a hold also in Ethiopia, but chances for this are low at the moment. Causes for local "militantism" lie not in poverty, but in oppression and militant ideology on both sides. Efforts for the reduction of poverty will help not to cause new problems, but to some degree only feed state institutions and in this way even help to avoid necessary reform; only a real change in the existing conflict systems and constellations, however, could change the degree of threat with terror. The War on Terror does not have this focus.

A reader of this paper may ask: Where is the problem with the "War on Terror"? The problem is the lack of differentiation and pragmatism - and the focus on US-interests only. This results from the idea of "evil", which is the basis for the ideology of the War on Terror. If we need to fight against the "evil", all methods seem to be allowed. Terror is "evil" – we all agree on that (even if I wish to suggest to drop quasi-religious terms like this one and replace them by "harmful" or similar terms). But: The fight against it creates new problems; it may even be evil itself. If we fight terror back, regardless of its causes, the fight may become an

---

[24] I thank Berndt Georg Thamm for his detailed information on this subject and the fruitful discussion we had while I was preparing this text. – S. also Berndt Georg Thamm, *Al Qaida, Das Netzwerk des Terrors* (München, 2005); Claudia Gomm (ed.), *Sicherheitspolitische Entwicklungen in Ostafrika*, Broschürenreihe der Bundesakademie für Sicherheitspolitik [BAKS] (Bonn, 2002).

endless one, if the causes are not understood. The fight itself can become one of the new causes. The "War on Terror" ideology provides some simple ideas, which provide governments a new legitimacy in their fight against a militant opposition; the necessity for a just and careful study of the causes fades away. With this we come back to the quotation in the introductory part of this text: One has to fight back "regardless of the cause" – if we mean by this that the fight against the evil is always justified, we tend to underestimate the causes of terror. The fight against the evil makes blind for the evil we do ourselves.

"Evil" is a question of perspective. Today's government of Ethiopia is composed of several former militant liberation fronts, forming the common coalition front EPRDF; they see their cause as historically justified. But what about the liberation fronts fighting against them today? If they are successful, their cause will also be judged as justified by those who control history then. From another perspective the terrorist looks like a resistant, liberation fighter and, thus, a hero. The ones who find all their justification in their fight against the "evil" use exactly the same pattern as those against whom they fight. The only way to escape from this vicious circle is an implementation of due process of law, justice and the practiced respect for divergent political projects; this does not exclude rapid and effective action of the state against those breaking the law. It requires more patience, but in the long term the risks are much lower; if there are less individual experiences of injustice (multiplied by a sense of collective humiliation), which is a key-cause of terrorism, terrorism has no breeding ground. In today's context, however, the War on Terror provides a framework within which numerous forms of oppression and humiliation are possible.

If one agrees that oppression is one of the great factors in creating instability, then one should also come to the following conclusion: Not only the *Networks of Terrorism*, but also the *networks of the War on Terror* are themselves an important factor in international and national destabilisation and as such constitute a threat to peace. The leaders of the War on Terror have forgotten (or know it, but do not accept it) that war creates injustice, suffering of the innocent and, by using at least a part of the methods of those against whom they fight, leave the consensus of humanity. This again creates a problem of legitimacy and for sure leads into militant resistance and the active creation of new opposition.

Bibliography

Abdulmejid Hussein, Statement at the 56th UN General Assembly on Agenda Item 166
        Measures to Eliminate International Terrorism, October 3, 2001
(http://www.un.org/terrorism/statements/ethiopiaE.html
Belachew Gebrewold, 'Deconstructing the Civilizing Process', 2006
        http://www.interpeacenet.org/peacestudies/deconstructing.pdf
Id., 'krieg ist frieden', 2006
        http://planet.gruene.at/index.php?seite=themen&tid=41735&PHPSESSID=70a682aec
        1b5e72ff9128353f182ed50
Country Reports on Terrorism 2005, ed. by the US Department of State (Washington, 2006),
        Chapter five: http://www.state.gov/documents/organization/65468.pdf
Fisher-Thompson, Jim, 'African Cooperation Growing on Anti-Terrorism, U.S. Report Says',
        April 29, 2006 (http://www.kinijit.org/content.asp?contentid=1571)

Foertsch, Volker – Klaus Lange (eds.), *Islamistischer Terrorismus, Bestands-aufnahme und Bekämpfungsmöglichkeiten*, Berichte & Studien der Hanns-Seidel-Stiftung München, 86 (München, 2005)

Gomm, Claudia (ed.), *Sicherheitspolitische Entwicklungen in Ostafrika*, Broschürenreihe der Bundesakademie für Sicherheitspolitik [BAKS] (Bonn, 2002)

Johnson, Dominic (compiled), *Krieg und Frieden, Gewalt und Intervention im Herzen Afrikas – von Kongo bis Sudan*, ed. by taz RechercheDienst (Berlin, June 2006)

Kinfe Abraham, 'Combating Terrorism in the Horn of Africa, Legislative and other Responses of IGAD Countries', Paper read at the Conference on Combating and Preventing Terrorism, Addis Ababa, June 25 – 27, 2003

Münkler, Herfried, Die neuen Kriege (Reinbek, 2002)

Rotberg, Robert I. (ed.), Battling Terrorism in the Horn of Africa (Washington, D.C., 2005)

Shinn, David H., 'Ethiopia: Governance and Terrorism', in Robert I. Rotberg (ed.), Battling Terrorism in the Horn of Africa (Washington, D.C., 2005)

Smidt, Wolbert G.C., 'Parlamentswahlen in Äthiopien', in *Afrika Spectrum* 2/2005, 319-330

Id., 'Ein demokratischer Versuch zuviel – zurück zur bewährten Diktatur? Äthiopien ein Jahr nach den Parlamentswahlen', in *Afrika Spectrum* 2/2006

swisspeace / FAST International Early Warning Program (ed.), *Ethiopia, Special Update January to June 2006*, FAST Update (Bern, 2006)

Thamm, Berndt Georg, 'Al-Qa'ida – Hydra des islamistischen Terrorismus', in *Deutsche Polizei* 9/2003, p. 6-15

Id., *Al Qaida, Das Netzwerk des Terrors* (München, 2005)

Trimingham, John Spencer, *Islam in Ethiopia* (London – New York – Toronto, 1952)

UN General Assembly Resolution 54/109 of 9 December 1999

West, Deborah L., *Combating Terrorism in the Horn of Africa and Yemen,* World Peace Foundation, Belfer Center for Science and International Affairs and John F. Kennedy School of Governance (Cambridge, 2005)

Woodward, Peter, *US foreign policy and the Horn of Africa* (London, 2006)

Id, *The Horn of Africa: Politics and International Relations* (London – New York, 1996)

Layers of Conflict in the Gambella Region:
An Interactive Approach

Dereje Feyissa

1. Introduction[1]

The Gambella region is located in western Ethiopia about 780 kilometers from the national capital, Addis Ababa. Its current land size covers 25,274 square kilometers, consisting of nine *weredas* (here after districts): Gambella, Itang, Jikaw, Akobo, Abobo, Gog, Jor, Godere and Dimma.[2] Two features stand out in defining Gambella as a physical space that has a direct bearing on the socio-political life of the region. Gambella is one of the hottest lowlands in the country with an average temperature of 37 degree and an altitude of 500 metres above see level, which stands in sharp contrast with its neighbouring highland regions that rise as high as 3000 meters (Ellman 1972). Above all, Gambella is a border region, covering one of Ethiopia's largest international boundaries with the Sudan. This physical setting partly explains its socio-economic marginality and political sensitivity.

The population of the Gambella region has been variously estimated. The 1994 national census estimated at 181, 862. There are five ethnic groups living in the Gambella region: the Anywaa, the Nuer, the Majangir, the Opo and the Komo. The Anywaa and the Nuer belong to the Nilotic language family whereas the Majangir, the Opo and the Komo belong to the Koman language group (Bender 1976). The population size of each ethnic group has remained very controversial. According to the census, the Nuer constitute 40 per cent; the Anywaa 27 per cent; the Majangir 6 per cent; the Komo and the Opo 3 per cent of the region's population.[3] Gambella is also home for migrant people who come from different parts of the country at various times. The migrants do not form an ethnic group per se. They are referred to by the generic term *degegna* (Highlanders), in reference to their place of origin in the highland regions of the country.[4] The Highlanders comprise 24 per cent of the region's population.[5] The majority of the Highlanders are ethnic Amhara, Oromo, and Tigreans and a variety of ethnic groups from southern Ethiopia.

---

[1] The data used in this paper is extracted from the anthropological fieldwork I carried out in the Gambella region at various times during 2000/2002 and 2004/2007
[2] A new district, Mengeshe, was created in the Majangir Zone in 2007.
[3] The Opo live in one kebele (peasant association) in Itang district, whereas the Komo live dispersedly in Gambella district.
[4] The Highlanders prefer to be called Habesha/Abyssinians, a more prestigious term which connect them with a 'Great' tradition in reference to the medieval Christian kingdom known as Abyssinia.
[5] Commuted from the 1994 National Census results.

Table 1.1   The Demographic Distribution in the Gambella Region

Group	Urban	Percent	Rural	Per cent	Total	Percent
'Indigenous' people						
Anywaa	9831	36%	34750	26%	44581	27%
Nuer	3014	11%	61459	45%	64473	40%
Majangir	64	0%	9286	7%	9350	6%
Opo and Komo	1067	4%	3735	3%	4802	3%
People from various highland areas of Ethiopia						
Amharas	4639	17%	7927	6%	12566	8%
Southerners	1334	5%	12170	9%	13504	8%
Oromos	5890	22%	4635	3%	10525	6%
Tigrayans	1341	5%	1255	1%	2596	2%
Total	27180	100%	135217	100%	162397	100%

Source: The 1994 Population and Housing Census of Ethiopia. Results for Gambella Region.
    Addis Ababa: Central Statistics Authority, 1995.

As a border region Gambella has also hosted a significant number of Southern Sudanese refugee populations since the 1960s. Once dramatically outnumbering the local population in the 1980s, currently the refugee population in the Gambella region is estimated at 51,374 distributed in three refugee camps. Nearly 50 per cent of the Southern Sudanese refugees are ethnic Nuer. Both the Anywaa and the Nuer live in Ethiopia and in the Sudan. The demographic structure of Southern Sudan is relevant in Anywaa-Nuer relations. The exact population size of each ethnic group in Southern Sudan is not yet established[6]. In comparative terms, however, the Nuer are by far a demographic majority in southern Sudan. This demographic imbalance is relevant as a social context within which the contemporary identity politics in the Gambella region is fought out. The political process in the Gambella region is indeed intimately tied with the politics of liberation in Southern Sudan ever since its commencement in the 1960s.

The Gambella region is one of the most conflict ridden regions in Ethiopia. Although there have been elements of reciprocity and complimentary socio-economic exchanges, the dominant pattern of inter-group relations in the region is conflict. Violence are expressed in various fields of social interaction: from villages to churches, from schools to political parties.

---

[6] The 1983 Sudanese census put the figures provincially. According to this census, the population size of the Upper Nile Province, where the majority of the Anywaa and the Nuer live, was 1.5 million. A conservative estimate put the population size of the Nuer in Southern Sudan half a million,   whereas on the basis of their settlement size, other scholars inflate the figure beyond a million (Yoh 2001: 94). The population size of the Anywaa in Southern Sudan is less disputed. Various scholars estimated it at 25,000 (Johnson 1986; Kurimoto 1997).

The manifestation of violence ranges from the complete destruction of villages to rioting in the schools; from the targeting of minors and the raiding of public transports to the crucifixion of individuals in order to humiliate the group to which they belong. In recent times, the conflict has assumed a more violent form involving bombings and massacres. Media and partisan representations of the conflict in the Gambella region give the impression as if the parties to the conflict are aligned in two blocks. A closer examination, however, reveals that the conflict is multi-layered and interactive. Some actors might have more agency than the others but the end result is murkier. These layers of conflict and their multi-directional interaction resemble more an arena than a dichotomy. The various collective, individual and state actors are acting towards serving their respective interest. The end result is, however, more than the sum of the individual actions. More over, none of the actors are fully in charge of the consequences of their own actions, let alone the sum total. In the following section I outline each level of the conflict situation to foreground the interactive pattern which will be the object of explanation in the following section.

2. Levels of conflict

2.1 Inter-Ethnic Conflicts in the Gambella Region

There are different levels of conflict in the Gambella region. One of these is inter-ethnic. This is evident in the protracted conflict between the Anywaa and the Nuer, and between the Anywaa and the Majangir. The Anywaa-Nuer conflict is the most prominent of all conflicts in the region. It dates back to the second half of the 19th century when a section of the Nuer (Jikany) migrated to the east from southern Sudan. The main driving force of Nuer territorial expansion are access to and control over vital natural resources, cultivation and pasture lands along the tributaries of the Sobat. The Anywaa and the Nuer are variously positioned in the distribution of these key natural resources and they practice different livelihood. The Anywaa are predominantly cultivators while the Nuer make a living on livestock production, although they are increasingly becoming agro-pastoralists. Anywaa areas are better endowed with natural resources since their major settlements lie along the banks of the rivers with lower population densities. This land type covers less than one percent of the landmass of the region. The Nuer have accessed these lands in two ways. Where there is a major Anywaa settlement, Nuer clans ally through inter-marriage or military alliances with the local Anywaa; and where the Anywaa settlement is small, movement to these pastures is regulated by 'effective occupation' among the various Nuer clans. The resource-driven movements of the Nuer have resulted not only in their territorial but also demographic expansion. Radically formulated assimilationist society that it is, the Nuer have absorbed many Anywaa into their society. In some parts of mixed settlement areas processes of ethnic conversion (Anywaa becoming Nuer) is under way[7]. In the long term, this has meant the expansion of the Nuer cultural space as well. This is very much resented by the Anywaa who have constructed a different identity system that emphasizes territoriality and purity of blood[8].

---

[7] This is particularly true in the Jingmir area, located between Akobo and Nasser in present-day Luakpiny County in the Upper Nile State, Southern Sudan.

[8] For a comprehensive analysis of the contrasting identity formations between the Anywaa and the Nuer, see Dereje, 2003. Ethnic Groups and Conflict: The Case of Anywaa and Nuer Relations in the Gambella Region, PHD Submitted to Martin Luther University, Germany.

The 1980s also saw struggle for political power among the Anywaa and the Nuer elites. On the basis of their settlement history, settlement pattern, greater competence in national culture and higher degree of education, the Anywaa elites expected a greater political advancement over their Nuer counterparts, which they didn't get. In the early 1980s disgruntled Anywaa elites established a liberation movement known as the GPLM (Gambella People Liberation Movement) to fight the Derg regime. With a political and military alliance with major armed groups (TPLF and OLF) the Anywaa took control over the newly constituted Gambella regional state in 1991. The Nuer who undertook an intense politics of recognition resented the Anywaa dominant political status and military power. The monopolistic closure of the Anywaa and the Nuer politics of inclusion brought about violent conflicts between the two throughout the 1990s.

There are at least three major violent conflicts between the Anywaa and the Nuer. The first occurred during the early years of the 1990s, locally known as the *girgir* (1991-2) when militant section of the GPLM committed atrocity against civilian Nuer in what appears ethnic reprisal. As a result, thousands of Ethiopian Nuer citizens trekked to the Sudan along with the refugees. From their bases in the Sudan, groups of armed Nuer mounted counter offensives, which resulted in the destruction of many Anywaa villages along the Baro River. The Nuer contestation of Anywaa political dominance resulted in yet another major war that broke out in Itang district in 1998. A more deadly conflict occurred in 2002 on issues related to succession to the office of the vice president, the Nuer preserve in the distribution of administrative power in the Gambella People National Regional State (hereafter the GPNRS). In these bloody conflicts many lives were lost, villages were razed to the ground and thousands of people were displaced.

The Anywaa legitimated their dominant political status on the basis of settlement history (indignity in Anywaa perspective) and contribution to regime change whereas the Nuer base their politics of inclusion on demographic-cum-democratic strategies. According to the 1994 census, the results of which is fiercely contested by the Anywaa, the Nuer constitute 40% whereas the Anywaa 27% of the region's population. This competing base of political entitlement is one of the root causes of the conflict situation in the Gambella region. The changing demographic structure of the region and its implication to political entitlement has magnified the Anywaa discourse on ethnic extinction. There is a strong belief among the Anywaa that the continuous territorial and cultural encroachments of the Nuer would result in their extinction. With multiple stakes, from political power, resources to identity maintenance, Anywaa politics in post 1991 Gambella has crystallised into the project of containment, a political project which reacts to the Nuer politics of inclusion. In that sense these political projects are mutually constituted and reinforced. The more the Nuer advance in their politics of inclusion, the greater the Anywaa fear, the more their political closure has become (Dereje, 2006).

Another inter-ethnic conflict in the Gambella region is between the Anywaa and the Majangir. In 2001 a major conflict broke out. The trigger to this conflict is the brutal killing of a Majangir woman in Abobo district where the Majangir and the Anywaa live together. The Majangir attributed this killing to an Anywaa man which the Anywaa refute. In Anywaa perspective, the conflict is instigated either by the Nuer to weaken their political standing in the regional politics or it is attributed to EPRDF'S divide and rule policy. On the assumption that the Anywaa brutally killed the Majangir woman, the Majangir retaliated by killing their Anywaa neighbours, followed by a spate of revenge killings from both sides. What started as an inter-personal affair engulfed the entire Majangir and Anywaa communities in Abobo and Godere weredas, which resulted in an estimated casualty of 200 deaths. Several Anywaa and Majangir villages were burnt. There are different object of the struggle in Anywaa-Majangir conflict. Traditionally, Anywaa-Majangir relations involve elements of hierarchy. The numerically larger and the politically more centralised Anywaa were more powerful than the fewer, scattered and politically in cohesive Majangir (Stauder, 1971). Anywaa are also more educated, thus have occupied administrative power in the Majangir areas. The Anywaa also encroach into the Majangir forestlands, which are well-endowed with bee-hives and commercial crops. In Post 1991 Gambella, the Majangir have been renegotiating these asymmetrical inter-ethnic relations. They aspire to create a wider political and administrative unit that combines all the Majangir who are parceled out by three regional states; Gambella, Oromiya and SNNPR. According to the 1994 census, the Majangir constitute 6% of the population, the third largest 'indigenous' group in the GPNRS. The political process in the Gambella regional state dominated by the two major players, the Anywaa and the Nuer, the contestation of their marginal status brought the Majangir into a violent conflict with the Anywaa in 2001[9].

2.2 Intra-Ethnic Conflict

Intra-ethnic conflict in the Gambella region is evident in the regional cleavages among the Anywaa; party politics among the Majangir and the political competition and resource conflict among the Nuer clans. The main faulting line in Anywaa politics is the Lull/Openo divide, those who live along the Baro River and the forest region, respectively. Struggle for political power among the Anywaa is often framed in the language of Lull against Openo. The Openo Anywaa are those who live along the River Sobat in Southern Sudan and its tributary Baro River in Gambella. Lull means in Anywaa language forest. When used as an ecological category it refers to the forest region within Anywaa country. Lull lies between the Openo and the Gilo River and ends in the east at the foot of the Ethiopian escarpment. In present-day Gambella the districts of Abobo and Gog are considered Lull regions but at its most political it is used by the Openo Anywaa to refer to all the groups outside of the Baro/Sobat basin. Perhaps the most important factor for the social cleavage between the Openo and the Lull is related to local political history. The Openo and the Lull regions also represented frontier zones for the two political systems of the Anywaa: the *kwaaro* (village headmen) and *nyieya* (nobles), respectively. At its most general, the term Lull refers to the south-eastern part of Anywaaland, which was the land of the *nyieya* (nobles) whereas the Openo area had many of the villages, which produced the *kwaaro*. The social cleavage is further reinforced with the differential introduction of Openo and Lull people to modern education. Modern education among the Anywaa was pioneered by the American Presbyterian missionaries who established the first school in Akedo village (Openo) in 1960. It was only ten years later that the first school was established in Bat Gilo in the Lull region. The facilities in Akedo were

---

[9] Some sources also indicate a Majangir- SPLA connection (Vaughan, 2003).

better where the missionaries established their headquarters. Ironically, more Lull visited the school than the Openo did such that there was a higher representation of Lull in the first generation of educated Anywaa elites. This is because many of the inter-village conflicts had occurred' among the Openo Anywaa[10]. Many of the new settlers in Pokwo village were, therefore, from Lull and the first Anywaa pastor was from Lull.

By the 1970s these Lull educated elites were ready to assume administrative positions, albeit as subordinates to the more influential and educated Highlanders who come from the centre. These elites were later on co-opted by the socialist regime that it used as avant garde in its so-called cultural revolution. Located within easy reach of the expansionist state, the Openo Anywaa received the brunt of state encroachments in cultural, social and economic terms. By 1970s they took up arms against the Ethiopian state and established the GPLM. Although Anywaa from the various regions later on joined the GPLM, the bulk of GPLM soldiers and leadership was extracted from the Openo. With the seizure of power by the GPLM in 1991, the Openo elites dominated politics thanks to their 'contribution' to regime change. The Lull faction in the GPLM took control of the leadership in 1995 with the political blessing of the federal state (represented by the Highlanders). Leadership changed side when an Openo Anywaa became the president late in 1997. The Openo-Lull cleavage was once again reopened with the establishment of an opposition party, the GPDC 1998 after an imposed merger between the Anywaa and the Nuer parties and formed the Gambella People Democratic Front. The bulk of the GPDC leadership comes from the Lull Anywaa, whereas the post-1998 GPLM leadership is from the Openo Anywaa. There is a renewed tension among the Anywaa power elites in the regional administration and within the newly constituted Anywaa party, the APDO (Anywaa People Democratic Organization). The upper echelon of the party structure was briefly dominated by the Lull which was later on replaced by the Openo upon the defection of the regional president after the December 13, 2003 conflict between the Anywaa and the Highlanders.

There is also a simmering tension among the Majangir on issues related to struggle for political power and the divergent reactions of the Majangir to land encroachments by their neighbours. There is an acute power struggle within the Majangir People Democratic Organization (MPDO). This power struggle is framed by one of the factions in terms of ethnic purity. Although both are extracted from the dominant Meelanier clan, the leader of one of the factions is half Majangir and half Sheko. This has raised the issue of ethnic purity issues in Majangir politics which collides with the 'greater Majangir' political project at the inter-ethnic level where they have sought to bring all Majangir and the related Sheko people from the Southern regional state into one administrative structure.[11] In the current power struggle, however, the issue of 'ethnic/regional purity' is inserted. The simmering tension between the two factions burst into violent conflict during the district sport tournament which the Majangir zone hosted in February 2007.

The most intense intra-ethnic conflict is among the Nuer. This is expressed at two levels: political competition among the tribal and clan elites and the conflict over scarce

---

[10] This is because of greater availability of firearms and relative land shortage in the Openo area. The Anywaa youth from the Openo areas did not feel safe enough to cross 'enemy' villages and come to Akedo

[11] In fact, the Majangir invited many educated Sheko from the South to work as civil servants in Majangir zone although there are many Highlanders who could have done the job.

natural resources among the villagers. The Nuer who live in the Gambella region (the Jikany) are divided into three tribes: The Gaajak, the Gaajok and the Gaaguang. The mode of political relation among the three tribes is competitive and at times very hostile. This is true particularly between the Gaajak and the Gaajok. The Gaajak resent the dominant political status of the Gaajok in the wider Nuer society particularly in Southern Sudan. On the basis of their larger demographic size in the Gambella region and a higher degree of incorporation into the Ethiopian state system, the Gaajak aspire a dominant status in Nuer politics in the regional state of Gambella. Intra-ethnic identity politics among the Nuer is also acted out in the emerging separate identity of the Thiang vis a vis the Gaajak.

There is also conflict over natural resources especially among the Gaajak clans. The resource-based conflict among the five Gaajak clans is a case in point. The Thiang occupy the best part of the rangeland. The permanent settlement of the Thiang in these lands deprived other Gaajak clans of their traditional avenues of expansion. Scarcity used to be addressed by the Nuer through a continual eastward expansion, mainly at the expense of Anywaa territories, where most of the dry season grazing lands and cultivation lands are found. An increase in population and a growing pressure on the riverine land, however, has generated competition over resources among the various Nuer clans, for they all compete for the same economic niche. Currently, there are intermittent conflicts between the Thiang and the two Gaajak sections, the Cieng Reng and the Cieng Nyajani on land-related issues.

2.3 Indigenes Vs Migrants

The Gambella region was incorporated into the Ethiopian state at the end of the 19th century. Prior to the arrival of the Ethiopian state, the region was inhabited by various groups of people who speak Nilotic and Koman languages. Today, they are survived by the Anywaa, the Nuer, the Majangir, the Opo and the Komo. Gambella is a lowland region that sharply contrasts the neighbouring western highlands. This is the reason why the migrants are called Highlanders. The first category of Highlanders who settled in Gambella is state officials and their families. Few traders followed suit. The bulk majority of the Highlanders who currently live in the Gambella region, however, came in the 1980s as part of the resettlement program. The introduction of coffee farming and timber production in the Majangir area has also encouraged new wave of migrants to the area. The 1990s saw yet another round of skilled migrants to the region. Given the fewer number of educated indigenous people, the newly constituted Gambella regional state encouraged educated Highlanders to come to the region and work as civil servants in the regional government. According the 1994 census, the Highlanders constitute 24% of the region's population and in some areas, particularly in the Majangir Zone and in the regional capital; they constitute more than 50% of the population.

There have been intermittent conflicts between the 'indigenes' and the 'migrants' in the past but the conflict has escalated since 1991. In 1992 more than 200 resettled Highlanders were killed in Ukuna village by armed Anywaa groups (Kurimoto, 1997). In the same year hundreds of Highlanders were massacred by armed groups led by the Nuer prophet Wutnyang. The Highlanders retaliated to both by indiscriminately killing 'black' people. Other than cultural differences, the boundary between the indigenes and the Highlanders is constructed in the language of color. The 'black' indigenes are contrasted with the 'red' Highlanders. This social boundary is reinforced by a new political boundary. In post 1991

Ethiopia, the various groups of people who live in the Gambella region are accorded with different degrees of political entitlement. According to the regional constitution, sovereignty resides in the five 'indigenous' nationalities, also called by the federal government national minorities. The Highlanders do not fit into this classification scheme. They are of diverse ethnic origins. The category of Highlander is elastic to the extent that any non-Nilotic people with brown skin color (red in local perception) wherever he/she is from considered as Highlander[12]. In terms of their ethnic identity, the majority of the resident Highlanders are ethnic Amhara, Oromo, Tigreans and Kembatta. In post 1991 political dispensation, the Highlanders emerge as a residual category because, by definition, they 'belong' to ethno-regional states other than Gambella on the basis of their respective ethnic identity. As a result, they do not have a political representation in the regional parliament despite their demographic size.

Despite their exclusion from the political process, the Highlanders dominate the business sector. They also provide more than 50 per cent of the skilled labour of the regional government although affirmative action has already produced a new generation of educated indigenous elite. Although the indigenous languages are promoted in the schools and are used as working language at the zonal and district administration level, Amharic is the working language of the regional government. Their better grasp of the language of the regional government has given the Highlanders an additional competitive edge in the skilled job market, if not in managerial positions and political offices, which are preserves of the indigenous elites. The sense of insecurity, however, seems to have generated an 'extractive' attitude, which above all is reflected in 'repatriation' of capital to 'homeland' regions. Amongst civil servants, the anxiety that they are likely to be replaced by the 'indigenes' sooner or later has generated a sense of apathy towards carrying out their professional responsibility. The Highlanders sense of relative deprivation is not only about their exclusion from political representation and economic insecurity but also what they consider lack of administrative justice. They see themselves as victims of 'local tyranny'[13].

There is also a resource dimension in the conflict between the indigenes and the migrants. This is particularly true in the Majangir Zone; one of the most forested regions of the country. In this forestland the Majangir have lived for centuries making a living through shifting cultivation, bee-keeping and hunting. In recent times there has been an influx of Highlanders into the area, attracted by the productivity of the forestland. Responding to these encroachments, the Majangir have adopted different strategies. Some left their traditional settlements and went deeper into the forest. Others have responded to the new economic incentives and started selling/leasing forestland, whereas a few Majangir have become coffee growers. All these reactions have adversely affected the forestland. Fleeing from Highlander's encroachment the first categories of Majangir cleared new forestland. Those who sold/leased their forestland to the Highlanders have put demographic pressure on other settlements. Land sale/leasing also brought about legal complications. According to traditional Majangir rules of

---

[12] The Highlanders are also variously called Habesha, Gaala, or Bouny.
[13] Some leaders of the MPDO, for instance, are widely known for their power abuse, evident in their sexual exploitation of Highlander women in the job market. Many Highlanders describe their situation as 'humiliation': "the only way our daughters get a job is by sleeping with Majangir officials".

resource use, the land is communally owned by lineages, clans or kinsmen. Most of the land sold or leased to the Highlanders is on an individual basis, without the consent of other claimants. Although land sale/lease goes through official registration after the deal, this is not recognized by the kinsmen. This has caused intra-Majangir tension and dispute. Even those who leased/sold the land still put a claim on what they consider their 'ancestral land'. This 'duplicity' is very much resented by the Highlanders who feel legally insecure should any land dispute arise between them and the Majangir, given their lack of political representation. As a result, the Highlanders, particularly those who are investing in coffee farming, have established interest networks that extend from the district administration, to the region up to the federal level. While ordinary Highlanders often run into trouble with the local administration, the big investors are getting away with their aggressive forestland encroachment. Here what we observe is the environmental cost of political exclusion. The political structure undermining a sense of belonging to the area with a sense of responsibility, the Highlanders economic behavior is informed by short term gains than environmental considerations.

2.4 The State against Ethnic Groups

A fourth level of conflict is largely related to the political conflict and military confrontation between the EPRDF and armed groups of Anywaa. The Anywaa and the EPRDF were initially allies. In what appears a memorandum of understanding, the EPRDF promised the GPLM political power over the Gambella region in post-Derg Ethiopia. The Nuer then perceived siding with the Derg; the Anywaa appeared a 'natural ally' for the EPRDF. As an independent political organization, however, the GPLM resisted EPRDF's hegemonic political behavior. The EPRDF demilitarized the GPLM in 1992, transformed it into a party in 1995 and the leadership was replaced by 'user-friendly' members. In 1998 the EPRDF further imposed a merger between the GPLM and the Nuer-based party, the GPDUP (Gambella People Democratic Unity Party) and established a more docile regional umbrella organization, the GPDF (Gambella People Democratic Front). This was resented, especially by the educated Anywaa who established an independent political organization, the GPDC, Gambella People Democratic Congress. The GPDC seriously challenged the EPRDF-affiliated GPDF during the 2000 regional election. Despite GPDC's electoral gains in Anywaa polling stations, the result was rigged and GPDC got a marginal political representation in the regional council. The pragmatic political promotion of the Nuer by the EPRDF, on the other hand, brought a new round of political tension within the GPDF. The EPRDF dramatically increased the political representation of the Nuer in the regional council in what appears 'thanks-giving' to their contribution during the Ethio-Eritrean border conflict (1998-2000). This political tension escalated into the 2002 deadly conflict between the Anywaa and the Nuer.

The federal government took a series of political measures as part of 'conflict resolution'. Senior officials, including the Anywaa regional president, were imprisoned; members of the regional police who were accused of inciting and participating in the violence (largely Anywaa) were jailed or dismissed from their jobs; the contentious multi-ethnic district of Itang was abolished and parceled out between the Nuer district of Jikow and the newly constituted Anywaa district of Openo-Alwero. The federal government has also identified the 'root causes' of the conflict situation in Gambella as the existence of 'too many' political parties. On that basis, all the existing parties were abolished in 2003 and were replaced by new ethnic parties modeled on EPRDF's PDOs (People Democratic organizations). These Gambella PDOs were organized by the EPRDF into a new umbrella political organization called the GPDM (Gambella People Democratic Movement)[14].

The political measures taken by the federal government has alienated a large segment of Anywaa society. In fact, what is dabbed as 'Anywaa banditry' (shifta) that gradually evolved into an armed rebellion was largely organized activity of ex- Anywaa police who were dismissed from their jobs. Failing to sustain their own family and claiming to represent Anywaa discontent, they resorted to violence against not only government establishments but also civilian Highlanders. This is so because of the categorical association between the Highlanders and the Ethiopian state. In the discourse of color the Ethiopian state falls on the 'red' side of the color spectrum because state agents who come from the centre readily fall into the category of Highlanders. In September 2003 six road construction workers (Highlanders) were killed. This was followed by a series of indiscriminate killing of Highlanders. On December 13, 2003 Gambella town witnessed an extreme form of violence when the Highlanders resorted to mob violence against the Anywaa residents of Gambella town. The trigger was the killing of eight government officials (Highlanders) on the same day. The individuals who carried out the attack have reportedly never been caught but it was widely assumed both by the Highlanders and the government that the ambush was the work of an armed Anywaa group (Human Right Watch, 2005). Whoever killed them, the manner they were killed was brutal. The severely mutilated bodies were brought to the regional council for a public display before they were taken to the hospital. Assuming that the murder was committed by an Anywaa and agitated by the sensational display of the bodies of the murdered, the Highlanders indiscriminately killed Anywaa male residents of Gambella town with rocks, machetes, and pangas. Some members of the federal army deployed in the region, manned entirely by the Highlanders, participated in the killing with automatic weapons. Estimates of the casualty vary. Anywaa sources and international human right organizations put the death toll to 420 whereas the government acknowledged only 67.

A spiral of revenge killings followed from both sides. Aggrieved by the complicity of the government establishments in the massacre, feeling vulnerable to more attacks and disappointed by the lack of protection from nor public apology by the government, more than a third of the Anywaa populace crossed the border to Southern Sudan where the various Anywaa armed groups were brought together and formed a politico-military organization known as the GPLF (Gambella People Liberation Front). From its base in Pochalla in Southern Sudan and the adjacent Anywaa territories on the Ethiopian side of the border, the GPLF has fought with the Ethiopian army with various degrees of success. The existing political tension between the Anywaa and the EPRDF is further compounded by the prospect of the discovery of strategic resources in the Gambella region and the issue of economic control related to that. The Gambella basin is one of the major petroleum potential areas in

---

[14] In a further political intervention, the EPRDF reorganized the GPDM in 2007 into the Gambella People Democratic Unity Movement (GPDUM).

Ethiopia. Currently a Malaysian oil company, Petronas, is undertaking exploration over the entire expanse of the Basin.

3.   *Objects of the struggle and interacting levels of conflict*

The aforementioned discussion has identified four levels of conflict in the Gambella region. The first level is inter-ethnic which is evident in Anywaa-Nuer and Anywaa-Majangir conflicts. This does not mean however that the ethnic groups are homogeneous with a constant interest to defend. All the ethnic groups contain within themselves different lines of differentiation not only bringing them into intra-ethnic conflict but also occupy different positions in inter-ethnic relations. There are also buffer zones with inter-ethnic links. Measured by the sheer magnitude of the casualties in fact more people are killed in intra than inter-ethnic conflict every year, evident particularly in the resource conflict among the Nuer clans. A third level of conflict is between the 'indigenes' and the migrants. Gambella as one of the least densely populated regions in the country it has attracted both spontaneous migrants and government sponsored resettlers. There has been tension between the indigenes and the migrants which occasionally erupts in to violent conflict. The conflict between the Anywaa and the Highlanders since December 2003 is an extreme manifestation of violent conflict whereas the potential for conflict between the Majangir and the Highlanders is very explosive. A fourth level of conflict is between the state and ethnic groups which is specifically acting out in the conflict between the Anywaa and the EPRDF.

In each level of the conflict there are various objects of struggle which could be summarized into three categories. The first prominent object of the struggle is natural resources, particularly the land. There are two land types which are competed by the various groups. The first land type is the riverine land along the Baro River. This land is both an agrarian and pastoral resource. The Anywaa and the Nuer who live in the area sustain their livelihood by growing food crops on the alluvial soils and after-flood pasture for the dry season. Fertile the area as it is, the riverine land is also the most scarce land type in the region, covering only 0.5% of the land mass. Access to the riverineland is one of the main pull factors for the Nuer migration into Anywaa areas. Nuer's main interest is the dry season pasture and water points for their cattle but as they steadily shift into agro pastoral livelihood strategy cultivation land has also become a contested resource at the inter-ethnic level. Given their differential access to the riverineland it is also contentious among the Nuer clans who also occupy different positions in Anywaa-Nuer relations. Pressure on the riverineland has been accentuated by the adverse impact of government development projects such as the disruption of the water flow for the downstream users during the dry season since the damming of the Alwero River in 1985. A different land type is contested between the Majangir and the Highlanders. The encroachment of the Highlanders into the traditionally Majangir inhabited forestland is one of the root causes of the conflict in the Majangir Zone. The forestland is an ideal ground for the cultivation of coffee and other commercial crops. In the conflict between political and military organizations which claim to represent the Anywaa and the EPRDF we find contestation over an imagined resource; petroleum. Although Gambella is one of the designated petroleum areas the results from the two wells drilled so far turned out to be dry. Be the intricacies of petroleum exploration as it may, the very potential and the exploratory measures taken by the government has already raised competing claims of the imagined but a strategic resource, further fuelling the conflict situation in the region.

A second cross-cutting object of struggle at the various levels of conflict is political power. This is particularly true since 1991. The new political context which engendered power struggle is the establishment of the Gambella regional state as part of EPRDF's ethnic federalism. The struggle for political power is evident at the inter-ethnic, intra-ethnic and indigenes and migrants conflicts. The conflict between the Anywaa and the Nuer could be largely made intelligible if it is viewed in terms of the way both have responded to the new opportunity structure. The Anywaa advance a political ownership right over the Gambella regional state on the basis of history, contribution to regime change and greater competence in national culture. The Nuer contest this with a demographic argument for political entitlement. They also back their power claim by their recent contributions to national wars. It is these unmediated competing bases of entitlement which brought the two communities into a protracted violent conflict. At the intra-ethnic level, the Lull/Openo divide; the Gaajak/Gaajok rivalry, and the issue of ethnic purity among the Majangir are aspects of struggle for political power at a lower scale. So is the conflict between the Anywaa and the EPRDF in as much as the main contentious issue is infringement of regional autonomy by the latter.

A third object of struggle is maintenance of cultural identity. This is true especially in Anywaa's and Majangir's relations with their neighbors. The Anywaa feel sandwiched by the Nuer in the west and the highlanders in the east while reflecting on the changing demographic structure of the region. Perceived or real the Anywaa fear that their survival is at stake. Their politics gravitates towards the project of containing their neighbors and in recent times the state as well. The Majangir are also grappling with a similar issue in their relation with their highland neighbors. The Majangir feel apprehensive about the steadily demographic growth of the highlanders who now make the majority in the area which they regard their home. The Majangir also fear they would be ultimately disowned their habitat (the forestland) by the cunning and more sophisticated neighbors. Underlying the identity anxieties of the Anywaa and the Majangir is also the new nexus between demography and political power in the context of electoral politics.

These various levels of conflict and objects of struggle not only operate by their own but also interact. The intra-Nuer conflicts, for instance, are directly linked to Anywaa-Nuer conflict. The inter-clan conflicts produced thousands of internally displaced Nuer who have resettled in traditionally Anywaa areas. As long as the intra-Nuer conflicts exist the Anywaa-Nuer conflict persists. Similarly the pragmatic mode of interaction between the Ethiopian government and the ethnic groups engenders and reinforces inter-ethnic conflict. The struggle for political power between the Anywaa and the Nuer elites throughout the 1990s is a function of the way the politics of entitlement is organized by the EPRDF. The Anywaa advance political ownership of the Gambella regional sate on the basis of history and contribution to regime change because there are precedents in post 1991 Ethiopia where groups are accorded with political rights over a specific region on the basis of the same principles[15]. Viewed against this background, Anywaa political demands appears a critic to the double standards that underlies EPRDF's modus operandi. The tension between the indigenes and the migrants is also related to the inherent contradictions of the new political structure. If empowering national minorities is enshrined in the constitutions so is citizenship rights which include the right to reside anywhere in the country with the democratic right to elect and to be elected. Both the indigenes and the migrants invoke the same constitution in their contestation over political rights.

The repercussion of institutionalized identity politics does not end at the inter-ethnic and indigenes/migrants level. It has also ushered in the social fragmentation within the ethnic groups magnifying and politicizing sub-ethnic units of identification. The Lul/Openo divide among the Anywaa; the purity issue among the Majangir and the inter/intra-tribal political competitions among the Nuer are manifestations of the janus-faced nature of the post-1991 identity politics in Ethiopia. On the one hand, identity politics has reinforced inter-ethnic boundary and fostered intra-ethnic solidarity. But the same process has also raised problems of where to draw the line in the definition of the 'self' and engendered intra-ethnic competition for political power and resources.

Bibliographie

Ellman, A. 1972. *An Agricultural and Socio-Economic Survey of South Sudan Refugee Settlements and Surrounding Areas in Gambella Awraja, Ethiopia,* UNHCR.

Bender et al. 1976. *Language in Ethiopia.* London. Oxford University Press.

Dereje Feyissa, 2006. 'The experience of the Gambella regional state'. In: Turton, ed. Ethnic Federalism.

--------------------2003. *Ethnic Groups and Conflict: The Case of Anywaa-Nuer Relations in the Gambella Region.* PhD. Dissertation submitted to Martin Luther University.

Human Rights Watch. 2005. *Targeting the Anuak: Crimes Against Humanity in Ethiopia's Gambella Region.*

Johnson, D. 1986. 'The Nilotic Frontier: Imperial Ethiopia in the Southern Sudan, 1898-1936.' In: D.L. Donham and Wendy James, eds. The Southern Marches of Imperial Ethiopia, 219-245.

Kurimoto, E. 1997. 'Politicization of Ethnicity in Gambella'. In: K.Fukui, E. Kurimoto and M. Shigeta (eds.) Ethiopia in Broader Perspective: Papers of the 13th International Conference.

Stauder, J. 1971. *The Majangir: Ecology and Society of a Southwest Ethiopian People.* Cambridge: Cambridge University Press.

Turton, D. 2006. 'Introduction'. In: Ethnic Federalism: The Constitution of the Federal Democratic Republic of Ethiopia. 1995. Addis Ababa.

Vaughan, S. 2003. Ethnicity and Power in Ethiopia. PhD Thesis. University of Edinburgh.

---

[15] This is the case, for instance, for the Harari who 'own' the regional state of Harar despite their smaller numerical size compared with the Oromo and the Amhara. By the same token, the political empowerment of the Agaw in the Amhara regional state represents a 'constitutional oddity' (Vaughan, 203).

Perceptions of Fairness Expressed in Contemporary Narratives of the Nuer living in the Ethiopian region of Gambella: their relevance to conflict transformation

Monika M Sommer

1   Introduction and Background

Gambella has become notorious for conflicts, many of which escalated and saw violent outbreaks. The most visible reaction from the government's side – but of course not the only one - has been the deployment of huge numbers of federal police forces in Gambella town and the National Defence Forces outside the town (for details see, Chan, 158) .

Different other players, local initiatives of civil society, such as churches and the mosque, and also international NGOs have been working on appeasing the situation in manifold ways. In more or less coordinated manners a number of communities were engaged in dialogues, aiming to facilitate understanding. Yet, there is some evidence indicating that many of these well intended initiatives remain somehow on the surface and do not really reach the participants.

This paper tries to uncover some of the local potential for justice, peace and reconciliation. It argues that values for conflict management and related strategies do not necessarily need to be 'imported'. Like every community – the Nuer in this case - has its own traditions which can be recurred to. This potential even exists despite the fact that people in Gambella do not have much experience with peace. Several generations grew up in a violent environment. If locally owned traditions won't be recognised, 'Peace' it at risk to become a political parole and a vocabulary to access international recognition and funds, rather than representing the original and humane urge for peace and justice. Each ethnic group though has been preserving traditions and folktales that deal with questions of fairness and justice. My basic assumption is that these tales that have been told to the children since generations have also shaped the perceptions of each single person profoundly. Therefore, any intervention or training in conflict resolution should take these perceptions into account and be built up upon them.

One way of viewing the Regional State of Gambella is to take a look at the area as an Ethiopian enclave in Southern Sudan[1], with a composition of population that in many respects has similarities with the Sudanese population across the border. The Sudanese connection is especially strong within the group of the Nuer, as many Nuer used to live in Southern Sudan, but came to Gambella during the turmoil of the different civil wars in Sudan (Anyanya I and II). According to the census results of 1994 (which were not undisputed) the Nuer form with 39.7% of the population the strongest ethnic group in the Regional State of Gambella (*Central Statistical Authority, February 1999,* see also Dereje in this volume). The overall population

---

[1]   The region comprises an area of about 23,862.69 square kilometres (Central Statistical Agency, <u>CSA 2005 National Statistics</u>, Tables B.3 and B.4).

size was 162,397 at the time. Based on this data official population projections came to an estimated population of 210,134 for 2000 (*Central Statistical Authority*, December 1995).[2]

The other four ethnic groups living in the region who are recognised as indigenous peoples[3] of the regional state are the *Anywaa*[4], the *Majangir,* the *Opo* and the *Komo.* Specifically with the Anywaa, the Nuer share a long history of fierce competition, but also of cooperation and assimilation (Johnson, 1980:73f).

Those inhabitants of Gambella who originate from different – usually less peripheral – regions of Ethiopia are commonly summoned up under the term 'highlanders'. The term combines diverse ethnic identities, such as the Oromo, Kambatta, Amhara and Tigrayans. Following the census of 1994 they form 24.1% of the population. As this stratum of the population is not the focus of this article - and also to avoid unnecessary repetitions - it may be sufficient to refer to the contribution of Meckelburg and Dereje (both in this volume). The former portrays in detail the so-called highlander population, while the latter explains the multilayered structure of the conflicts in Gambella.

Conflicts in Gambella are multilayered and complex. What today is known as the Regional State of Gambella has a history of marginalisation within the Ethiopian central state and as an area bordering British Sudan (see Dereje Feyissa 2005: 2 and in this volume). Gambella belonged to the so-called "southern" periphery (Bahru Zewde, 1991: 16-17). Without going into details of the conflicts of the 20th century, it can be said that in local narratives and in the perception of people of Gambella, the time since the end of the Dergue-regime, and the introduction of a new (ethnic-based) federal system, is one of the most conflict-ridden and violent periods in history (Dereje Feyissa 2005: 10; Esei Kurimoto, 2001: 267). Even when taking into account that it is only human to idealise previous periods which are less fresh in memory, the time since 1991 – the time when the central socialist government was overthrown - has seen a remarkable escalation in conflicts.

With all simplification and inaccuracies related to this, it can be stated that the conflicts are multilayered indeed. The main causes of conflicts can be traced to access to power, land and participation in political and social life. With the implementation of the Federal Constitution in 1995 (Proclamation No. 1/1995, *Federal Negarit Gazetta*), ethnicity has become an asset related to political and social entitlements. Moreover, a sense of ethnic belonging and identity is certainly been strengthened.

During the last decade, the Nuer have managed to become recognised partners in the leadership of the regional state. But still, the experience of violence has been a permanent trait in the life of Nuer families and all other inhabitants of Gambella. Conflicts not only erupted

---

[2] The size of the population is highly contested, as its size is the base for numerous privileges, first and foremost seats in the regional government, positions in local administration, access to schools, affirmative action in higher education etc. For details see Sommer (upcoming), Ethiopian Federalism Seen from the Perspective of the Regional State of Gambella: cause of conflict and fierce competition or access to resources and democratic participation?, working paper, Bremen

[3] The term "indigenous" as such is not well defined. The most widely-accepted formulations, which define the term "indigenous peoples" in stricter terms, have been put forward by international organizations, such as the United Nations, the International Labour Organization and the World Bank. Specifically in the African context (see, the Indigenous Peoples of Africa Co-ordinating Committee - IPACC) the term "indigenous" is widely associated with characteristics of previous political and economic marginalisation.

As in the case of Ethiopia, national and regional constitutions contribute "ownership" to those who are considered to be indigenous to a certain area.

[4]   sometimes referred to as Anuak; this article follows Sato Kurimoto, which is closest to the way the Anywaa call themselves

among the Anywaa and the highlanders, but also between Anywaa and Nuer and among different Nuer clans, mainly based on disputes over access to grazing land or – subsequently - motivated by vengeance and retaliation. Moreover, it frequently happens that the long and porous border with Sudan takes its tribute. In the dry seasons of 2006/2007 for instance, young Murle men, from a nomadic group residing in Southern Sudan, repeatedly raided cattle along the border. They were said to be equipped with modern Sudanese weaponry and uniforms from the North. These insurgencies have left numerous communities of mainly Nuer, but also Anywaa background homeless and internally displaced within the Regional State of Gambella. These recent events are mentioned here because they show the specific vulnerability of the people living in the region.

2   Study questions and objectives

In the complex social and political context only superficially sketched out above, research on the different players and diverse ethnic groups needs special emphasis. A deeper understanding of the dynamics of the conflict will only be attained, when local considerations of the events are valued and expectations of the people concerned are met when developing strategies of possible interventions. The study questions therefore are:

- *What do local narratives reveal about perceptions of justice and peace?*
- *How, according to these stories, shall peace be re-established after violations of life, property or rights?*
- *How do these perceptions relate to 'modern' concepts of justice and peace-building?*

This contribution is part of a more comprehensive study with the objective to develop a concept of peace-building which can be approached together with the people concerned and which truly will be owned by them. It is an attempt to build upon the strengths of the society itself and on its cultural heritage. Local actors will not be taught in peace-building strategies which have been developed in the western world, based on western perceptions. On the contrary, the role of an external facilitator will be the one to help local actors to literally dig out their own capacities for peacemaking and to rely on them. As a matter of fact, each ethnic group residing in Gambella has traditional ways of dealing with conflict in the life of the community and society (Sommer 2005). These methods are practiced mainly internally though, and often seem to fail when mechanically applied in cross-ethnic conflicts (interview 11-02-08). The objective of this study therefore is to look beyond the forms of conflict resolution and to understand the underlying values and perceptions. Hence narratives and folktales are expected to be transmitters of a common understanding of how conflict should be transformed in a given society.

The Nuer are regarded as one of the best researched population groups in Sub-Saharan Africa. This reputation goes back to Evan Prichard who did his social-anthropological research back in the 1930s, mainly in the Sudanese part of Nuer-land. He described in detail the procedures of preventing retaliation and compensation of loss after violence occurred (Evans-Pritchard: 1969/1940). Many of these procedures are still alive within the Nuer-communities (Sommer: 2005), but have the tendency to fail when it comes to inter-ethnic violence and conflicts. In the multi-ethnic environment of Gambella, more and more conflicts arise beyond the limits and limitations of one ethnic group. Space becomes narrower and opportunities to meet and dispute are more numerous. Therefore the specifications of these somehow internal procedures as such are not the main focus of this paper.

3   Questions of theory and method

In this paper the terms justice and peace are used almost interchangeably. One reason is the interconnectedness of justice and peace in the sense that no lasting peace will be achieved without having met the basic needs for justice of any given community (Galtung 2000). More importantly though, the narratives do not clearly distinguish between two concepts – one of peace and another of justice. As social tales, which are meant for teaching, they rather deal with individual and collective behaviour in a rather comprehensive way. The research had to take this character of oral tales into account.

Moreover, the terms (folk-)tale, lore and narrative are going to be used in an almost interchangeable mode. Finnegan (with reference to Bascom) defines folktales as 'prose narratives ... regarded as fiction. (...) They are not considered as dogma or history, they may or may not have happened .... (They) may be set in any time and place.' The terms are clearly connected, narrative being the broader term, potentially crossing the boundary to written prose (Finnigan 1992: 149).

In the interpretation of lore continuing methodological tensions can be observed. For our purposes the structuralist approach, in its particular form of narratology seems to be the most appropriate method of interpretation and of coming close to the meaning of the narratives (Finnegan 1992: 39, 183; Czekelius 1993: 121). Thus the topics to be investigated in the analysis include:

1. Patterns in the roles of narrative characters (the lion, the hunter, pp).
2. Structure of plots.
3. The varying voices and viewpoints in the narration.
4. The interaction of fiction and event.
5. The social context of storytelling.

The author is well aware of the specific risk that lies in the quest for meaning while analysing narratives: There might be several meanings; meaning may change through time and depending on specific occasions. Stories may be also multilayered. There are different 'parties' involved in the construction of meaning: starting with the people who created the earliest versions of the story to the researcher who collected the tale – these two points mediated by numerous storytellers in uncountable social situations. In an attempt to cope with this complexity, the dialogic nature of the storytelling will be taken into account. 'Meaning' is understood as an emerging process.

The narratives that are being analysed in this paper are basically understood as social and moral teachings, and as a presentation of the collective knowledge of the self in the world (identity). Thereby the different characters in the stories will be analysed, as each character represents a specific identity and point of view in the narratives, especially in the fables. The approach is focussed on the content and symbolism of the stories, the contextual analysis, and the symbolisms within a given cultural context. The latter is being done based on focus-group discussions and on literature studies (see methods below).

The field research was carried out during several visits to Gambella between 2005 and early 2008 - in all covering a period of about ten months. The research was based on a qualitative methodology, comprising open in-depth group and individual interviews and observation. Interviews were conducted in Gambella town and district villages, such as Kwergen and Lare in the case of the Nuer.

Interview-partners were selected randomly according to judgement and convenience. People were asked whether they could tell stories that were passed from generation to generation, especially those stories that were told to children to teach them right and wrong and to develop a sense of fairness. Sometimes the researcher then would be introduced to others, who assumingly knew better than the one approached in the first place. This random selection cannot claim to be representative, but still reflects a broad segment of society.

A series of interviews were conducted among the Nuer, women and men. From the stories I collected I used those which to me seemed most relevant. After listening to the stories I asked the storytellers what the story meant to them and which significance it carried for them. In a second step I asked other members of the same ethnic group whether they knew the specific story and whether it was significant for them (focus-group discussions). All in all I conducted an open interview type of review, which included the respondents' discussions and reflections in relation to the stories and questions of justice in general. Some of these group discussions were conducted in Addis Ababa, where I met some Nuer women when they visited the capital. In gaining the acceptance of the interviewees the researcher benefited from her previous role as an advisor for a local inter-ethnic and inter-religious peace initiative, the Gambella Peace and Development Council (GPDC). Friends and kin of friends at different stages arranged and facilitated ways of meeting individuals, both women and elders of the area.

4   Nuer stories on fairness and justice

In many occasions when stories were told I found that Nuer preferred stories that deal with history – either in the form of the mythical past, but also in the type of retelling recent events, thus either glorifying the actors, or in order to understand and attribute some meaning to history.

In 2005 for instance many people – mainly women and children when taking a bath or collecting water – were killed by the crocodiles in the Baro river. While talking about this dramatic increase in deaths among innocent people, a Nuer man told me the following story[5]:

'Do you know that the crocodiles sometimes only appear to be crocodiles? Sometimes the dead transform into crocodiles in order to retaliate, when their family did not revenge them after they were killed. After a person is killed at least compensation should be paid.(...) There are reported cases, in the old times that someone was killed, but his family did not grab hold of

---

[5]   Recorded October 2005 (Lare), Dobuol Malual

the killer. He may have left the area and in the case I am talking about now, he had fled downstream, where he settled at the river Baro. But the victim transformed himself into a crocodile. It followed the man way down from the tributary to the Baro-river – close to Itang – where he then found and killed him. After that the crocodile vanished for ever.

You know, now, as there were many people killed during the incidents in Gambella in December 2003, people believe that the deceased victims are retaliating. This started exactly after the incidents. Who knows when it will stop?'

The story teller refers to an old myth, which is also known to the Anywaa. He tries to give meaning to the dramatic increase of losses of human life. Taking a bath in the river - and even more fetching water – is part of daily life and a normal household-chore in Gambella-town. The horror of this advent is connected with another horrific incident, when Anywaa men were killed by an agitated mob of mainly 'highlanders', assisted by federal soldiers in 2003: There was no open discussion about the event at the time, inquiries into the event were politically undesirable or had the undertone of being manipulated. The sense for basic justice made way for explanations that reaffirmed the absolute need for retaliation and revenge. The narrator though acknowledged eventually *'the crocodiles eat everyone – irrespective of family, clan or ethnic belonging. This is not the way real justice should be done!'*

The following stories are of the genre of fables and were told when I directly asked for stories that relate to fairness.

In the following story [6] the fox and the camel crossed the river, where they expected to find more food. The camel carried the fox, as the latter could not swim. They both eat their favourite foods. But as the fox was much smaller than the camel, he was already full, when the camel was still eating sugarcane. The fox insisted to return immediately. *'As the camel did not react, he started howling with all his might. This alerted the local farmers, who came to chase the fox. But the fox had hidden away in a ditch, and the farmers found the camel instead of the fox, eating their crop. They started beating the camel badly and left it as dead. The camel survived though, and the fox came back from his hiding place, suggesting to return to the other side of the river. The camel asked, 'Why on earth did you start howling? You alerted the farmers and they nearly killed me'. But the fox only replied, 'This is what foxes do upon finishing their meals'.*

The camel accepted the fox to climb on his back, but when they reached the deepest point in the middle of the river, he said, 'I feel like twirling in the water'. And as the fox anxiously asked, 'Why on earth do you want to do it right now! I'll be drowning!' The camel only replied, 'This is what camels do upon finishing their meals'. The camel span round into the water and the fox sank into the floods and died. '

The narrative characters are the camel, the fox and the farmers. The protagonists are the animals, whereas the farmers are presented as posing a potential threat to the animals. They are the owners of the crop and may beat and kill them. The structure of plots is constructed in a circular way. The main characters go out for an excursion, which can be seen as a state of normality and equilibrium. But then one betrays the other out of pure selfishness. Things are getting out of order; the betrayed part comes close to death. The initial order is been

---

[6] 'Fox and Camel', recorded October 2005 (Gambella town-Yacob Nyal Gatluak); like all other stories it has been reduced to the pure content and shortened out of practical reasons (limited space). Unfortunately, but naturally the narrative looses its dynamics and suspension in this process.

reinstalled by retaliation: in return it is the camel who tricks the fox, this time with fatal result. The 'tit for tat' gives the listener a sense of safety and reinstalled order.

The story is relatively easy and straight forward – injustice will be punished instantly.

Anther story where the fox plays a prominent role is the following, in which the fox deceives mankind[7] :

'One day, the Moon called an insect and said to him, go to the people of the earth and tell them that I, Moon tell you as follows, 'You people you will die, but you will live again, as I, Moon die and rise again every evening.' Insect started his journey to the people of the earth. On his way, he met with fox (...)'. In the course of the following conversation the Insect reveals his mission and Fox offers in return, *'As you are not fast, let me take this good message to the people of the earth!' Insect agreed. Fox came to the people of the earth, and said, this is the message that Moon said, 'You, people of the earth, when you die you will not come back to live again – that's the difference between you and me!'*

After that he returned to the Moon. Moon asked him, 'What did you tell the people of the earth?' Fox replied, 'I told them that when they die they will not return again, unlike the moon and the stars that return'. Moon became furious. He took a rod and beat the nose of the Fox. That is why the nose of the Fox is still bent.

After telling this story, the narrator as well as the audience agreed that many Nuer until this day trust that this is the reason that people have to die without returning to life. The vicious fox is behind it.

Here again we meet the mean fox. This time he is also attributed with tremendous power. He poses as the messenger of a god-like figure, the moon and changes the fate of humankind! The plot is not circular in the sense that full justice will be reinstalled. The fox is been beaten with lasting effect. The more important effect though, the mortality of mankind, is not reversed. Eventually the wrongdoer went away with minor injuries and could triumph. The relationship between Moon and the people remains distorted.

Again, the following story is about animals who steal food from the gardens of men[8]. In this case monkeys came to the garden to eat the farmer's peanuts:

' one day, the man made a plan to give a warning to the monkey. He took a big gallon and filled it with mud and sand. On the sand then he put some peanuts. Then he left and hid himself. (...) When the monkeys came, one approached the gallon and stuck in his hand. He grasped as many peanuts as he could. But – he could not get his hand out! He started pulling and pulling .... But his fist was stuck! No way! The other monkeys joined him. Seeing his misfortune, they started screaming and bawling. (...) Hearing the noise a giraffe came.' The giraffe failed in convincing the monkey to let the nuts go and escape. Eventually the farmer killed the monkey, while the other animals escaped. *'What do you think killed this Monkey?'*

The educative question at the end was seemingly part of the story. In the following discussion listeners and participants agreed that it was greed and stinginess that killed the monkey. That it was important to be flexible and to listen to good advice. The giraffe here, as the camel

---

[7] 'Moon, Insect and Fox', recorded July 2006 (Moses Wawich)

[8] 'A Foolish Monkey', heard at different occasions, the following version is Moses Wawich, June 2007

before, is presented as a caring character. But she cannot help amid the rigidity, stupidity and greediness of the protagonist, the monkey.

The characters are the man (the owner of the nuts), the monkey and the giraffe. The man is presented as the lawful owner. In the version recorded here, it is even mentioned that he finds it unfair not to be able to enjoy the fruits from his labour in the garden.

The story devolves in a somehow circular way, when considering the reestablishment of a formal order. In the parallel linear progression, the monkey dies. This line is dramatically marked by the giraffe's intervention that brings the opportunity to change the course of the story three times. The monkey has the threefold option to decide about his fate.

An interesting side-remark to this story is that I found a similar one in a collection of Arabic tales (Sellnow: 43, who quoted Peseschkian). The first plot, the unwillingness to open the hand and to let the bounty go, was identical. But then the protagonist – a human being in the Arabic case, a man – was open to advice and learned to let go. Confronted with this different variation of the story, one of my informants, an elderly lady of about 60 years commented, *"This story does not sound real for me. It seems to be made up! (...) Our story tells the real problem. That is you can be killed, if you do not listen to advice. He could have left the nuts and find another way later. But he was too dogmatic, sticking to the nuts in his hand. It can happen that you'll die out of stupidity".*

The fox as a mean character and possibilities to deal with his cruelty are also represented in the following story in which the crocodile population is endangered by his assault[9]. In this case

> 'Fox felt that he could live freely and in a peaceful environment if all Crocodiles had gone (...)' He told them that there was a better place to stay, where the water was cooler. He brought even a sample of the water, 'Wow how cold. Wow how cold! Wow how cold! We have to settle there (...).' The crocodiles were so enthusiastic that they took everything, all their eggs and offspring. But the fox led them towards the nearby savanna with thick dry grass, where he set fire on the grass. A small bird, called Kat managed to save two baby crocodiles and dropped them into the river. '(...)As time passed, the two crocodiles reproduced themselves and became many again. When they grew up, they started looking for their enemy, the Fox. Fox realized that the crocodiles were looking for him. Therefore, he stopped coming close to the river. In order to drink, he even invented a long pipe, made from a stick. Instead of going down to the river, he would sit on a tree at the riverside and drink with the pipe from the distance.'

Here we meet the fox again, an evil crook, mean like ever. No one can trust him. His business is not only egoistic but deadly. His outstanding intelligence in thinking up the expulsion of the crocodiles from their original habitat makes the good-humoured crocodiles easy victims. Crocodiles are important animals in Nuer myth of origin. At least one clan – the Ciani – believe that from their mother's side they stem from a female crocodile: the crocodile transformed into a woman, gave birth to a son – Ciani – and returned to the waters after two years[10]. In this story, the crocodiles are close to be massacred and exterminated completely. Only the unexpected intervention of the bird gives the narrative a sense of hope. Eventually this small bird is able to save the whole species! With this unforeseen intercession of the small outsider the story manages to create the plot: eventually the species survives. Fox's

---

[9] 'Fox and Crocodiles', recorded July 2006, Moses Wawich
[10] The origin of the Ciani, recorded Tibang Lam, January 2008

access to the water is even more restricted than it was before. He is not able to enter the water at all any more.

An interesting aspect is that the crocodiles – big and generally feared animals – are saved by a very small bird on the one hand. Evenly important though seems the fact that the survival of the species as such is accomplished by the own potential and reproductive resources of the crocodiles. The latter aspect apparently pertains to the role reproductive strength plays in the social life of any Nuer – male and female alike.

There are some stories of the genre of fables that show the lion to be weaker than much smaller animals. The smaller animals can be mosquitoes (a full swarm that kills the arrogant lion) or a mouse, as in the following story. Considering the limited space, I selected the shorter one, which is the very popular story of '*The mouse and the lion*'[11]:

> '*One day the lion went for hunting. When he became tired he rested under a big tree. While he was asleep, the rat came. The lion woke up, and instantly caught the rat. He felt disturbed. The mouse apologised and begged, 'Father, I did not want to upset you. It was not intended. Please, let me go. It might be that one day it will be me who helps you.' The lion had a good laugh, 'ha, ha, ha, (....) You will help me? But I will let you go, as you are so small. You will not even fill one tooth in my mouth!' Happily the rat ran away.*
>
> *Another day the lion was trapped in a net which was lied out by hunters. He was tightly bound, and the more he moved and tried to get out, the tighter the net became. The lion roared loudly. All animals heard him without knowing what to do. Besides, they were afraid of the lion. But the rat came. 'Do not be afraid,' the rat said when approaching the lion. 'I will help you.' And he started cutting the nets with his teeth, until the lion could come out!*'

In this and another focus group discussion the participants compared the story of the lion and the mouse with the one of the lion and the mosquitoes (where the lion eventually dies). Both stories are about the power of the small. The first story of the mosquitoes though emphasized more on the pride of the lion, whereas the one with the mouse is about might. This story tells us that even the smallest one can contribute, and can help even the mightiest among the animals. Both stories tell people that even small creatures can do something and have power. Any mighty person should be aware of that.

The story of the lion and the mouse seems to be extremely popular among Nuer as well as among Anywaa. Both communities refer to the lion as 'the king of the animals'. Also for the Nuer, who do not know kingdoms, the lion represents the mighty and powerful in Nuer society. '*It is a metaphor. Sometimes these powerful men may abuse the property of the weaker. And this story tells them to be aware of the power of the weak. That your pride may kill you, if you forget about this*'(Gambella town, 22-01-07)

Another story that is similarly known among Nuer and Anywaa is the story of the vulture, the lion and the fox[12]:

> 'Once upon a time, *the lion and the vulture were living together. The lion had an ox, the vulture a cow. They (...) used to take turns in herding the cattle and leading them to the pasture. (.....) the cow became pregnant. At the time when the time for delivery came, the lion arranged that he would take care of the cattle. (...) When the cow delivered, the lion took the*

---

[11] recorded, June 2007

[12] In the Anywaa story the main characters are the hyena, the lion and the monkey; the following version wa recorded in Kwergen (Lare), January 2008

placenta and put it on the anus of the ox. When the vulture came back home, the lion received
her carrying the calf, and said proudly, 'see, my ox delivered this beautiful calf!' (...) The
vulture said, 'you are cheating me!'
As they quarrelled, they called upon the community. The community were some other animals.
(...) The problem was new in the community. Everyone came. Fox came late, though. The lion
was angry, 'Why are you late? We have been waiting for you, fox!' Then fox looked at
everyone and said, 'You know why I am late? I had to boil water for my uncle, who just gave
birth to a son!'
The lion said, 'How can a man deliver a son?' And the fox said, '... and how about your ox?'

The story was allegedly told by the elder to emphasise how important it was to call upon the
council of elders and to find a just solution. Contrary to this intention though, the council as
such plays a subordinate role. The real hero is the fox. Only his intelligence and subversive
cunning makes it possible to oppose the might of the lion. The structure of the plot is circular;
justice is been reinstalled by the smart intervention of the fox.

There is some evidence that this story might not necessarily be originated among the
Nuer. It is not known widely among the Nuer; it is more lively narrated among the Anywaa
and has more variations (Sommer, upcoming). Moreover, the character of the fox is different
from his usual personality. In this story he acts for the common good, on behalf of the vulture
who is been cheated. We have seen that this is quite unusual for the fox, who tends to be just
mean and selfish in other stories. Nevertheless, the story shows that fables travel among
communities, and might be adopted, when there is a need to adjust to new challenges. The
characters get as much as possible adopted into the own system (the hyena transforms into
vulture, the monkey into the fox) , a process that indicates a serious adoption into the own
cultural repertoire. The adoption of this story may therefore hint at the depth of the
interchange between Anywaa and Nuer, and at the same time reflect the felt need to come to
some form of collective decision making process also among the Nuer. At least the
explanation given by the narrator points into the latter direction.

5   *Storytelling in contemporary life*

The following story of Gatluak, the cannibal, was recorded during an interethnic workshop
(Nuer and Anywaa) in Abol, 26 September 2007. Storytelling was not requested as such. The
participants were rather encouraged to share their respective attitudes and traditions towards
peacebuilding in social life.   The following story is already shortened. It reflects many
elements of contemporary life experience. Moreover, it is an excellent example of living lore.
It reveals much about the ambiguity towards peace of the narrator, but also the experiences of
fight, flight and bare abandonment. The community experienced difficult times before they
arrived in the present location, traditional Anywaa territory. Here is the story of the cannibal:

The first part of the story narrates a failed bride-abduction (without her consent) by Gatluak
and his brothers. After this Gatluak left his brothers and told them to leave him alone.

'(...) Then he went to a lake, where he knew that all people would pass by. That pond was crossed by the main road that led to the town of Kaldak[13], which at the time was the headquarters of the SPLA. Whenever someone passed that road with his spear on his back, he then would approach him saying, 'Come on!' 'Where are you going?' Then the person would say, 'I am going to Kaldak.' But Gatluak would say, 'You'll never reach Kaldak! Because I am going to eat you...'. That village is called Kal, indicating that people without cattle live there. And then the name was modified to Kaldak, because people never reached there, after passing that point. (...)

As Gatluak continued killing people at the checkpoint, he realised that he could not eat all immediately, so he started drying their meat on the trees along the road. After the meat dried, he tied it up and went to the market to sell it. (...)' Eventually Gatluak was arrested, but he did not eat in prison. The guards therefore decided to give him a person who was sentenced to death as food. *'This person had to die anyway.(...) But before he killed the condemned man, he asked, 'What have you done to receive the death sentence? Tell me, before I'll eat you!' The man replied, 'I killed my brother. I am a murderer like you. Only that I killed only my brother.' Then Gatluak said, 'If it is like that I will spare you.' He was now in a dilemma and did not really know what to do. (...) Gatluak said, 'ok, ok'. In the morning he reported to the government saying, 'Sorry, but I cannot eat this man. His flesh is poisoned.' The man was released after that.(...)'*

The story continues with the description of the constant trouble he caused in prison. He continued eating human flesh, whenever he could get it. The clou of the story was, when the narrator unleashed the point, *'If we come to the background of Gatluak, he was a Dinka!'*, a disclosure that was followed by heavy turmoil.

After finishing this story the narrator continued explaining his story,

'The reason why I tell this story is: If the condemned man was not clever, he wouldn't have survived. From childhood onwards Gatluak has never forgiven anyone! When he lost his girl during her flight into the tree, his heart got even more infested by hatred.' (...) 'The reason why I am talking about this is: we are sitting together under the same tree and we are one family. If your brother is against you – be patient! Then he'll realise that you are patient, because you are his brother. If you are offended and start retaliating rather than being patient, you'll only show your ignorance. From our ancestors, our mothers were the same. Now we form different ethnic groups, but still we have these common roots. Some people – even from different ethnic groups – have the same nature and the same manners, so that they harmonise. The Anywaa and the Nuer – knowing that we are from the same family – we have to work together. Even if there are problems, or if we get sick, we have to call one another and call them.' (Abol, September 2007)

The story filled various listeners with considerable horror. In many respects this seemingly ruthless and cruel narrative is one of the most complex stories I ever heard during my research.

It turned out to be well known among Nuer, who even claim that the story is real, and that the full name of the person was Gatluak Panyual.

---

[13] Kauda? in South Kordofan was indeed as a local SPLM-headquarters for some time; many Nuer later confirmed that the name of the town was Kaldak, located in Southern Sudan, but no one could trace it on any map

Patterns in the role of the characters: Gatluak first seems to be an ordinary Nuer. Nuer give this name to a child who is born during the construction of the big byre that dominates every hamlet. But he is a trouble maker from the beginning. The story starts with the attempt to raid a bride. He does not bother to pay bride wealth. He is influential among his brothers because he is the strongest among them, based on pure power. When leaving his brothers, thus totally abandoning the social order, he becomes a cannibal, someone who eats his own kind. The dogs, the companions of humans, handed him over to the police. But cannibalism had already become a habit. It was only interrupted when confronted with his own self – the murderer. He is the only one he could not less but identify with. He could not kill him.

The structure of the plots is linear. We follow the protagonist through different stages and adventures. There is no point of return. No initial order, no return to a state of harmonic order. The threat remains. But with the final plot – the revelation that Gatluak is a Dinka – the threat is externalised. The threat is the 'other' – the ethnic group not present in the meeting, in Abol or Gambella. Gatluak is a threat to everyone. He does not have real friends; even his brothers support him reluctantly. But as a powerful loner he can survive.

Ogres, monsters and giants appear in traditional Nuer stories, too. The interaction of fiction and events though is particularly interesting here. The narrator refers to real places. Gatluak is a real man who has a name. The places refer to the Sudanese civil war and to the competition between Dinka and Nuer within the structure of the SPLA/M.

The Nuer in Abol arrived there within the last 10 years. They fled upstream along the river from the area around Jikow, where their livelihood was destroyed during the fighting within the civil war. Many men have a background in the SPLA. The story might even refer to the experience of Ananya 2, which another Nuer, who faught with the SPLA, explained to me as follows (Kwergen, January 2007): 'I was demoralised, because the soldiers began fighting among themselves. I was not happy with that. Nuer and Dinka started killing each other within the army. My friends were Dinka, Shilluk, of different tribes; but now started abandoning the cause we were fighting for. Instead of Arabs we killed each other. It was then that I started to continue my education. (…) (The cause of the separation) was the political goal of having a united Sudan on the one hand – or an independent State of South Sudan. That was the reason.'

At last the storyteller refers also to the myth of the creation of Thiang-Nuer and Anywaa, "our mothers are the same". This myth is very popular, and this is the short version[14],

> *(…) You know that the Thiang-Nuer are descendents of the Anuak? At least from the mother's side.'* It follows the story of Ochudo, the Anywaa myth of origin, where the mythical person (God?). Ochudo impregnated the daughter of the Anywaa king. In the Nuer version though, before leaving the village, *'the man started talking: (…) you will be pregnant with two boys. After giving birth you will open a calabash, remove the inside and place one of the boys inside. You will see the different colour of the face of that boy. (…) She gave birth and put one of the sons inside the calabash. The father added a stick, a spear, hammer and a leopard skin. The calabash was thrown into the river as advised and flowed down the river towards the tribe called Luo. (…) They found the calabash floating in the water and collected it. (…)* A Nuer

---

[14] Lare district, January 2007

girl slept with the offspring of this union, and their descendants are the Nuer clans Gajok, Jok,and Thiang *(Antilop)*. *'The mother of Jok died. The boys remained with the father. The Thiang are now carrying the spear, Jok is carrying the skin. His successor is Duol Korion. He is a very young man. He is living here, not far from here.(... continues the story of the spear)*

In many instances Nuer refer to different myths of creation. This myth is of specific interest, because it is identical with the Anywaa myth in its first part – the appearance of the stranger and the impregnation of the girl. In the Anywaa myth the girl gives birth to one boy only, who later on becomes the first king and source of wisdom for society.

The myth of the common lineage between Anywaa and Nuer through the maternal line is inherited only with the Nuer and seems to be unknown in the Anywaa myths. When the Nuer narrator in the context of Abol – in a situation of still unsettled strives for land – mentions this myth, he strongly urges for their understanding. The seemingly brutal story tells the story of the Nuers' Odyssey until they arrived there; the story suggests that they have overcome and survived incredible hardship – even survived being killed in the bloody civil war (portrayed in Gatluak, the cannibal). Where people eat their own kind and institutions of justice could not cope with the beast. In the context of Gambella depicting the Dinka as the cruel 'other' also served the purpose to unite and to find a common understanding among the local residents – Anywaa and Nuer.

It remains an open question though whether all Anywaa present in the meeting understood the full significance of the story. Many seemed to be quite scared by the image of the bloodthirsty Gatluak, whom they identified as a Nuer. But as the whole group encouraged the storyteller to tell it again for the plenary – and also to make sure that I understand it – I assume that they understood the basic message – to be accepted as one of them, as a human being in need of a new place to live after an adventurous past.

6   *Some common features*

Nuer narratives deal with history, of the own family, the clan and the people. Many of these stories are not presented here, as their focus seemingly is more on building a common identity. They show survival and give hope in desperate situation (the story of the crocodiles). Moreover, as the story of Gatluak the cannibal shows, stories are multilayered and complex as life. They may encapsulate history as well as moral teachings. And they show ways to deal with power. The stories of the lion deal with the relative might of pure power.

The fox we meet again and again. In only one of the collected examples (Moon and Fox) full restitution of the initial state cannot be given – the question of return after death remains an open one. In all other sample stories related with the shrewd, but false and traitorous fox, it is eventually his adversary, the more reliable character that triumphs.

7   *Preliminary findings*

Returning to the initial research questions the following reflections may contain some interim conclusions.

What do local narratives reveal about perceptions of justice and peace?

Justice, in the fables and tales collected, mainly comes from outside – the bird who rescues the crocodiles – or through direct retaliation (the camel who kills the fox). Very often though unfairness prevails and the mean principle wins. Legal institutions (in a broader sense, including prisons and the police) are portrayed as helpless, not able to fully protect the community (prominently in 'Gatluak'). When we look into the process of how justice is supposed to be found, only in one of the stories grievances were brought to the attention of a council of elders (respectively the council of all animals).

Many stories deal with the origin of Nuer and mankind as such, and with kinship ties. These stories, too, give some insight into perceptions of fairness that are of indirect relevance: these stories strongly suggest that fairness is something to be applied within one group of common origin – not necessarily towards the 'other'. Just as the rites and procedures of compensation are strongly internal, the underlying perceptions appear to share this character of ethnicity.

The stories though create a space, where gradual understanding can be achieved in a longer process of exchange. The story of Gatluak may give a basic understanding of Nuer's suffering to the Anywaa listeners.

The adoption of Arab or Anywaa stories shows the vital state of storytelling. The "imported" Arab story for instance, of the greedy monkey who cannot let go – and dies because of his stinginess, met a trait in the psychology of the Nuer which allowed them to absorb and integrate it as their own heritage. By assimilating new elements gleaned from the contact with other groups, they are able to preserve their own culture in a creative process. When I heard it the story seemed completely included into Nuer repertoire. When Anywaa stories are adapted by Nuer in other instances, a process is under way that creates a new space of shared values.

How, according to these stories, shall peace be re-established after violations of life, property and rights?

Some stories re-establish the fair social order. Others clearly reflect the desperation amid the inability of police and the judiciary to effectively deal with brutalised and abusive characters – like with Gatluak, the cannibal. This seemingly is a relatively young story. Several of my informants claimed that Gatluak lived during the time of their grandfathers. The reference to the SPLA in the story could support this. In contrast to the story of Gatluak though, the – almost certainly - older fables re-establish order. The lion fails in many stories, when he becomes too arrogant. These fables deal with the satisfaction of the powerless in overcoming might. In the review group someone said, "We would tell this story (about the lion and the mouse) when someone in power becomes too arrogant!"

The perception of fairness revealed in the stories is certainly not a stable one and is not carved in stone. It is subject to changes and is been modified with new collective experiences in contemporary life.

Story telling is still part of social life as shown before. It will be used not only in teaching the youth, but also in arguing in public discussions. In the perception of people the stories reveal undisputable truth. At the same time they seem to make it easier to criticise the authority.

How do these perceptions relate to 'modern' concepts of justice and peace-building?
The stories collected so far are not always optimistic in achieving justice. Sometimes coincidence helps; very often the seemingly weakest and least important character intervenes for the lucky outcome, like the bird that rescued the young crocodiles, the mouse who saved the lion. When justice is done, it is very often because of the honesty, fearlessness, skills and dedication of one of the main actors.

In most stories, there is not anything like "absolute" justice. Farmers (legal) rights might be violated, but the fellow invaders (for instance the fox and the camel) should behave as companions – not leaving the other alone. The owner of a field of crop does not find our sympathy, but the camel that was cheated by his fellow, the fox. The retaliation is morally fully sanctioned in the story.

Compared with modern concepts of peacebuilding, which is very much based on the definition of well defined interests (Saner 2005; Pfaffenholz 2001; Avruch 2002), such a strategy of negotiating interests may appeal to the Nuer sense for wit, skill and cleverness. The one, who is able to present his interests and even convinces his adversaries, can be respected. Whether or not the outcome of such a process would be sustainable and acceptable in the long run, remains doubtful, after analysing the traditional lore. In many narratives justice comes mainly by coincidence. Thus it needs to be met with scepticism whether Nuer would easily stick to a negotiated agreement. With the next upcoming opportunity it might rather look like 'fate' had turned and required a new strategy. Nuer here seemed to be extremely flexible and prepared to adjust to the slightest development – and to changes and shifts in power.

8   Outlook

It may be legitimately questioned whether any serious conclusion can be drawn from the analysis of the tales collected during my fieldwork. First of all it might be questioned whether the art of story telling is still alive, or rather overshadowed by "modern" means of communication and entertainment. To my experience the art is still alive, and in development. Modern life takes its tribute, of course. But as most Nuer villages and settlements outside the town of Gambella until very recently were still without electricity. But even now mass-media have not yet reached the general population in the towns and villages of the region. People need to entertain themselves – they tell the old stories and they develop them further.

Secondly, doubt might be legitimate, as to which conclusions could be seriously drawn from a collection of a number of tales and fables. Is the collection of the stories not just as arbitrary as the later interpretation? I tried to reduce this risk by introducing the review groups as a second step (after the collection of the stories). The review groups consisted of listeners of the same ethnic group. These groups in many cases came up with very clear interpretations how they understood the stories and what they meant to them.

Thirdly, it needs to be further clarified, in which way the underlying perceptions of the stories will be instrumental in developing policies towards justice, healing and peacebuilding. One level of application could be the invention of story-telling in grass-root community dialogues. Telling stories – thereby communicating depth and values of their own culture – broadens the horizon and has shown a healing effect in different circumstances (Zupan 2004: 338). At a second level though the stories reveal to the attendant observer priorities in approaching justice and peace of a group of people. Ideally this knowledge can be transformed into programs towards understanding and creating peace which are responding to the needs of the people.

In summary, I still feel that it is worthwhile trying to analyse the material, which can give us some understanding about the feeling of the people of Nuer towards truth, justice and peace.

In the limited sense of creating a new and joined space of shared values, storytelling may help to facilitate communication between segregated and divided groups. They can establish links and understanding, thus contributing to more peaceful relationships and modes of dealing with conflicts of interest in the society of Gambella.

Older conflicts will be transformed only when a basic sense of justice will be met. Each group has specific perceptions about justice and peace which are rooted in history, culture and tradition. The whole picture of the potential of the different ethnicities in unfolds itself in the concert of the group, as the comprehensive study, which is under way, will show. So far it can be stated that Nuer society, in its dilemma to cope with what is often perceived as modernity may need to mobilise its own traditions and engage in a constructive processes of change. These traditions may change in the process, but can contribute to society to become fitter – and less vulnerable – when confronted with globalisation in its various forms.

Bibliography

Bahru Zewde (1991), *A history of modern Ethiopia, Eastern African Studies*, London

Central Statistical Authority, *Housing and Population Census, 1994*, February 1999, Addis Ababa .

_____, *Statistical Report*, December 1995, Addis Ababa.

Chan Gatkuoth (2007), *Gambella Conflicts: The Role of the Government in Preventing and Resolving Conflicts*, in: Wolbert G.C. Smidt - Kinfe Abraham (eds.): *Discussing Conflict in Ethiopia, Conflict Management and Resolution. Proceedings of the Conference "Ethiopian and German Contributions to Conflict Management and Resolution"*, Addis Ababa 11 – 12 November 2005, Lit-Verlag Münster.

Clapham, Christopher (2002), *Controlling Space in Ethiopia*, in: Wendy James, Donal L. Donham, Eisei Kurimoto, Alessandro Triuzi (eds.), *Remapping Ethiopia*, Oxford.

Czekelius, Annette R. (1993), *Of 'Meaning' and 'Significance': The Emic Interpretation of a West African Tale*, in: *Arican Languages and Cultures*, Vol. 6, No. 2. (1993), 121-132.

Evans-Pritchard, E.E. (1969/1940), *The Nuer, A description of the modes of livelihood and political institutions of a Nilotic people*, Oxford University Press, Oxford, NY.

Falge, Christiane, (2006), *The global Nuer. Transnational Modes of Livelihoods*, Martin-Luther-Universität Halle-Wittenberg, Halle.

Dereje Feyissa (2004), *Events leading to the December massacre and its aftermath*, paper

Dereje Feyissa (2005), *The experience of Gambella Regional State*, Osaka

Finnegan, Ruth (1992), *Oral Traditions and the Verbal Arts*, Routledge, London, New York

Galtung, Johan (2000), *After Violence: 3R, Reconstruction, Reconciliation, Resolution: Coping With Visible and Invisible Effects of War and Violence,* http://www.transcend.org/TRRECBAS.HTM

Johnson, Douglas H. (1980), *Nuer expansion and the Ethiopian Empire,* in: Donham, James (eds), *Working Papers and History in Imperial Ethiopia:* The Southern Periphery from the 1880s to 1974, African Studies Centre Cambride

Johnson, Douglas H. (2003), *The Root Causes of Sudan's Civil Wars,* James Currey, Oxford.

Meckelburg, Alexander (2007), *Ethnische Gewalt in Süd-Westäthiopien: Konflikte, Akteure, Perzeptionen,* unpublished master-thesis, University of Hamburg

Pankhurst, Alula (2002), *Surviving Resettlement in Wellega,* in Wendy James ed al (ed.), Oxford.

Saner, Raymond (2nd ed., 2005), The Negotiation Expert, Martinus Nijhoff Publ, The Hague.

Sellnow, Reinhard (2004), *Die mit den Problemen spielen: Ratgeber zur kreativen Problemlösung,* Stiftung Mitarbeit, Bonn.

Sommer, Monika M (2007), *Traditional instruments of conflict resolution and mediation among the people of Gambella, Ethiopia,* in: Wolbert G.C. Smidt - Kinfe Abraham (eds.): *Discussing Conflict in Ethiopia, Conflict Management and Resolution. Proceedings of the Conference "Ethiopian and German Contributions to Conflict Management and Resolution",* Addis Ababa 11 – 12 November 2005, Lit-Verlag Münster.

Sommer, Monika M (upcoming), *Perceptions of Fairness and Justice Among the Anywaa living in the Ethiopian region of Gambella: their relevance to conflict transformation,* contribution to the 2nd European Conference on African Studies, ECAS, Leiden, June 2007.

Young, John (1999), *Along Ethiopia's Western Frontier: Gambella and Benishangul in Transition,* in: The Journal of Modern African Studies, Vol. 37, No 2 321-346.

Zupan, Natascha (2004), *Facing the Past and Transitional Justice in Countries of Former Yugoslavia p 327-342 ,* in: Berghof Handbook on Transitional Justice, Berghof Research Center for Constructive Peace Management, Berlin.

Some Preliminary Considerations on Collective Violence, Identity and Conflict and their Coherence: The Case of Gambella, Western Ethiopia

Alexander Meckelburg

This essay focuses on the description and analysis of collective violence in the Gambella Regional State, Ethiopia's western-most regional state (here after Gambella)[1]. In scientific debate, conflict research in Gambella has primarily focused on the relations between the two major groups in the region, those of the Anywaa and the Nuer. This paper takes a closer look at the relations of one of these indigenous groups, the Anywaa[2], with another group locally referred to as Highlanders[3], who are settlers, workers and businessmen from different parts of the Ethiopian highland plateau. Historically, these two groups have entered into violent conflicts in different constellations and for different reasons. This history of violence has created a burdened coexistence and made violence a reoccurring component of their relations. By analysing two exemplary violent events from the recent history of the two groups, this essay wishes to contribute to the understanding of the nature, the past and maybe even the future of the conflict as such[4].

Gambella: History, Peoples, Conflicts

Gambella is one of Ethiopia's classical peripheral border-regions[5]. It looks back onto a history of conflict and violence that has involved different groups at different times. Serving as a hunting ground for slave traders in the late 19th century, it swung back and forth between two governments, the British-Sudanese and the Christian-Ethiopian empire, due to their struggle for control over the region. Later, during the second Sudanese Civil War (the war in the southern Sudan restarted in 1983), the Southern Peoples' Liberation Army (SPLA) used it as a training and recruitment base and for cross-border incursions. Accordingly the trade of arms affected the security situation of the local population. During the same time, the region's

---

[1] The Regional State of Gambella, also Gambella Peoples' Regional State (*yägambella hizzbočč killil*) was lifted to the status of a regional state in the new framework of federalism since 1991. Before, it had belonged to Illubabor province as an *awraja* (sub-province).

[2] The Anywaa are also found in literature under the names Anuak or Anyuak.

[3] On this term see next page

[4] This essay is for its most part the essence of my MA thesis submitted to the Institute of Ethiopian Studies (Afrikanistik/Äthiopistik) at the University of Hamburg, Asien-Afrika-Institut in September 2007. The thesis is based on two field-trips in the late summer of 2005 and 2006. I am thankful to everybody at the *Gambella Peace and Development Council*, where I was given the opportunity to work and be part of a local peace-building initiative for some time, which enabled me to learn about the perceptions on peace and violence of some of the people in Gambella.

[5] Gambella lies approximately 700 km south-west from the national centre of Ethiopia: As a border-region I define here a place that is regarded as having played no direct role in the state-building of the Ethiopian empire, and that was used as a resource-base for material goods including slaves. It's conflicts are directly intermingled with those across the border, in the case of Gambella, with that of the Sudan and - from a demographic perspective - ethnic groups are living on both sides of the border.

demography severely changed when up to 60, 000 famine affected people were relocated to the region from the northern highlands of Ethiopia, Wollo and Tigray, and from the southern highlands during the nation-wide resettlement campaign. With the collapse of the socialist regime known as the Derg[6] and the introduction of the ethnic-based federalism as the current constitutional framework, the two major indigenous groups, the Anywaa and the Nuer, repeatedly entered into violent conflicts with each other, between 1991 and 2002 (Dereje, 2003; Sommer 2005). Currently, the constitutionally recognized people in the region are the Nuer (40% of the population), the Anywaa (27%), the Majangir (6%), and small ethnic groups of Komo and Opuo (each 3%) (1994 national housing census of Ethiopia; quoted from Sommer, 2005). A group of non-indigenous people, locally referred to as the Highlanders[7], are contributing to the demography in Gambella, too. Today they constitute 24% of the population (ibid.). While the Nuer are predominantly agro-pastoralists with an increasing tendency to a sedentary lifestyle, the Anywaa practise agriculture along the fertile banks of the rivers that run through Gambella and into the Sudan. Both Anywaa and Nuer play a crucial role in the local political scene, the administration and the police force. The Majangir make a living from hunting and collecting honey and practise shifting cultivation to some extent. The Opuo and Komo[8] groups practise shifting agriculture and keep only small numbers of cattle. The Highlanders are engaged in different forms of economics. Many run the local businesses in the few centres such as Gambella-town, Bonga, Itang, Pinyudo and such like. Others are working in the local administration. Out of the many thousands that were brought to Gambella during the time of resettlement in the 1980's, only a small number is still living from agriculture. Additionally the Highlanders constitute the core of the large contingents of the ENDF (Ethiopian National Defence Forces) stationed in the region.

Theoretical framework: Conflict, Violence and Identity

The terms "conflict" and "violence" and "identity" are in daily use, even though the terminology in social sciences and its understanding gravely differs from scholar to scholar.

---

[6] After Ethiopia's last emperor Haile Selassie I was deposed by a military coup, a transitional military
government, generally referred to as *Derg*, which is the Amharic word for *committee*, was in power between
1974 and 1991.

[7] The Highlanders are an ethnically heterogeneous category of people from several ethnic backgrounds defined first an foremost by the fact that they belong to groups living in the Ethiopian highlands (cp. *däga* amhr.: highland; *dägañña* amhr.: highlander) The Anywaa refer to these people as *gaala* (cp. *Galla*) which emphasises the lighter pigmented skin colour of most of the Cushitic and Semitic highland inhabitants compared to the darker pigmented skin colour of the nilotic groups. In return the Highlanders may refer to the Anywaa and other nilotic groups from the lowlands as *tiqur* or *shanqilla*, rather derogative terms that emphasise the skin colour (*tiqur*, i.e. black) or the history of slavery these groups fell prey to: *shanqilla* (i.e. slave).

[8] Although it would be worth taking closer consideration of these small ethnic units, which has hardly been done, these groups, together with the Majangir, do not play a significant role in this paper. While the Majangir contribute to the conflict map of Gambella since conflicts erupted into violence between them and Anywaa as well as Highlanders, the Opuo and Komo are part of the wider conflict map since they are in close contact with both Anywaa and Nuer due to their own group size. Some Opuo men for example were fighting, until recently, along with the militant Anywaa based Gambella Peoples' Liberation Movement/ Front (GPLM/F) in the region along the river Jikow.

Due to this preconception, I have tried to generate some essential thoughts, inspired by different scholars, pragmatically to come to a framework for discussing violence in the case of Gambella. This attempt reflects the difficulty between theory (the framework) and practise (retelling stories on violence) and mirrors the limits of being preoccupied with violence itself. Conflict, by definition, is a social fact, characterized by the disputes of two or more factions over natural, political, or social resources or opinions that are based on the structural imbalance of the two groups (Imbusch, 2006: 69). Conflicts therefore do not necessarily involve violence. But if violence occurs, uncontrolled, controlled or purposely, it can be understood as a medium of conflict. Violence and conflict therefore are connected. Conflict may occur without violence, however violence rarely occurs without conflict. Accordingly, the analysis of violence may contribute to the analysis of the conflict itself.

Violence as a scientific term is controversial according to its content. Scholars distinguish political, structural or physical violence. One might also argue that violence in different cultural settings is perceived differently (Grabbert, 2004). In the words of Carolyn Nordstrom (1997: 6), "writing about violence is not a simple matter. The subject is fraught with assumptions, presuppositions, and contradictions. Like power, violence is essentially contested: everyone knows it exists, but no one agrees on what actually constitutes the phenomenon." Here I intend to discuss violence as a social interaction that uses physical force and is intended to cause bodily harm or kill: While violence is not the most frequent form of conflict manifestation, it is considered its most fierce (Grabbert, 2004). Neither primitive nor abnormal, violence is the "narrowing of the available forms of action and at the same time it is a strategic choice" (Elwert, 2000: 9), an obstacle for the utilization of compromises since the death of people in violent conflicts changes the very nature of the conflict and makes it more difficult to be solved (Bar-Tal, 2000: 67). Furthermore, violence is a marker, a signal of social contradictions, and its analysis can contribute to the understanding of the contradictory social and political circumstances in which it emerges.

Specifically, this paper deals with collective violence, a direct form of violence which involves groups on the side of the perpetrators and the victims, and to a certain extent modes of control (Imbusch, 2006: 92).

There are several questions that can be applied to the understanding of violence in a society: Who uses violence? How is the violence used? Who are the victims of violence? (Imbusch, 2006: 83-85). One may also question the meaning of violence for conflict: The occurrence of violence leaves enduring impressions on any given society. It will result in the persistent will to revenge, delegitimisation and victimisation of the perpetrators as well as among the victims (Bar-Tal, 2000). It will elevate the conflict to a level more likely for violence to appear again. Given that fact, if violence once occurred, it will most probably reproduce itself. This will happen along difficult social circumstances, which have been described by Ervin Staub (1999: 195): "[...] such as severe economic problems, intense political conflict or rapid and substantial social change". Staub (ibid.) concludes that such circumstances lead to desires in human beings, such as the need for security or rebuilding of group esteem.

„This form of need fulfilment may also turn them against others. By devaluating and scapegoating others people defend their identities and views of themselves and escape feelings of responsibility for their own and their group's inability to protect them and their families." (Staub, 1999: 196).

With the above mentioned, several aspects and preconditions of collective violence are denominated.

The other key term in the headline of this paragraph is identity, which in this context points to ethnic identity. Ethnicity in the Gambella region is, as far as my evaluation is concerned, the catalyst for violence. If this is true, it also comprises the political setting in which violence occurs since ethnicity has been lifted to an all-embracing political concept of today's Ethiopian politics. Ethnicity today is largely understood in a functional way. The primordial view of ethnicity defining it by language, territory, belief-systems and descent beliefs, has roughly changed to the understanding that ethnicity is more a vehicle to group-mobilisation, and the boundaries of ethnicity are defined by the elite's will to recruit followers (Kaufman, 2001: 17). Additionally another approach seem fruitful for the Gambella case and that is, that ethnic conflict emerges along group comparison and juxtaposing group worth (Horowitz, 2000: 166). Groups use stereotypes of the other group to distinguish between "them" and "us" and accessorily a feeling of being "backward" compared to an "advanced" group (ibid.) disburdens the use of violence for the alleged backward group.

Violence, conflict and ethnicity are interwoven in several ways. Ethnicity is a medium of the conflict, while violence may be its form. If conflicts between groups use ethnicity to distinguish the enemies, violence manifests the "ethnic" boundary between them. Violence then may produce ethnic victims and ethnic perpetrators. The more violence is involved, the more difficult these boundaries may be crossed. It is more likely for ethnic conflicts to erupt in violence when ethnic fears of extinction or foreign infiltration are met and "myths" are being created to justify the violence (Kaufman, 2001). This is to say that violence needs ancient (ethnic) hatreds that are not necessarily ancient by definition but are renewed and reproduced generation after generation (Schlee, 2001).

Anywaa and Highlanders: A History of Violence

The purpose of the following paragraph will be to shed some light on the interaction between the Ethiopian state and Gambella as a periphery. Furthermore, I will discuss several features regarding the common history of Anywaa and Highlanders in the region. The settling of Highlanders in Gambella may be divided into three historic processes:

It seems that, during the imperial period, the main function of Highlanders coming to the region was that of agents of the government, soldiers and traders.

Almost one hundred years later, during the socialist period in the 1980s, the region served as a point of arrival for up to 60,000 Highlanders who had been forced to move in the course of the nation-wide resettlement program (sub-chapter 1).

Today, the Highlanders are stationed in the military or run local businesses, work in the administration and only few are left as agriculturalists on the countryside (sub-chapter 2).

Early contacts between Anywaa and the Oromo from the western highlands of Ethiopia reach back to the 17th and 18th century, when the Oromo marched to the western escarpment of the Ethiopian highland plateau and the Anywaa settled on the foot of the highlands. The use of the Anywaa word *gaala* (a word which is by now widely used for the Highlanders as well as for the Ethiopian government) goes back to this period (Dereje, 2003: 285). These early contacts were peaceful and resulted in mutual and tight trade relations in the 19th century (Bahru, 1976: 26).

Only the *Shoan* expansion of the Ethiopian empire under Menelik II institutionalized the relations between the two groups. The leader of the Leeqa-Oromo Jote Tullu had loosely incorporated parts of the Anywaaland into his realm. After his submission to Menelik II he became tributary toward the emperor and extracted such tributes from peoples within his reach. Thus, the constellations of power in the region had changed. In terms of power the Amhara stood on top followed by the Oromo and than again followed local Anywaa chiefs (Dereje, 2003: 287).

Ethiopia was foremost interested in the region's goods, namely slaves and ivory. Extracting both, the Anywaa were, on the one hand, directly affected by slave raids but on the other hand the need for ivory brought sufficient modern weapons to the region, from which the Anywaa could participate. Thus they could save themselves from the expansion of the Nuer and several expeditions of suppression by both the Ethiopian and the British-Sudanese administration (Evans-Prichard, 1940: 13-15).

Despite the fact that the Anywaa have been able to exploit the rivalries between the British and the Ethiopian government to some degree, the incorporation into the Ethiopian empire has left lasting impressions on the Ethiopian Anywaa society even today: Still alive in the Anywaa's perception of the state is the memory of slavery[9] and political and economic marginalisation (Dereje, 2006: 210). Furthermore through the "remarkable success" (Dereje, 2003: 292) of the Anywaa in resisting the colonial powers as well as their pastoral enemies, the Nuer, the Anywaa developed strong ethnic pride and "a collective memory that kept the spirit of resistance alive" (ibid.).

The Resettlement Program and the Conflict

Throughout the imperial period, the conflicts between Anywaa and Highlanders remained in periodic conflicts. The resistance of the Anywaa was focused on the state and the Highlanders, since the state was represented by their appearance as governmental agents for example or as police. Shumet (1985) has collected several protocols of Anywaa raiding imperial police stations during the 1950's. The resistance towards the tax-policy of the regime had inspired such raids. The revolution of 1974 brought lasting changes to Ethiopia in general and to Gambella in particular. Contrary to the imperial regime of Haile Selassie, the new military junta was more conscious of the ethnic contradictions in the multi-ethnic Ethiopian empire (Clapham, 2002: 14). Its political aim was to subdue all ethnic groups under an omnipresent state, devoted to the construction of socialism (ibid.). Accordingly, nationalism

---

[9] In return the stigmatization of the Anywaa as former people falling prey to slavery is also kept alive by the Highlanders, in form of the terminology *shanqilla* and *barya* (i.e. slave)

and the emergence of the national liberation movements like in Tigray, among the Oromo or the Somalis were portrayed as the major obstacles for socialism (Merera, 2003).

Christopher Clapham has defined the politics of the Derg as *encaderment* :

> "It [the Derg] amounted to a project of encaderment, or incorporation into structures of control, which was pursued with remarkable speed and ruthlessness. It sought to intensify the longstanding trajectory of centralized state formation by removing the perceived source of peripheral discontent and espousing an ideal of nation-statehood in which citizens would equally be associated with, and subjected to an omnipotent state". (Clapham, 2002: 14).

On the political level, this project meant the establishment of a single-party state and the suppression of any form of opposition (Dereje, 2003). On the social level, the project was embarked through the *zämmäjja* (Development through cooperation campaign). Students and teachers were sent to the countryside in order to alphabetise the rural masses and help them to be free from the former *yoke of tyranny* (i.e. the former feudalism embodied in the *gäbbar*-system). As a matter of fact, it was a way to set in motion the cultural revolution (Dereje 2003, Clapham, 2002). Lastly, on the economic level, the project focused on the resettlement and villagisation program.

The politics of the Derg had various serious effects on the Anywaa. From the perspective of modernisation, especially the traditional markers of the Anywaa society such as traditional leadership, marriage system, and rituals were banished as backward and anti-revolutionary (Kurimoto, 2001; 2002; Dereje 2003). Especially the traditional system of leadership fell prey to the Derg's politics "to crush any alternative forms of power, from the imperial kingdom to centralised indigenous political systems of ritual leaders" (Dereje, 2003: 304). These politics had mixed effects on the Anywaa, while the attempt to change their traditional system led to a rebellion in 1978, led by the *kwaaro*[10] Amed Umed, that was violently crushed by the Ethiopian government some years later. In the course of the rebellion, some militant Anywaa had turned violently against teachers from the highlands and Derg officials in the region (Dereje, 2003: 307). For others among the Anywaa, the political change brought new opportunities. Women were most directly affected by the change, as they were no longer subdued to traditional roles (Kurimoto, 2002). For young men, the changes brought more freedom in marriage and the educational training meant the chance to be sent to Addis Ababa or Eastern Europe for political training (Dereje, 2003: 309).

The aspect of the resettlement's effects is most important, as it is also a little discussed aspect of the history of Gambella.

The Gambella Settlement Project was carried out on behalf of the socialist government through the Relief and Rehabilitation Commission. Most of the settlers (96%) came from those regions that were most heavily affected from the occurrence of famines: Wollo (63%), Shoa (18%) and Tigray (15%) (Pankhurst, 1992:56). Those regions with the smallest population density had to host the most participants of the nation wide settlement project. In Gambella, consequentially, the number of settlers made up one third of the population (Pankhurst, 1992: 57). Five settlement complexes were being established in the region: Ukuna, Tata Zuria, Perpengo and Ubala, and additionally a so-called mixed integrated

---

[10] The Anywaa's traditional political system is defined by two integral political offices that of *kwaaro* and that of the *niyeye*.

resettlement scheme known as the Baro-Abol Rehabilitation and Support Program (BARSP) (Dereje, 2003: 312)[11].

Until today, the period and the forceful campaign to resettle "foreigners" in the lands of the Anywaa is being seen as the starting point to exterminate the Anywaa, a plan carried out by the socialist government and its successor. This is also an integral part of the human rights advocacy of the Anywaa diaspora. These views and the fears of foreign infiltration, extermination and loss of land, were also seen by international observers, namely the NGO *Cultural Survival*:

> „Genocide is conducted against the Anuak people in Ethiopia by several means: (1) by dispossessing them of their lands through the resettlement program; (2) by undermining their resource base through destroying their agricultural fields, prohibiting hunting and, possibly, by ecologically degrading the Gambella area; (3) through attempts to interbreed them with northern Ethiopians in integrated resettlement; (4) by destroying their traditional way of life through confiscating domestic animals and such accoutrements as marriage beads; and (5) by using them as cannon fodder in various civil wars." (Cultural Survival Quarterly, July 31, 1981; Issue 5.3.).

Such accounts of incidents are told with passion among the Anywaa of Gambella today. One citation from an interview conducted in Gambella-town on October 16th 2006 features many of the same memories:

> „But some of the Anywaa said that they [i.e. the government] want to assimilate the Anywaa. In Gok, Potchalla, in all Anywaa areas, they came to destroy the Anywaa community. They made their militia and started to kill Anywaa. Also Anywaa were organized in militias. But there was no resistance since the Anywaa were only armed with sticks. (...) They [i.e. the Highlanders] brought alcohol to make the people [i.e the Anywaa] drunk. They brought prostitution and theft. By the use of alcohol they made Anywaa men go to bed with highland girls. They wanted to extinct the black colour. (...) Students were forced to build houses. And people were forced to clear their living grounds. I was working in Pochalla. Under control of the military there was no water and no sleep. Food was rationed. Many were forced to work. Many houses were built and the old ones were forced to cut the forest. I was among the student union. There were educated people [i.e. Anywaa] like Agwa Alemo[12] who told the people that Highlanders came to Anywaaland to destroy the Anywaa. But the Anywaa did nothing. They could not. When my life was getting terrible I was made a soldier and then fought in Asmara. I came back to Gambella only ten years before."

In this account we find not only confirmation for the descriptions of the aforementioned *Cultural Survival* but also confirmation on how alienating the resettlement program was

---

[11] Apart from devastating effects on the ecology and the fauna of Gambella, the Anywaa lost large lands to the sites. According to Kurimoto (2001: 267), the Anywaa used to describe those times with the acronym of the 4Ks: *kac* – hunger – *kwac* – begging – *kap* – prostitution – *ku* – theft, expressing the effect the infiltration of Highlanders had on their lives.

[12] Agwa Alemo has worked as a district commissioner for the Jikaw district. He was dismissed from his job, since he was accused to be cooperating with the Gambella Peoples' Liberation Movement (GPLM). He fled from Gambella and joined the Front that operated from the Sudan. Later, Agwa became the organisation's chairperson. (Dereje, 2003; Chan 2006).

perceived. It was neither planned with, nor discussed with Anywaa. Instead of being consulted, the Anywaa were forced to contribute to the "incorporation of foreigners" and to accept profound changes in the land they saw as their inherited home.

The settlers' perspective is, to a certain extent, different. Some of them have had to leave their homeland due to the famine and others, who, in search for new opportunities, had believed to take advantage of the government's offer to settle in the south, they were disappointed when they reached the area.

The following accounts have been collected in Shebo[13] in late October 2006. Interviewees were either members of the settlement campaign, who had been relocated to Shebo from other settlement sites in Gambella, or refugees who had fled to Shebo after the wave of attacks by the Anywaa, which occurred mainly during the breakdown of the socialist government (see further below).

For the settlers, the situation was difficult indeed. They had to struggle with insufficient living conditions and diseases which before had been unknown to them. Many of the people I interviewed had not been forced to go to Gambella, but followed the government's propaganda saying that virgin lands were waiting for them to be settled, where the government and its associated organisations would ensure the availability of huts and cattle. But as soon as the settlers reached Gambella, things looked quite differently. Apart from diseases, the huts the people met were ill-constructed. Some recalled building loft beds, since during the raining   season the huts were flooded with water to such an extent that it became impossible to light a fire. Considering the living conditions, the relocation to Shebo meant a lot of benefits for the life of the settlers: The fields were easier to cultivate, the rivers were further away, and still the land was fertile. However, like in other resettlement sites (see also Pankhurst, 1992; Wolde-Selassie, 2003), the social living conditions were hard. Work routine was imposed and the settlers were under constant control of the PA (Peasant Association) militia. An interviewee tapered the situation ironically by saying, "Without permission, you were not even allowed to cross the muddy street". The settlers had to work up to seven days a week for the collective farm, but in return they were only given a small amount of land for their own use. The worship of religion was restricted. While worshipping the Ethiopian Orthodox belief was only restricted, other religions were completely banned. As a former settler and pastor of the *qalä hiwot* church recalled, the worship had to take place secretly, and he himself has been arrested several times by the settlers militia. When informants were asked to describe the relationship between the Anywaa and the settlers, the general tendency was to emphasise the harmonic and peaceful relationship between the two groups: both settlers and Anywaa benefited from the offered educational facilities in the settlements. Their relationship was additionally assured through trade, and even the existence of marriage relations has been mentioned.

---

[13] To my knowledge. Shebo is the last existing settlement complex in the Gambella region. There, apart from some settlers who are still living in the region of Pinyudo, the Highlanders (most of them Kambattaa) are still making their living from agriculture. Shebo was eventually designed by the Derg authorities in response to the inhospitable living conditions in the other settlement complexes. After the outbreak of collective violence against the settlers at the time of the breakdown of the socialist regime, many settlers fled to Shebo for refuge, since the place did not exactly belong to the catchment-area of the Anywaa.

However, this peaceful coexistence did not last too long. The establishment of the Gambella Peoples' Liberation Front (GPLF) led to onslaughts on different settlement complexes in the region. The Front was essentially established in response to the ongoing alienation of the Anywaa from regional power (Dereje, 2003). As the involvement of the Derg regime in the Sudanese civil war gradually increased, the SPLA used the Gambella region and its refugee camps as training and support camps. As a consequence of a steady strengthening relationship with the Ethiopian government, the SPLA was assigned to administer the region. This produced a power imbalance between Anywaa and Nuer. Furthermore, the Anywaa became more and more alienated by the Nuer's increasing numerical dominance. The discontent grew with the harsh measures the SPLA used in administering the region. Here, Kurimoto (1997) sees a clear connection between the behaviour of the SPLA and the continuous violent relations between the two groups.

An interviewee, a Nuer, recalls the behaviour of the SPLA troops:

> „When there was fighting among the people or murder, the SPLA would come. Everybody involved in the fight would have to line up. The soldiers would kill one or two, whether they were involved in the fight or not, did not matter. Then the soldiers would take all the cattle from the two parties involved as a punishment. That was how the SPLA kept the peace among the people (Interview, September 20th 2005, Gambella-town)."

The Anywaa's resentment on the SPLA and the fear of foreign infiltration resulted in the establishment of the GPLF, which was soon supported by other ethno-nationalist movements like the Tigray Peoples' Liberation Front (TPLF) or the Oromo Liberation Front (OLF):

> „On top of political grievances that alienated the Anywaa elites as well as the ordinary men and women, the GPLM drew on cultural rhetic for political mobilization, particularly appealing to the emotive dimension of territoriality [...]" (Dereje, 2003: 315).

Liberating the region from the Nuer and the Highlanders was part of the political program of the Front and resulted in onslaughts on settlers' complexes and government officials.

The settlers faced a more extreme form of collective violence when, with the downfall of the socialist regime, the sites were attacked by civilian Anywaa and militias.

The connection between resettlement and violent ethnic conflict is not new. The situation described by Wolde-Selassie (2003) for Mettekel very much mirrors the situation in Gambella at the same time:

> „The relations between Gumuz and state-sponsored resettlers are characterized by worse hostilities, causing bloody conflicts that have claimed lives on both sides. The ethnic conflict, mistrust, and hatred continued slowly throughout the period up to the fall of the Derg. The already volatile relations between the two groups then burst out into open ethnic conflict that resulted in bloodshed claiming considerable human lives on both sides immediately after the 1991 political change in the country." (Wolde-Selassie, 2003: 255/56).

It is also true for Gambella at the same time, "When Mengistu had fled to Zimbabwe" (this expression is common to describe the time and the downfall of the regime), the settlement complexes were swept with violent attacks. The Anywaa demanded back their territory. Some interviewees remembered ultimatums that the Anywaa gave them as to when and how they had to leave the land, leaving all property behind. Then they were told to "return to where they came from". In other cases the settlements were attacked. The Anywaa looted the properties, burnt the huts of the settlers and killed indiscriminately.

A woman, 15 years of age by the time of the Anywaa attacks, recalls:

> „On Ginbot, 23 in 1983[14], Ukuna was attacked. In Ukuna so many people have died. But I don't know why. We had nothing, no water and no food. Some who killed were fellow students. We were in grade five together. They killed the people by knife and gun. They killed fathers, mothers, children. In some houses everybody was dead. It was when there was no government that they started to kill. Maybe it was envy. The settlers had markets, trade and tea-houses. Ukuna was in the middle of the forest. There were four villages. In three they killed everybody. Only in *village three* some people survived. I don't think there is a connection between Ukuna and December 13th [the onslaught on Anywaa civilians in Gambella town on the 13th December 2003; see the following chapter]. [...] Highlanders and Anywaa cannot live together. The Highlanders are afraid".

Resulting from the destruction of the settlement sites, the settlers fled to Gambella town, went back to their original homes, and only a few found refuge in Shebo, where they still make a living as farmers. Despite being alienated and afraid of further violence, a farmer concluded his feelings of home in comparison to Gambella:

> „Once you are out of your mother's womb - can you go back? It is like that. For us, the old, it is easy. We could go back. But what about our children? Is this not their home? They have adopted the life, the climate and the food."

December 13th 2003: The Symbolism of Violence

Further alienation came along with ethnic federalism successively introduced since 1991. In terms of violence, the new constitutional framework caused severe effects. On the side of the Anywaa-Nuer relations, the birth of the Gambella Peoples' Regional State saw bloody confrontations. Kurimoto (1997: 807) describes the situation as follows:

> „It seems as if hatred and hostilities which had been accumulated during the Derg era exploded all at once when the powerful centralised regime collapsed and there was a sort of power vacuum." (Kurimoto, 1997: 807).

The group's relations were marked by the violent confrontation of the group's elites and their struggle for political control of Gambella's regional politics (Dereje, 2003; Sommer, 2005). Consequently, as Dereje (2006) has pointed out, Gambella became the case to exemplify the weaknesses of Ethiopia's federal experience.

Also on the side of the Highlander-Anywaa relations the changing political framework enforced violent confrontations. Non-indigenous settler groups, such as the Highlanders in Gambella, have suffered a declining status due to the political changes. The transition of political power to the indigenous elites has had similar effects in several regional states. Asnake (2004) has pointed to the deportation of settlers in the regional states of Oromia, and Dereje (2006) has described comparable situations for the states of Somali and Beni-Shangul-Gumuz. Basically, these conflicts resulted from age-old ethnic animosities and aimed at

---

[14] Ginbot is the ninth month of the Ethiopian calendar, comprising the 9th of May until the 7th of June of the Gregorian calendar. The year 1983 E.C. corresponds to the year 1990 G.C.

expelling the settlers from the states and sending them back to their states of origin corresponding to their ethnic background. Similar attempts have been made in Gambella, as a consequence of conflicts between the Gambella Peoples' Democratic Congress (GPDC) and the Gambella Peoples' Democratic Movement (GPDM)[15] (*abyotawi demokrasi*, p. 10).

Essentially, the Highlanders occupy an undefined role in the new constitutional framework. In the sense of the constitution, they are not a recognised group. Despite this, they are still playing a major role in the administration of the Regional State and in the economy of Gambella. Because of their better knowledge of Amharic, which has been determined as the continuing working language of the administration, they constitute up to 40% of the skilled labour in the administrative apparatus (Dereje, 2006). They run all transport and logistics as well as the service sector. Nevertheless, they may currently be regarded as *semi-citizens*, a term originally applied to the Anywaa by Douglas Johnson (1986) to describe their unfulfilled integration into the Ethiopian society. The government ironically defined the former resettlers as relicts of the old regime, largely chauvinists and did not care much about them (Dereje, 2003). Additionally, governmental intervention made ethnic animosities more likely when an administrative reform was put in place in 2003 changing the preference from the status of being indigenous to those better trained. This change brought more Highlanders in governmental jobs and on the other hand left many formerly employed indigenous police and governmental workers unemployed, which led them to take up arms and make a living as *shifta*[16] (Chan, 2008). Ambushes on busses increased, which also had an ethnic component, as their victims were mostly Highlanders.

Notwithstanding the tense relations between the two groups and the reoccurring outbreaks of violence on both sides, the history of the conflict reached a peak of violence in a pogrom on the 13th December of 2003, when a mob of highland civilians backed by the military indiscriminately killed civilians of the Anywaa community. Without wanting to talk down what happened, at this point I wish to emphasise the collective violence between civilians, not denying, though, that a reasonable intervention of the armed forces had occurred. As the military is largely recruited from Highlanders, group alliances were at stake, and in the best case the military did not do enough to stop the onslaught in an organised manner[17], which is within their responsibilities. What happened on the 13th of December in the small town of Gambella is difficult to reconstruct. This is due to both the nonexistent will of the Ethiopian government to report on the events - on the contrary, the first reaction of the government was to blame the massacre on a violent clash between Anywaa and Nuer - as well as the current advocacy of the Anywaa diaspora and some NGOs, whose work tends to describe the massacre of 2003 as a starting-point of a *genocidal* campaign with the aim to destroy the Anywaa population as a whole.[18] Both current states obstruct a free and impartial look into what had happened.

---

[15] The GPDM was manufactured under the auspices of the EPRDF to settle the struggle between the Nuer and Anywaa factions. The GPDC was established in response by alienated Anywaa and Nuer.

[16] *Shifta* is the Amharic term for bandit. In the local context it serves to describe armed groups responsible for highway robbery and has also become a term to stigmatize the Anywaa as a whole.

[17] This perception has been promoted by workers at the local office of the World Food Program and has been partially publicized in an unofficial document.

[18] Such assessments of the situation are currently easily accessed on the Internet. The most prominent pages include: www.anuakjustice.org; www.gambellatoday.com; the most influential report of Human Rights Watch is found under: http://hrw.org/reports/2005/ethiopia0305/ethiopia0305text.pdf; several other organisations have

In the morning of the December 13th, eight corpses of workers of the Administration for Refugees and Returnees Affairs (ARRA) were brought to town by the military. They had been found on the road between Jikaw and Itang. Their vehicle had been ambushed, and all passengers had been killed. When their bodies were brought to town, the word had spread rapidly that they were heavily mutilated. However, instead of bringing them directly to the hospital, the drivers paraded with the catafalque pick-up through the town, initiating a procession that many Highlanders joined in walking behind the truck. The bodies were taken to the regional government, and the parade gave rise to an outrage of the participants. When they reached the regional government, stones were already flying, and cars were being crashed in rage: The demonstrators were trying to articulate long standing demands for security, as they were feeling threatened by militant Anywaa. But instead of doing so in a moderate and articulated way, they started a bloody precession, which claimed the lives of many innocent Anywaa civilians[19].

What occurred was a pogrom, an outbreak of collective violence, in which Highlanders with the support of several armed soldiers killed Anywaa men, destroyed Anywaa property, burned down huts, and overran the Anywaa neighbourhoods of Gambella town. The mob killed men and boys (probably at weapon-grade age), but spared women and children. Witnesses recalled the same situation again and again: when the perpetrators came to the houses, they ordered the men to come out. They were beaten (some to death) or ordered to run away, only to be shot by individual soldiers. The pogrom lasted for several hours (there are different accounts), violence eventually erupted in Itang and Pinyudo, following similar patterns as in Gambella. In the aftermath, there were several cases of revenge and counter revenge: Highlanders were killed for what had happened in Gambella, and then again Anywaa were killed for what had happened to these Highlanders. Since the incidents of 2003, several NGOs have reported on recurrent violence by the Ethiopian National Defence Forces against Anywaa civilians:

The "International Human Rights Clinic" (Harvard Law School's Human Rights Program) has recently documented (for the time between 2004 and 2006) 46 incidents of extrajudicial killing, 14 rapes, and 64 incidents of physical violence by the Ethiopian military against Anywaa civilians[20]. Reasonable counter-attacks by Anywaa militants under the flag of the GPLM/F (obviously founded on January 10th 2004[21]) include an ambush on the police-station of Gambella town on October 30th 2005, when several policemen including the security chief were killed and prisoners were released from Gambella police station. It was followed by a successful attack on the town of Abobo on November 30th 2005[22]. Various armed confrontations are recorded in several GPLM/F press releases until late January 2006[23].

---

undertaken related investigation such as Human Rights Clinic and Genocide Watch. The reports focus on the severe human rights abuses by the National Defence Forces against the Anywaa population.

[19] The numbers are more than blurry: conservative estimates start at 67, while HRW and other activist groups following them put the number at 425.

[20] http://www.law.harvard.edu/programs/hrp/clinic/documents/ETHIOPIAREPORT.pdf; last access: 17.11.2007

[21] http://www.gambelatoday.com/modules.php?name=News&file=article&sid=224; last access: 17.11.2007

[22] http://www.gambelatoday.com/modules.php?name=News&file=article&sid=229; last access: 17.11.2007

[23] http://www.gambelatoday.com/modules.php?name=Search&author=&topic=0&min=0&query=GPLM/F&type =&category=0; last access: 17.11.2007

For the Anywaa, the December massacre has a very symbolic character: It dramatically alienated them from the Ethiopian state. Since the perpetrators were Highlanders and as such directly associated with the Ethiopian state, the pogrom embodies the exclusion from the Ethiopian state. When they where asked whether the Anywaa would fight for Ethiopia again if the war with Eritrea broke out again, every interviewee answered with the same characteristic question: "Why should we go to war for a government that is killing its own people?" For many Anywaa there is a direct link between the pogrom and the former resettlement: Given the fact that the massacres are conceptualised as an extension of the government's plan to eradicate them, the settlers must have been brought to either assimilate or oust the Anywaa. We have come full circle, as the Anywaa conceive the former settlers as part of the violent mob that has ambushed their group's members on the December 13th. This is embodied in a statement I got from a middle aged Anywaa women in late September 2005: "If they [i.e. the settlers] would have gone back to where they came from, they would not have killed our men."

Conclusion

In this essay, the focus on violence has served as a specific approach to the conflicts in Gambella. This approach was chosen in addition to the "root causes" in order to clarify further conflict generating patterns beyond the political and social setting. The question what exactly violence is remains and thus the difficulty to conclude from a fact to a cause.

The identity of the Anywaa is largely based on resistance. Violence needs ancient hatreds and the fear of extinction, as Kaufmann (2001) has pointed out. These roots of hatred have to be renewed throughout the generations to accomplish their fate. As we have seen, the relations between the Highlanders representing the Ethiopian state and the Anywaa have already turned violent some one hundred years before, when the Anywaa experienced slave-raiding and occupation. These old animosities were renewed through time and culminated in the violence during the socialist time. The violence was then driven by the Anywaa's fear of extinction, and it's exploitation by their elites, who considered the settlers to be collaborators of the Derg regime. This violence that swept the settlement sites was symbolic in character and points to the meaning of liberating one's country once and for all from the foreign infiltration. The extent of violence reflects how threatening the resettlement program was perceived as an act of foreign infiltration induced by the Derg's politics.

The reoccurring violence has shaped the identities of the groups. Violence by the Anywaa, targeting a government embodied by the Highlanders, consolidated the Highlanders' "ethnic" identity as a group of their own. The boundaries of groups are manifested by the rise of one group against another. What emerges is a cycle of violence that gets harder to break each time a group member is killed.

The second event emphasised in this paper were the atrocities of 2003. Here, too, we find the strengthening of identity through violence. The Anywaa's identity is framed by the feeling of exclusion; the Highlanders become a group of perpetrators. The violence again shows signs of symbolism, the will to punishment and the group-stigmatisation of the Anywaa as *shifta*, since the targets were only male. The destruction of properties points to the will of group-punishment. The demonstration before the beginning of the pogrom points to the Highlanders' discontent, structural insecurity, and fear of being targeted by bandits. The fact that the bodies of the aid workers were being paraded through town, which initiated the violent outbreak, shows how much the confrontation with violence is likely to start counter-violence itself, and therefore, how self-reproducing this phenomenon is. It may also show which role violent specialists (this term is borrowed from Charles Tilly (2003)) play in guiding it. It reflects the fact that violence is not "always already" (Nordstrom, 1997) existent in a society, but needs people to exploit it, hoping to benefit from the construction of animosities (Schlee, 2006) and from pitching groups against each other. This fact has led the advocates of human rights, who are concerned with the Gambella situation (Diaspora groups, human rights groups, and human rights journalists), and many Anywaa in Gambella to believe that December 13th was the starting point of a *genocidal* campaign organised by violent specialists of the Ethiopian government and profiteers of the political Anywaa elite in Gambella (like the regional president), campaigned under an operational name and carried out by the Ethiopian Defence Forces with the help of Highlanders, first and foremost to get rid of the Anywaa to ensure full control of the resource-rich regional state of Gambella. This is the language of genocide and human rights in the Internet globalising a local conflict. But listening to the speechlessness of the victims of violence, Anywaa and Highlanders alike, one must come to a different conclusion: Violence in Gambella has a self-reproducing component, which the regional and federal government are not strongly committed to consider, while the civilians, due to discontent, fear and the experience of violence, are more easily exploited to narrow the means of conflict mitigation through the use of violence.

Bibliography

Asnake Kefale, 2004, 'Federalism: Some Trends of Ethnic Conflicts and their Management in Ethiopia.' In: Nhema, Alfred G. (Ed.), 2006, *The quest for Peace in Africa. Transformation, Democracy and Public Policy.* Addis Abeba: OSSREA. pp. 51-58.

Bahru Zewde, 1976, *Relations between Ethiopia and the Sudan on the western Ethiopian Frontier. 1898-1935.* PhD-Dissertation: University of London.

Bar-Tal, Daniel, 2002, 'Die Kultur der Gewalt.' In: Kempf, Wilhelm (Ed.), 2000, *Konflikt und Gewalt. Ursachen-Entwicklungstendenzen –Perspektiven.* Studien für europäische Friedenspolitik, Band 5. agenda: Münster. pp. 66-81

Chan Gatkouth, 2008, 'Gambella Conflicts. The Role of the Government in Preventing and Resolving Conflicts.' In: Kinfe Abraham & Wolbert Smidt, 2007, *Discussing Conflict inmidst of Conflict: Proceedings of the Conference on German and Ethiopian Contributions to Conflict Prevention and Resolution.* Hamburg, Münster: Lit Verlag.

Clapham, Christopher, 2002, 'Controlling Space in Ethiopia.' In: James, Wendy & Donald Donham (Eds.), 2002, *Remapping Ethiopia. Socialism and After.* Addis Ababa, Ohio: James Curry. pp. 9-32.

Dereje Feyissa, 2003, *Ethnic Groups and Conflict. The Case of the Anywaa-Nuer Relations in Gambella Region, Western Ethiopia.* Dissertation. Martin Luther Universität Halle Wittenberg.

Dereje Feyissa, 2006, 'The Experience of Gambella Regional State.' In: Turton, David, 2006, *Ethnic Federalism. The Ethiopian Experience in comperative Perspective*. Addis Ababa, Ohio: James Curry. pp. 208-230.

Donham, Donald, 1986, 'Old Abyssinia and the new Ethiopian Empire. Themes in social history.' In: James, Wendy & Donald Donham (Eds.), 198, *The Southern Marches of Imperial Ethiopia*. Cambridge. pp. 3-48.

Elwert, Georg et al., 1999, *Dynamics of Violence. Processes and De-Escalation in violent Group Conflicts*. Berlin: dunker und Humblot.

Evans-Pritchard, Edward E., 1940, *The political system of the Anuak of the Anglo-Egyptian Sudan*. New York.

Grabbert, Wolfgang, 2004, 'Was ist Gewalt? Anmerkungen zur Bestimmung eines umstrittenen Begriffs.' In: Eckert, Julia M., 2004, *Anthropologie der Konflikte. Georg Elwerts konflikttheoretische Thesen in der Diskussion*. Bielefeld: transcript. 88-101.

Horowitz, Donald L.,2000, *Ethnic Groups in Conflict*. Berkeley and Los Angeles, California: University of California Press.

Imbusch, Peter & Ralf Zoll, 2006, *Friedens- und Konfliktforschung. Eine Einführung mit Quellen*. Opladen: Leske und Budrich

Johnson, Douglas H., 1986, 'On the Nilotic Frontier. Imperial Ethiopia in the Southern Sudan, 1898-1936.' In: James, Wendy & Donald Donham, 1986, *The Southern Marches of Imperial Ethiopia*. Addis Ababa, Ohio: James Curry. pp. 219-245.

Kaufmann, Stuart J., 2001, *Modern Hatreds. The Symbolic Politics of Ethnic War*. Ithaca and London: Cornell University Press

Kurimoto, Eisei, 1997, 'Politicisation of Ethnicity in Gambella.' In: *Ethiopia in a Broader Perspective. Papers of the 13th International Conference of Ethiopian Studies*. Vol. II. Kyoto: Kyoto University. pp. 798-815.

Kurimoto, Eisei, 2001, 'Capturing Modernity among the Anywaa of western Ethiopia.' In: Kurimoto, Eisei, 2001, *Rewriting Africa: Towards Renaissance or Collapse*. JCAS Symposium Series, No. 14: Osaka. pp. 262-280.

Kurimoto, Eisei, 2002, 'Fear and Anger. Female versus Male Narratives among the Anywaa.' In: James, Wendy & Donald Donham, 2002, *Remapping Ethiopia. Socialism and After*. Addis Ababa, Ohio.

Merera Gudina, 2003, *Ethiopia. Competeting Ethnic Nationalism and the Quest for Democracy 1960 – 2000*. Addis Abeba, Chamber Printing House.

Nordstrom, Carolyn, 1997, *A different Kind of War Story*. Philadelphia : University of Pennsylvania Press

Schlee, Günther, 2000, 'Die soziale Konstruktion von Feindschaft.' In: Max Planck Institute for Social Anthropology Working Papers 5. Halle/Saale.

Schlee, Günther. 2006, *Wie Feindbilder entstehen. Eine Theorie religiöser und ethnischer Konflikte*. München: Beck Verlag.

Shumet Sishagne, 1985, 'The Economic Basis of Conflict among the Nuer and the Anuak Communities.' Paper prepared for the Third Annual Seminar of the Department of History. Addis Ababa University, Bahr Dar. April 17-22, 1985.

Sommer, Monika M, 2005, *Transforming Conflict in the Multi-Ethnic State of Gambella in Ethiopia – Mediation in a Divided Society*. M.A. Thesis. Institute Universitaire Kurt Bösch.

Sommer, Monika M, 2007, 'Perceptions of Justice of some of the People living in the Ethiopian Region of Gambella: Their Relevance to Conflict Transformation.' Paper presented at the 16th International Conference of Ethiopian Studies, Trondheim, 2-7 July 2007.

Staub, Ervin, 1999, 'Predicting collective Violence: The Psychological and cultural Roots of Turning against others.' In: Summers, Craig & Eric Markusen, 1999, *Collective Violence. Harmful Behaviour in Groups and Governments.* Lanham, Boulderf, New York, Oxford: Rowman and Littlefield Publishers

Tilly, Charles, 2003, *The Politics of Collective Violence.* Cambridge.

The Kara-Nyangatom War of 2006-07:
Dynamics of Escalating Violence in the Tribal Zone

Felix Girke[1]

Introduction

The Kara, an agropastoralist group living on the banks of the Lower Omo, have a long history
of conflict as well as an equally long history of contact and cooperation with the Nyangatom,
their western neighbors. The events of what I call the "war"[2] of 2006-07 between these two
sides therefore present only an artificial segment of an ongoing contact situation in South
Omo, but indicate the dynamics of the conflict, and the interplay between traditional and
state-sponsored modes of mediation. Despite the cut-out character of the time-span chosen,
the paper shows how the rules of engagement have been and are continuously changing, as
new actors and new resources make their impact felt.

Conflict in the Lower Omo area of southern Ethiopia has been written about before,
(especially by Jon Abbink, Uri Almagor, Jan-Åke Alvarsson, Serge Tornay and David
Turton), and even conflict between Kara and Nyangatom. The account presented here shifts
the discussion which dwelled mostly on events of the 1970s and 1980s into the present, and
puts special emphasis on ecology, oral history as political charter, and the concept of the
"tribal zone". The question of ecology is central because while the stakes of the war were
precisely access to land and water, the issue was disregarded in the policies and plans NGOs
and the local administration developed for the resolution of the conflict. Furthermore, the
different stages of the conflict can be correlated with different phases of the natural and
agricultural cycle, which sheds light on why fighting was more or less intensive at times, and
why interest in peace-making emerged when it did. To look at the various histories which deal
with the past relations of Kara and Nyangatom, and which provide frames of reference for the
current situation, is central for understanding the language of the conflict, the symbolic
gestures made, and the way in which agreements were put. In addition, the events will be
discussed as an example of a "war in the tribal zone": with this term, Ferguson and Whitehead
(2000) describe areas at the fringe of empire which are shaped by the dominating power,
while not being controlled by it. The war between Kara and Nyangatom might thus look like a
merely local issue, but its modalities (such as underlying causes, the resources at stake, and
the ways of mediation) were all transformed and complicated by sometimes barely visible
influences exerted by the proximity of the Ethiopian state institutions.

I base this paper mainly on observed events and public debates which I attended, and
less on de-contextualized interview data. Also, I cannot give a balanced account in the sense
of letting the Nyangatom and Kara speak on equal terms; while it would have been valuable

[1] The author is PhD Candidate at the Max Planck Institute for Social Anthropology in Halle, Germany. I am
    grateful for the comments of the IDOCO group at the MPI, especially for the suggestions from J. Beyer, M.
    Höhne, and M. Laszczkowski.
[2] The term *shauki* designates a defensive condition which can escalate into generalized *banko* (also "spear"),
    usually interspersed by *sulla*, small-scale attacks.

to gather data from both sides synchronously, this was impossible for me during this particular research stay, being firmly grounded in the "Kara side". My objective is not to give an account of the "truths" of the war, or attempt to explain its hidden structure; instead, I present a focused view on the internal goings-on of a community which sees itself under attack. The wider relevance of the paper beyond the field of regional studies lies primarily in the patterns of social dynamics I describe, and in the example of the "tribal zone" still extant in South Omo.

Kara and Nyangatom – The Need for Enemies?

The relationship between the Kara and the Nyangatom is complex, as can be expected between such close neighbors, and impossible to do full justice to here. Accordingly, I will merely highlight a few items, historical and economic relations which merit special attention as they contribute to the salient context of the events of 2006-07.

These relations are not something which connects separate ethnic entities, not something groups "have" or "don't have", which is external to them: they are, in so many ways, what defines the groups. The Kara are only Kara vis-à-vis their neighbors, Nyangatom, Moguji, and Hamar[3]. So even though the external affairs of the Kara have been overshadowed by the growing power of the Nyangatom "at the fringe of the state" (Tornay 1993), the discussion is never only about "inclusion and exclusion" – the Nyangatom matter to the Kara, not only as a threatening Other, but also as a source of cherished cultural elements, as a challenge, as a rewarding engagement. The most visible signs of this are Nyangatom terms which are used in Kara for utensils, for classifying livestock, in song, in naming and other domains. I do not see this as a result of Nyangatom "cultural imperialism" following Kara defeats in the 1970s (Alvarsson[4] 1989: 33), since the tenor in which the Nyangatom terms are used resonates with nostalgia and fascination. Old men might switch in mid-conversation from speaking Kara to speaking Nyangatom, demonstrating a pleasure of mastery and a fondness of the more guttural, throaty sounds.

It is also important to keep in mind that group relations in the Lower Omo are often at odds with relations between individuals, who cultivate friendships across boundaries irrespective of the larger polities. Bailey's statement that "[a]nimosity is a feature of the political person, the one engaged in a contest for power, not of the whole person" (Bailey 1998: xi) rings true here; public talk about "the Nyangatom" is very different from behavior towards individual Nyangatom. Such partners, also called "bondfriends", through their mutual trust and support display the autonomy of the individual as opposed to the coercive dynamics of the group (see Girke 2008), and in an interesting reverse movement are accorded respect for taking such a stand from the very groups they spite. Through such friendships, the Nyangatom have been providers of much sought-after goods such as beads and metal-work,

---

[3]   As Kara would be wont to use it, "Hamar" here stands for all "mountain people" (gemerr-ed), and in general conversation the distinction between Hamar, Banna (also atula) and Bashada (also banno) is often glossed over.

[4]   Even though he spent little time on research on-site, Jan-Åke Alvarsson's report on the conflicts of South Omo (1989) provides a broad summary of the anthropological discussion, detailed accounts of actual goings-on in the 1980s and before, as well as some insightful commentary.

which even today the Kara firmly associate with their western neighbors. So while the Kara fight with the Nyangatom, they see them simultaneously as much more than just "enemies". Oral history from Kara provides some motifs which illustrate the relations between the two groups.

A Mythical Charter

The Kara report in a story as if found in Kopytoff (1986: 49, 55) how they came to be the dominating power in the Lower Omo. However, two apocalyptic catastrophes, the *tobolo* (a deluge) and the *gind'o* (sleeping sickness), probably towards the end of the 19th century, which wiped out all but a few adults according to oral history, severed the Kara from their earlier past, accounts of which are fragmentary today. As eminent middle-men of the river valley, they were rich and powerful; the stories about their wealth and glory are corroborated by accounts from among the Kara's neighbors (Strecker 1976; Alvarsson 1989: 31, 43, 101; Sobania 2000) as well as by the early explorers like Bòttego. What might come as a surprise is the narrative about how they fought the Turkana in the Kibbish area, and finally chased them away. At this time, so the Kara, the Nyangatom were few and poor, and huddled pathetically in a nearby forest. The victorious Kara in their magnanimity called them forth to Kibbish (also *Naqwa*), rubbed fire sticks together, and gave the burning kindling to the Nyangatom, telling them that this was to be their land from now on.

Tornay (1979: 98) tells a more sober story of how the Nyangatom "within living memory" expelled the Turkana from Kibbish. But history is not necessarily about what was, but about how people converse about it. Tornay's suggestion that the peoples of the Lower Omo "have no official historians and no history books. They are not, in other words, totally bound by their past" (1979: 113) thus requires qualification – there are always histories being told which precisely are attempts to rhetorically bind people to a certain charter[5]. It pays to bear in mind that anthropologists, in recording situated, implicated accounts of what has been, now join those voices and become part of ongoing conversations.

The on-stage Kara history maintains that they lost their numerous cattle through some disaster[6]; there are vivid stories of how they fought amongst themselves, and only in this way could be brought low.[7] In backstage situations, younger Kara confided to me that they had doubts themselves about many specific stories and items of lore.

---

[5] Here, Tornay casually implies a gap between "them" and "us". I merely want to point out that the divergence of the accounts from both sides is considerable, even though people on both sides will be aware of their Other's ideology. In the space provided, I cannot do full justice to the complex question of the voices in oral histories.

[6] Today, there are few Kara who again have sizeable herds of cattle; others do not even own a significant number of small stock. A visitor to Kara might be misled by the massive number of cattle seen grazing between the foothills and the river; these will as a rule belong to Hamar herders who drive them into the lowlands for grazing and water. While these "mountain people" and the Kara have a generally cordial relationship, recently Kara have become more and more irritated by the ever-growing herds which they blame for their country turning into a desert, as well as by the increasing opportunistic thefts by herders. There is a connection of this recent disgruntlement with the war over the Omo river; the Kara now feel hemmed in even by their friends, up to the point that they insinuate that the Hamar would not mind taking over their country for good.

[7] It is fitting that neither the Ethiopian conquest nor the Italian occupation occasioned particular stories of trauma and terror. The first apparently bypassed Kara, and the few stories of the second which survive tell of

In conversations about the relations with the Nyangatom, I often encountered an attitude of derision and condescension. "They are our *kaissi*, our slaves", was said with conviction, and I assumed this to refer to the ancient time of Kara supremacy. Such statements stand in stark contrast to Alvarsson's claim that the Nyangatom had achieved "some type of recognized influence over the Kara" (Alvarsson 1989: 71) after destroying the Kara village of Kundamma[8] in 1973 and killing over a hundred people. Trying to reconcile this disjunction, I found that this "serfdom" of the Nyangatom was not an ancestral myth, but referred to the years directly preceding the massacre at Kundamma, when the "Omo Nyangatom" (who supposedly lack cattle) had been allowed by the Kara to settle on the western banks of the Omo, cultivate some fields the Kara were not needing, and in return provided services such as scaring away birds for their hosts (see Tornay 1979: 105; Alvarsson 1989: 50). Thus oral history is made: the situation escalated after thefts and similar trouble, and the Kara (along with the Hamar) proceeded to kill between 80 and 100 Omo Nyangatom in order to get rid of the troublesome neighbors. Even though they in turn suffered the devastating counterattack on Kundamma, the serfdom of the Nyangatom *kaissi* is well-remembered and often referred to: "We killed them, just like that" – the fact that even more Kara were killed in return is completely sidelined. Kara self-esteem and "group face" was restored when they subsequently massacred the inhabitants of two villages of the Nyangatom Ngaric section. Alvarsson (1989: 71), who gathered his data in Nyangatom mostly, assumes that this was more a gesture from powerlessness than a true show of strength: the villages affected were peripheral to the Nyangatom, the Ngaric merely the descendants of the Omo Murle (see Tornay 1978), absorbed in former times. In contrast, the destruction of Kundamma hit a Kara stronghold, fundamentally challenging their position on the Lower Omo.

So despite this defeat, the way the Kara present themselves in their charter cannot be disregarded as mere grandstanding and boasting which they performed for an outsider in order to aggrandize themselves – many young Kara are raised on these precise stories, and are nurtured by these very sentiments. The rhetoric is directed inward as much as outward.

Recent Developments in the Tribal Zone

The Karas' routine in dealing with the steady stream of tourists and their subsequent accumulation of capital, the rise of some young Kara in the district (*woreda*) administration and in the rank and file of NGOs, the expanding *mahaber* trade associations, the young Kara boys who are being trained as athletes in Addis Ababa, even the two Kara who made a career in the Ethiopian armed forces, all these examples bear witness to how the region has been changing, and how the local people have adapted and appropriated offered innovations.

Despite these considerable transformations in terms of education, mobility, participation, monetarisation etc. since the 1970s (which serve as a period of comparison for

---

running battles and an exile of several seasons in a forest up north, but nothing like the *banda* horror familiar from other parts of southern Ethiopia (e.g., Strecker 1976: 20).

[8] As so often in South Omo studies, the names of places and even ethnonyms appear in wide array of variation in various publications. Tornay and Alvarsson use "Kurdam", which seems to me to be the Nyangatom version. Alvarsson (1989: 26) provides a decent overview over alternative ethnic designations which is, however, far from exhaustive, especially if one figures in sections of groups which might at times act quite independently.

the discussion at hand), state institutions are still discussed as external agents, even where Kara have achieved positions within them. Struggles over implementation of policies and regulations (such as the ban on hunting) are common, compliance with them is superficial and only as far-reaching as necessary. So while within the borders of the Ethiopian state, the Lower Omo lies in the tribal zone as postulated by Ferguson and Whitehead (2000).

In public debate as well as in private talk, Kara often bemoan their subordinate position within the state structures - "we have become the highlander's wife" is used not to indicate cooperation and endearment, but a sense of powerlessness and frustration (see Naty 1992: 258). They are aware of the gradient of wealth, infrastructure and power, and despite their abilities to appropriate innovations on their terms, they are aware about their location at the outmost periphery (see also Turton 2002).

Their resilience and cleverness (*pachalmamo*, a common Kara trope) was challenged in 2006 at an unprecedented scale through a specific development brought about by state interference[9]: the *Kuraz Woreda*, formerly shared by Nyangatom and Dassanetch was dissolved, and the establishment of a separate *woreda* for the Nyangatom was set into motion. The justifications I gathered for this administrative measure ranged from "the Nyangatom are so many now, they need it" over "the two are always squabbling, we have to separate them" to "the government needs the support of the Nyangatom because of border issues with Sudan" (cf. Matsuda 2002; Vaughan 2006: 184ff); all of these are equally plausible in the context of Ethiopian ethnic federalism. The establishment of the new *woreda* impacted the Kara through the demarcation process, as the zonal government was bent on conveniently taking the river Omo as the boundary. As an administrator told me: "We have to look where the people live now. West of the Omo, are there any Kara living there?" This argument conveniently leaves out even the recent past – the last permanent Kara settlements on the western bank were abandoned (only around 15 years ago) precisely due to the constant threat from the Nyangatom, who with their superior armament and numbers threatened to overwhelm the Kara. In this way, the Nyangatom expansion and aggression, and the resulting pattern of residence which is still felt as anomalous, was to be retroactively legitimized by the central administration. This proposition was unacceptable to the Kara, who never felt that they had given up the areas in the west (and especially their fields on the western bank) for good. When these news made the round in Kara in April and May, and after the administrator (a Nyangatom himself) had given me oral confirmation of the plans in early June, the Kara were too stunned to even be upset: "If they really do this, there will never be peace", a young man told me matter-of-factly.

The experience of state intervention aggravating conflicts between the local groups is not a new one: "The Ethiopian conquest of the Lower Omo area (1898-1903) both exacerbated and confused inter-tribal rivalries" (Tornay 1979: 112). Ferguson and Whitehead, in their comprehensive treatment of the "edge of empire", describe the tribal zone as an area which is transformed by the "intrusive state system" (2000: xii) without said system gaining a monopoly on force. Taking care not to romantically glorify pre-colonial times, they show the dangerous fallacies in assuming that conflict between indigenous groups is due to internal reasons – the classical barbarians needed to be fierce precisely because of their contact with

---

[9] I choose this loaded term because the state apparatus was mobilized by individuals who were recognized as biased stakeholders, much rather than impartial arbitrators.

an overwhelmingly strong empire (2000: 11-16). With the implementation of the policy of ethnic federalism, which imposed "top-down" a vision of identity and aligned administration along externally determined "ethnic lines" (cf. Vaughan 2006: 184), group boundaries are becoming enhanced and rigid in the struggle for resources. The traditional ways of negotiating conflict are superseded by much more anomic, unregulated permanent states of crisis.

So it is precisely because "Ethiopian Government administration ... has always been weak in these southwestern lowlands" (Fukui/Turton 1979: 2; cf. Strecker 1976: 30) that the conflicts of the late 20th century have often escalated.

Fighting over and across the Omo, 2006-07

The Omo River has been described as a "life line" for the region (Alvarsson 1989: 80), and this is equally true for the Kara, the Mursi, the Nyangatom, the Dassanetch, the Moguji and Kwegu. With the seasonal fluctuation of the river levels according to rainfall in the higher catchment areas in central Ethiopia, both the river banks and the occasionally inundated flats further inland provide fertile farming grounds. Beyond the importance of the river for agriculture[10], it provides more potential for conflict as the Omo is the only reliable source for watering the herds. In the case of Kara, these are mostly merely domestic herds of small stock. The Nyangatom, though, while no pastoralists in the narrowest sense of the word[11], are forced to bring their cattle herds to the Omo river regularly, as they have been cut off from other pastures through the cordoning off of the Ilemi triangle and constant, ongoing fights with the Turkana, and as the Kibbish river waterholes are dangerous and unreliable.

Thus, control of their section of the Omo is a major factor in the Kara presumptions of supremacy and their stories of past grandeur. Since in an average year, five months of work can provide all the staple food necessary to survive the rest of the year, they occupy an extraordinary ecological niche. Kara mythology tells of how they, arriving at the riverbanks, tricked the innocent and naïve Moguji, the "true autochthones" according to legend, into signing away all rights to the land; and up till today, the lands on both banks of the Omo are unambiguously demarcated and clearly assigned to particular owners, be they Kara, Bogudo or Gomba[12]. The distribution of these fields is far from even; some individuals hardly have

---

[10] Other activities in securing livelihoods are also dependent on the Omo – opportunistic hunting in the riverine forest, apiculture, fishing. While some of these are ideologically tainted, and some ritual prohibitions still obtain (but see Strecker 1976, Alvarsson 1989: 31), they all provide important contributions to nutrition and social satisfaction for the surrounding groups.

[11] According to strict definitions, none of the groups in South Omo is pastoralist, as the numbers of livestock per capita and the percentages of dairy products to general nutrition are far too low. Almagor claims that "[t]hough agriculture plays an important role in their lives, they should be viewed as they view themselves, as pastoralists" (1979: 121; see Turton 2002: 150 on self-perceptions of Mursi and Kwegu). While this helps us to understand symbolism, metaphors and discourse much better, it detracts from our understanding of the current land issues. The discussion gets interesting again when he turns towards the Dassanetch-Amhara relations, their views on agriculture vis-à-vis herding, and issues of taxation (2002: 267 fn.17; Strecker 1976: 49 on the Hamar case).

[12] The Gomba, like the Bogudo, are submerged remnants of earlier groups which have been absorbed by the Kara after gind'o and tobolo, and no longer exist as politically autonomous entities. All these groups, while nominally Kara, have their own sets of rules regarding ritual matters; it is remarkable, though, that despite the political weakness especially of the Bogudo, none of these two land-owning group has ever been stripped of its holdings. Moguji, however, even around their settlement of Kuchurr, ever since their mythical surrender of the riverbanks to the late-coming Kara (cf. Kopytoff 50, 55), have no tenure of farming lands.

any claim to any section of the riverbank, while others hold so much that they regularly invite other Kara to farm sections of their fields. In good years, it has been common to also allow Hamar or Nyangatom access to fields.

The Timeline

Any attempt to segment the war of 2006-07 as a separable chain of events is fallacious. A look at a timeline of attacks, negotiations, rumors, and meetings still yields some insights into connections and the dynamics of violence.

The relation between Kara and Nyangatom had been on an upswing recently, and both groups had farmed the western banks of the Omo together during the agricultural season which began around September 2005. This did not last long: a young Kara man, whose wife had been killed by Nyangatom in 2003, decided that he needed to get personal revenge. Already after she had been shot by a sniper from across the river, he had traveled upstream with some friends and fired indiscriminately at a village near Kopirye (also *Kopriye*). Even though seven people died, these killings where not satisfactory, as he said. To count as a true killer in Kara, one either has to touch the body of the victim, or bring back any of their belongings: "Gonde dazadei", it had not really tasted well, he explained to me. During the intervening years, some elder Kara had persistently hassled him by insinuating that his revenge was still incomplete. Despite the fact that others had tried to calm him down and had asked him not to collect on his "debt" (the Kara term *bazza* translates quite literally, with all the connotations of payback and outstanding dues), he decided at the worst possible time, namely, just before harvest, to finally put to rest all doubt. He crossed the river, killed two Nyangatom herding boys (of the *sookhol* section[13]), and returned home, bearing their bloody clothes as proof.

This happened some weeks before I reached the Lower Omo in March; I have been unable to ascertain an exact date. Both groups reacted in a predictable way: the Kara immediately returned to the eastern side of the river, and the Nyangatom evacuated the riverbank as well, so that the sorghum, in part already harvested and ready for threshing, was left lying in the fields. There were some tentative negotiations between individual Kara and their personal Nyangatom friends, who had farmed together, on whether the Kara might be allowed to cross and collect some of the grain, but apparently, these all petered out, and the sorghum was eventually recovered by the Nyangatom. The Kara, accordingly, had to make do with the grains they could harvest on the eastern banks. For a while, a tense silence hung over the Omo valley. In April, this silence was broken. I somewhat arbitrarily divide the subsequent time into three segments according to the respective tenor of the conflict. I was present at several of the events listed here, and occasionally facilitated transport.

April - June: Hot war, cold war
On April 7, a shot is fired from the Nyangatom side near one of the hamlets of southern Kara.

---

[13] Tornay gives the name of this section as "Ngisakol" (1979: 100). The Kara pronunciation differs from this transcription. Over the last years, the name *sookhol* has been used to metonymically evoke all negative aspects ascribed to the Nyangatom in Kara.

On April 12, four Kara snipers ambush a group of Nyangatom who approach the Omo river from the south and, shooting across the river, kill or wound four.

A little later, some Kara women who stealthily creep down the river bank at night to fetch water come under fire after the sloshing water inside a jerry-can alerts watchers in the dark. They scatter and escape. Some Kara youths return shots and injure one Nyangatom.

On the night of May 1, the Kara ritual leaders lay out protective arcs of selected plants across a few symbolic paths, shielding the country from invasion.

On May 1, while the Kara are celebrating a wedding in the central village Dus, shots are heard from the waterline, as Nyangatom fire at Hamar cattle drinking from the river. The government-appointed leader of the Dus-*kebele* is nearly hit, several heads of cattle are lost. The entire male population of Dus rushes to the riverine forest at the Kalime fields, and shots are traded back and forth for the better part of an hour. Apparently, there are no casualties on either side. The *kebele*-leader drives to the safari camp Murule at Naumur and transmits the news to the *woreda* officials by radio.

On May 2, a car arrives from the *woreda*, carrying the head of police and some minor officials, in which the Kara protest against being left alone in this fight. They are admonished to remain calm and not act in revenge.

On May 6, there is a night-time war dance in Kara, through which the young people demand to be given permission to fight a more proactive war. The war dance leads to the donation of eight goats by various elders, which are to be slaughtered at a proper *osh*, a war council.

On May 8, the *osh* is held at Dus. Representatives from the different parts of Kara country participate, as well as numerous Hamar who – after the incident with the cattle – display considerable eagerness to take revenge. The spokesmen of the Kara assent to the demands and encourage the young warriors to go out and kill.

On May 14, a Kara lying in ambush shoots a solitary Nyangatom through the chest who descends the riverbank on the other side; he is assumed to be a scout, doing reconnaissance for a later attack. Weeks later the information arrives that the bullet has pierced a lung.

On May 19, around 40 young Kara assemble and move south, planning to cross the Omo river and to exterminate a herding camp of the Nyangatom. This band is beset by bad omens, and while they are waiting for a more favorable divination, a respected elder is sent from Dus to catch up with them and eventually convinces their leaders to desist. Despite grumblings of the young fighters, the group, robbed of its heads, disperses.

On June 7, a group of Kara from the southernmost village waylays a truck bound for Nyangatom territory, turn it back towards Kara and unload 100 sacks of coffee husks. The owner, a Nyangatom trader, is abandoned at the Murule safari camp. He later claims to have had a large amount of cash stolen as well.

Late June - Early October: Under the shade tree

On June 26, police arrive in Kara in order to transport some Kara negotiators to a peace meeting in Omorate (Dassanetch territory). They also discuss the return of the coffee, but cave in to the Kara refusal, thus acknowledging the claim that the coffee had been taken as restitution for the loss of the sorghum harvest earlier this year.

After a preliminary debate among numerous elders under a big shade tree in Dus on June 27, the Kara and Nyangatom emissaries meet at Omorate on June 29 and 30. Mutual provocations and resentment dominate the event.

On July 8, a second round of meetings begins in Turmi (Hamar territory), which turns out somewhat more conciliatory. There, it is agreed that the required ritual for the establishment of peace has to be held either at Dus or at Kibbish, the center of Nyangatom land (cf. Abbink 2000).

In the subsequent weeks, the Kara wait for news and for a date to be fixed; eventually, some elders returning from Turmi inform the community that a date has been set. The long period of waiting is fraught with rumors and informal debates about the projected course of events.

On August 31, the long-expected cars arrive, after transportation had been funded by the Selam-C project of the Pact Ethiopia NGO. In an arduous journey, the negotiators travel to Kibbish, where talks are held on September 1. The ritual sealing the peace is performed on September 2. One focal point of the meeting was the announcement by government representatives to from now on collect 80 heads of cattle and 40 heads of small stock as compensation for any homicide.

Around the middle of September, several Nyangatom call for their Kara friends, asking permission to farm on the western bank. The Kara respond reluctantly and ultimately decline.

On October 1, two Nyangatom visit their Kara bond-friend at the irrigation site of Kundamma, drink beer with their host and bring a few bullets to trade away.

On October 2, a delegation from the (Ngu-)Kumama section of the Nyangatom reaches the south of Kara, were they are amiably hosted. The elders from both sides hold a joint *osh*, and affirm future cooperation and peaceful coexistence.

October – January: Peace in our time?

On October 6, word spreads in Kara that the Nyangatom have demanded blanket assent by the Kara to their demands to farm the western bank of the river. Without permission being given, Nyangatom arrive at the river in numbers, establish themselves and begin clearing the land.

On November 18, Kara fire two bullets into the air at Kundamma after guns were exchanged; shortly afterwards, Nyangatom demand satisfaction since supposedly the bullets had injured some cattle. This is quickly recognized as a insubstantial provocation.

In the following weeks, many Kara express annoyance upon seeing their fields being occupied by the Nyangatom. This is exacerbated as the Kara are firmly warned by some Nyangatom to no longer cross the river to collect salty soil and salt-bearing bushes from the Lokulan area across from Kundamma.

Around December 24, a school teacher assigned to Dus decides that the increasing tensions are bound to lead to more fighting, and organize a hasty meeting at Kundamma, which then takes place on December 27 and 28. Grievances are voiced on both sides, and despite some further provocations, mutual assurances of peace are finally issued. The Nyangatom invite some Kara to cross the river the next day and together they feast on a sacrificed oxen.

In the middle of January, a young Kara administrative clerk who had come to visit, fires some shots as a gesture of mourning when entering his father's brother's camp on the riverbank. Within minutes, armed men come rushing from the nearby village, ready to defend their land, thinking the shots signals of an attack.

This summary indicates not only the various actors and their plans, but also the varying degrees of intensity which characterized the period.

Ecological Backdrop

It is a simple matter and highly insightful to correlate the timing of the stages outlined above and especially the timing of the peace conferences with the ecological and agricultural cycle dictated by the rise and the fall of the Omo waters. "Hami Karassa wakitum", the fields are the cattle of the Kara – Kara livelihood, as well as that of all other groups living on the Omo, depends on riverbank cultivation for secure subsistence (see Matsuda 1996). Briefly, the Omo river rises from around January, were it is at its lowest, in irregular intervals up until around August, when it can even spill over the banks, and pools can be found surprisingly far inland. This period from February to August is the time of plenty, the time after the harvest. People leave their small hamlets close to their farms, and slowly return to the larger villages. Major rituals such as weddings are held, there is time for leisure and maintenance, travel, invitations, and trade. The youths, dispersed for a long time due to the hard work in the field, celebrate their reunion in dancing and playing – the "social rhythms based on oecological [sic] changes" described by Evans-Pritchard (1939: 192) are clearly in evidence here.

As the river level starts receding, carefully observed and untiringly discussed every morning by the elders sitting in the sunrise on a cliff, one by one families start to head off to the sections of the river they have decided to farm this year. The small hamlets are getting repopulated, and as soon as the inundated flats and steep banks are becoming accessible, slash and burn cultivation begins. As the grain ripens, often as not the last year's stores are slowly used up, and the sweet sorghum cane and the opportunistically harvested maize provided welcome food especially for the children.

Looking at the suggested stage model of the war, a correlation becomes apparent: The time after harvest, the fat, leisurely lived time, was when tempers were most heated, when a raid was planned and nearly executed, when shots were fired, and many men were willing to fight. The second stage "under the shade tree" corresponds to the end of this time of plenty, and marks the onset of the return to the fields. Finally, the last stage, of an uneasy, worried peace, was a period where the boon of harvest was taking shape but could still be spoilt; Kara and Nyangatom saw each other every day across the river, and the final, consolidating peace conference in Kundamma took place mere weeks before harvest. This was the time when the river was so low in places that it might even be crossed on foot by an enterprising posse; as the Kara and Nyangatom were depleting their stores, both desired an additional assurance of truce for the last few days necessary to gather up the grain, and to abandon the exposed fields and return into the more easily defensible villages. This is no abstract pattern gleaned through anthropological analysis; in Kara the discussion of river levels, warfare and farming often went together as people are highly aware of the connections. Thus, the thrust of the argument lies not in the simple "discovery" of this correlation, but in its consequences.

While plausible in the example of 2006-07, the model is not strong enough to predict individual behavior – as it had not been in early 2006, when the Kara widower crossed the river at the most inopportune time possible and killed his fill. Analysis of the communal resolution of the conflict, however, needs to take these ecological aspects into account (see also Tornay 1979: 97). In some way, the conflict of 2006-07 supports the hypothesis postulated by Alvarsson (1989): "Starvation and peace or food and war?" is the question he dares to ask, and using data from the 1970s and 1980s, he makes a strong argument that aggression between the groups of the Lower Omo was in fact highest when there was precisely no food insecurity. This is a direct challenge to simple economic-ecological models which are based on the assumption that scarcity provokes conflict (1989: 16f, 73f), and he suggests that "cultural motives" for warfare such as pride (in times of plenty) are salient factors in the escalation and prolongation of conflicts, whereas hunger can drive warring groups to the shade tree visibly quicker (1989: 107). His numbers reflect a perspective over several years, indicating that in the fattest years violence peaked, whereas the data from 2006-07 encourages the application of the same hypothesis over the different stages of a single year.

Causes and Triggers Considered

The issue of the individual who triggered the war was not an issue for the Kara themselves; even though people were ready to condemn him for his trespass, resignation won the day - "you cannot fix a broken clay pot" was an oft-repeated phrase. Accordingly, there were no official sanctions on the killer, even if some of his close friends expressed their displeasure by not attending the ceremony in which he was decorated with a killer's name. But as push came to shove, other members of the political body showed commitment to the situation he had caused as if they themselves had been responsible, just as the Nyangatom would hold any Kara liable for the trespass of one individual[14]. The demands by the police for surrendering him were thus openly scorned – ever since a Kara who was handed over to the police in the 1990s for murder mysteriously disappeared from his arrest cell (in Nyangatom territory, no less), there has been little faith in the legal system, and the state is not reliably enforcing its rules at this point. In this sense, the Kara upheld the individual's right to make his own decisions, even against the group's obvious interests, and at considerable opportunity costs. But while Kara and Nyangatom accept the individual's action as in some way binding for the group, their communities are hardly able to constrain such actions to accord with the group's will. So even with war triggered by an individual, peace can only be re-established communally, and not through police action, be it prison sentences or blood money.

The assumption on the side of the NGO representatives who facilitated the peace meeting at Kibbish was that the regional conflicts derive solely from revenge killings (and cattle raids), and that to implement the policy of blood money would be a strong discouragement to hot-headed pastoralist warrior youths. To work from this assumption means turning a blind eye to issues of demographics and ecology, and blaming only the savage nature of the shankilla, the "blacks" of southern Ethiopia, for any conflict.

Additionally, the proclamation of this policy indicates a considerable lack of historical awareness of its proponents. The peoples of the Lower Omo have been familiar with the

---

[14] For a well-phrased analogy from another part of the world, see Rafael (1967: 311). However, despite the seeming automatisms in the rules of engagement, over the year it became apparent that there were appreciable differences between sections both on the Kara side and the Nyangatom side in how firmly they committed to fighting the war.

concept of livestock fines for homicide for a long time, and had already learned that it was neither reliably enforced, nor conducive to peace, as already Tornay reported: "In August [1972] the Ethiopian police drove 86 skinny cattle to Kibbish as compensation from the Dassanetch [for an earlier killing], a response which was, of course, received ironically by the Nyangatom." (1979: 104) This shows not only that the concept of a blood price was no revolutionary innovation for South Omo, but also that people have learned not to rely on the administration's capabilities (or willingness) to actually enforce the rule to any appreciable degree. During the Kibbish meeting, a Kara spokesman also took such an ironical stance as he demanded that the originally suggested 80 heads of cattle were not enough, and that 40 heads of small stock should be added on top – the irony being that one would be hard pressed to collect 80 heads of cattle from all of Kara in total already. The Nyangatom and Kara present shared the joke, while the NGO delegation saw it as a positive reception of their policy. So while indeed the fighting of 2006 was triggered by a "revenge killing", the ecological and demographical pressures along the Omo mean that whatever the sanction on killing, violent friction will likely keep occurring until the pressure is relieved in some way – which was not acknowledged by the facilitators of the Kibbish meeting.

Was the peace ritually sealed in Kibbish, then, a "stranger's peace" (Fukui/Turton 1979: 12), which was bound not to last long? Government representatives as well as NGO workers did not believe so – in fact, they argued that they had merely facilitated the intentions the local people had held themselves, working "bottom up". They failed to take into approach that while true ritual leaders of Kara and Nyangatom had gone through the correct motions, the events never lost aspects of charade. When NGOs are staffed with highland Ethiopians who often have no liking neither for their posting nor for their "client" populations, and when they are accompanied by government officials, it is inevitable that both Kara and Nyangatom will prudently do what is expected of them. Nobody wants the blame for doubting the peace be shifted on their shoulders – while government control lacks finesse, it can be heavy-handed. In the end, the Kara had to be satisfied to go home from Kibbish with the hope that they could at least start cultivation before new fighting would occur.

> "It is too early to make peace now. It has not hurt enough yet, neither us nor the Nyangatom. Let it go on, let some more people die, so that everybody feels the pain. If we make peace then, it can last." (Kara man of the Nyiramaley age-set)

Outlook

As I have indicated above, the parameters of conflict over and across the Omo river have changed from the time when Tornay and Almagor were discussing issues of warfare and expansion. Even if in 1979 Fukui and Turton were able to state that "territorial expansion is not the expressed motive of such wars", but merely their consequence (1979: 10), such attitudes have decisively shifted today. Also Tornay's finding that "[t]erritorial conquest , in fact, is a characteristic of sedentary peoples... For nomads or semi-nomads, gaining access to a place is more important than occupying it" (1979: 115) has to be reconciled with the reality on the ground: if for example the Nyangatom are becoming more interested in settling on the Omo (instead of merely accessing it seasonally for watering and pasture) by displacing other populations, they will have to be thought of as a sedentarizing population. The events of

2006-07 suggest that while Tornay talked about the "Omo Nyangatom" as a small group of "poor" folk (1979: 98, 105), today a much larger section of the Nyangatom is in need of farming land. It is no longer the case that "[a]lthough the prize of war is access to localized resources, this seems to be 'forgotten' by the antagonists" (1979: 114); it is the administration and NGOs who are forgetting it.

A visible sign of the changing times, and during 2006-07 (and likely well into the future) the most problematic stimulant to conflict, was the attempt to formally demarcate the boundaries between Nyangatom and Kara under the aegis of the regional government and the newly-established *woreda*. I do not have the data to allow me to fully analyze the events around the establishment of the new Nyangatom *woreda*; most relevant, though, seems the change in demographics. While the Kara have sustained their population, the Nyangatom numbers are staggering. In 1979, Tornay speaks of about 5000 individuals, and sees them in crisis, as the constant state of war had cost them "400 to 500 people every five years" (1979: 111). But then, texts from the 1990s put their number at around 13,000 (Tornay 1993: 152), and I was told by Nyangatom officials that in a recent census they had surpassed 33,000. This number might be skewed as there is often an advantage to be found in terms of fund allotment and NGO help if one can claim a larger population. But rumors have it that many of today's Nyangatom were or still are Sudanese Toposa[15]. If this is the case, the Nyangatom demographics are readily explained, as well as the awesome pressure they exert on all their neighbors.

What about the balance evoked in Turton's and Tornay's text now? "Woti *chip* amidi!" was a recurring statement in Kara: "We are squeezed in!" Nearly twenty years ago, Alvarsson perceptively pointed out the basic characteristic of the "tribal zone" was in place - that while there had been little "direct" transformation of the area through the Ethiopian state, conflicts were already aggravated through the "lack of territory for expansion" (1989: 85), which became felt precisely in times of population and herd-size growth (see Almagor 1979: 128 for the Dassanetch perspective).

This heightened sense of crowding, to use a behaviorist metaphor, is manifested in the dissolution of buffer zones which Kara and Nyangatom patterns of cultivation and herding had let emerge. That the "encroachment" by the Nyangatom on the Kara's territory (Tornay 1979: 114) received official sanction subsequent to the establishment of the new *woreda* is an indication that there was no appreciation of the benefits both groups received from not having a boundary guaranteed by the armed forces of the state apparatus. The definition of the Omo River as the boundary has pushed the Kara literally with their backs against the wall. As a pernicious side-effect, this policy decision might have rendered mediation and negotiation obsolete, depriving the Kara spokesmen of their capacity to influence the future of their people substantially: the coming years will show whether Nyangatom, backed by the zonal government, will even bother to communicate, or whether they will simply insist in their demands, uncompromising and proud (cf. Turton 2003 for the Aari-Mursi example, and Abbink 2000 for a caustic analysis of the Suri-Dizi case).

Instead of equable agreements, places were thus simply appropriated, and even unwitting dunces were used in order to cement a claim: the "Nyangatom" episode of the BBC

---

[15] Toposa and Nyangatom have largely amiable relations and are considered perpetual allies (Tornay 2001: 40); both belong to the group of "central Paranilotes" (2001: 9), and are linguistically and culturally similar.

show "Tribe" (screened in 2005) showed the Nyangatom spokesman Eyjem on the top of the hill Lokulan. He visualized the predicaments of his people. Pointing in all directions, Eyjem declared that everywhere there were enemies, from the Mursi over the Kara to the Dassanetch (with the lone exception of the Toposa in the west). To do this standing on Lokulan (an extremely photogenic location) is a powerful move, considering that even for Tornay (1979: 103), the area around the hot springs of the hill Lokulan was clearly Kara territory. But with the permanent Kara settlements on the western bank terminated, the issue became open to competing definitions of the situation. In 2006, access to Lokulan, with its salt deposits and the salty herbs growing around its base, was a highly divisive issue of the entire peace process, especially during stage three (as discussed above). The irony of the situation, that the BBC team was actually exploited by the Nyangatom who thus managed to naturalize their claim to the area in front of millions of viewers, was lost on the BBC and its adventuring show host Bruce Parry[16].

Alvarsson starts his report on the "Aspects of Armed Conflict in South Omo" with a surprised remark: traditional conflicts between "small ethno-linguistic groups, interrupted decades ago by a Pax Britannica or other similar phenomena in the surrounding areas, [have] persisted in the Lower Omo" (1989: 13). He ends it by stating that in case the conclusions of Turton on the nature of the "uncentralized political system", which is based on mutual respect depending on displays of autonomy, group agency and aggression are correct, end to bloodshed can only be attained by precisely such an outsider's peace, enforced through violence and occupation (1989: 87, 104). This he terms the road to "cultural extinction" and "the end of these people as 'free pastoralists'" (1989: 107); and while he falls prey to the romantic stereotype, his statement drives home the point that in the "tribal zone" all interventions are fraught with danger.

South Omo conflict studies present a severe challenge to development discourse and practice, as well as to assumptions of casual modernization, and the biased or underinformed measures of integrating these marginal areas into the Ethiopian state. The data from the 20th century shows that while scarcity and hunger have aggravated some situations, it was in times of plenty that groups acted out their expansionist tendencies most harshly – indeed, already Alvarsson states that the mere fact that white people (the missionaries from the Swedish Philadelphia Church Mission/SPCM) had settled near Kibbish, and had begun to support the local population on a permanent basis, had helped trigger feelings of superiority among the Nyangatom (1989: 101).

Further developments are difficult to predict. One remedy to the ongoing warfare was suggested by the provincial administration: that on the western bank of the Omo a joint *kebele*, managed by Kara and Nyangatom, should be established. By being common stakeholders, it was argued, this could become the germ of a new era of cooperation and peace[17]. But then, how to persuade the Kara that it would be safe for them to settle among Nyangatom, some of whom could be Toposa from the Sudan, who would not even see neighbors in the Kara, and would not have individual friends among them? How to assure

---

[16] See *Anthropology Today* 21 (2), 22 (2-3) for discussions of this series.
[17] Tornay makes a similar suggestion in pointing out some cultivable areas which the Nyangatom could clear jointly with Hamar or Kara (1993: 153); however, no such project, as is wont, is likely to last when the first shot is fired.

them that once a quarrel broke out, they would not be massacred before they had a chance to reach the other side of the river? As seen in the discussion of blood money, simple solutions are bound to fail.

Post Scriptum

On March 17, 2007, a month after I had left my field site, Kornan Naqwa from Kara was shot dead from ambush by a Nyangatom, while drinking coffee in the homestead of a friend on the western bank of the Omo River.

Bibliography

Abbink, Jon, 1993, 'Ethnic conflict in the "tribal zone": the Dizi and Suri in southern Ethiopia.' In: *The Journal of Modern African Studies*, Vol. 31(4), pp. 675-682.

Abbink, Jon, 2000, 'Violence and the crisis of conciliation: Suri, Dizi, and the state in South-West Ethiopia.' In: *Africa*, Vol. 70(4), pp. 1-22.

Almagor, Uri, 1979, 'Raiders and elders: a confrontation of generations among the Dassanetch.' In: Fukui, Katsuyoshi, and David Turton (eds.), *Warfare among East African herders*, Osaka: National Museum of Ethnology.

Almagor, Uri, 2002, 'Institutionalizing a fringe periphery: Dassanetch-Amhara relations.' In: Donham, Don and Wendy James (eds.), *The southern marches of imperial Ethiopia. Essays in history and anthropology*, Oxford: James Currey.

Alvarsson, Jan-Åke, 1989, *Starvation and peace or food and war? Aspects of armed conflict in the Lower Omo valley*, Uppsala Research Reports in Cultural Anthropology Vol. 8.

Bailey, FG, 1998, *The need for enemies. A bestiary of political forms*, Ithaca: Cornell University Press.

BBC Wales, 2005, *Tribe. Series 2: Nyangatom*, Television documentary.

Donham, Don, and Wendy James (eds.), 2002 [1986], *The southern marches of imperial Ethiopia. Essays in history and anthropology*, Oxford: James Currey.

Evans-Pritchard, E. E., 1939, 'Nuer time-reckoning.' In: *Africa*, Vol. 12(2), pp. 189-216.

Ferguson, R. B., and N. L. Whitehead (eds.), 2000 [1992], *War in the tribal zone: expanding states and indigenous warfare*, Santa Fe: School of American Research Press.

Fukui, Katsuyoshi, and David Turton (eds.), 1979, *Warfare among East African herders*, Osaka: National Museum of Ethnology.

Girke, Felix, 2008 (forthcoming), 'Ecology, exchange and cultural neighbourhood – themes in South Omo bondfriendship.' In: Gabbert, E.C., and Sophia Thubauville (eds.), *Modalities of cultural neighbourhood in South Omo*, Köln: Rüdiger Köppe.

Kopytoff, Igor, 1989, *The African frontier: the reproduction of traditional African societies*, Bloomington: Indiana University Press.

Matsuda, Hiroshi, 1996, 'Riverbank cultivation in the Lower Omo Valley: the intensive farming system of the Kara, southwestern Ethiopia.' In: Sato, Shun and Eisei Kurimoto (eds.), *Essays in Northeast African studies*. Osaka: National Museum of Ethnology.

Matsuda, Hiroshi, 2002, 'Political visibility and automatic rifles: the Muguji in the 1990s.' In: James, Wendy (ed.), *Remapping Ethiopia: socialism and after*, Oxford et al.: James Currey.

Naty, Alexander, 1992, *The culture of powerlessness and the spirit of rebellion among the Aari people of southwest Ethiopia*, PhD Thesis, Stanford University.

Rafael, Karsten, 1967, 'Blood revenge and war among Jibaro Indians of East Ecuador.' In: Bohannan, Paul (ed.), *Law and warfare*, New York: Natural History Press.

Sobania, Neil, 1980, *The historical traditions of the peoples of the eastern Lake Turkana Basin c. 1840-1925*, PhD thesis submitted to the School of Oriental and African Studies, University of London.

Strecker, Ivo, 1976, *Traditional life and prospects for socio-economic development in the Hamar administrative district of southern Gamu Gofa*, A report to the Relief and Rehabilitation Commission of the Provisional Military Government of Ethiopia.

Tornay, Serge, 1978, 'L'énigme des Murle de l'Omo.' In: *L'Ethnographie*, Vol. 119(N.S.), pp. 55-75.

Tornay, Serge, 1979, 'Armed conflict in the Lower Omo Valley, 1970-1976: an analysis from within Nyangatom society.' In: Fukui, Katsuyoshi, and David Turton (eds.), *Warfare among East African herders*, Osaka: National Museum of Ethnology.

Tornay, Serge, 1993, 'More chances on the fringe of the state? The growing power of the Nyangatom, a border people of the Lower Omo Valley, Ethiopia (1970-1992).' In: Tvedt, Terje (ed.), *Conflicts in the Horn of Africa: human and ecological consequences of warfare*, Uppsala: Department of Social and Economical Geography/EPOS.

Tornay, Serge, 2001, *Les fusils jaunes. Générations er politique en pays Nyangatom (Éthiopie)*, Paris: Société d'Ethnologie.

Turton, David, 1993, '"We must teach them to be peaceful": Mursi views on being human and being Mursi.' In: Tvedt, Terje (ed.), *Conflicts in the Horn of Africa: human and ecological consequences of warfare*, Uppsala: Department of Social and Economical Geography/EPOS.

Turton, David, 2002, 'A problem of domination at the periphery: the Kwegu and the Mursi.' In: Donham, Don, and Wendy James (eds.), *The southern marches of imperial Ethiopia. Essays in history and anthropology*, Oxford: James Currey.

Turton, David, 2003, 'The politician, the priest and the anthropologist: living beyond conflict in southwestern Ethiopia.' In: *Ethnos*, Vol. 68(1), pp. 5-26.

Turton, David, 2004, *The meaning of place in a world of movement: lessons from long-term field research in southern Ethiopia*, RSC Working Paper No. 18, University of Oxford: Refugee Studies Centre.

Vaughan, Sarah, 2006, 'Responses to ethnic federalism in Ethiopia's southern region.' In: Turton, David (ed.), *Ethnic federalism. The Ethiopian experience in comparative perspective*, Oxford et al.: James Currey.

Human Rights and Conflicts of Street Children in Ethiopia

Anna Lena Johannsen[1]

1   Introduction

The aim of the research is to understand the street children phenomenon by critically looking at development and human rights concepts. Strengths and weaknesses of process based on the Poverty Reduction Strategy Papers (PRSP and approaches of non-governmental-organisation's (NGO) are analyzed. Different kinds of conflict impacting on street children are discussed. Also some conflict mechanisms of life on the street are presented. Having scrutinized these different levels, an attempt is made to answer the following questions: Which concepts and development strategies offer the most convincing, effective and sustainable solutions for the street children phenomenon? Are street children's most pressing needs reflected in the Ethiopian PRSP? What are the economic and social impacts of globalization on street children? Is the Human Rights concept a helpful tool for the improvement of the situation of street children?

The number of street children in Ethiopia has reached an alarming proportion with an estimated 200,000 street children — and around 100,000 in the capital Addis Ababa alone. One quarter of them are girls who are particularly vulnerable to various kinds of abuse[2]. The NGO Forum on Street Children estimates that the number of street children continues to increase by 3% each year because the conditions that give rise to the phenomenon do not improve[3]. The ministry of labor and social affairs estimates another 500,000 children to be at risk of ending up on the street. There are a number of reasons for children living on the streets: family violence, family breakdown, rural-to-urban migration, poverty or death of parents from HIV/AIDS. Street children often run away from their homes to reduce the burden on the family or simply because the family cannot cope with another mouth to feed. The problem is made worse by the increasing drought problem. Streetism is an inter-related phenomenon with complex roots. Street children rely on state assistance and require specifically targeted programs. These state programs still lack in Ethiopia, leaving the community or charitable NGOs responsible for street children.

One has to be aware that a Western concept of childhood dominates most literature on the phenomenon of street children. A child migrating to the city and working on the street might, for example, be culturally legitimate. Many children have been pulled out of school by their parents who could not afford education fees, or the parents needed their children's labour to supplement family income[4]. In particular, the cultural constructions of the boy-child

---

[1] Anna Lena Johannsen earned a European Master's Degree in Human Rights and Democratisation University of Maastricht, she lives in Padua, Italy

[2] UN Office for the Coordination of Humanitarian Affairs, IRINnews, *ETHIOPIA: UNICEF concerned over round-up of street children*, http://www.irinnews.org, 26.7.2002.

[3] Addis Tewlid, *the lost generation?*, Abebe, M., http://www.addistewlid.com, 15.4.2003.

[4] B. Rwezaura, *Law, culture and children's rights in Eastern and Southern Africa - Contemporary challenges and present-day dilemmas,* in W. Ncube (ed.), *Law, culture, tradition and children's rights in eastern and Southern Africa,* Dartmouth, Ashgate, 1998, p.292.

might enhance the likelihood of boys to become street children[5]. In my opinion, the increasing number of street children is an expression of the negative impact of globalization on the poorest, including the promise of a better life in the city with less hardship than in the countryside. The loss of traditional family values and the adoption of individually-shaped urban life and monetisation aggravate streetism due to the rupture of community bonds[6]. My hypothesis is that the microcosm of streetism is an expression of aggression on other levels (private, national and international level); namely inhuman and unjust relations of inclusion and exclusion and the lack of a social net and will to take care of the weakest in family, society and in international economic and political relations.

2   Street children — a definition

Street children are children who are abandoned or neglected and for whom the street has become their home[7]. Children living on the street can be distinguished into *street children* (who decide to stay on the street) and *abandoned children* (who have no alternative). They can be categorized into children *on* the street and children *of* the street. Some 15,000 (of about 100,000) children in Addis Ababa are believed to be children *of* the street, which means they work 12 to 14 hours a day and then go home[8]. However, most street children live their entire lives on the streets[9]. The use of such terms clouds over the diversity of experiences of the children that populate the streets[10]. Although classified as a group, street children are heterogeneous. Instead of a uniform profile, the different motives and backgrounds must be considered. Neither the poor in general, nor street children in particular, are a homogenous group.

The majority of street children are between 8 to 14 years old, but some are much younger or even born onto the street. Due to socio-cultural reasons, most of the street children are boys. It is more common that boys look for work outside their homes. Some relatives even encourage boys to look for work in the city. It is a dream of a more *modern* life, which is synonymous with job opportunities and making a fortune. They leave their miserable family situation in the countryside, where many families do not have enough food for all their children, and follow their illusion about a better life in the city[11]. Once in Addis Ababa, the disillusionment of being without income is great and the only alternative becomes a life on the street. Often children become victims of child labour, sometimes working for a businessman who offers their parents money. But mostly they never earn any money and instead work long days for a handful of food and a place to sleep on the floor. Without the socially accepted alternative to return home, a life on the street is perceived as a life at least in

---

[5] B. Rwezaura,…op.cit,pp.298-299.

[6] A. Invernizzi,…op.cit.pp.94-95.

[7] G. Van Bueren, *The International Law on the Rights of the Child,* Boston, Martinus Nijhoff Publishers, 1995, p.284.

[8] UN Office for the Coordination of Humanitarian Affairs, IRINnews, *Ethiopia: more and more children forced onto the streets,* http://www.irinnews.org, 30.4.2002.

[9] G.Van Bueren,…op.cit.p.284.

[10] A. Invernizzi, *Straßenkinder in Afrika, Asien und Osteuropa – eine kommentierte Bibliographie,* Bonn, Zentralstelle Weltkirche der Deutschen Bischofskonferenz, 2001, p.79.

[11] Interview with Gizachew Ayka, director of the NGO Hope For Children, 19.4.2003.

independence and free from hard work. Often that is what they ran away from in the first place: violence, abuse or too hard work at home.

3   A view from within

What do children *learn* when living on the street? How do street children deal with the conflicts they have? What kind of conflicts do they have and with whom? The street can be a place of exclusion and marginalisation but also a place for socialization and integration. For some children, the street is a place of identity, solidarity and belonging. In many cases, the subculture of the street becomes a substitute for family or community life. The context is different from person to person. Therefore, it is essential to listen to the children's conceptualization of their situation and relationship to life on the street in order to understand their needs. The cause of streetism and the consequence of it have to be differentiated. The street mostly is a place of gang membership and group pressure. The laws of inclusion and exclusion are rigorous. There is now other authority they could turn to or that takes care of them or their problems. In order to survive, one needs to have a clear belonging, which *leader* one adheres to and which place to defend. Once in conflict with a group member, violence and fighting are means of *solving the conflict*. The winner can stay but the looser must leave and look for another place to live – to become member of another group, in another area. If you are new to the street, you have to submit to a group leader and work for him[12]. It is the law of obedience and of the survival of the fittest. The groups are organized hierarchically and there are clear gender roles. Most conflicts are due to personal disputes (jealousy, disobedience) or maybe someone took the food of the other, sleeps in the place where the other used to sleep or comes to an area without permission where others rule. Next to this inter-personal level, street children are of course in conflict with authorities on the street: the police, shop owners, people in society who mistreat them etc.. They are in fact *in conflict with society in general*. "Sometimes the street children become aggressive to people who mistreat them but most of the time they try to leave things behind", reports Gizachew Ayka from Hope for Children in Ethiopia. Most of the time the children see themselves outside the societal system due to the values society puts on them[13]. Because of that they create their own social system with unwritten rules and regulations. It is predominantly the perception of the public that discriminates and excludes the street child[14]. Street children also frequently experience violence by local police and are subject to external pressure they cannot influence. Stigmatization and violence against street children drives them into identifying themselves as delinquents. Many street children live outside official norms and often find themselves criminalized even though they did not commit any crime. On the street they learn how to live in a group, how to avoid conflicts, how to share and of course how to use different drugs. If they get into conflict with the police, these simply move them to another place – sometimes they even brutally deport them far outside the city. Then they have to walk back long ways to

---

[12] Interview with Gizachew Ayka, director of Hope for Children, 2.2.2007.
[13] Interview with Gizachew Ayka, director of Hope for Children, 2.2.2007.
[14] A. Invernizzi,...op.cit.,p.99.

return. Their "illegality" makes them subject to harassment and to the constant threat of eviction[15].

4   The relation between poverty, conflicts and street children

The street children phenomenon cannot be considered in isolation. It must be seen as a consequence of other underlying problems. It is a symptom for underlying poverty that is aggravated by the global relations of inclusion and exclusion. For understanding the complexity that causes the phenomenon, a holistic approach including poverty, discrimination, social relations and culture is necessary[16]. Poverty alone is not an explanation for streetism. Street children are not a mono-causal phenomenon but an example of the intensification of economic and social marginalization. They are victims of an unequal economic and social system. Thus, only if grasped multi-dimensionally can we change the street children problem. Due to the complexity of the streetism phenomenon, various levels and factors that impact street children have to be considered. Both national and international relations have to be addressed for finding sustainable solutions. It becomes ever clearer that solutions for the problem of streetism consist in addressing the causes of the migration to the street. Rural conflicts (conflicts at the borders with Eritrea, Somalia, Sudan, Kenya, but also within the regions – e.g. the South or Oromo dominated areas etc.) and poverty causes the rural populations (mostly from the North, Gojam and Gonder area) to move to urban areas in the hope for employment and a better future. But the unexpected challenges of city life enhance the breakdown of many families[17]. In order to reduce the number of internally displaced people, conflicts must be solved to a peaceful end. Therefore, it is my conclusion that family values, children's right to a family and childhood, underlying conflicts and rural poverty must all be addressed to prevent streetism.

Children flee their homes due to conflicts and poverty, which are the main causes for children living on the street. An unjust distribution of land, no access to production and ruthless laws of inclusion and exclusion, lead to some peasants not being able to feed their children. Poverty has many dimensions. It depends on the perspective and context and is above all a cultural construction. It manifests itself in low income, poor health, missed education, social and political marginalization and deprivation. This needs to be considered in the design of development strategies for street children. Poverty has an undermining effect on children and is the main reason for children leaving their homes and becoming street children. Poverty, discrimination and exploitation aggravate the marginalization of street children, and certain solutions lie in economic and social reform. Existing social politics and equipping children and their caretakers with basic capabilities to escape poverty have been insufficient to stop this negative trend[18]. Social security and justice for children and disadvantaged groups

---

[15] J.Hardoy, *the urban child in the Third World: urbanization trends and some practical issues*, Innocenti Occasional papers, Florence, UNICEF, 1992, p.3.

[16] A. Invernizzi,...op.cit.,p.87.

[17] Shorter, A. and E.Onyalcha, *Street Children in Africa*, Limuru, Kolbe Press, 1999, p.12.

[18] Deutsche Welthungerhilfe and terre des homes, *Die Wirklichkeit der Entwicklungshilfe, zehnter Bericht 2001/2002 Eine kritische Bestandsaufnahme der deutschen Entwicklungspolitik*, 2002, p.28.

is a pillar for sustainable development[19]. The United Nations Children's Fund (UNICEF) estimates that 40% of children in developing countries live in extreme poverty. They are disproportionately represented among the poor. The poverty of children is increasing, especially in sub-Saharan African states. A child born in sub-Saharan Africa is more likely to be malnourished than to go to primary school and is as likely to die before the age of five as to attend secondary school[20]. Poor children are likely to pass on poverty to their children, perpetuating the poverty cycle[21]. Children are hit hardest by poverty because it causes lifelong damages to the development of their minds and bodies. There is no second chance for child development. In order to reduce poverty, it is necessary to create a secure and child-friendly environment to enable children to live with dignity[22]. Therefore, without the realization of children's rights, poverty cannot be reduced. This means ensuring access to basic education, health care, nutrition, water, sanitation and human rights — such as freedom from want and discrimination, which is the basis for social protection and effective participation[23]. Basic and quality education is a vital element in eliminating discrimination and exploitation of children and part of the solution to reducing poverty. The failure to reach this goal means that the poorest children remain in the risk to continue living in situations of exploitation [24]. Thus, preventing and solving streetism is about finding effective poverty reduction measures and conflict solving mechanisms.

What could be sustainable approaches to the reduction of child poverty? To alleviate the poverty of a few, like NGOs do, can be criticized as being a "drop in the bucket." Long-term poverty reduction implies improving the structures that cause poverty. It is necessary to apply a holistic approach towards the street children phenomenon. Neither the top-down nor the bottom-up approach can be successful by itself. Both complement each other. For poverty reduction to be effective and for development to be sustainable, large-scale development strategies have to become compatible with grass-root needs. Poverty reduction and development need to be formulated according to the ideas of the affected. NGOs and civil society must improve their roles as mediators and advocates so that the rights and needs of the grass root are truly taken into account at the international and national level. I believe that a new nationally and internationally shared responsibility for street children could constitute a convincing approach for tackling the phenomenon since many layers are part of the problem and of the solution. Human rights herewith can serve as a very suitable framework. Poverty does not just mean lack of income; it means the denial of basic human rights. A human rights approach to poverty reduction provides a framework for promoting and protecting the human rights of people deprived of their basic rights. The actions of all power holders — the government, IGOs, trans-national companies (TNCs), NGOs and civil society — need to become formulated in the best interest of the child, focused on the protection of children and the prevention of child-poverty. Societal and global structures that aggravate conflict, poverty and inequality, and thus also the street children phenomenon, need to be addressed. This

---

[19] Deutsche Welthungerhilfe and terre des hommes,...op.cit, p.38.
[20] A.Shorter and E. Onyalcha, *Street Children in Africa*, Limuru, Kolbe Press, 1999, p.20.
[21] UNICEF, A UNICEF policy review document: *Poverty Reduction Begins with Children*, New York, The United Nations Children's Fund, Division of evaluation, policy and planning, 2000, p.1.
[22] UNICEF, *finance development invest in children*, Division of Policy and Planning, New York, The United Nations Children's Fund, 2002, p.3.
[23] UNICEF, *Poverty Reduction Begins with Children*, ...op.cit.p.3.
[24] Ibidem., p.28.

includes fundamental changes of not only unfavourable international trade-relations and negative impacts of globalization but also harmful national and socio-cultural structures that enhance poverty, inequality, conflict, discrimination, exclusion and stigmatization.

5   The Human Rights approach

Poverty of street children needs to be understood as a violation of basic human right, above all in the sense of being socially excluded and discriminated against. The human rights concept is helpful because it defines neglect as a human rights violation. The Preambles of the International Covenant on Civil and Political Rights (ICCPR) and the International Covenant of Economic, Social and Cultural Rights (ICESCR) underline that human rights derive from the inherent dignity of the human person[25]. For street children, having rights first and foremost means being entitled to respect and dignity. Human rights are a tool to formulate basic needs into rights and duties. Human rights can be an effective long-term tool for solving the situation of street children because they address the various dimensions of poverty and social exclusion. Human rights also hold states accountable for the promotion, protection and fulfilment of basic human rights for street children. This accountability towards basic human rights can be a tool for breaking the poverty cycle. The eradication of widespread poverty entails the full exercise of human rights and fundamental freedoms — especially non-discrimination towards the poorest. Human rights are also a useful tool for the empowerment of street children. The right to basic education for women and girls is crucial for breaking the poverty cycle (the more educated women are, the fewer and healthier children they have[26]). Targeting the needs and rights of children would thus constitute a long-term investment in future sustainable poverty reduction and development. But human rights still have to become peoplelized and truly globalized to become a framework for lasting social transformation.

The human rights understanding of poverty addresses the daily assaults on human dignity and vulnerability. A human rights based approach means not only viewing poor people in terms of welfare, but also in terms of obligations to respond to violations of their rights[27]. Since poverty means a denial of human rights and human dignity, poverty reduction obviously involves more than crossing an income threshold[28]. The integration of human rights norms into anti-poverty strategies is crucial. When human rights are introduced in policy making, poverty reduction no longer only derives from the fact that the poor have needs but is based on the rights of poor people — entitlements that give rise to obligations on the part of others that are enshrined in law[29]. Governments are under an obligation imposed by international law to take special measures for effective protection against discrimination of the most vulnerable, discriminated and socially-excluded groups, including street children.

---

[25] United Nations, *A Compilation of International Instruments,* New York and Geneva, United Nations, 1994, pp.8 & 20.
[26] UNICEF, A UNICEF program policy document: *Human rights for children and women: How UNICEF helps make them a reality,* New York, The United Nations Children's Fund, 1999, op.cit.p.15.
[27] UNICEF, *Poverty Reduction Begins with Children, ...* op.cit.p.3.
[28] Ibidem., p.39.
[29] The Office of the High Commissioner for Human Rights, *Human Rights, Poverty Reduction and Sustainable Development - a Background Paper,* World Summit on Sustainable Development, Johannesburg, 2002, p.4.

In theory, a large number of human rights protect street children — the Convention on the Rights of the Child (CRC) being the most specific convention. In practice however, the rights are neither protected by the state — which is the first institution to be held accountable — nor by civil society at large. The CRC (Convention on the Rights of the Child) is the first global instrument to recognize the child possessing rights and the state to respect and ensure them. It defines universal principles for the status of children, providing them with fundamental human rights and freedoms. The CRC was adopted by the UN General Assembly on 20 November 1989 and entered into force on 2.September 1990 — from then on it was considered to be binding. It is a unique international human rights treaty because it has nearly universally been ratified (except for Somalia and the USA) and because it reflects the indivisibility of civil, political, cultural, economic and social rights and emphasizes their mutually reinforcing nature[30]. Upon ratification, States commit themselves to fulfilment of the rights. The Convention does not, however, establish directly enforceable rights. It obliges States to undertake measures to implement the Convention's rights. States have to report to the UN Committee on the Rights of the Child, which monitors the State parties obligations. The CRC lists both direct and indirect obligations of states towards the child. The meaning of the Convention, however, is not primarily legal but, above all, political. The Convention on the Rights of the Child reflects international consensus on children's rights. It is innovative in that it expresses a new attitude towards children in terms of inherent rights and not in the form of charity[31]. The child is no longer merely a part of a family, but a person of his or her own. The international community, however, is far from agreeing on a universal definition of childhood. Childhood is a cultural construction — children are not children "by nature"[32]. The image of "child" changes through time and from culture to culture[33]. This needs to be taken into account when tackling the street children phenomenon from a human rights perspective.

6   *Ethiopian street children deprived of their rights*

The international provisions of the Convention on the Rights of the Child have not yet been implemented to a satisfying degree in Ethiopia. The Committee on the Rights of the Child has expressed a strong concern about the status of the CRC in Ethiopia. In Ethiopia, there is still a gap between the convention and national law and also between practice and theory. Implementation of children's rights has not sufficiently happened, as the case of street children in Ethiopia shows. In theory, human rights instruments ensure accountability, but in practice the state is failing to provide an adequate complaint procedure for child victims of abuse, ill treatment and neglect. Street children in Addis Ababa do not receive any particular care from the state; they are predominantly left to their own destinies. An improvement has been the start of thinking in human rights terms for children, as the State reports to the Committee reflect. Violations against street children have, however, insufficiently been

---

[30] L.LeBlanc, *The Convention on the Rights of the Child – United Nations Lawmaking on Human Rights,* Lincoln and London, University of Nebraska Press, 1995, p.76.

[31] M.D.A. Freeman, *The Limits of Children's Rights,* in M. Freeman, P. Veerman (eds.), *The Ideologies of Children's Rights,* Boston, Martinus Nijhoff Publishers, 1992. pp.4-5.

[32] G. Van Bueren,...op.cit.pp.33-38.

[33] Verhellen, E., *Convention on the Rights of the Child – background, motivation, strategies, main themes,* Leuven-Apeldoorn, Garant Publishers N.V., 1997, p.11.

addressed so far. The implementation system can have a trickle-down effect to make the Convention known to the public at large, and it can (ideally) become a means to involve children in political consideration. At large though, the issue of children's participation in the implementation of the Convention has received insufficient attention, and street children are still deprived of a range of fundamental human rights.

There is need for recognition of the inter-related reality of children's rights and economic, social and political developments. A new strategy for children's rights requires a new perception of children as whole human individuals with needs, capacities and rights to be protected from public and private forms of violence. All levels of society have to realize that they contribute to the situation of streetism by neglecting the phenomenon. Only if grasped multi-dimensionally, it is possible to change it — including the fulfilment of civil, political, economic, social and cultural rights. There have been significant improvements in the protection of children's rights, but the survival and development of children is still not given sufficiently high priority. The thinking in human rights terms has to become part of Ethiopian culture and practice. Law and practice have to be harmonized, otherwise the concept of human rights for street children remains hollow. After having scrutinized existing standards and instruments, the conclusion has to be that they are not sufficiently focused on street children but nevertheless constitute the frame for something that yet has to be implemented.

7   The PRSP-approach

The Sustainable Development and Poverty Reduction Program (SDPRP) prepared by the Ethiopian Government was delivered to the World Bank in August of 2002. The objective of the government's poverty reduction strategy is to reduce poverty through macroeconomic stability. Whether economic growth benefits the poorest is questionable. It is important to ensure that rapid economic growth does not lead to higher levels of inequality. A pro-poor growth strategy, promoting growth with equity, actually gaining the poor, is essential for rapid poverty reduction[34]. It is the government's overriding objective to ensure that growth also has a positive social impact and that poor people are the prime beneficiaries of economic growth and development[35]. The PRSP process is coloured by many promising words, but concrete ways of implementation are still missing. Fundamental improvements need to be made in order for poor people to genuinely participate in the PRSP processes. Accountability and transparency must be improved within the World Bank and IMF, and the poor people must be heard in a genuine and transforming way[36]. The PRSP attempts to include the poor with a voice in the decision-making process. The participatory assessment of the PRSP is a chance for acknowledging poor people's rights. However, there is no established culture of consulting the poor. There is a pressing need to institutionalise participation of non-state actors in policy, planning and monitoring development.

---

[34] Ethiopia's PRSP: *Sustainable Development and Poverty Reduction Program (SDPRP)*, Federal Democratic Republic of Ethiopia, Addis Ababa, Ministry of Finance and Economic Development, 2002, pp.25-26.
[35] Ibidem., p.36.
[36] see Christian Aid, *Ignoring the experts - Poor people's exclusion from poverty reduction strategies*, http://www.christian-aid.org.uk, 18.5.2003.

Does the Ethiopian PRSP benefit street children? Children and childhood poverty are not discussed explicitly in the Ethiopian PRSP. The Ethiopian PRSP neither specifically targets children nor an urban policy that aims at the prevention of streetism. Instead, a strategy suggested by the Ethiopian PRSP states that beggary and working poor should be discouraged and stigmatized. And traditional means of giving alms to the poor, such as street children, should be transformed into a fund that creates employment for street children[37]. The institutionalisation of the stigmatization of street children, as suggested in the Ethiopian PRSP, must be criticized because it fosters the severity of marginalization already experienced by street children. And instead of creating alternative job opportunities for street children, an investment should be made in education, rehabilitation and social inclusion. A focus on the prevention of child poverty is not dominating the PRSPs, even though it is fundamental for breaking the poverty cycle. Street children's most pressing needs are still not targeted enough in the Ethiopian PRSP. The Ethiopian PRSP still needs to include a pro-child-dimension, specifically targeting the needs and rights of children, including street children. This would, at the same time, be a long-term investment in future sustainable poverty reduction and development.

8   NGO initiatives

NGOs are playing an increasingly important role for development at the local level. Many have made significant contributions to participatory development. They seek to alleviate poverty and inequalities by empowering the poor, strengthening their capabilities to become masters of their own destinies, building on indigenous know-how and cultural sensitivity, promoting self-reliance and self-sustainability[38]. A great number of NGOs and local initiatives actively change the situation of extremely poor children in Ethiopia for the better. But they do not have a cumulative effect to bring about change towards the overall street children phenomenon. Many NGOs face problem with the registration at the government. Every third year their NGO status must be requested anew. The government does not support the NGOs in their work, but makes life more difficult for them many times. It is e.g. very difficult to get access to an available ground (e.g. the compound Hope for Children had build its school on was taken away from them again!). The purchase of tax free items is very limited even though this should be the case for charity NGOs (we wanted to give the NGO our car, but the government would not allow a tax free import!).

Networking among the various initiatives could have a synergetic effect, touching the various cultural and political layers of the problem. "Ethiopian child rights NGOs have started creating forums and this has already helped solving some problems", mentions Mr.Ayka from Hope for Children. It is essential to find structural solutions because the street children phenomenon is the expression of a complicated web of social and economic problems that forces people to live on the edge of society. These also include changes in culture, mentality and attitudes. The public opinion has a strong impact on children's living conditions. All levels of society (government and civil society) have to realize that they contribute to the situation of streetism by neglecting the phenomenon. It is thus important to understand the

---

[37] Ethiopia's PRSP,...op.cit.pp.126-127.
[38] Brohman, J., Popular Development, Oxford, Blackwell, 1996, p.254.

strengths and weaknesses of the socio-cultural context. In my opinion, solving the street children phenomenon is about changing societal structures that produce neglect into structures that value children. The reintroduction of collective responsibility for the upbringing of children into African societies, for example, can be promising for the prevention of streetism. Therefore, the advocacy work of NGOs in raising awareness of the responsibility for street children in the community at large is a promising approach for finding sustainable solutions.

In Ethiopia, the majority of direct actions to help street children are undertaken by NGOs and religious organizations. Many NGOs have ethical or religious motivations for their work. While religion and NGO-work do not necessarily contradict, the combination can have a manipulative affect on the beneficiaries of aid. NGOs and groups of young Ethiopians who go out and talk with street children are those who concretely do something for street children. Many NGOs do not attempt to take the children off the street, but aim to bring sympathy. Some organizations work directly with the children while others work with the local community. In spite of good intentions of numerous programs for street children, the attitude of the public remains largely negative. The hostility towards street children explains to a large extent why the public is not committed to solving the problem. Advocacy aimed at the education of the general public should be central to NGO activities. Therefore, human rights NGOs have an especially crucial role to play. "Society has gotten used to the street children phenomenon and thinks it is normal", a staff member of the NGO Hope for Children (HFC) explains. "They have gotten blind and do not see the misery anymore. They perceive them as lower, non-human and non-worthy, as thieves and criminals and treat street children like garbage. The dumping of street children outside the city, which human rights groups criticize, is just the peak of mistreatment", Y. Tsefaye from HFC says[39]. Worse is the daily neglect and disrespect by society and the perception of street children as outcasts, delinquents and disturbers, which result in depression and suicidal thoughts on the part of street children. To overcome the feeling of neglect and helplessness, of I am not useful anymore is essential[40]. Therefore, it is just as important that the state increases investment into the structures that promote peace and stability, and a better living for very poor and neglected children (education, health, family, etc.) as to change people's ways of thinking about street children who they see daily on the street. A positive change from the perspective of a street child starts in the heads of the people passing by: that people do not pass by and look away, but that they see the children, respect them and protect their human rights.

9   Résumé

The phenomenon of street children has not been understood as a social problem in need of multidimensional community strategies yet. First and foremost, policies that attempt to effectively aid street children must build on the experiences of the street children themselves. A social program for street children can fail simply because people do not share the results of it. Therefore, it is important that the targets are defined together with the street children and that the socio-cultural context is understood. It is decisive that development targets are

---

[39] Interview with Yonas Tsefaye, worker at the NGO Hope For Children, 18.4.2003.
[40] Interview with Gizachew Ayka,…op.cit..

defined together with the street children themselves in order to be legitimate and really respond to their needs. Secondly, a child-focused development is crucial for sustainable poverty reduction and for alleviation of the street children problem. But a focus on the prevention of child poverty is not dominating the Ethiopian PRPS, even though it is fundamental for breaking the poverty cycle. And the most pressing needs of street children are still not targeted enough in the Ethiopian PRSP. Thirdly, urban child-poverty must be targeted in any sustainable poverty reduction strategy, and rural life has to become economically more stable for preventing children taking to the streets of the cities.

Conflicts at the root of children taking to the streets must be settled to a child-friendly solution. On a private level, reducing conflicts on family level could prevent the children from leaving their homes. This could be achieved through family counselling and support for parents to take care of and responsibility for their children. Once on the street the children should not be left to their own *laws*, but sensitively taken care of by professional social workers and by a functioning legal system. It is important that the police are trained to respect the laws, to understand street children's behaviour and humanly treat juvenile *delinquents*. In order to reduce conflicts with society, the public must learn to respect the way the children live and/or find ways out of the misery together with the children. Awareness raising programs, fostering understanding, tolerance and the respect for life and the value of children, are needed. This is the responsibility on a political level. Last but not least, fairer international (trade) relations, lessening extreme poverty aggravating the street children phenomenon are an international responsibility (the MDGs are an example of good will, but effective action must follow).

Coming back to the initial question of the best concepts and development strategies that offer the most convincing, effective and sustainable solutions for the street children phenomenon: While World Bank development strategies have a large-scale approach towards poverty reduction, NGOs address specific needs of the deprived. Both approaches tackle the problem from different ends; both are insufficient as such. While the PRSP development concept offers a long-term solution for the street children phenomenon, the NGO approach predominantly offers short-term solutions. Neither takes underlying conflicts into consideration. The locally run projects mostly have a direct impact on poverty reduction. Service-providing NGOs offer shelter, food, clothing, health, parental and brotherly love and a sense of belonging. These aspects well reflect the importance of street children's physical and spiritual needs, which Hope for Children successfully tries to combine. Particularly street children need emotional support and a new opportunity to change their lives. Hope for Children has a promising concept towards resolving the street children problem, due to its multidimensional and people-oriented approach. It makes a contribution for changing the situation for a significant number of street children who would otherwise be neglected and forgotten. NGO work can achieve a great deal, empower the poor and make a difference, but they nevertheless do not have enough strategic capacity and financial power for large-scale changes. None of these excellent NGO-initiatives does more than offer a palliative for this immense social problem, as Shorter and Onyancha mention[41]. The projects are coping with the consequences, rather than looking at the causes of the problem itself. NGOs make the life of street children endurable but do not remove the cause of their situation. In addition to

---

[41] Shorter, A. and E. Onyalcha,...op.cit.p.91.

addressing the symptoms, it is essential to change the local and global relations that cause them. This means also to address conflicts and foster political peace. It is crucial that the Ethiopian civil society realizes its full potential to monitor and criticize the (non-) investment of the government in the social sector of development. Currently, Ethiopian civil society largely lacks this capacity[42]. The NGO group for the CRC encouraged the creation of national NGO coalitions to improve coordination and cooperation[43]. Networking is a means also to control accountability and to prevent corruption[44]. It offers a chance for NGOs to work more efficiently and effectively, but this has not become common practice yet. Greater coordination between agencies working with street children would prevent more children slipping through the cracks[45]. A functional consortium of street children organisations would constitute a powerful pressure group for policies on poverty alleviation and for legislative and educational changes in front of national and international bodies. In particular, the political will, to change structures fostering conflicts, inequality and marginalisation, has to improve. Next to that, the view from within makes clear that poverty is not only measurable in terms of economic poverty, but must also be understood as social exclusion – often due to conflicts, stigmatization and hopelessness. The human rights approach shows potential to change society's negative attitudes and to encourage people to take responsibility for street children and their inherent rights. In my understanding, the human rights approach makes clear that neither strategy can be successful without thinking in terms of rights and duties.

Bibliography

Brohman, J., *Popular Development,* Oxford, Blackwell, 1996.

Bueren, G., Van, *The International Law on the Rights of the Child,* Boston, Martinus Nijhoff Publishers, 1995.

Deutsche Welthungerhilfe and terre des hommes, *Die Wirklichkeit der Entwicklungshilfe, zehnter Bericht 2001/2002 Eine kritische Bestandsaufnahme der deutschen Entwicklungspolitik,* 2002.

Ethiopia's PRSP: *Sustainable Development and Poverty Reduction Program (SDPRP),* Federal Democratic Republic of Ethiopia, Addis Ababa, Ministry of Finance and Economic Development, 2002.

Freeman, M.D.A., *The Limits of Children's Rights,* in M. Freeman, P. Veerman (eds.), *The Ideologies of Children's Rights,* Boston, Martinus Nijhoff Publishers, 1992.

Government of Ethiopia, *Ethiopia: Development Framework and Plan of Action 2001-2010,* presentation of the GFDRE on the third UN Conference on the LDCs, Brussels, 2001.

J.Hardoy, *the urban child in the Third World: urbanization trends and some practical issues,* Innocenti Occasional papers, Florence, UNICEF, 1992.

---

[42] Government of Ethiopia, *Ethiopia: Development Framework and Plan of Action 2001-2010,* presentation of the GFDRE on the third UN Conference on the LDCs, Brussels, 2001, p.18.

[43] NGO group for the Convention on the Rights of the Child, *A guide for non-governmental organizations reporting to the Committee on the Rights of the Child,* Geneva, Defence for Children International, 1998, p.3.

[44] Shorter, A. and E. Onyalcha,...op.cit.pp.108-110.

[45] see UN Office for the Coordination of Humanitarian Affairs, IRINnews, *Ethiopia: more and more children forced onto the streets,* http://www.irinnews.org, 30.4.2002.

A. Invernizzi, *Straßenkinder in Afrika, Asien und Osteuropa – eine kommentierte Bibliographie*, Bonn, Zentralstelle Weltkirche der Deutschen Bischofskonferenz, 2001.

LeBlanc, L., *The Convention on the Rights of the Child – United Nations Lawmaking on Human Rights*, Lincoln and London, University of Nebraska Press, 1995.

NGO group for the Convention on the Rights of the Child, *A guide for non-governmental organizations* reporting to the Committee on the Rights of the Child, Geneva, Defence for Children International, 1998.

B. Rwezaura, *Law, culture and children's rights in Eastern and Southern Africa - Contemporary challenges and present-day dilemmas*, in W. Ncube (ed.), *Law, culture, tradition and children's rights in eastern and Southern Africa*, Dartmouth, Ashgate, 1998.

Shorter, A. and E.Onyalcha, *Street Children in Africa*, Limuru, Kolbe Press, 1999.

The Office of the High Commissioner for Human Rights, *Human Rights, Poverty Reduction and Sustainable Development - a Background Paper*, World Summit on Sustainable Development, Johannesburg, 2002.

UNICEF, A UNICEF policy review document: *Poverty Reduction Begins with Children*, New York, The United Nations Children's Fund, Division of evaluation, policy and planning, 2000.

UNICEF, *finance development invest in children*, Division of Policy and Planning, New York, The United Nations Children's Fund, 2002.

UNICEF, A UNICEF program policy document: *Human rights for children and women: How UNICEF helps make them a reality*, New York, The United Nations Children's Fund, 1999.

United Nations, *A Compilation of International Instruments*, New York and Geneva, United Nations, 1994.

Verhellen, E., *Convention on the Rights of the Child – background, motivation, strategies, main themes*, Leuven-Apeldoorn, Garant Publishers N.V., 1997.

Internet sources:

Addis Tewlid, *the lost generation?*, Abebe, M., http://www.addistewlid.com, 15.4.2003.

Christian Aid, *Ignoring the experts — Poor people's exclusion from poverty reduction strategies*, http://www.christian-aid.org.uk, 18.5.2003.

UN Office for the Coordination of Humanitarian Affairs, IRINnews, *Ethiopia: more and more children forced onto the streets*, http://www.irinnews.org, 30.4.2002.

UN Office for the Coordination of Humanitarian Affairs, IRINnews, *Ethiopia: more and more children forced onto the streets*, http://www.irinnews.org, 30.4.2002.

UN Office for the Coordination of Humanitarian Affairs, IRINnews, *Ethiopia: UNICEF concerned over round-up of street children*, http://www.irinnews.org, 26.7.2002.

Chapter 3: Eritrea

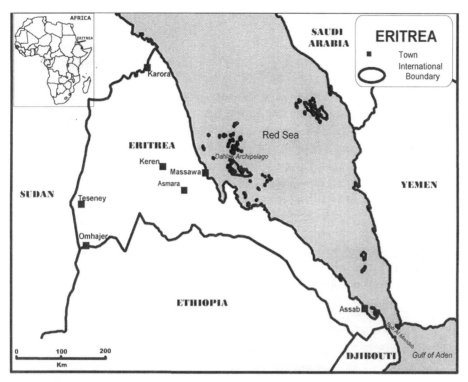

The delineation of the international boundaries shown on this map must not be considered authoritative

Eritrea, the USA, and the "War on Terrorism": Internal Challenges and the International Dimension

Nicole Hirt

1 Introduction

This article analyses the foreign relations of Eritrea towards the United States of America in the context of the dynamics of the global "war on terrorism", considering local and regional dimensions of insurgency in the Horn of Africa. Additionally, it attempts to illustrate the once ambiguous relations between Eritrea and the U.S. and the reasons for their steady decline, which are based on both countries' engagement in the Somalia conflict on opposite sides and America's increasingly open support of Ethiopia in the border dispute with Eritrea.

As Eritrea's foreign policy is strongly shaped by the narrow circle of the leadership of the PFDJ (People's Front for Democracy and Justice), it may be assumed that personal and psychological factors have an impact on its foreign policy, like the political elite's disappointment of the negligence of Eritrean positions and interests by the United States during the Eritrean liberation struggle.

The first section deals with the role of the opposition within the country, including Jihad Eritrea, as it was instrumentalized by the government to claim the existence of an internal terror threat while it was a supporter of America's anti-terror strategy (from 2001-2004). Since independence, the state has been run by a one-party regime, which has turned into an autocracy at least since 2001, the time of the September 11 events in the United States. By a mix of popular support or at least obligance towards the EPLF/PFDJ[1] that brought about independence, political repression and traditional norms and values fostering conflict avoidance, the government was able to maintain its internal monopoly of power and there were relatively few acts of insurgency within the country, given the size of the diasporic Eritrean opposition in Sudan and around the globe.

As to transnational insurgency, the government of Eritrea's strategy to support opposition forces in neighbouring countries, mainly Ethiopia and the Sudan, and since recently, in Somalia, is no regional exception. It is hard to discover links to international terrorism in this regard. Eritrea follows a long-standing tradition within the Horn by trying to destabilise its neighbouring countries through the support of militant opposition movements. It is a new strategy to link such activities rhetorically to the support of or the fight against al Qaida, reflecting the new realities created by the United State's anti-terror campaign.

Regarding internal violence in Eritrea, the government itself is the main actor, using force to extinguish both violent and non-violent opposition within the country. With its power stabilized, the main vulnerability of the government is not its lack of a power monopoly, but its lack of material resources, and in spite of its ideology of self-reliance, the regime needs foreign support to shore up its hard currency reserves, preferably in form of unconditional budget support. At this point, the interests of Eritrea and the United States seemed to match

---

[1] The Eritrean People's Liberation Front (EPLF) led the country to independence in 1991 and renamed itself into Popular Front for Democracy and Justice (PFDJ) in its third congress in 1994.

during the immediate post-September-11 period: the U.S. needed a country in the geographical position of Eritrea willing to meet its demands in the fight against actual and potential terrorism, while Eritrea's poor human rights record did not seem to be an obstacle to a nation that considers Guantanamo and CIA prisons as adequate means of "pre-emptive self defence". And Eritrea needed an international partner supplying it with the much needed hard currency without asking too many questions.

Therefore, after 2001, attempts were made from both sides to set up a common anti-terror strategy, but finally, the whole process failed. Section three of the article analyses Eritrea-U.S. relations in the context of their historical development and their actual failure in the framework of the "war on terrorism". The aim is to present an example of mutual misperceptions and instrumentalisation of interests in the context of anti-terrorism, leading to dangerous and unforeseeable developments and further destabilisation of the Horn.

2   Internal and Regional Dimensions of "Terrorism"

The roots of internal insurgencies in Eritrea date back to events during the independence struggle, when the EPLF ousted the ELF (Eritrean Liberation Front) from the field in 1982. During the following years, the remnants of the ELF split up into numerous factions, with the ELF-RC (ELF-Revolutionary Council) emerging to be probably the strongest among the different factions and unrelated to Islamist activities. As many former ELF-fighters remained in Sudan as refugees prior to and after independence, a potential base for future acts of sabotage was created. After independence, the EPLF/PFDJ government missed the opportunity to reconcile with the opposition forces, which can be seen as one first step towards political authoritarianism. Similar to the secular opposition, the Islamists are divided into several organisations. The Eritrean Islamic Jihad Movement (Harakat al Jihad al Islami al Eritria/EIJM) was formed around 1980, a second one is the Islamic Salvation Movement. It is said that only a small part of the supporters of Islamist organisations are radical supporters of terrorism[2], but when Osama bin Laden stayed in Sudan and trained fighters for his purposes in the 1990s, it is likely that a number of Eritreans joined his training camps (Mengisteab and Yohannes 2006:209). Links between the Eritrean Islamist movements and al Qaida were allegedly discovered during the investigations into the first World Trade Center bombing in 1993[3], but it is unclear if and to what extent these links still exist.

Today, Jihad Eritrea constitutes one part of the country's exiled opposition, but it is difficult to trace back the events of sabotage and terror that took place in Eritrea during the 1990s and early 2000s to one single opposition group, a fact which is partially due to the lack of transparency of the government's information policy.

The continuous planting of land mines during this period caused casualties among military personnel and civilians alike; but explicit acts of terrorism have been relatively rare. The following incidents highlight the issue in some detail:

In 1996, some Belgian tourists and their driver were killed near Merara, a village situated in the eastern escarpment north of Asmara. The incident was not reported by the

---

[2]   MIPT Terrorism Knowledge Base, www.tkb.org/Group.jsp?groupID=4535
[3]   Mineweb – South Africa: Nevsuns's Eritrean Tragedy – too little, too late? (dehai news archive/apr-may03)

Eritrean state media at that time. However, in 2001, Dr. Amare Tekle as representative of the Office of the President claimed that "(...) a terrorist organisation with a multinational membership had begun to terrorise Eritreans and visitors from abroad along one of its borders. Among its despicable crimes was the cold-blooded murder of 5 Belgian tourists and their Eritrean escorts. It was for this reason that Eritrea made the war against terrorism one of the corner-stones of its nascent foreign policy"[4]. The speech was held few days after the arrest of the G15[5] and aimed at gaining support from the United States as a reliable partner in the fight against terrorism, and probably to divert attention from the internal developments in the country. The term "terrorist organisation with multinational membership" seems to refer to al Qaida or Islamist forces in general, which seems doubtful in relation to the attack on the Belgians. The incidence did not take place near the border (of Sudan), and according to rumours it could be traced back to an ELF splinter group.[6]

During the Independence Day celebrations in 1997, there was an alleged failed assassination attempt against President Isaias himself in the surroundings of Keren – the suspect being a Sudanese army captain and the National Islamic Front (NIF) government of Sudan was blamed by Eritrea to be responsible[7]. The exact circumstances of the event remained, however, unclear.

In 2003, a Canadian employee of the Nevsun mining company was killed near Bisha in the western lowlands. The government blamed the Eritrean Islamic Jihad Movement for the killing, while the British Ambassador to Eritrea, contradicting this assumption, remarked that there would be no speculation about the reasons of his death.[8] In the same year, a hotel was bombed at Tessenei near the Sudanese border, and the Eritrean Islamic Jihad Movement (EIJM) claimed responsibility for this act of sabotage, as well as for several attacks on military personnel during the same period.

In May 2004, a bomb attack took place during the independence celebrations in Barentu, the capital of Gash-Barka, killing 5 and wounding 88 people. This time, there was public reaction and the government arrested several suspects, claiming they were trained by "groups sponsored and trained by Ethiopia and the Sudan"[9]. There was no direct reference to the Eritrean Jihad Movement. Both Khartoum and Addis Ababa denied to be involved in the attack. ENA (Eritrean National Alliance), the umbrella organisation of the Eritrean opposition, condemned the attack on innocent civilians and claimed that the Eritrean government itself was behind the attacks for the purpose of "giving it international dimensions in an attempt to break out from the regional and international isolation that it lives in"[10].

---

[4] Speech at the Plenary Meeting of the 56th Session of the United Nations General Assembly on Agenda Item 166, „Measures to Eliminate International Terrorism", New York, 4 October 2001.

[5] The so-called G15 comprise a group of high-ranking critics within the PFDJ, indluding former Ministers and Generals who were arrested in September 2001 after having written a critical letter to the President demanding a move towards democratisation

[6] Personal communication in 1997

[7] Alfajr, Vol.1, Issue No 6 Wednesday, 18 June 1997: Confession of captain Nesredin Babakar Aba Alkaharat member of general sevice of security of NIF government in Khartoum charged with attempting to assasinate President Isias Afwerki

[8] Eritrea. British National Killed. IRIN, 17 April 2003

[9] Reuters Nairobi, Kenya, quoting government spokesman Yemane Ghebremeskel, 27 May 2004

[10] Sudan Tribune: Eritrean Opposition ENA Condemns Barentu Bombing. June 7, 2004

To sum up, acts of sabotage and terrorism may be attributed to opposition forces who found a save haven in Sudan and partially in Ethiopia, namely ELF splinter groups and the Eritrean Jihad Movement, but given the degree of suppression and lack of civil liberties in Eritrea, the intensity of violence is low, and international actors of terrorism like al Qaida do not seem to play any significant role in this context. A possible reason is that the western lowlands bordering Sudan are the closest region for militant activists, but the (predominantly Muslim) civilians living there are potential supporters of the opposition, making it counter-productive to attack civilian targets. At the same time, military presence of the government is high, rendering it difficult for small insurgent units to attack military targets - while land mines might strike civilians or National Service recruits as well.

Generally, the acts of sabotage and terror committed in Eritrea were undertaken by opposition groups having their base in neighbouring countries, mainly the Sudan, and are probably supported by both the Ethiopian and the Sudanese governments. This is no surprise, as in a transnational or regional dimension, Eritrea, Ethiopia, the Sudan, Somalia and to a small degree even Djibouti are mutually involved to varying extents in supporting each other's armed opposition groups, thus contributing to the destabilisation of the region. To support the enemy of one's enemy is not a new development in the Horn, and ethnic and religious factors play an important role in this aspect. The next section deals with a new dimension of international involvement in the region, namely the United States' engagement in the "war on terrorism" and its links with the Eritrean government.

3   Relations between Eritrea and the United States – Foes or Partners in the "War on Terror"?

3.1   Pre-Independence Relations
In order to assess the ambiguity of Eritrea-U.S. relations, it is necessary to take a glance at the role the United States played during the times prior to Eritrean independence and its attitude towards the Eritrean liberation struggle. It is well known that the U.S. openly favoured the option of Eritrea joining the Ethiopian Empire during the time of the British Military Administration (1941-1952), when the future of the former Italian colony was discussed at the United Nations. The United States regarded Eritrea as a strategically important place because of its closeness to the Middle East and therefore, the Americans planned to entertain military accommodations related to Cold War activities on Eritrean territory, like supervising troop movements of Arab states which were considered to be potentially harmful to the West. As Emperor Haile Selassie was considered a reliable ally of U.S. interests, the Federation between Ethiopia and Eritrea was constructed by the combined efforts of the Ethiopian Government, the Orthodox Church and U.S. lobbying in the international arena, utilising the support of Eritrea's Christian highlanders who were promised a privileged position under the new arrangement (Negash 1997, Trevaskis 1960). When the Federation was proclaimed in 1952, it was obvious for most international observers that it would be short-lived. In fact, Eritrea was annexed by Ethiopia in 1962 without any audible sign of protest coming from the international community, let alone the United States, while the Eritrean struggle for independence was launched in 1961 in the western lowlands, initially mainly supported by the

Muslim population who did not share the attachment of the Christian Tigrinya speaking highlanders to the Abyssinian culture. But gradually, attempted cultural domination by the Amhara-dominated Ethiopian ruling class, accompanied by economic and political deprivation of all Eritreans alike led to a growing influx of dissatisfied Eritrean Christians to the Eritrean Liberation Front, especially after the Derg overthrew Haile Selassie and extended its terror machine to Eritrea, targeting not only the Front, but all kinds of civilians who were suspected of supporting the case of Eritrean independence. During the early 1970s, three groups split from the ELF to form organisations that merged into the EPLF (Eritrean People's Liberation Front) in 1975, many of its members being highland Christians. The organisation soon came under the leadership of Isaias Afewerki, who determined the ideological outset of the EPLF as well as its foreign relations (Markakis 1987, Yiob 1995).

The Derg finally split from the U.S. in 1978 and turned to the Soviet Union. Thus, the EPLF as a Marxist-oriented movement found itself in diplomatic isolation, as its potential ally, the USSR, for obvious reasons turned to extend support to Ethiopia's new ruler Mengistu Haile Mariam[11]. Naturally, controlling Ethiopia including the strategically important Eritrea as one single entity was clearly preferable to any superpower compared to the option of a small and unstable Eritrean nation-state. While the ELF had interpreted its foreign relations in the framework of its affiliation to the Arab countries, the new EPLF-leadership under Isaias was much more reluctant in this regard, as the Tigrinya highlanders did by no means identify themselves as a part of the Arab world, unlike their Muslim counterparts who were linked to Arab culture by religion, culture and language, and using Arabic as their *lingua franca*.

Haile Selassie claimed that the Eritrean struggle was attributable to Arab interests, using the liberation movement as a proxy, and Israel as an ally of the Emperor was also deeply involved in military training of Eritrean counter-insurgency units with the financial support of the U.S.. There are unconfirmed rumours that the Americans tried to weaken Eritrean-Arab relationships by supporting the emerging EPLF against the ELF, but it is certain that they never favoured Eritrean independence but kept to their paradigm of one united Ethiopia including the Red Sea coast, even if Ethiopia had meanwhile fallen under the hegemony of the Soviet Union. The EPLF unsuccessfully attempted to turn the minds of the Soviet Government by claiming that its support of the Derg was to be considered as an "historical mistake" in order to leave a back door open to finally gain the support of the Eastern Bloc. In fact, the EPLF found itself very much in international isolation, and thus the leadership came up with the ideology of self-reliance which attracted numerous leftist admirers from the West.

After several military ups and downs, the EPLF finally emerged victorious over the Derg military apparatus, which coincided with the dissolution of its ally, the Soviet Union, and the end of the Cold War. Attempts by American diplomacy, led by former President Jimmy Carter in 1989 to secure Eritrea's membership in the Ethiopian nation as an autonomous region[12] failed due to the obvious political and military decline of the Derg. The military victory in 1991 was facilitated by the strategic alliance between the EPLF and the TPLF (Tigray People's Liberation Front) that started its uprising against the Derg in 1975.

---

[11] However, a new ally, namely the Tigray People's Liberation Front (TPLF) emerged within Ethiopia and rose in 1975 to oppose the Derg regime, strengthened by EPLF support
[12] The New York Times, Nov. 24, 1989: Ethiopia-Eritrea Peace Talks

Another noteworthy aspect in this regard is that the relationship between the TPLF, which initially was striving for secession and the EPLF, which supported a unified Ethiopia (apart from its own declaration of independence) after the fall of the Derg-regime had been uneasy from the beginning.[13] Nevertheless, after the retreat of the Ethiopian army in 1991, when Eritrea became de-facto independent and the TPLF took over the government in Ethiopia, both movements appeared to the public to be close allies able to create lasting peace between the new-born State of Eritrea and the Republic of Ethiopia.

3.2   From 1991 – 1998

The immediate challenge for the newly independent country Eritrea under the leadership of President Isaias Afeworki and that of Ethiopia under the TPLF-led Ethiopian People's Revolutionary Democratic Front (EPRDF) with Prime Minister Meles Zenawi as its leader was to find a place in the emerging New World Order. It is interesting to note here that Eritrea tried very much to imitate Ethiopia's strategy in this regard. The EPRDF simply revived the situation that had prevailed under Haile Selassie, turning back to the United States as its main supporter and establishing close ties with Israel as well. And as regards the TPLF, it immediately shifted its stand from a Marxist-oriented, isolationist movement   into a seemingly open-minded, pro-Western government and established an ethnically-based federal constitution. Being a minority regime, this strategy helped stabilise its power[14], and the Meles-Government secured the much-needed support from the international community, including the USA and Europe, in spite of its gross human rights violations.

The Isaias Government copied the same strategy in Eritrea, trying to establish close relations to former adversaries like the United States and Israel (Mengisteab and Yohannes 2006:192-201). In 1987, the EPLF had declared a political shift from socialism to a mixed economy and controlled democracy at its second congress, and thus equally became eligible for Western support. After having to swallow Eritrea's independence as a matter of fact on which both EPLF and TPLF insisted alike, the USA accepted the new reality and supported the Eritreans politically and economically, but in much more reluctant terms than neighbouring Ethiopia (Mengisteab and Yohannes 2006:167). This positive attitude towards the new nation was followed by the Europeans alike, fostered by some prominent supporters of the Eritrean independence struggle[15], but not accompanied by the same intensity of strategic thinking as could be observed from the U.S. and Israel, as European military engagement in the region has been limited after World War II.

Although substantial parts of the Eritrean population favoured close relations with the Arab world, President Isaias remained reluctant by continuously rejecting membership in the Arab League. In fact, at this point of time, Eritrea's relation with the Sudan deteriorated and diplomatic relations were cut off in 1994, while border skirmishes took place with Yemen and

---

[13] Young, John 1996: The Tigray and Eritrean People's Liberation Fronts: A history of tensions and pragmatism, in: Journal of Modern African Studies, 34,1.1996

[14] Trivelli, Richard M., 'Divided histories, opportunistic alliances: Background notes on the Ethiopian-Eritrean war', in *Afrika Spectrum* 33/3, 1998, 257 – 289.

[15] One example is the German MP Uschi Eid, a member of the Green Party, who was a supporter of the EPLF during the independence struggle and fostered German-Eritrean relations during the first years of independence. Several Norwegian organisations, reaching from the Communist Party to the Church,were also active supporters of the Eritrean struggle.

Djibouti in the following years. Relations between Eritrea and Libya remained exceptionally close from the time of independence until the present. Although Eritrea officially maintained its policy of self-reliance and put restrictions on international aid organisations and Non-Governmental Organisations (NGOs), especially since 1997, it secured loans from the World Bank, the EU, the UN, and received bilateral aid from USAID and various European donors, as well as from the Arab Development Bank. It can thus be concluded that before the war with Ethiopia broke out, Eritrea followed a cautious policy of diversified international and regional integration (Hirt 2000:150-157).

3.3   Relations during the war with Ethiopia, 1998 –2000

A violent border conflict between the two countries broke out in May 1998, taking the international community by surprise, and the USA tried unsuccessfully to mediate by presenting the U.S.-Rwanda peace proposal, which was rejected by Eritrea for reasons beyond the scope of this article[16]. While Eritrea lacked the diplomatic skills in presenting its stand to the international community effectively, Ethiopia on the other hand was successful in doing so, accusing Eritrea as the aggressor, thereby leading to Eritrea's increasing international isolation. One major fact beyond the art of diplomacy was that Eritrea had alienated possible supporters during the pre-war period through the President's harsh language on the international parquet. He had criticised both the Organisation of African Union (OAU) and the UN shortly after independence for their lack of support for Eritrean independence. There is no doubt that Isaias was right in his arguments that both organisations turned a blind eye on the suffering of the Eritrean people under the previous Ethiopian regimes, and the UN especially had miserably failed in protecting the Federation between Eritrea and Ethiopia which was born under its auspices. Nevertheless, his criticisms were not helpful in creating sympathy for the new-born nation among members of those institutions (Hirt 2001, Wrong 2005).

The Sudan, former facilitator of the independence struggle, had been declared as a supporter of Islamist movements in Eritrea, while the latter supported all kinds of groups opposed to the National Islamic Front (NIF) Government, from the Sudan People's Liberation Army (SPLA) to the National Democratic Alliance (NDA). With the exception of the close ties to Libya, links to the Arab world, given the rejection of Eritrea to become a member of the Arab League[17], were not strong enough to create decisive Arab support during wartimes. New allies like the Europeans had been treated with suspicion prior to the "border war", because the government feared they could undermine its self-reliance approach by sending NGOs insisting on their own conditionalities, and by promoting civil society organisations which the PFDJ government did not want to tolerate. And it would have been naive to believe that the USA and its ally Israel with its strong historical ties to Ethiopia would favour tiny Eritrea and risk losing Ethiopia[18].

---

[16] The US-Ruanda proposal suggested the withdrawal of Eritrean troops from the region around Badme they had occupied in May 1998 (and which were declared as Eritrean territory by the Eritrea Ethiopia Boundary Commission in 2002), and the employment of Ruandan military observers (Brüne/Heinrich 1999:151)

[17] Eritrea has an observer status at the Arab League since 2003

[18] In 1995, Israel and Eritrea signed an agreement granting Israel access to the Dhalak Islands in the Red Sea in order to establish military facilities. It seems, however, that this engagement did not materialise although there are Arab sources claiming that Israel is actually in the process of re-establishing military ties with Eritrea by creating a naval base on the Dhalak Islands and thus resuming military cooperation disrupted by the border war

It can be assumed that Eritrea over-estimated its own military strength and its regional importance for international actors, as well as its capacity to rely on its own force.

3.4 From 2001 to 2005 – September 11, the "Coalition of the Willing" and the CIA – ups and downs in Eritrean-American relations

After the end of the "border war", Eritrea survived as an independent nation, yet, ended up in humanitarian and economic misery and lost its image as one of the new hopes of Africa. Internal rifts within the PFDJ became obvious, and a short-lived "Prague Spring" (Wrong 2005) evolved. Then, the USA was hit by the September 11 attacks of 2001 and almost simultaneously the Eritrean reformers ended up in jail. It was the beginning of the age of the "war on terror". And, as it seems, the beginning of Eritrean hopes to re-establish U.S.-Eritrean ties on a new base in order to get its support against the Ethiopian government under Meles Zenawi, while relations between Eritrea and most of its neighbours, including Sudan, remained strained[19].

Eritrea further alienated Western supporters because of its rapidly deteriorating human rights record. This alienation included the State Department of the U.S., which was additionally angered by the imprisonment of two Eritrean employees of the American Embassy during the same period[20]. Moreover, the Isaias government claimed that the G 15 were spies for both Ethiopia and the CIA and therefore traitors, and blamed U.S. envoy Anthony Lake, who had mediated in the conflict, for interfering in Eritrea's internal affairs and called him a person who has 'no shame'[21]. But at least the Pentagon tried to maintain good relations by sending high-ranking military commanders to the region, including Eritrea, searching for possibilities to establish new military facilities in the "war on terrorism". Of course, Eritrea's geographical situation close to Yemen and Saudi-Arabia and its access to the sea would have made it an ideal partner in the anti-terror campaign. But finally, the choice to set up an American military base at the Red Sea fell on Djibouti in 2002, a fact which probably disappointed the Eritrean government. In the same year, the Ethiopia Eritrea Boundary Commission (EEBC) declared that Badme, the starting point of the border war, belonged to Eritrea, a verdict which up to now Ethiopia has not accepted, without facing much pressure from the international community to accept the "final and binding" nature of the ruling. Eritrean foreign relations suffered from continuous relative isolation, aggravated by its human rights violations from the viewpoint of the Western nations, and its continuous involvement in regional affairs by supporting opposition movements of neighbouring countries. Echoing the term "axis of evil" by which President Bush branded Iraq, Iran and North Korea, Eritrea declared an "axis of belligerence" consisting of Ethiopia, the Sudan and

---

(Muhammed Salahuddin, Arab News, August 31 2006: How Israel casts its dark shadow over Horn of Africa. www.arabnews.com, retreived on September 28, 2007).

[19] One exception was Djibouti. Eritrea had cut its diplomatic relations with the small neighbour due to its support to Ethiopia, which had shifted its trade from the Eritrean ports of Massawa and Assab to the port of Djibouti, but relations improved soon after the end of the war.

[20] Two local members of the US embassy were arrested in 2001, allegedly for having translated texts criticising the government from Tigrinya into English. They remain in prison without charge. In 2005, two more local staff members of the American embassy were imprisoned, this time for alleged human trafficking. Human Rights Watch 2006

[21] The Herald, Winter/Spring 2002-2003, Number 27, p 9. Lake had publicly criticized the arrest of former Minister of Foreign Affairs, Haile Woldetensae, a member of the G15

Yemen[22]. The Sudan accused Eritrea of supporting the SLA (Sudan Liberation Army) in Darfur, while Eritrea claimed that Sudan supported militant Jihadist groups in Eritrea.

Yet, in another attempt to improve its relations with the U.S., Eritrea joined the "coalition of the willing" in the war against Iraq in 2003. Ironically, both Eritrea and Ethiopia joined this coalition unlike the overwhelming majority of African states. As a response, Donald Rumsfeld and Tommy Franks, commander of the U.S. central command, visited Eritrea in 2003 and lauded its role in the fight against terrorism and its support for the war in Iraq, but it seems that no further results were reached beyond verbal support[23].

Since then, U.S.-Eritrean relations have deteriorated from bad to worse. For example, President Isaias accused the Americans, especially the CIA, as traitors during the border war who had co-operated with the Ethiopians to bring down the Eritrean government. The United States on its part continued to criticise human rights violations in Eritrea, especially the persecution of Evangelical religious communities, a claim that was denied – against obvious evidence - by the government[24]. One can notice that especially since 2005, the move towards an anti-Western and anti-American position of the government has accelerated. Eritrea restricted the movements of the UNMEE peace mission, expelled all European and American nationals among the mission's staff, as well as USAID, which had provided substantial amounts of food aid. The State Department was accused by Eritrean media of being involved in election fraud in Ethiopia[25].

On the side of the U.S. administration, the person who may foremost be held responsible for the deterioriation of relations with Eritrea is Assistant Secretary of State for African Affairs, Jendayi Frazer, who entertains an exceptionally amicable stand towards PM Meles Zenawi and holds a view of the EEBC border decision which is far from the diplomatic neutrality and respect for international law which should be demanded from a person in her position. In early 2006, Frazer fell out with President Isaias, when she required unsuccesfully to visit the contested border area to find out a "workable boundary" based on the principle of "*ex aequo et bono*"[26], disregarding the final and binding nature of the EEBC decision. She was then granted access to the border area from the Ethiopian side[27]. John Bolton, former US ambassador to the UN, revealed Frazers's point of view in the recent publication of his memoir[28]: "For reasons I never understood, however, Frazer reversed course and asked in early Febuary [2006] to reopen the 2002 EEBC decision, which she had concluded was

---

[22] UN Security Council, 31 October 2002: Letter from Eritrea Ministry of Foreign Affairs to the UN Security Council, S/2002/1218, citing a press statement of the Eritrean Government: „An axis of belligerence cannot be tolerated"

[23] Sudan Tribune, 2 September 2003: President Isayas accuses Sudan of embracing „terrorist groups"

[24] IRIN, 1 May 2003: Eritrea: Government denies religious persecution

[25] During the Ethiopian election campaign, Eritrean state media supported the CUD, disregarding its hardline position towards the border conflict and the projected incorporation of Assab into Ethiopia.

[26] Ex aequo at bono (Latin for „according to right and good" is a legal term of art in the context of arbitration. Article 38 of the Statute of the International Court of Justice provides that the Court may decide cases ex aequo et bono, but only where the parties agree thereto. The ICJ has never decided such a case to date (2007). Source: Wikipedia.org

[27] Ghidewon Abay Asmerom: Commentary: U.S. Officials stop demonizing Eritrea, a young and principled African nation. Shabait.com, August 17, 2007. See also: BBC News, January 18 2006: Doubts over US Eritrean Visit

[28] Bolton, John: Surrender is not an Option: Defending America at the United Nations and Abroad. Threshold Editions 2007

wrong, and award a major piece of disputed territory to Ethiopia. I was at a loss to explain that to the Security Council, so I didn't" (Bolton 2007:347).

Apart from the border issue, Jendayi Frazer did her best to prevent the U.S. House of Representatives from tieing aid to Ethiopia to improved conditions of human rights, a move which was even criticised by supporters of the Bush Adminstration.[29] Besides being the main supporter, if not originator of the plan to put Eritrea on the list of states sponsoring terrorism (see below), she went as far as suggesting "regime change" as one possible option to avoid this threat. Ken Menkhaus, a leading American scholar on the Horn of Africa, put it as follows: "Recent statements made by the Assistant Secretary of State for African Affairs, Jendayi Frazer, may have aggravated an already tense situation in the Horn. She made a statement about the government of Eritrea – in order to stay off the list of states sponsoring terrorism, one of the ways to do that would be regime change. By using that expression, that sent a message throughout the region that looked like the United States was implicitly accepting the possibility of an Ethiopian attack [on Eritrea] (...)".[30]

3.5   The Somali Issue

Simultanously, a new and peculiar turn in Eritrean foreign policy became manifest in 2006, which aggravated the historical low in Eritrea-U.S. relations: On the one hand, President Isaias repeatedly condemned the Bush administration for its involvement in the Middle East and the Horn of Africa[31], and stated that human rights as an issue were merely used as an excuse for interference in other nation's internal affairs in order to establish world domination. This can be seen as a sign of frustration in the diplomatic field, as there has not been any progress towards border demarcation between Eritrea and Ethiopia since the 2002 verdict of the EEBC.

At the same time, a shifting of stance towards the former enemies, the Islamists, can be seen, which now became Eritrea's new allies – a move ostensibly aimed against its arch-rival Ethiopia. In 2005, the government reconciled with the formerly much hated head of the Sudanese NIF government, General al Bashir and, in another surprising ideological shift, allied itself with the United Islamic Courts (UIC) in Somalia. The UIC took control over Mogadishu in June 2006, and since then, the Ethiopians have been militarily involved by supporting the Provisional Government of Somalia against the UIC, as they fear for the stability in their own Eastern province Ogaden, which is inhabited by ethnic Somalis. At the end of 2006, the Ethiopian army entered Somalia with the support of the Provisional Government and ousted the UIC from its military positions. The latter chose to avert open battles and turned to guerrilla tactics. The Ethiopian military support of the Provisional

---

[29] Yohannes Woldemariam and Okbazghi Yohannes: War Clouds in the Horn of Africa. Sudan Tribune, 12 November 2007

[30] VOA, 26 October 2007: UN Move on Ertitrea-Ethiopia Border Issue Raises Fears of Stalemate Collapse

[31] Sudan Tribune, August 25, 2007: Eritrea sets conditions to improve relations with the USA: „In an interview as broadcast by Eritrea's state-run radio, Isayas Afewerki said that the USA should suspend ‚activities aimed at harming our national interests. If the situation has to really change for the better, then the Americans must change their ways of thinking. They should stop making all manner of threats against us. They have to stop all activities aimed at harming our national interests. Regional peace is being threatened through their interference'.

Government (PG) was massively backed by the United States, who saw the UIC being dominated or at least infiltrated by al Qaida elements. Since then, both Ethiopia and the U.S. have been involved in the Somalia issue without any convincing political strategy to overcome the chaos created by their military tactics.

The above demonstrates the classical "enemy of my enemy is my friend" position of Eritrea, which now actively supports the Islamic forces in Somalia, allegedly with military support[32] – an obvious reversal of stand in which it declared a few years ago that the Islamic fundamentalists were enemies for the national unity and integrity of the country. In fact, there may have been unofficial support for the Islamic al-Ittihad movement in Somalia by the PFDJ in previous years, but what is new is the public support for the UIC by the Eritrean government, although it denies having sent military supplies to Somalia. The explanation for this diplomatic shift given by the government through its internet outlet shabait.com is interesting: In an article published in July/August 2006, the shabait commentator[33] equates the Provisional Government of Somalia with "the warlords who don't represent others than themselves", while the Islamic Court Union (I.C.U.) is described as "a reliable political entity that can withstand the warlords". The reason of the Eritrean government's sympathy for the Islamic Court becomes clear when the article further explains that "(T)he warlords (...) fell under the wings of the U.S. and Ethiopia and were given ministerial posts in the interim federal government". The United States is further accused of using the warlords to fight against what it calls terrorist elements (a statement which undeniably contains some truth). However, according to shabait.com, "the main objective of the U.S. administration is not what it officially declares to be fighting terrorism but there is some other hidden agenda behind it." Unfortunately, there is no further explanation clarifying this point[34]. Not surprisingly, Ethiopia is described as a "designated agent of the U.S. in the Horn", while, according to shabait, the most remarkable thing about the UIC is that "it has battered the warlords and their militias without any outside or international assistance".[35] The fact remains however, that the U.S. involvement in Somalia siding with Ethiopia has brought in frictions in relationship between Eritrea and the U.S. Besides, it has also brought about increased instability in the region as is explained below.

The brief period of UIC domination in Somalia, which led to considerable stability in the shattered country, came to an end when Ethiopian troops entered Somali territory at the end of 2006 to re-establish the rule of the Provisional Government. Since then, the Islamic movement has changed its strategy and is engaged in guerrilla-style insurgency against the PG, which is unable to maintain any form of power monopoly in the country. The United States, who supported Ethiopia's military move into Somalia, resorted to bomb attacks on Somali territory to destroy "elements of al Qaida" involved in the Kenya attacks on the U.S. embassy back in 1998, which resulted in the death of innocent civilians[36]. Moreover, after a UN report, which claimed that Eritrea had supplied the UIC and its military wing, the Shabab

[32] UN Security Council Report S/2007/436
[33] Shabait is the official media outlet of the Eritrean Ministry of Information
[34] The ‚hidden agenda' might refer to America's support of Ethiopia to establish it as a hegemon in the region.
[35] Shabait.com: Commentary. A Ray of Hope amidst the Dark Episode of Somalia: The Recent Developments in Somalia and the Repercussions – Part I, July 29, 2006 and Part II, August 2, 2006, retreived in October 2006
[36] US launches new Somalia raids. Guardian Unlimited, 9 January, 2007. The exact numbers of casualities is unclear, but the suspects wanted by the US Government were not among them.

militias, with military support, the United States threatened to put Eritrea on the list of states supporting terrorism[37] (along with Iran, North-Korea, Syria, Sudan, and Cuba). The Eritrean government in retaliation hosted a large congress of the UIC and other Somali opposition groups in Asmara in September 2007, where 400 members convened, including its leader Hassan Dahir Aweys, who had not appeared in public for months. The U.S. government believes he is an active supporter of al Qaida and seeks to arrest him. The congress in Asmara ended in the election of a new leadership of the UIC and other opposition forces and the formation of the 'Alliance for the Re-Liberation of Somalia' against the Provisional Government. Following these events, Eritrea has been described by the international media as a state harbouring insurgent movements from all surrounding countries and the re-establishment of American-Eritrean ties is further away than ever[38].

As has been mentioned in the introduction to this article, it makes sense to seek an explanation of the support of Islamic forces by the Eritrean leadership by considering both tactical and psychological aspects: As Ethiopia entered a coalition with the United States in fighting "terrorism" in the form of the United Islamic Courts in Somalia, Eritrea has no other option than supporting their enemy's foe, a shift which is not easy to explain from the secular point of view the Eritrean government strongly insists on. Therefore, the UIC is described as a force that fits into the Eritrean doctrine of self-reliance, being able to batter the friends of Ethiopia and the U.S. without outside support, just as the EPLF did during the independence struggle. Such an explanation is given in Part II of the mentioned shabait document: The direct or indirect support of the U.S. administration "pinched hard the feeling of every Somali", and therefore "(...) residents of Mogadishu were forced to help the I.C.U. during the confrontation [with the war lords]." And finally, "the strategies and methodology of war that the I.C.U. had applied in the fight against the warlords are factors that challenged the plans of the U.S. administration as well as the TPLF regime".[39]

The description of the Islamic Court Union given by shabait probably aims at making it possible for pro-government Eritreans, mainly in the diaspora (the principle readers of this internet site), to understand the ideological shift of their government and interpret the Islamic movement in Somalia in a positive way, as it has been attributed with virtues of the EPLF, like self-reliance, military strength, and discipline. Shabait also criticised the plans of the African Union (AU) to deploy peace-keepers in Somalia, reminding its readers of the failure of the OAU to support Eritrea's right to self-determination back in 1962 and explaining that supporting the UIC, which opposes AU-involvement, means weakening Ethiopia, as "the new consciousness of the Somali people (....) is becoming a disturbing development to the TPLF regime [the Ethiopian EPRDF government], and the powers that back the regime"[40]. This

---

[37] On the record briefing on U.S.-Eritrea relations, Jendayi Frazer, Assistand Secretary for African Affairs, Washington DC, 17 August 2007
[38] Interestingly, the ambassador-designate to Eritrea, Ronald McMullen, explained his wish to „reestablish cooperation with Eritrea" in a statement before the US Senat's Foreign Relations Committee, not mentioning his government's threat to put Eritra on the terror list: Statement of Ronald K. McMullen, Ambassador-designate to the State of Eritrea, 19 September 2007. http://usinfo.state.gov/xarchives, retreived on 21 September 2007
[39] Shabait.com, op.cit., Part II, retreived in October 2006
[40] Shabait.com: Editiorial. "Deploying AU peacekeepers in Somalia", to what end?, September 20, 2006, retreived in October 2006

sentence clarifies that Eritrea's foreign relations are increasingly following the goal of weakening the Ethiopian government and causing trouble for its ally, the United States.

4   Conclusion

As the latest developments show, the unresolved conflict with Ethiopia and the disappointment of the Eritrean government about the pro-Ethiopian attitude of the United States play a major role in shaping its regional foreign relations and its attitude towards the "war on terrorism". It seems that the past four years have shown a gradual shift towards a complete break of relations with the United States and a political move towards those regional forces who are opposed to the Ethiopian government and its ally, the U.S..

This leads to a specific definition of terrorism from the Eritrean side: "Terrorism" is simply seen as an attitude opposing the Eritrean government. Islamic forces are seen as terrorists as long as they turn against the government of Eritrea (like the Eritrean Jihad Movement), while they become friends when they oppose Ethiopia and the Americans, like the UIC in Somalia. The internal opposition (the G15) are seen as agents of the CIA and therefore, from the current point of view of the Eritrean leadership, the United States are seen as an evil force involved in attempts to bring down the government with the help of internal and external forces opposed to it (an attitude which might also be described as "terrorist").

At the time of writing, U.S.-Eritrean relations are at a historical low. Eritrea's attempt to co-operate in the "war on terrorism" was short-lived and has definitely come to an end. It seems that the Jihadist movements within the Eritrean opposition are too insignificant to pose a threat perceived strong enough by the United States to justify the Pentagon's ambition to co-operate with an uncompromising government like the Eritrean leadership. Additionally, from an American point of view, Eritrea contributes to the destabilisation of the region by its involvement in the general game of mutual insurgencies prevailing in the Horn, especially in the case of Somalia, where it openly supports the opponent of the Ethiopian- and U.S.-backed Provisional Government. At the same time, it should be stressed that the Americans have been caught in ambiguous policies towards Eritrea before and beyond independence, being aware of the country's strategic importance, but always favouring larger Ethiopia whenever a crisis arose. This was facilitated by the elaborated diplomatic efforts of the Ethiopian government, which plays its own game in the "war on terrorism", consuming U.S. resources by pretending to defend common interests while it is trying to stabilise its internal power base.

Since September 11, 2001, the American-led "war on terror" has not significantly contributed toward the stabilisation of the affected regions outside the United States and has been far from successful in extinguishing radical opinions and strategies. In the Horn of Africa, it led to the instrumentalisation of prevailing power struggles in the name of anti-terrorism in order to extract resources from the U.S. budget, thus contributing further to the destabilisation of an already more than unstable region.

Bibliography

Brüne, Stefan/Heinrich, Wolfgang, 1999, Der äthiopisch-eritreische Krieg, in: *Jahrbuch Dritte Welt 2000*, München, pp 145 –163

Hirt, Nicole 2001, *Eritrea zwischen Krieg und Frieden. Die Entwicklung seit der Unabhängigkeit*, Hamburg

_____ 2000, 2001, 2002, 'Eritrea', in Hofmeier, Rolf; Jakobeit, Cord (eds): *Afrika Jahrbuch 1999, 2000, 2001, 2002*, Opladen

_____ 2004, 'Eritrea', in Hofmeier, Rolf; Mehler, Andreas (eds): *Afrika Jahrbuch 2003*, Wiesbaden, pp 246 -251

_____ 2006, 'Eritrea', in; Mehler, Andreas; Melber, Henning; van Walraven, Klaas: *Africa Yearbook 2005*, Leiden, pp 287 - 295

_____ 2007, 'Eritrea', in; Mehler, Andreas; Melber, Henning; van Walraven, Klaas: *Africa Yearbook 2006* , Leiden (forthcoming)

Kidane Mengisteab and Okbazghi Yohannes 2005, *Anatomy of an African Tragedy. Political, Economic and Foreign Policy crisis in Post-Independence Eritrea*, Lawrenceville

Markakis, John, 1987, *National and Class Conflict in the Horn of Africa*, Cambridge

Matthies, Volker 2005, *Kriege am Horn von Afrika. Historischer Befund und friedenswissenschaftliche Analyse*, Berlin

Prunier, Gérard, *Somalia ist nicht Afghanistan. Übergangsregierung und Islamisten kämpfen um die Macht – doch beide Lager sind in sich zerstritten* (Le Monde diplomatique, 15.9.2006). www.monde-diplomatique.de/pm/2006/09/15

Ruth Yiob 1995, *The Eritrean Struggle for Independence*, Cambridge

Tekeste Negash, 1997, *Eritrea and Ethiopia. The Federal Experience*, New Brunswick

Trivelli, Richard M., 1998, 'Divided histories, opportunistic alliances: Background notes on the Ethiopian-Eritrean war', in *Afrika Spectrum* 33/3, pp 257 - 289

Young, John, 1996, 'The Tigray and Eritrean People's Liberation Fronts: A history of tensions and pragmatism', in *Journal of Modern African Studies*, 34,1

Woodward, Peter, 2006, *U.S. foreign policy and the Horn of Africa*, London

Wrong, Michaela, 2005, *I didn't do it for you. How the World Betrayed a Small African Nation*, New York

Continuity and Change in Eritrea-Sudan Relations: Trends and Future Scenarios*

Dr. M. Venkataraman

The Past

This section brings out the historical relationship albeit briefly for it helps understand the rationale behind the current relations better. Historical linkages could be seen in many ways and it existed even before the coming of colonialism. The existence of Kingdoms and the struggle for power between them is one such example of the linkages. Writing on the topic, Bereket Habteselassie argues that there was struggle for dominance by both the people in the region.[1]

Other noteworthy aspects are the spread of the Kingdom of Sennar, (540 A.D - 1820 AD), which was the dominant kingdom in Eastern Sudan into the Northern Eritrean Coasts of the Red Sea. Northern Barka, Sahil, and Semhar (what is called today as Gash Barka), Anseba, and Semenawi Keih Bahri were all incorporated into this Kingdom. Also at the time of the Mahdi movement in Sudan when the British occupied the Sudanese port of Sewakin,[2] the Mahdists were cut off from the outside world and the only way by which they could continue their economic activities with the outside world was through the small Eritrean port called Massawa in Red Sea.

Economically also there have been lots of interaction since ancient times and it is believed that many of the economic activities have been informally carried out. In recent times this had expanded and Eritrea's major exports to Sudan include skins, meat, live sheep and cattle and it is estimated that in 2002 majority of exports were to Sudan (Library of Congress, Federal Research Division, 2005, p. 10)[3]. Earlier, Eritreans were employed in many of the Sudanese agricultural projects; construction activities etc., On their part, Sudanese nationals also entered Eritrea with the coming of the British and the defeat of the Italians in World War II. In their effort to administer Eritrea, the British brought a number of civil servants, traders, teachers, police and other professionals from its colony – Sudan.[4] These

---

* Some parts of this article has been borrowed from my earlier version entitled "Eritrea's Relations with the Sudan since 1991", published in Ethiopian Journal of the Social Sciences and the Humanities, Addis Ababa University, College of Social Sciences, vol.3, no. 2, December 2005, pp. 51-76

[1] Bereket Habteselassie says, "parts of Western Eritrea were the subject of invasion and conquests from neighboring nations throughout history. The reverse is also true, in that some of the north-western ethnic groups have crossed over to Sudan". Bereket Habteselassie, Behind the War in Eritrea, (Nottingham: The Russell Press Limited, 1980), p.33

[2] Interesting to note in the occupation of Sewakin, is the involvement of Indian army troops. See Helen Chapin Metz, ed. Sudan: A Country Study,Washington: GPO for the Library of Congress, 1991. Sahel now partially belongs to Anseba and Semenawi Keih Bahri (Northern Red Sea), Semhar to Northern Red Sea.

[3] It should be noted that this is no more the case now. Exact estimates are hard in the period after Eritrea's independence owing to both lack of appropriate official data and the border between them closed on and off due to frequent clashes.

[4] Based on the interview conducted with Mohammed Seid Nawud, Research officer, Eritrean Center for Strategic Studies in Asmara, 14th February, 2002

people have now settled and have intermarried with the local people in Eritrea. They have become Eritreans now. The areas they lived have been named after Sudan known as Hilat Al-Sudan, which means Sudanese settlement or home. Such places are still found in Keren, Agordat, and Barentu etc.,[5] Import – export activities were actively carried out and this was the situation even when their relations were on the lowest ebb.[6] Generally speaking, one can observe that many a time, irrespective of the type of political relations that exist between the capitals, economic relations continue without any hindrance at least in border areas and in this Eritrea and Sudan are no exceptions.

Even before Sudanese independence was achieved in 1956, there have been lots of political links as well between the two countries. It is important to note that Eritreans had participated in the political and administrative positions of the Sudan. Some were in police forces and others were mobilized in the Sudanese army. Consequently, they became advocators and strong supporters for the independence of the Sudan. In fact, some Eritreans had also lost their lives for Sudanese independence.[7]

Before moving into the discussion of the role of the Sudan in Eritrean liberation struggle, it is pertinent to observe here that domestic political and economic pressures in both countries have had serious impact on their bilateral relationship. Their political systems have been marked by instability and lacks legitimacy, so to say, to the extent of deriving mass support from their respective populations. More importantly, the two major religions in both the countries viz: Christianity and Islam are not 'politically situated' equally in the sense that while the Sudanese government has declared itself as an Islamic state, Eritrea hosts a secular government with representation from both the Christian and Islamic communities – the majority being the Christian representation in the government. As will be seen in subsequent paragraphs, it is this strange combination that defined their path to follow.

Sudan's support during the Eritrean liberation struggle

This section reveals the several dimensions during the phase of Eritrean liberation struggle, which has continued in many ways to dominate Eritrea's post-independent relationship. The aim here is to establish the connections.

Firstly, Eritrea got active support from the Sudan during its liberation struggle. The Sudanese government announced its intention that it will support the Eritreans' in their cause against imperialism and domination of Ethiopia and its allies and allowed the formation of a liberation movement in Sudan called the Eritrean Liberation Movement (ELM) in 1958 probably due to the impact of Sudan's independence couple of years earlier. Eyasu Gaim (1993, p.519) succinctly points out the necessity with which Sudan was compelled to support the cause of Eritrean liberation movement. To quote him:

---

[5] Interview with Mohammed Seid Nawud, Ibid
[6] These are basically informal economic exchanges as there are no official statistical figures to substantiate this.
[7] Mohammed Sied Nawud, who was a member of the Sudanese Communist Party, is an example. He is now working in the Eritrean Center for Strategic Studies, Asmara.

The government of Sudan had difficulties in distancing themselves from the crisis in Eritrea since Sudan was a vital transit route for channelling the Islamic support to the Eritrean Liberation Front.

The support extended by the Sudan is worth emphasizing here for this brought in the involvement of the Arab world into the picture. The special emphasis of ELM to lure the support of the Arab world describing it as a movement of Arab liberation facilitating support of diverse Arab governments was a valid reason for the Sudan to continue to support the Eritrean cause. The repercussion of this was that while the Sudan supported the Eritrean cause openly, Ethiopia lent its support to the southern Sudanese guerrilla movement due to "Sudan's support for Eritrean secessionists" (Johnson: 2003, p.36) and especially after Sudan's strong support to the Arabs in the 1967 Arab-Israeli war. Ethiopia got entangled, so to say, in the process. It is interesting to note this aspect of the tit-for-tat policy exhibited by these countries, which continued even after Eritrean independence. The support of Sudan to the ELF as well as to other opposition groups that emerged within Ethiopia such as the OLF a little later in 1975 angered Ethiopia and hence Ethiopia started retaliating by supporting the southern Sudanese opposition groups. In fact, when the then regional Minister for Information of Sudan visited Ethiopia in 1976, he was told by the Ethiopian Foreign Minister that "unless the Sudan ceased supplying the Eritrean rebels, Ethiopia would give active support to the Anyanya remnants in Ethiopia" (Johnson: 2003, p.59).[8]

In view of the above reasons, the Eritrean independence cause was viewed as an Arab concern initially. Haggi Erlich notes that "the struggle over Eritrea and the Horn of Africa should be viewed as an integral part of the Red Sea and Middle Eastern affairs rather than as an African conflict" (Erlich: 1983, p.48). During the time of the Dergue action against the Eritrean liberation forces, Sudan served as the nearest refuge and the then government of Sudan helped the ELF in providing sanctuaries and military aid.[9] The regime in Sudan due to its alignment with the Arabs as well as due to its Islamic notion therefore inevitably had to play a constructive role in its support to the ELF. It is this 'religious aspect' that defined their bilateral relationship in the 1990s too.

Another dimension of the Sudanese support to the Eritrean liberation struggle is that it encompasses a religious dimension, which has continued up until today. In this regard, mention should be made of the split in the Eritrean Liberation Movement, which comprised mostly of Muslims while the Popular Front for the Eritrean Liberation otherwise called Eritrean People's Liberation Front (EPLF), that was formed in 1975comprised mostly of

---

[8] For details on the Addis Ababa Agreement and the Anyanya remnants, see pp. 38-42
[9] This was done for several reasons. The involvement of the U.S. as part of the "Cold War" in the Horn in support of Ethiopia was one such cause for concern. It is more so due to the inimical relationship that the Arab countries had with Israel, which was considered as a threat to Arab security. The other important reason was the considered view among many Arab countries that the Eritrean Liberation Front could act as a bulwark towards the formation of an Arab state in the Red Sea coast. This view prevailed among many Arab countries so long as the ELF associated its cause as an Arab cause through its campaigns. This can be seen from the argument put forward by Bowyer Bell who also opines that the Eritrean revolution was increasingly seen to be associated with revolutionary Arab nationalism by which "under increasing Ethiopian pressure, the ELF began to associate their cause with the Arabs collecting support from conservative Imams for Islamic reasons, and from radical regimes for ideological ones". Bowyer Bell, The Horn of Africa – A Strategic Magnet in the 1970s, (New York, Crane Russak and Company, 1973), pp. 13-28

Christians (Young: 1996, p.107). Rivalry among these two fronts invited external manoeuvring thereby complicating the whole scenario. The uprising against the then Ethiopian regime of Mengistu Hailemariam (the Dergue) by the Tigray People's Liberation Front (TPLF) coincided with the uprising by the EPLF. According to Tesfatsion Medhanie, the joint EPLF – TPLF offensive against the ELF, for all practical purposes, was seen by some Muslim groups as a unified action of Christians to dominate Eritrea thereby inspiring some Muslim Eritreans to form a religious movement to halt that domination (Medhanie: 1994, p.95). One can see the religious dimension coming into play here. Splinter groups from ELF such as Jihad Eritrea continue to operate even today complicating the situation even more.

The political ideology of the EPLF in fact did not prove to be negative in terms of the support it received from the Arab states. It was possibly assumed that the EPLF could invite opposition from among the Arab states, as it was a Christian dominated front and having its ideology based on Marxism-Leninism. But the reverse was true. [10] Surprisingly to many, Sudan and the Arabs did not oppose the emergence of the EPLF and later on its dominance (Legum and Lee: 1979, p. 122).

One can see changes in Sudan's policy in later years particularly towards the second half of 1970s when Ethiopia threw a diplomatic offensive by attempting to improve its relationship with the government of General Jafaar al-Numeiry, declaring that Ethiopia recognized the unity and integrity of Sudan. This had implications in the sense that it meant in effect not supporting the Sudanese opposition forces. By this Ethiopia intended to take the 'wind out of the sails' of the Eritrean Liberation forces operating from inside the Sudan. As was expected, corresponding to the new Ethiopian declaration, the Numeiry government expressed its support to the unity and integrity of Ethiopia ignoring the Eritrean movement and thereby cutting of its main logistical base (Pateman: 1998, p.104). For Al-Numeiry, the reason for taking Ethiopia's gesture to the extent of cutting off ties with ELF was the split in the movement itself, which discouraged Sudan to continue any kind of support.[11] Eyasu Gaim (1993: p.53) added another reason for that matter. According to him:

> In July 1970 there was a coup attempt against Al-Numeiry which is believed to have been inspired by Iraq, and where the leaders of the ELF were implicated in the process, and this became a factor for the Sudanese government to stop its support to the ELF.

---

[10] Reasons for the above volte-face could be attributed to the intricate nature of Cold War politics in view of the political changes that took place in Ethiopia and the corresponding shift in support by the U.S. and the Soviet Union. With the coming of the Dergue to power in 1974 overthrowing Haile Selassie regime, Soviet Union saw it as an opportunity to get into the Horn in view of the regions geo-strategic importance then not to mention now. The Soviets made a swift move to get into Ethiopia at a time when the U.S. was getting outside of it. The ELF viewed the role of Soviet Union in the region as one of strategic ally and not an enemy because it thought that it was following a more practical Soviet style communist ideology.

[11] Sudan's volte-face had other reasons such as Ethiopian gain in the war against Somalia and Eritrean liberation forces and the Soviet support to Ethiopia, which feared the Sudan in view of the repercussions to the Southern Sudanese groups that Ethiopia supported.

In the war against Ethiopia, therefore, one can see two different liberation movements not just along different ideological lines but more importantly along religious lines too. It was the EPLF forces, which was successful in overpowering the ELF.

Whatever the motivation of EPLF vs ELF is, the fact remains that there emerged two opposing forces hostile to each other, the remnants of ELF being spread out into neighboring countries. Arguably though, external events, notably the 1979 Iranian revolution and the strengthening of Islamist political movements in the Middle-east not only acted as a source of inspiration but also provided an impetus to the Eritrean Muslims to organize a religious movement.

Changes and Continuity in the 1990s

The 1990s brought a new phase of relationship guided by sovereignty and independence. This section analyzes the extent to which continuity and changes, as revealed in the previous sections, could be seen.

Positive changes were in the form of the enthusiastic greeting of Eritrea's May 1991 victory and its subsequent de-jure independence by the Sudan. The defeat of the Dergue regime in Ethiopia in effect meant the defeat of SPLA (Southern People's Liberation Army) due to the (on and off in fact) support that the latter received from the Dergue. This meant that establishing friendly relationship with the new government in Ethiopia as well as with Eritrea would take 'the wind off the sails' of SPLA and thereby contribute towards consolidating its rule. The SPLA could no longer continue its war efforts against the Sudanese government as it was able to do before. In fact, Tesfatsion Medhanie notes that "in 1990 the EPLF took part in the war between Sudanese regime and the SPLA…it attacked the SPLA inside Sudanese territory affecting the military balance in favour of the Sudanese regime" (Medhanie: 1994, p.94). This adds testimony to the initial cordiality in Eritro-Sudanese relations. It is worth noting here what the then Secretary General of the Peoples Front for Democracy and Justice (PFDJ) Ato Alamin Mohammed Seid said on the situation. To quote him:

> Our victory and achievement of peace and stability in our region is the result of the friendship of the Eritrean revolutionaries and the Sudan, and hence the victory of the Eritrean people is the victory of the peoples of the Horn of Africa and especially the people of Sudan.[12]

The early 1990s, therefore, was a period of friendship and cordiality for both Sudan and Eritrea and they concentrated on issues relating to security given the fact that both were not well positioned and feared armed opposition. As was feared, the independence of the State of Eritrea did not stop the ELF to continue its armed opposition from the Sudan against it and hence this became a thorny issue between them. On the part of EPLF (now PFDJ), the existence and operation of such groups or factions was considered irrelevant. It did not see any reason for their existence not only in Eritrean soil but also in the Sudan. Writing on this issue, Tesfatsion (1994, p.93) comments that:

---

[12] See Hadas Eritrea, Asmara, Ministry of Information, 2, October, 1991, p.1

> Upon the liberation of Eritrea in May 1991, the EPLF demanded the closure of the offices of the Eritrean opposition forces in the Sudan. The NIF regime closed down the offices, halted the political activities and confiscated the property of these forces.

From the above, one can understand that the government in Sudan took practical steps to halt the activities of these forces in its soil, which otherwise could have been a challenge to the EPLF although the extent of such efforts to completely remove the ELF cadres from operating inside Sudan is questionable. The effort was a good will gesture made in order to establish cordial relations with Eritrea, for which Sudan needed to clear EPLF's threat perceptions. This aspect defined their bilateral relations at least during the initial years and measures were taken to improve bilateral relationship. For example, in January 1992, when the EPLF attacked the opposition forces in Western Eritrea, Sudan participated in it. To quote Tesfatsion Medhanie (Ibid: p.94) again:

> A contingent of the Sudanese government forces crossed the border, moved inside Eritrea, and attacked Eritrean opposition forces including the Jihad Islamic Movement. They captured some leaders of the Islamic Jihad Movement and handed them over to the EPLF.

This indicates that both countries worked closely to eliminate the Eritrean opposition forces.[13] When the Eritrean referendum was conducted in April 1993 and results announced a Sudanese delegation headed by the Chairman of the NIF regime visited Eritrea to congratulate the people and government.[14] When Eritrea was officially proclaimed as an independent and sovereign state on May 24, 1993 shortly after the referendum, Sudan was among the first country to recognize it. The Sudanese President who was present on the occasion expressed his strong support for Eritrea.

The active role played by Eritrea to resolve the long-standing civil war in Sudan, along with the heads of Ethiopia, Kenya and Uganda to bring the different factions of SPLA into an agreement by establishing a committee in mid-1993 and which continued in the early years of 1994 and culminating in 1995 with a declaration in Asmara is a land mark development that exemplifies the extent of cordiality and mutual concern and cooperation between the Horn countries. Notably, this was done as part of Inter-Governmental Authority on Development (IGAD – earlier IGADD to include Drought) talks that was held in different places.

Revisiting the past

The strategic concerns of both these countries in terms of how to manage their relationship smoothly without interfering in each other's internal affairs became a difficult task. It was unavoidable for both of them, so to say, to continue their past tactics given the nature of their respective domestic set up. For the Sudan the resumption of the war with the SPLA (coupled

---

[13] The 30th anniversary of Eritrean armed struggle in September 1991 was attended, amongst others, by top army officials from the Sudan in which they affirmed that "...from today we shall share with our brothers in Eritrea every small morsel of food and every book and every dose of medicine and every thing our dear people in Eritrea need in material, human and moral support". See Sudanese support, Horn of Africa Bulletin, vol.3, no.6, September-October 1991, pp. 7-8

[14] See speech made by the President of Sudan on 24 May 1993 in Hadas Eritrea, May 26, 1993, p.2

with the continued presence of some of the remnants of ELF cadres inside Sudan) had its fall out upon Eritrea. In other words, it only enticed both governments to involve in each others affairs. Sudan's professed export of Islamic tenets in to neighboring countries in the Horn is a decisive factor. In fact, it could be said that the NIF government in Sudan squandered the advantage of taking into its fold the political debt that both Eritrea and Ethiopia owed to the Sudan by its continued support of Islamic revolution to groups in Eritrea. The assassination attempt on the Egyptian president Hosni Mubarak during his visit to Addis Ababa in 1995 adds testimony and convinces the view of the danger posed by the Sudan in the form of export of Islamic revolution into neighboring Horn countries.

Talking about the crisis in the Sudan in April 1994 at the VII Pan African Congress in Kampala, Uganda, President Isaías Afewerki declared: "although colonialism is the root of the crisis (in Sudan) later ...the regimes of the north of Sudan are mainly responsible for the conflict in the south of that country".[15]

Hence some of the latent irritant issues between them came to the fore and resulted in break up of diplomatic relations. In a statement issued by the Eritrean Foreign Ministry issued on 23 April 1994, the Eritrean government made it clear that the relations are not that cordial. It went on to accuse the NIF government in Khartoum saying that it wished to control a force in Eritrea and towards that end formed a group called the Islamic Jihad of Eritrea and has continued to support this group leading to deterioration of relations.[16]

By December 1994 diplomatic relations between them broke down and Yemen tried to mediate the conflict without any result. On December 24 1994 the Eritrean press announced that:

> According to reports from Sudan the government of that country is taking hostile measures against Eritrean nationals residing in that country, (refugees) ...tales like illegal detention, terrorism and looting of property.[17]

The tense relationship can be gauged from a statement made by the Eritrean Minister for External Affairs who declared that:

> the main cause for the deterioration of the relations is the government of the National Islamic Front that works actively to subvert the peace that Eritrea enjoys...has created obstacles to our diplomatic ties by carrying out such activities... and (therefore) starting from today (December 5) Eritrea declares diplomatic relations with the government Sudan broken".[18]

Given the above, it is not surprising that both entered into polemics accusing each other of harbouring hostile opposition forces. For example, in January 1995, addressing the Eritrean journalists, the Minister for External Affairs mentioned that:

> The regime of Khartoum has once again revealed its intentions of extending its hegemonic ambitions in the region's politics ...Sudan is the one undermining the peace and the stability of Eritrea and of the whole region.[19]

---

[15] Eritrea Profile, 9 April 1994, p. 1
[16] Horn of Africa Bulletin, vol.6, no.3, May – June 1994. See also www.europaworld.com, p.7
[17] Eritrea Profile, 24 December 1994, p. 1
[18] Eritrea Profile, 10 December 1994, p. 1 The United States also played a role in this regard, as they armed both Ethiopia and Eritrea at this time to reward them for their anti-Islamist position
[19] Eritrea Profile, 7 January 1995, p. 1

The Eritrean President joined the accusations, which is revealed from an interview with Arab News Daily in which he mentioned that the main cause for the breakdown of diplomatic ties was created by Sudan. To quote him:

> We know that the NIF was organizing the Jihad movement and other groups, we tried to solve it by dialogue. We told them: what is the logic of supporting these people, we are on the verge of achieving victory and if you want to support the independence of the country you have to support the population, don't meddle in our internal affairs.[20]

The support that the NIF regime was giving to the opposition groups of Eritrea, in short was the main obstacle to Eritro-Sudanese relations, though the latter denied this.[21] In other words, as rightly put by Ruth Iyob, "the emergence of the Eritrean Jihad Movement with overt support of the Sudan's ruling party, the NIF, led to strains in Eritro-Sudanese relations culminating in the severance of diplomatic ties" (Iyob: 1997, p.666).[22]

What can be discerned from the way both governments sought to tackle the problem is to increase their respective support to each other's opposition groups and thereby threatening the fragile peace of the Horn. In retaliation to the NIF governments' increase in support to Eritrean opposition groups in Sudan, the former sought to coordinate and unite all Sudanese opposition groups in the form of a National Democratic Alliance (NDA) with its base in Asmara. The Economist underlined President Isaias as saying "we are out to see that this government is not there any more. We are not trying to pressure them to talk to us, or to behave in a more constructive way. We will give weapons to any one committed to over throwing them".[23] The publication in the Eritrean press on 17 June 1995 indicated further that:

> A conference of Sudanese political forces will be inaugurated today. The participants are: The Democratic Unionist Party of Osman al-Mirghani, the Popular Liberation Movement of John Garang in the South, the Party Umma represented by Omar Nur al-Daim, the Sudanese Legal Command of the armed forces represented by the general Fathi Ahmed Alí, the Communist Party of Sudan represented by Dr. Al-Tijani al-Tayib, the Coalition Party of the South of Sudán of Al-Yaba Suror, the Bedja Conference of Al-Said Mohammed Tahir Abu-Beker and the Sudanese Alliance Forces represented by Brigadier General Abd the-Aziz Khalid.[24]

---

[20] As quoted in Eritrea Profile, 17 June, 1995, p.4

[21] Although the Sudanese government denied the accusations of Eritrea, it had later on admitted its support to these groups. As was published in the Eritrean profile, the Sudanese President al-Bashir revealed that the "main reason for the breakdown in relations was not a result of Eritrean doing but of factionalism within the Khartoum government. The Sudanese policy towards Eritrea was not constructive. The Sudanese government was, because of serious internal rifts, saying one thing and doing another". Eritrea Profile, 25 December 1999, p. 1

[22] Colin Legum reported President Isaias as saying "clandestine cells of fundamentalists continued to be formed; safe houses were sought by the Sudan Embassy in Asmara; and at least one group of ten young fundamentalists was shot trying to cross the border into Eritrea. See Colin Legum, "Afeworki on the War Path", New African, February, 1996, no. 56, p. 38

[23] The Economist, October, 14, 1995

[24] Eritrea Profile, 17 June 1995, p. 1

On the same day when the above was published in the Eritrean Profile, an interview given by
the Eritrean President Isaías appeared. Talking about the achievements and challenges of the
country, the Eritrean President mentioned regarding the relationships with Sudan that:

> The National Islamic Front of Sudan, (NIF) is a minority group and it has been there for
> more than 40 years ...the NIF has organized this jihad and other groups ...and NIF says that it
> fights against imperialism. If they want to fight against America (USA) why don't they fight
> against them there instead of Eritrea, Ethiopia or Somalia...[25]

In fact until the breakdown of diplomatic relations, Eritrea pursued a two-track strategy one
aimed at continuing the diplomatic dialogue with the government and the other supporting the
opposition in the Sudan. It is the considered view of many that Eritrea started supporting the
Sudanese opposition militarily since January 1996 soon after the breakdown of diplomatic
relations.

It should be added that during this time Sudan was accused of giving refuge to many
terrorists, including the now "in-famous" Al Qaeda leader Osama bin Laden. Douglas
Johnson adds that Osama bin Laden had a number of construction and other projects in the
Sudan and operated training camps for the militants of Lebanese Hizbullah and Palestine
Hamas (Johnson: 2003, p.137). And this should be viewed in terms of the Christian-Muslim
dichotomy in Eritrea and how the portrayal of Sudan as one of exporting Islamic ideology
coupled with its so-called support to "terrorists" can have its impact on the presumptions of
the Eritrean government. Understandably, this would not be taken lightly by Asmara.

The offensive from the opposition forces against the government of Sudan was made
during the same time when the meeting of the Council took place in Asmara in 1996, thereby
leading to the accusation by Sudan that Eritrea carried out military operations in its territory.
Asmara responded that they were groundless accusations. In an interview given to the daily
Sharq al-Awsat in August 1996, President Isaías responded that Eritrea does not have the
ability nor the resources or ambition to pursue expansionist policies in the Sudan. When asked
about the Sudanese accusation of the existence of opposition groups in Asmara, the President
answered that Eritrea has historical relationships (even before its independence) with different
Sudanese groups but this does not mean to intervene in the internal matters of Sudan.[26]
Although the President denied any involvement in the internal affairs of Sudan, it is quite
evident from the above statements made by officials of the Eritrean government that Eritrea
did support the opposition in Sudan. In fact, when the Sudanese Embassy was vacated in view
of the breakdown in diplomatic relations, Eritrea allowed the opposition National Democratic
Alliance (NDA) to occupy Sudanese embassy premises.

It is also evident that the Sudan also supported the Eritrean Jihad Movement ever since
Eritrea formally became independent. For example, the NIF regime invited the Eritrean Jihad
to the popular Arab and Islamic Conference in November 1993 in Khartoum. This is
particularly disturbing since there were about 400,000 Eritrean refugees waiting to be
repatriated to Eritrea. The possibility of these refugees coming into Eritrea with Sudan's
ideological indoctrination as well as support from the Eritrean Jihad Movement is very much
there. Berhane Woldegebriel writing in the Review of African Political Economy opined that

---

[25] Eritrea Profile, 17 June 1995, p. 1
[26] Eritrea Profile, 7 September 1996, p. 6

"there are reliable reports that Sudanese security officers have been discouraging Eritrean refugees from returning home, but persuading them to join the Islamist Organization"(Woldegebriel: 1996, pp.87-88).

The polemics continued in 1997 (and in fact even after diplomatic relations were restored) with Sudan accusing Eritrea of downing a helicopter in its territory. On January 18, 1997, Sudan repulsed an attack by Eritrea inside its territory killing 250 Eritrean soldiers.[27]

Towards normalization

As was pointed out earlier, Eritrea – Sudan relations are also defined and closely tied up with developments in the region as well as concerns shown by countries outside the region. Also, their attempts at bringing about peaceful coexistence very much depend upon how they could define their relations with countries like Ethiopia. This section reveals this aspect of it.

The deterioration in relations with Ethiopia facilitated rapprochement with Sudan. In other words, so long as Ethio-Eritrean relations were normal, Eritro-Sudan relations suffered. But when Eritro-Ethiopian relations got worse, Eritrea's relations with Sudan got normalised. This was so because of the sympathy with which the SPLA received from both Eritrea and Ethiopia, which Sudan wanted to remove. And the best opportunity came when Eritrea's relations with Ethiopia worsened to the extent of going to war. To Sudan, this was a blessing in disguise for it could now lure Eritrea to its side thereby breaking its support to the SPLA. On the part of Eritrea also, national interest considerations prompted the Eritrean government to make a move towards Sudan and normalize relations with it; for Asmara could not afford to devote hostility on both sides of its borders. As rightly pointed out by Dan Connell, one of the winners of the Eritrean war with Ethiopia is Sudan, which reached an agreement with Asmara (Connel, p.205).

The whole normalization process took place in May 1999 at a tripartite meeting in Doha, Qatar, which was attended by the Heads of State of Eritrea, Sudan and Qatar where President Isaias and his Sudanese counter part General Omar al-Bashir agreed to normalize their bilateral relations under which they agreed to resume diplomatic ties.[28]

The process towards normalization started in November 1998 when Qatar took the initiative of mediating the conflict between Eritrea and Sudan. The reason why Qatar took the initiative in bringing both to a settlement was because Qatar has a wide range of oil exploration interest in the Sudan. Political stability and security in the Sudan was sought as a pre-requisite for Qatar to explore its economic ties with the Sudan in a big way. Besides, Eritrea at that time was on the move to approach the Arab countries to join the Arab League to which the Sudan voiced its opposition. The entry of Eritrea to the League could possibly guarantee a psychological rest at least since the League members fear the alliance of Israel and the U.S. with Eritrea and influence the Red Sea region. [29] Whatever the different

---

[27] Official Press Release by the Ministry of External Affairs, **Eritrea Profile**, 18 January 1997, p. 1

[28] See www.europaworld.com p. 7. See also, **Eritrea Profile**, 8 May 1999, p.1

[29] The Libyan interest in this can best be answered by the way in which Libya under Col. Ghadaffi was increasingly becoming inclined to interfere in African affairs in order to project itself as the leader of the African countries. The recent initiatives by Libya for establishing an African Union at par with the European Union should be seen in these terms.

motivations might be, the fact remains that Eritro-Sudanese relations once again underwent changes and this time for the better. A six point agreement was signed in Doha[30]

After the agreement, air communication resumed between the two capitals and diverse committees were created to watch over the bilateral relationship, and on 3 January 2000 the embassies in both capitals were reopened. As mentioned earlier, the visit by the Sudanese President General Omar el-Bashir to Asmara on 18 January for the purpose of consolidating the friendly ties was the highlight of the bilateral relations. This visit was reciprocated by the Eritrean President in the following month of February the same year and announced that he would take measures to repatriate about a million Eritrean refugees in Sudan. Since Eritrea's independence, about 197, 000 Eritrean refugees have been repatriated and re-settled. The relations have improved to a great extent after the Doha Agreement, which was implemented. Diplomatic relations were quickly resumed to the Ambassadorial level by April 2000.

Recent Developments

The restoration of diplomatic relations has not been consolidated and tensions have continued. New developments – both within Sudan and Eritrea and in the region – have once again opened up 'Pandora box' revolving around the same issue of how best to manage their "strategic concerns" to each others benefit. This section elaborates some of these new developments in some detail.

Firstly, at the systemic level, changing configuration of relations particularly the 1998-2000 war between Eritrea and Ethiopia had its fall out upon Eritrea-Sudan relations. Ethiopia's mending of relations with Sudan, meaning relinquishing support to the SPLA, contributed to aggravating Eritrea-Sudan relations.[31] The issue was once again accusations of interference in internal affairs when a string of territorial gains was achieved by the rebel forces in Sudan in late 2002, which the Sudanese government considered it as an Eritrean military invasion of its eastern border region.[32] Eritrea was accused of supporting the Southern Liberation Movement in Sudan as well as rebels in East Sudan, who were fighting the Sudanese government for greater autonomy.[33] The Sudanese Foreign Minister, while rejecting the mediatory role of Egypt at a press conference in Cairo, went on to accuse that "Eritrea opened training camps for the opposition and rebel movements, supported them with

---

[30] Eritrea Profile, May 8, 1999, p.1 The third, fourth and sixth points of the agreement were the most important and determinant in the relations of the two states. This is because the main cause for the problem between them was harbouring hostile elements.

[31] See John Young, "Armed Groups along Sudan's Eastern Frontier: An Overview and Analysis", Small Arms Survey, HSBA Working Paper No: 9, Geneva, November 2007, p. 7.

[32] See UNMEE Media Monitoring Report, 12 November 2002, p. 5

[33] Rebels belonging to Beja Congress and Free Lions Rebel Movement have been waging a low-intensity guerilla war with the Central government in Sudan since 1997 and they were supported by Eritrea training them and giving them sanctuary in Asmara. See for details on this, Dorina Bekoe and Nirina Kiplagat, "Peacemaking and Peacebuilding in Eastern Sudan", United States Institute for Peace, http://www.usip.org/pubs/usipeace_briefings/2006/0927_eastern_sudan.html September 2006; See also John Young, "Armed Groups along Sudan's Eastern Frontier: An overview and analysis", Small Arms Survey Working paper no: 9, Geneva, November 2007. For an analysis on the rise of rebel movement in East Sudan and Eritrea's role in it see, John Young, "The Eastern Front and the Struggle Against Marginalization", Small Arms Survey, working paper no.3, Geneva, May 2007

tanks and artillery, gave them a radio station, passports and our embassy".[34] As has been the case, these were rejected as lacking foundation by the Eritrean government.[35] Following this development ambassadors were withdrawn and the border between them closed.

Another development that affected their relationship was the summit meeting between the leaders of Sudan, Ethiopia and Yemen in October 2002, which although discussed the situation in Somalia, the crisis in the Middle East and the Southern Red Sea security, nevertheless, was called as an alliance of convenience aimed against Eritrea. It was in other words called the mini-axis of belligerency against Eritrea.[36] This development gave rise to new tensions between the two governments, as can be seen from the measures taken by the authorities of Kassala in Sudan to move Eritrean refugees far from its camps, and the accusations against the illegal detention of innocent Eritreans in Sudan.[37]

Normal relations returned once the problem within Sudan was solved. The signing of peace agreement between the North and the South Sudan in January 2005 contributed to normalizing relations between Eritrea and the Sudan. Once normal relations were restored, Eritrea made subsequent attempts to mediate the problem in East Sudan and in October 2006 a peace deal was signed between the government of Sudan and the East Sudanese rebels in Asmara.[38] Besides, Eritrea also actively pursued its diplomatic strategy to bring about an end to the ongoing conflict in Darfur in West Sudan by attempting to unite the various rebel factions in Darfur and unite them.[39]

As mentioned above, as and when the opposition forces gains ground in its fight with the government in Sudan, tensions between them increase for each of them blame the other of supporting their respective opposition forces with arms. As noted by the U.S. Assistant Secretary for African Affairs in a briefing on U.S. – Eritrea relations, "Eritrea is a major player on Sudan, but again, they're a major player because they're sponsoring and supporting the rebel groups".[40] The continuity of this aspect is noteworthy here. However, it should also be noted that Eritrea has denied existence of any opposition forces in the country. The

---

[34] Ibid. Eritrea's support to East Sudan rebels including the Beja Congress, apart from its support to other groups such as Oromo Liberation Front, Gambella People's Liberation Front, Somali Islamic Courts, has been confirmed by Human Security Baseline Assessment, (HSBA). See, "The Militarization of Sudan: A Preliminary Review of Arms Flows and Holdings", Small Arms Survey, Geneva, http://www.smallarmssurvey.org/files/portal/spotlight/sudan/Sudan_pdf/SIB%206%20militarization.pdf

[35] www.irinnews.org/report.aspx?reportid=3495

[36] For more reasons on this see www.shaebia.com, 30th October 2002

[37] Eritrea accused Sudan of arresting its nationals and closing community centres used by Eritreans in Khartoum. See, "Eritrea- Sudan Relations Plummet", http://news.bbc.co.uk/2/hi/africa/3400575.stm 15, January, 2004; Eritrea's neighbors accused it for de-stabilizing the region. See "Eritrea-Region's Trouble Maker", http://news.bbc.co.uk/2/hi/africa/3353313.stm, December 2003

[38] See "Sudan: Gov't Eastern rebels sign peace agreement", IRIN, http://www.irinnews.org/report.aspx?reportid=61338, December 2007; the full text of the agreement is given in Sudan Tribune, http://www.sudantribune.com/IMG/pdf/Eastern_Sudan_Peace_Agreement.pdf

[39] See "Eritrea Hopes to Unite Darfur Rebels", http://www.sudantribune.com/spip.php?article22157, June 2007.

[40] Jendayi Frazer, Assistant Secretary for African Affairs, "Briefing on U.S. Eritrea Relations", http://www.state.gov/p/af/rls/spbr/2007/91231.htm, August 17, 2007

Eritrean president in an interview to Al Arabiya Satellite T.V. emphatically denied the "existence of opposition forces in the country....all foreign plans to create a political opposition were foiled".[41] The Eritrean president further added that relations with Sudan have now become stronger than before. To quote him:

> Our relations with Sudan are strategic and cannot be imposed or changed by the political circumstances or events. Our relations are historical and date back to the era of struggle. Relations after independence were good, but due to some political and ideological reasons these relations stumbled but later returned to normal. These relations are now growing and taking the form of strong bilateral relations and joint work to find solutions to even the problems of the region. [42]

This goes to show not only the changes in perception but also the contradictory picture of the above-mentioned aspect.

Relations have since improved between the two as Eritrea joined Libya in extending its mediatory role in bringing about an end to the conflict between Chad and the Sudan in February 2007 following which a high level joint military committees from Eritrea, Sudan, Chad and Libya have been formed to bring about peace in West Sudan's Darfur crisis.[43]

Trends and Future Scenarios

Studying the interaction between Eritrea and the Sudan is interesting for it reveals several trends. At the outset, it could be understood from the above analysis that their bilateral political relations have swung between extremes. What comes to light then is that the inability to maintain cordial relationship can be attributed to factors like a) domestic problems in the Sudan; b) political instability- meaning absence of representative governments in both countries; c) religious antagonisms and d) developments in the Horn and maybe: e) foreign intervention, mainly of the U.S. In fact, it is the interplay of these factors that has contributed to trends in ups and downs in bilateral relations.

Another informative aspect that emerges from their bilateral relations is that in a way both countries have produced a "common category" of political leadership concerned only with how to retain their respective power base. From the ashes of the protracted independence struggle with Ethiopia came the leadership in Eritrea that was initially praised for its new outlook and dynamism, which soon faded having got entangled and lured into the game of "power politics" and straining relationships with all neighbouring countries in the Horn. And from a long-drawn out domestic conflict between the North and South Sudan rose a kind of leadership (not in any way different from previous leaderships especially Al Numeiry) also entangled in power-struggle. So, the commonality in these countries is that governments in these two countries are not representative enough and have been subject to problems leading

---

[41] "President Afeworki says no political opposition in Eritrea", Sudan Tribune, http://www.sudantribune.com/spip.php?article21830, 12 December, 2007

[42] Ibid

[43] The high level joint military committee met recently in Asmara in December 2007. See "Eritrea: President Receives High Level Joint Military and Security Committee", www.allafrica.com 11 December 2007; for the full text of the meeting see, "Chad-Sudan: Tripoli Security Meeting", Africa Research Bulletin, vol.44, issue 8, September 2007, pp. 17182-17190.

them to focus on consolidating their political power by adopting strategies like exporting Islamic ideology and supporting opposition groups. While Sudan had invariably extended its Islamic support to Eritrean Jihad Movements (as well as to other countries in the Horn), Eritrea rendered its support to the rebel movement in South Sudan as well as in the East of Sudan. In other words, peaceful coexistence has not been possible and it is the struggle for peaceful coexistence that has led them to adopt such inimical policies against each other.

Changes in governments have not in way produced different outlook or policies. For example, in spite of a strong historical basis for mutual gains through economic cooperation, these countries have exhibited the primacy of political relations meaning consolidating bilateral economic ties have not been taken up. Rather, they have been guided by their respective politically motivated concerns without looking at the economic dimension. They have been subjected to narrow outlook and lack of farsightedness.

The governments in both the countries have not changed and so are the possibilities of renewed tensions cropping up once again. Concern is also there with regard to the large presence of Eritrean refugees who had fled the country at different times – in the past due to Dergue oppression and in the 1990s after Eritrea's independence due to political repression within the country. The issue is whether these can contribute to any kind of stable political atmosphere given the Sudan regimes' religious support. The presence of these refugees itself raises the question as to what extent it can act as a glue in solidifying political relations between the Sudan and Eritrea given the doubts exhibited by the Eritrean side on the indoctrination of these people. This is indeed a thorny issue yet to be resolved amicably and can rake up possibilities of renewed frictions between the two countries as can be discerned from the past trend.

One consequence of the improved relationship between the two governments is the deporting of young Eritreans by the Sudanese government who are trying to escape the Eritrean governments' conscription attempt en masse back to Eritrea (many of them Christians!!). The Kassala (Eastern Sudan) regional government has been acting as an agent of the Eritrean government since the peace agreement with the Beja rebels supported by the Eritreans and even allows Eritrean troops to enter Sudanese territory to deport refugees.

Bibliography

Books

Bowyer Bell, 1973, *The Horn of Africa – A Strategic Magnet in the 1970s*, New York, Crane Russak and Company.

Colin Legum and Bill Lee, 1979, *The Horn of Africa in Continuing Crisis*, New York, Africana Publishing Company.

Country Profile-Eritrea: Library of Congress, Federal Research Division, September 2005, p. 10.

Douglas H. Johnson, 2003, *"The Root Causes of Sudan's Civil Wars"*, Indiana, Indiana University Press.

Eyasu gaim, 1993, *The Eritrean Question: The Conflict between the Right to Self-determination and the Interests of States*, Uppasala, Iustus Forlag.

Haggi Erlich, 1983, *The Struggle Over Eritre 1962-1978: War and Revolution in the Horn of Africa,* Stanford, Hoover Institution Press.

Roy Pateman, 1998, *Eritrea: Even the stones are burning,* Asmara, the Red Sea Press.

Tesfatsion Medhanie, 1994, *Eritrea and its neighbors in the new world order,* Sweden, Bremen Munster.

Journals, Magazines and Internet Sources

Ruth Iyob, *"The Eritrean Experiment: A Cautious Pragmatism"*, The Journal of Modern African Studies, vol.35, no. 4, 1997, p. 666.

Berhane Woldegebriel, *"Briefing Eritrean Refugee in Sudan"*, Review of African Political Economy, 1996, pp.87-88

Colin Legum, *"Afeworki on the War Path"*, New African, February, 1996, no. 56, p. 38

John Young, *"Armed Groups along Sudan's Eastern Frontier: An Overview and Analysis"*, Small Arms Survey, HSBA Working Paper No: 9, Geneva, November 2007, p. 7.

John Young, *"The Tigray and the Eritrean Peoples Liberation Fronts: A History of Tensions and Pragmatism"*, The Journal of Modern African Studies, vol. 34, no.1, March 1996, p. 107

Hadas Eritrea, Asmara, Ministry of Information, 2, October, 1991, p.1

Eritrea Profile, 9 April 1994, p. 1

Horn of Africa Bulletin, vol.6, no.3, May – June 1994. www.europaworld.com, p.7

The Economist, October, 14, 1995.

UNMEE Media Monitoring Report, 12 November 2002.

Human Security Baseline Assessment, (HSBA). *"The Militarization of Sudan: A Preliminary Review of Arms Flows and Holdings"*, *Small Arms Survey*, Geneva, http://www.smallarmssurvey.org/files/portal/spotlight/sudan/Sudan_pdf/SIB%206%20 militarization.pdf; www.irinnews.org/report.aspx?reportid=3495; www.shaebia.com, 30th October 2002

Gender-Specific Violence in Eritrea – Perception and Reality

Asia Abdulkadir

"Women and donkeys need the stick."
"You must hit an ox at every turn and beat your wife every three days."[1]

1.   Introduction

The massive participation of women and girls in the Eritrean liberation struggle arose international attention and inspired a number of publications.[2] It was not only the high number of female EPLF-fighters - according to Pateman women constituted approximately forty percent of the EPLF - that nurtured the impression that gender relations were undergoing a thorough change. Also various spectacular measures of the EPLF, like allowing women to occupy high ranking positions in the military, banning female genital mutilation (FGM) and facilitating access to land, made Eritreans and outside observers conclude that the EPLF policy has led to a relatively high degree of equality between women and men.

Notwithstanding certain improvements there is a considerable imbalance in the power relation between men and women. Women and girls are subordinate by custom and practice. A women's status depends on being married and girls tend to marry at a very young age. Also it is generally considered more important to educate boys than girls and therefore a higher percentage of boys go to school than girls. But in a society where war and armed conflict are endemic, another aspect of gender relations deserves particular attention: the existence and degree of violence. What can be said about the extent and nature of and the possible response to violence against women?

Research conducted by the National Union of Eritrean Women (NUEW)[3] indicates that various forms of sexual violence against women, including severe forms of Female Genital Mutilation (FGM)[4], spouse abuse, sexual exploitation, rape and attempted rape have been occurring for generations within the Eritrean society.

My PhD research project[5] - on which this paper is based - was looking at the perception of gender-based violence[6] in the Eritrean society, especially occurring in the Eritrean army after the so-called border war with Ethiopia (1998-2000). I will also discuss the root causes of gender-based violence. My research did not produce quantitative results

---

[1]   Tigrinya proverbs from the Eritrean highlands which imply an acceptance of violence against women.

[2]   Most of the publications on women in Eritrea – with Armit Wilson (1991) being the classic example – described that the major changes occurring among Eritrean women are probably the most decisive of the revolution.

[3]   See the qualitative study on "Sexual and Gender-Based Violence in Debub", which was conducted by *Haben* and *CARE International* in May 2002. Page Nr. 9.

[4]   My previous research on Female Circumcision in Eritrea has found out that 98% of Eritrean girls and women have undergone this practice.

[5]   This research was completed in the year 2007.

[6]   Gender-based violence is violence directed at an individual female or male, based on her or his specific gender role in society, such as in the case of women and girls, being forced to cook and clean.

concerning the extent of the problem, for two reasons: first because of the absence of relevant statistics and the refusal of both the government and the society to recognise the existence and dimension of the problem, and second because due to political restrictions and insecurity I was not able to conduct my field research in Eritrea but had to do it in Sudan where I interviewed young Eritrean refugees and deserters. However, the study tries to provide valuable insight into the nature of violence against women and more importantly, how Eritreans as individuals and as a society perceive it and respond to it.

During the 1998-2000 war between Eritrea and Ethiopia, the Eritrean government in its national TV programs addressed rape cases of Eritrean women by Ethiopian soldiers while sexual violence and abuse against women in the Eritrean army are still considered taboo. Nevertheless, the US Department of State Country Report on Human Rights Practices in Eritrea (2006) describes a state of pervasiveness of violence against women, including spousal abuse, female genital mutilation, prostitution, unequal access to education, employment and control of economic resources. Moreover, it notes that

"there were reports that some women drafted into the service were subjected to sexual harassment and abuse".[7]

In Eritrea many young women suffer from unwanted pregnancy, unsafe abortion, sexually transmitted diseases (including HIV).Sexual and gender-based violence has acute physical, psychological and social consequences. Survivors often experience psychological trauma: depression, terror, guilt, shame, loss of self-esteem. Women and girls who are raped suffer also significant loss of social status, as the result of this study shows.

Generally, both among scholars and among practitioners, it has been accepted that the root cause of gender-based violence lie in gender relations, which worldwide are marked by the domination of men and the subordination of women. Violence against women occurs in varying contexts – at the domestic and community levels, in situations of armed conflict, and under repressive governments, among others. Although the relationships between these issues and contexts such as between war and domestic violence are complex, in many cases, violence against women is part of a conscious policy. Rape and physical violence are also carried out by opportunistic persons taking advantage of the prevailing climate of impunity and the culture of violence against women and girls.

While all Eritreans suffer from the climate of impunity and a very repressive regime, women pay a particularly heavy price for a system that is often unable or unwilling to respond adequately to all forms of gender-specific violence (Bailliet 2007:495).

Thus this article discusses several elements of the problem of gender-specific violence. First, it offers an overview of gender based violence and attempts to provide a theoretical understanding of violence. Second, it discusses the root causes of gender based violence. In particular, it highlights some of the ways in which violence is legitimated by community and other social institutions. Third, the article examines the perception of sexual violence against women in the Eritrean army looking at the impact of their socio-cultural and political environment.

---

[7] US Department of State, 2006, "Country Report on Human Rights Practices in Eritrea" Bureau of Democracy, Human Rights and Labour, 6. March.2007.

2.   Theoretical understanding of gender-specific violence

It is necessary to enunciate the underlying conception of violence on the basis of which I trace and analyse various brutal actions that encroach on people's lives. Contrary to some theorisations of violence, which distinguish between domestic, physical, emotional, or sexual assault, I argue that it is important to operate with a broader conception of violence. Such a concept must take into account a multitude of other forms of violence, including institutional and state violence.

In the analysis of violence towards women it is important to differentiate between culturally induced individual oppression by men and the way this is made possible by societal structures based on gender inequality (Brückner 2002:27). The latter leads to the phenomenon of many forms of male violence simply not being perceived as such, so that perpetrators have little or nothing to fear and only very rarely feel guilty (Godenzi 1996:80). Therefore one aspect that deserves closer attention is the societal structure that underline hierarchical family relations as well as the individual acts of men (and for that matter women). Both dimensions need to be addressed in order to ensure human rights for women.

The vast extent of gender-specific violence can be interpreted as an extreme consequence of the hierarchical construction of gender relations, which seem to justify a personal and sexual subjugation of women. Carol Hagemann-White highlights this issue:

> "The specificity of gender violence is, that the perpetrator acts upon his advantage as structurally stronger person." (Hagemann-White 1997:23)

Without this structural component individual violence would not all together fade away, but would lose its societal and cultural back-up. Cross-cultural studies show the interconnection between a comparatively equal gender structure and little gender and generation violence and vice versa (Levinson 1988:440). This finding is reaffirmed by a representative Swiss study (Gillioz et al. 1997:17) which shows that male violence corresponds with a demanding position and a strong conviction of male dominance including the idea of possession of one's wife, including her body and of having the right to control her actions. That means the majority of violent men are convinced of their legitimate right to enforce women's subordination.

Since both men and women play an active part in shaping their relationship (,,doing gender"), which also goes for the social praxis of the reproduction of a hierarchical structure, it is important to also look at the traditional image of women. The traditional female role stresses the responsibility of the woman for a happy family and a content husband, suggesting that it is her duty alone to ensure and invest in this by sacrificing her own interests if required, in order to serve others (Brückner 2000:7).

The situation of women combatants in Eritrea presents a complex picture of the interplay of the doggedness of social structures despite changing demands on women. The following statement of one interviewed Eritrean women substantiates how the traditional role of women is sought to be maintained within the Eritrean army: "As a woman within the

Eritrean army you take the role of either mother or sister. This is a widespread view and it expects from women to serve their male colleagues as they would be treated at home".[8]

Gondenzi (1996:85) notes that this kind of caring behaviour of women may make women dependent, while at the same time making the other dependent on oneself. However to assume a constellation of mutual dependence is illusory, since the relationship remains a hierarchical one. The realization of a man's dependency on a woman could potentially make him even more aggressive in the relationship.

Thus a definition of violence that is comprehensive and useful when examining violence against women is one that not only covers the physical and psychological manifestations but also the root cause of violence against women, namely gender inequality. A useful definition seems to me to be the following:

> Gender-based violence is a form of discrimination that seriously inhabits women's ability to enjoy rights and freedoms on a basis of equality with men. [...] gender-based violence is directed against a woman because she is a woman or that affects women disproportionately. It includes acts that inflict physical, mental or sexual harm or suffering, threats of such acts, coercion and other deprivations of liberty.[9]

This is one definition of violence which is generally accepted by researchers and practitioners. The first step in responding to and preventing violence against women is to recognize it in all its subtle forms. The term "sexual violence" is used in my study to refer to all forms of violence of sexual nature, such as rape, attempted rape, sexual assault and sexual threat.

3. Methodology

This sub-section provides a background on the unique setting in which this study was researched as well as on the contribution that former soldiers have made to share their experiences during the military service.

As in any study on the subject of violence against women, the greatest challenge lies in the methodology employed. Qualitative research in the form of problem-centred interview (PZI) was deemed most appropriate for fulfilling the objective of this study. Qualitative research is especially relevant when little is known about the target population and the topic under investigation, since it allows the interviewer the flexibility to explore each area of interest in depth and to include additional questions where appropriate.

Since it was impossible to conduct field research in Eritrea due to the government's denial of this social problem, I interviewed 15 former Eritrean Soldiers who are now refugees in Sudan. The interviews were conducted between October 2003 and March 2004. I also conducted eleven informal interviews with experts working with Eritrean refugees and Eritrean organizations based in the Sudan.

The issues that were explored in the interviews include:
- definitions of violence against women by female and male respondents in relation to their experiences and observations concerning gender based violence;

---

[8] Interview with a former member of the Eritrean army Nardos (pseudonym), Khartoum, February 2004.
[9] Convention on the Elimination of All Forms of Discrimination against Women, General Recommendations No. 19 (Eleventh Session, 1992).

- reasons for women not wanting to speak about their experiences;
- problems experienced by women victims of gender-based violence when seeking help, and
- the role of the family in shaping perceptions of gender based violence.

Since only former female and male solders were interviewed, the findings are not meant to indicate the extent of violence against women in the entire population. Being interested in the perception of gender-based violence of recruits, I decided not to ask whether the women I interviewed had actually experienced gender based violence. This decision was also supported by the tenet of not talking to women survivors[10] of violence without any professional guidance. Due to the stigmatization of victims of gender based violence, women affected did not want to be identified as victims of sexual violence although all of them confirmed that sexual violence and abuse were widespread in the Eritrean army.

As with any research, there are limitations and strengths inherent in the methodology used to obtain the data. However, when conducting research of such a sensitive nature and about which there are no baseline statistics for sampling, the major ethical constraints of confidentiality and safety of the respondents must be addressed before the more academic considerations of representation and randomness. The strength of this methodology was that it protected the respondents from a breach of confidentiality and secondary trauma, while giving a voice to participants who might have experienced violence and torture as far as possible.

In order to guarantee the confidentiality of all information and reflecting the wishes of respondents, the names of interviewees have been changed.

4   The findings

In the study, participants were asked to define violence against women and whether they ever witnessed gender-based violence during their military service. Rape, wife beating, and the inability to refuse sex, were named as types of gender-based violence that women have to face.

While rape was described as the most serious crime possible; most respondents could not estimate the extent of its prevalence, instead describing it as "common" or "quite common". An Eritrean female asylum seeker in Norway attested:

"Sawa in particular, is a horrible place for women. Women serve to give pleasure to the old men. Young girls have unwanted babies or are forced to marry men much older to them."[11]

Participants of this study were asked if women speak about such experiences. The results showed that survivors did not generally speak out, or if at all, only to family members or friends. While providing a safe environment to speak out, families often advised women to keep silent on their problem, therefore in effect disempowering them. Some participants in this study indicated that the reluctance to speak about abuse was based on the perception of

---

[10] Women and girls who have been raped can be presented and/or perceived either as victims or survivors and there is an ongoing debate as to which is the more appropriate term. In this article both terms are used interchangeably without significant distinction.

[11] See, Bailliet 2007:489.

what was "appropriate" behaviour on the part of the survivor herself. It is equally possible that women simply did not feel free to talk about abuse, a conclusion that may be drawn from the remark of the majority of the interviewees, who acknowledged that they knew women who had experienced sexual violence but sought to distance themselves from this with the value judgement such as: "Well, it happens to those who are willing". Furthermore, they said many women are taking advantage of it.

4.1   Social and legal obstacles to reporting violence and seeking redress

There are a number of factors that explain the public silence on violence against women in Eritrea. It is considered taboo to discuss family matters outside the house and only family members are involved in settling disputes that arise between husband and wife. On the other hand, it is a commonplace assumption that the husband has a right to discipline his wife and domestic violence is seen as a disciplinary act, and not as an abuse.

Eritrean women and girls rarely report to the authorities. This is true regardless of whether the crime is spousal abuse, child abuse, rape or incest. The low rate at which women and girls report such crimes is a symptom of the significant social and legal obstacles towards meaningful gender-based violence prevention and response in Eritrea. Women and girls who report abuse to the authorities find themselves confronting a system that prioritizes the reputation of their families in the community over their own well being and lives.

Based on my interviews and other research, I found that two primary obstacles stand in the way of enhanced protection against violence for Eritrean women and girls: discriminatory law that condone and perpetuate such violence and the absence of institutionalized policies to prevent violence, assist victims and hold perpetrators accountable. One informant described the situation as follows:

> "Essentially, victims of violence pay the price for the abuse they suffer, while the perpetrators usually go unpunished".[12]

She went on to say that:

> "cultural norms prevent women from reporting these types of incidents, and no one
> was charged or prosecuted for sexual harassment".[13]

The answer of the government to reports of rape is to encourage the perpetrator to marry the victim. The law currently in force includes provisions to provide clemency to rapists who agree to marry their victims from any criminal prosecution.[14]

As one of the interviewed stated:

> "If the perpetrator of the rape comes from the victim's religion or ethnic group
> the parents will ask him to marry the pregnant girl, however, if the perpetrator
> is from a different religion her parent mostly will not accept the marriage".[15]

Eritrean criminal laws do not effectively prohibit or adequately punish violence against women and girls. These laws include provisions that provide a reduction in penalty to men

---

[12] Interview with a former member of the Eritrean army, Senait (pseudonym), Khartoum, January 29, 2004.
[13] Ibid.
[14] See in Berhe. P.4-5. Berhe, M. discusses the subject in his undated study „Rape, Domestic Violence, Marriage and Female Genital Mutilation (FGM) under Eritrean Law".
[15] Interview with a former member of the Eritrean army Nardos (pseudonym), Khartoum, February 2004.

who kill or attack female relatives committing adultery; or as mentioned above, mercy from criminal prosecution to rapists who agree to marry their victims.

One of the informants of the study said:

> "In fact, the laws in particular and the way in which they have been interpreted and applied in practice have led to virtual impunity for perpetrators of violence against women and girls".[16]

The formal frames for sanctioning gender-specific violence are described in the Transitional Penal Code of Eritrea (TPCE). Since Eritrea's independence, a transitional law has been passed which is explained in the study „Rape, Domestic Violence, Marriage and Female Genital Mutilation (FGM) under Eritrean Laws."[17] The transitional laws in Eritrea today are a combination of the following sources:

- EPLF directives from the time of the independence movement;
- amended Ethiopian laws;
- customary laws;
- islamic law (Schari'a) and
- laws in force after independence.

Although the legal Transitional Penal Code does not offer a clear definition of sexual violence and harassment, article 589 of the Eritrean penal code defines rape as follows:

- There must be force or violence committed in the alleged rape.
- The compulsion must be against a woman to submit herself to sexual intercourse.
- The forced sexual intercourse must be out of wedlock.
- The use of force may be through rendering a woman unconscious or incapable of resistance."[18]

Article 589 of the Eritrean Penal law, in which sexual violence is treated, thus does not recognize sexual violence committed within marriage as a punishable offence. Furthermore, from a feminist perspective, it is a very problematic formulation of legislation, as it requires evidence of extreme violence and imposes a high evidentiary burden on the victim.

To add to these legal and social barriers, discriminatory legislation in force in Eritrea described in the sub-sections above, neither acts as a deterrent to violence, nor does it provide victims with adequate redress for the abuse they have suffered.

4.2 Women in the Eritrean army

A closer look at the position of Eritrean women in the army allows for a nuanced analysis of their controversial roles within the army. As elsewhere in the world, the ideology of national security in Eritrea serves to justify not only a military presence but the militarization of the

---

[16] Interview with a former member of the Eritrean army, Saba (pseudonym), Khartoum, February 2004.

[17] Berhe, M. discusses the subject in his undated study „Rape, Domestic Violence, Marriage and Female Genital Mutilation (FGM) under Eritrean Law".

[18] Berhe Page Nr. 3

entire society. Therefore the military plays a very important role in the country. Eritrea is one of the most militarized countries in the world.[19]

Women have been crucial contributors to war efforts and the war machinery during the war between Eritrea and Ethiopia. Needless to say, women, like men, can be strong defenders of nationalist ideology. Eritreans have gone to war against Ethiopians to defend values that bind them together as a people.

Article 8 of the National Service Proclamation (Proclamation No 82/1995) states that "all Eritrean citizens aged 18 to 50 have the duty to fulfil the 'Active National Service'." Active National Service means the 6 month regular military training given at a base in addition to participation in 12 consecutive months of active national service and development programmes under the armed forces, thus comprising a total service of 18 months. Although the period of compulsory military service is 18 months by law, the government has prevented any of the recruits to leave the armed forces since 1997. While the government and the National Union of Eritrean Women (NUEW) perceive the participation of women in the army as a sign of women's emancipation, it is a controversially discussed issue among the Eritrean population. Initially the population at large were in favour of the compulsory conscription, with nationalistic aspirations ranking high. However, in recent years this view has changed, with Muslims parents from the Lowlands first objecting to women serving in the army. This was followed by objections from parents from different parts of the country to sending away their young children. From a social point of view, there are two reasons for objections to women serving in the army: Firstly, it is seen as "masculinizing" women. This is particularly with reference to women combatants from the Eritrean People's Liberation Front (EPLF), who in the past have explicitly rejected traditional cultural practices that subordinate and severely oppress women throughout Eritrea. Such attitudes towards women soldiers were further confirmed by my informants when asked to give their opinion of women serving in the army. They stated that women combatants are not feminine enough for the norms of Eritrean society, because they had become too independent and would not follow orders from their husbands, thus deemed a high risk for marriage. They were also described as too rough and too old, in addition to doubts cast about their past sexual behaviour.

The second objection to women's participation in the armed forces alluded to the fear of unwanted pregnancies amongst unmarried women and girls in the army as a result of rape. The consequence of this, so the interviewees stated, were that these women would not easily find husbands in the future and thus risked remaining on the margins of society.

The only existing mass-based women's organization and para-governmental organization, the National Union of Eritrean Women (NUEW) is very supportive of women serving in the military. In that it believes women's commitment to the national struggle is an important factor in their emancipation (Tesfa G. Gebremedhin 2002:87).

What further complicates the debate is that recruitment criteria in the Eritrean army are different for men and women. They could be described as follows:

- Conscription excludes married women and women with children. This criterion does not apply to men, which demonstrates the double standards in the system regarding the

---

[19] Eritrea is among an exclusive group of countries (the others are Oman, Syria, Burma, Sudan, Pakistan, and Burundi) that spends more on the military than on health and education combined. See the UNDP's *Human Development Report 2003* (New York: UNDP, 2003).

equality of men and women. In fact, both men and women could claim discrimination within the system. Men could argue that the system gives women preferential treatment in some regards.

- In addition there are gender differentiated tasks for men and women within the military. Generally women are assigned mainly to administrative jobs, cooking, serving as nurses whereas men are given higher military positions such as Generals and Commanders.

This gender specific treatment within the Eritrean military obviously prevents women from obtaining higher ranks or having access to positions of power and decision making. According to the respondents I interviewed there were suggestions that high-ranking male officials selected female recruits for their specific roles based on their physical appearance. They were indirectly expected to not only perform their assigned duties but also carry out additional personal favours such as cleaning, washing clothes of their superiors, and in some cases these demands extended to sexual services. One can conclude from this that the construction of femininity within the military is to subjugate women as domestic servants and as sex objects. Furthermore, objections to women's involvement in the military are based on the normative expectation for women to behave in a traditional manner, as is the common practice within the civilian population.

In principle the compulsory conscription for women could have been an opportunity to advance equality between women and men by emphasising women's rights in placing them on the same scale as men, but in reality the armed forces in Eritrea are extremely exploitative of women. The case of rape and its juridical consequences shows just how difficult it is for women to break out from the traditional folds, allowing women to be raped without any formal consequences for the perpetrators and yet continuously placing demands on women's conformity to tradition. The treatment of women in the Eritrean armed forces is therefore not a step towards their emancipation, but in fact a mirror image of the way women are treated in the society as a whole.

The male-dominated structures of the military and of society as a whole and the lack of women in leading positions within the military and other institutions could be one of the indicators for the lack of justice for women and the military's indifference to their problems. In the following cited interview there was a further tendency to blame those women who encountered sexual violence for inviting and creating their own suffering, as it were. This must be contextualised against the lack of any open debates on the issue and the government's consistent position of complete denial. It is not surprising, then, that the general public and the some member of the army themselves are not aware of the seriousness of this issue. One of the male informants interviewed stated that

> "Women who have encountered abuse in the military should not be surprised as this is a natural consequence of the tough life and as they have left their homes to pursue a male dominated profession. These problems are not avoidable in the army."[20]

20

In a trivializing mode characteristic of government policy on the whole, he went on to claim that „if women and men come together it is impossible to avoid such incidents".[21]

The majority of the participants of the study stated that violence against women exists. At the same time, a number of the participants claimed that if a woman truly wanted to avoid sexual intimidation or sexual violence she would well be capable of doing so. The following statement by an interviewee further supports this accusatory claim:

> "There are a lot of women in the military who are able to protect their honour."[22]

Some interviewees also alleged that women in the army "tolerated" sexual violence or intimidation from their superiors in order to gain material benefits or get home leave from their superiors.

It is important to point out that both men and women who were interviewed, placed the blame and the responsibility on the women, to protect themselves against such harm. It is equally significant to note that women rather than men were more open to reflect on their own personal experience with abuse. They spoke of how they faced a similar situation of sexual intimidation. However, this relative openness was combined with self-protective mechanisms. E.g. women stressed that they were able to avoid being harmed and they usually refused to see themselves as victims of abuse. Therefore, while women are more open to discuss the issue, they refrain from admitting their personal affection by these problems due to the stigmatization of rape victims and the threat of becoming social outcasts.

Some former soldiers described the impact of the taboo on the question of violence against women, whereby women who became pregnant as a result of rape were rejected by their families, thus left to fend for themselves on their own, often forced to go to another town in order to raise their children and escape from further stigmatisation under the protection of anonymity. Such problems did not exist in the eyes of the government and indeed for the society as a whole.

This victimization of the victims, combined with the lack of a critical public discussion of the broader issues of violence against women, and the lack of recognition of their rights, discourage women from admitting their suffering or pursuing legal justice.

Conclusion

Although the participants of my research could not provide any quantitative information about the prevalence of violence against women, they were able to share from their own accounts and value systems and thus give insights into the existence of violence against women in the military.

According to the statements of the interview partners, violence against women is a fact and an every day reality in the Eritrean Army; even though it is taboo to admit it. Furthermore, many stated that sexual abuse and sexual harassment are widespread amongst both recruits and civilian women. There is a thick layer of silence surrounding the issue, although they admit that such abuses are common practice. On the surface it would appear

---

[21] Interview with a former member of the Eritrean army Nardos (pseudonym), Khartoum, February 2004.
[22] Interview with a former member of the Eritrean army Nardos (pseudonym), Khartoum, February 2004.

that this social problem does not exist in Eritrea, since even the ones affected by it claim to be unaware of the fact that it is happening to them or tend to deny it as a social problem by blaming the victims of violence.

There is a lack of knowledge about the nature and the impact of abuse generally and specifically of how to respond to survivors of these acts. Therefore, Eritrean women who are victims of abuse suffer under immense prejudice against them. Changing this perception is not an easy task and not enough is being done to address this.

Although it is currently not realistic to foresee major, short-term changes in the nature of violence against women in Eritrea, it is a cause of concern that so many women are still not able to access the criminal justice system in order to seek redress. The study indicates that this is the most important current challenge, not least in order to prevent further violence against women through deterrence. Most of the respondents said that victims speak about their experiences of violence at some point in time, usually to family or friends. However, very few take the problem to the criminal justice system even if there is no immediate threat of further harm from the perpetrators.

In effect, women who are victims of violence outside of the army's domain are also affected by the culture of public silence over violence as a social problem. The research findings confirm that violence against women is a "hidden problem" in Eritrea which makes intervening difficult. Family members do little to assist them in accessing the justice system. The study revealed that all too often, survivors and their family members believe that abuse is not a matter that can or should be resolved by the criminal justice system or by other agencies or public bodies. Therefore, if preventing violence against women requires changing attitudes towards gender-relations in society, those to whom survivors turn for help should be key targets for such initiatives.

There is a need to convince victims that accessing the services of the police and the courts could be of benefit to them and could thus help to change gender-relations in society. Government agencies in Eritrea and organizations working in the field do little to improve victims' access to the criminal justice system.

However, the effective eradication of gender based violence requires not just institutional change; it also requires a change of mindset and attitudes among individuals and state actors. Dealing with mindsets and age-old cultures and behaviour in most cases entails a long process and struggle for change which has to be rooted in and driven by civil society.

Finally, any criticism of the military as an institution is considered an offence against the Eritrean national security doctrine. Thus, violence against women within the army remains a taboo, effectively silenced by the almost sacred status of the military.

Bibliography

Bailliet, Cecilia M., 2007, Examining Sexual Violence in the Military Within the Context of Eritrean Asylum Claims Presented in Norway. Oxford University Press, pp. 471-510.

Berhe, M., undated, Rape, Domestic Violence, Marriage and Female Genital Mutilation (FGM) under Eritrean Law.

Brückner, M., 2002, Wege aus der Gewalt gegen Frauen und Mädchen. Frankfurt a. M.:
    Fachhochschulverlag.

Brückner, M., 2000, Gewalt im Geschlechterverhältnis - Möglichkeiten und Grenzen eines
    geschlechtertheoretischen Ansatzes zur Analyse „häuslicher Gewalt", in: Zeitschrift
    für Frauenforschung und Geschlechterstudien, 4, pp. 3-19.

Gillioz, L., De Puy, J., Ducret, V. and Belser, K., 1997, Gewalt in Ehe und Partnerschaft in
    der Schweiz - Resultate einer Untersuchung, in: Schweizerische Konferenz der
    Gleichstellungsbeauftragten (ed.): Beziehung mit Schlagseite. Bern: eFeF, pp.13-76.

Godenzi, A., 1996, Gewalt im sozialen Nahraum. Frankfurt a. M.: Helbing & Lichtenhahn.

Hagemann-White, C., 1997, Strategien gegen Gewalt im Geschlechterverhältnis, in:
    Hagemann-White, C., Kavemann, B. and Ohl, D. (eds.): Parteilichkeit und Solidarität.
    Bielefeld: Kleine, pp. 15-116.

Levinson, D., 1988, Family Violence in Cross-Cultural Perspective, in: Hasselt, V.B. et al.
    (eds.): Handbook of Family Violence. New York: Plenum Press, pp. 435-455.

Pateman, R., 1990, Liberte, Egalite, Fraternite: Aspects of the Eritrean Revolution. The
    Journal of Modern African Studies. 28(3), pp. 457-472.

Tesfa G. Gebremedhin, 2002, Women, Tradition and Development in Africa: The Eritrean
    Case, Asmara: The Red Sea Press.

Vlachova, M. & Biason, L., 2005, Women in an Insecure World (Geneva Centre for the
    Democratic Control of Armed Forces.

Zones of Peace under Threat in a Region of Conflict and Crisis.
*The Role of Eritrean Civil Society Reviewed**

Nicole Hirt and Abdulkader Saleh Mohammad

1 Introduction

During the 1990s, the new-born State of Eritrea was often considered one of the new hopes of Africa. This positive image changed rapidly due to the border war with Ethiopia, and the government's style of ruling since 2001.

Against this background, characterizing Eritrean society as a "zone of peace" is an assumption not easily comprehensible to the reader at first glance. We want to make clear that our definition of "zone of peace" (an imperfect translation of the German term "Friedensraum") is based on the analysis of social interactions of Eritrean society, and should be differentiated from the analysis of government policies.

The term "zone of peace" highlights the capacity of a society to resolve conflicts and promote internal stability using a deeply rooted culture of mediation without resorting to uncontrolled violence or civil war[1]. We are talking about a society subjected to various forms of rule over the past centuries – in most cases coming from outside: Turkey, Abyssinia south of the Mereb[2], Italy and Britain. All of them had in common that they followed their own interests and cared little about the local population. Throughout long periods of time, Eritrean society existed as an entity with functioning laws and regulations more or less independent of the respective governments. It developed distinguished mechanisms of conflict avoidance and resolution on a territory inhabited by a variety of social groups separated by culture and religion. These traditional forms of civil society[3] continued to function after independence and have so far minimised the spread of social anomie[4].

---

* This article is based on the research project "Friedensräume in Eritrea und Tigray unter Druck. Identitätskonstruktion, soziale Kohäsion und politische Stabilität" (Rainer Tetzlaff; Nicole Hirt and Abdulkader Saleh Mohammad/Eritrea, Wolbert Smidt /Ethiopia), University of Hamburg). The research design was developed during the period immediately following the end of the Eritrea Ethiopia war (2001), before the structural changes caused by increasing militarisation could be foreseen. Under the given circumstances, the role of traditional civil society turned out to be one of the decisive factors concerning the maintenance of inner-societal peace.

[1] There were two civil wars between ELF and EPLF during the liberation struggle in the 1970s and early 1980s, but they were initiated by the leadership of the fronts and opposed by the majority of the population and most probably the rank and file of the combatants.

[2] The river Mereb seperates Eritrea from Tigray, the northern Province of Ethiopia and had a seperating function long before the establishment of Eritrea as a territorial entity by Italian colonisation (Smidt, Wolbert 2007: Märäb Mellaŝ, in: Uhlig, S. (ed.): Encyclopaedia Aethiopica, Vol. 3. Wiesbaden)

[3] We define traditional civil society as a form of social organisation reaching beyond the extended family, but distinguished from state institutions – involved in regulating land and family disputes, thereby stabilising the social order. Traditional mediators are village or lineage heads and religious elders, as well as respected personalities asked to perform procedures of mediation (such mediators are called Shemagelle).

[4] The term social anomie goes back to Emile Durkheim and is defined as a lack of social orientation deriving from a lack of commonly respected norms and values (Durkheim, Emile 1897: Suicide)

Since independence, Eritrean society has faced the task of rebuilding a society deeply disrupted by 30 years of war against Ethiopian occupation, only to be confronted with another extreme challenge during the war with Ethiopia 1998-2000, followed by an internal policy of militarization. During the "border war", about one third of the population (1 million people) was displaced, 76.000 Eritreans were deported from Ethiopia and had to be integrated, while the economy was severely disrupted. Our assumption is that without the traditional system of conflict resolution and social stabilisation, the society would not have been able to face these extreme difficulties and maintain its internal order.

When we talk about a "zone of peace", we do not mean a space where absolute peace ("positive peace"[5] in the sense of Galtung) prevails. This would be an unrealistic assumption. But there should be more than "negative peace", i.e. the mere absence of war. Certainly, there are deep rifts within Eritrean society, but since independence, this has not led to an outbreak of violence among the people. There may be a certain degree of mistrust among the different ethnic, regional and religious groups, but so far the feeling of belongingness to one nation has been stronger and violent struggles over scarce resources or cultural values were not an option for the overwhelming majority of the people. "Peace" in our context can be defined as a very low level of violence and a high level of mutual respect in every-day life, the confidence that one can usually trust one's neighbour or business partner. It means the confidence that there are institutions one can turn to in case of conflicts – namely the well-established systems of mediation by traditional elders, and that there are systems of mutual support in times of dire need, which compensate the weakness of state institutions in this regard.

2   Background

The Horn of Africa is infamous as a region of continuous civil and bilateral warfare. For centuries, it has been characterised by wars and strives between local leaders, aggravated by the involvement of external powers. On the other hand, societies in some parts of the Horn developed remarkably successful strategies of peaceful coexistence, conflict resolution and survival in an environment marked by ethnic, religious and cultural heterogeneity. We define such territories as zones of peace. The English term "zones of peace" is commonly defined[6] as territories or local communities threatened by violent conflicts surrounding them or being imminent in a specified area. In some cases, they are established from above, like the unsuccessful "Safe Zones" in Bosnia-Herzegovina during the conflict in former Yugoslavia. In other countries affected by violent conflicts like the Philippines, Columbia and El Salvador, zones of peace appeared through grassroot level initiatives. In such cases, the communities declared themselves as off limits to war and armed hostility.[7] Eritrea is not a

---

[5] For Galtung, positive peace means the absence of structural violence

[6] For various definitions of "zones of peace", see Subedi, Surya P. 1996: Land and Maritime Zones of Peace in International Law. Oxford; Kacowicz, A.M. 1998: Zones of Peace in the Third World. South America and West Africa in Comparative Perspective. Albany, NY. Hancock., Landon (ed.) 2007: Zones of Peace. Bloomfield, CT; Nordstrom, Carolyn 1994: Warzones: Cultures of Violence, Militarisation and Peace. Australian Peace Research Centre, Working Paper No. 145. Canberra; Zones of Peace International Foundation (ZOPIF); www.zopif.org

[7] Hancock, L.E. and Iyer, Pushpa 2004: From Fear to Sanctuary. A Typology of Zones of Peace. Institute for Conflict Analysis & Resolution, George Mason University, Fairfax

zone of peace in this sense. But as a high degree of social stability can be observed, we suggest a new approach.

We suggest the following definition: A zone of peace (in our sense) is a space where, through formal or informal agreements supported by normative value systems, internal stability and relative absence of violence can be maintained within an area of widespread inter- or intra-state violence. Zones of peace are characterised by the existence of traditional or modern forms of civil society institutions which are in the position to regulate the allocation of scarce resources and mediate conflicts either independently from, or in cooperation with the government. They may work even in environments where governments are not able or willing to install legal and political mechanisms to guarantee participation and adequate juridical systems for peaceful conflict resolution.

It is important to note that zones of peace should not be regarded as a "paradise on earth", where violence does not occur at all. So far, there is probably no part of human society which is absolutely free from direct and, equally important, structural violence. What distinguishes zones of peace from zones of war or societies affected by state failure is the existence of practical mechanisms deeply rooted in the society to deal with existing conflicts in order to find resolutions that keep bloodshed, deprivation and other forms of violence at a minimum. Whenever conflicts occur among members of the society, there should be institutions they can turn to in order to find a solution to their problem without resorting to violent means – institutions with the ability to come up with solutions respecting the rights and interests of all conflicting parties involved. In the absence of a government able to implement such mechanisms by the rule of law, traditional mediators can play an important role in stabilising societies.

Zones of peace are not necessarily politically progressive societies – they may keep their stability by using deeply conservative concepts, while "Western" ideals of individual rights and freedoms may not play an important role. Traditional civil society may be instrumentalised by authoritarian governments to maintain "law and order", thus indirectly preventing the population from engaging in active protest against the government[8].

As to the concept of violence, we suggest the following:

- In any society of the world, physical (and psychological) violence exists at an individual level, although its frequency differs widely. This includes criminal acts like aggravated assault, rape, robbery and murder.
- There has been no society so far which is free from structural violence in the sense of depriving individuals from equal access to opportunities. In zones of peace, structural violence does exist – but inequality is reduced by mechanisms of social solidarity guaranteeing minimal social security to all members of society.

---

[8] A striking example for a zone of peace is Somaliland in comparison with the rest of Somalia. Here, internal peace is maintained by traditional authorities, while other areas, especially around the capital Mogadishu have fallen into social agony. That is not to say that Somaliland is a democratic society in the "Western" sense, but seems to be a successful model in maintaining the dignity of the individual under the given circumstances of state failure (see: Brons, Maria 2001: From Statelessness to Statelessness? Utrecht)

- Institutional violence is based on durable relations of submission based on physical sanctions, usually exercised by the state (these measures may be legitimate, i.e. regulated by law, or illegitimate).

- Conflicts resulting from disputes between different interest groups (e.g. social classes, ethnic groups) concerning the distribution of scarce resources are frequent in most parts of the world, but many societies established mechanisms of managing such disputes peacefully, making use of institutionalised procedures, while in other societies, the same conflicts may lead to outbreaks of violence.

- War-lordism and "markets of violence" (Gewaltmärkte, see Elwert 1997) are often found in societies where the state is too weak to maintain its monopoly of power.

- In countries affected by civil war, violence is widespread throughout the country (although some regions may be excluded) and is exerted between military groups and against the civilian population[9].

According to these principles, we suggest that the term "zones of peace" includes territories or social spaces where levels of criminality or deviant behaviour are low, structural violence is reduced by traditional social networks, where disputes between different interest groups can be managed peacefully through established mediation mechanisms, and where war-lordism and civil wars as forms of organised violence are absent.

We consider Eritrean society as one such example. The country became independent in 1993, after 30 years of struggle against Ethiopian domination. Eritrea is inhabited by 9 ethnic groups and its population is almost equally divided between Muslims and Christians. Before its colonisation by Italy in 1890, Eritrea had no centralised structures of government. Parts of the territory were controlled by Ethiopian rulers who extended their power to the Mereb Mellash, the Eritrean highlands. The Ottoman Empire and later the Egyptians at times controlled the coastal regions and their hinterland. But still, local leaders remained in power and formed shifting alliances with external powers. Even under Italian domination until 1941, local leaders kept some political influence. A system of predominantly indirect rule was applied by the Italian colonisers and the succeeding British Military Administration, which lasted until 1952. Then, Eritrea was federated with Ethiopia, only to be totally annexed by the Empire in 1962. Both the autocratic Emperor Haile Selassie and the military government of Mengistu Haile Mariam tried to monopolise political power over the Eritrean population. This strategy was unsuccessful and caused an uprising of the people, leading to political independence. While the liberation movement remained affected by ethnic and regional divisions under the dominance of the ELF[10], the EPLF[11] introduced a Marxist ideology in the mid 1970s in an attempt to (at least nominally) overcome subdivisions of Eritrean society along lines of ethnicity, religion, region, and gender[12]. It was successful in introducing a

---

[9] For a discussion of different concepts of violence, see van Riel, Raphael 2005: Gedanken zum Gewaltbegriff. Drei Perspektiven. Forschungsstelle Kriege, Rüstung und Entwicklung, Uni Hamburg, IPW, Arbeitspapier Nr. 2/2005

[10] Eritrean Liberation Front. It initiated the armed struggle in 1961.

[11] Eritrean People's Liberation Front. The EPLF was formed in 1975 after the unification of 3 movements that had split from the ELF.

[12] The EPLF itself was not free from ethnic disparities, as it was dominated by Christian Tigrinya highlanders. Therefore, its policy of national unity may also be seen as an attempt to establish its power monopoly over all parts of the Eritrean population (Markakis 1987:133).

feeling of equality amongst the fighters, in spite of its centralised authoritarian political and military leadership. This structure was later transformed into the political system of the independent state.

Research on Eritrean history and its political dynamics was carried out by numerous scholars. But researchers often neglected how these political structures affected Eritrean society at the grass-root level, namely the local population groups and their leaders, who played a decisive role in keeping stability and guaranteeing survival in a hostile environment dominated by power struggles between the political elites. In pre-colonial times, raids and counter-raids of different regional groups were common in conflicts over scarce resources like land and water. But at the same time, each local community developed detailed mechanisms of conflict resolution and arbitration including the active participation of parts of the population[13]. These procedures have survived for centuries up to present times. They guarantee the cohesion of local communities, sometimes against the interest of the political elites, especially the Ethiopian rulers, who often applied divide and rule strategies. In spite of these attempts and Eritrea's social diversity, the level of internal violence has remained relatively low since the time of Italian colonisation. When outbreaks of violence took place, they were usually caused by the political instrumentalization of differences by ruling elites.

One example is the conflict between Orthodox Christians and Muslims during the time of the British Military Administration and the Federation. The Ethiopian government instrumentalised the Orthodox Church and some highland elites to motivate the UP (Unionist Party)[14] to commit numerous atrocities against supporters of independence (at that time mostly Muslims). Due to rising military pressure of the Mengistu regime, including acts of terror against all groups of Eritrean society, the feeling of nationalism increased and the population seemed to have overcome local disparities for one common cause: liberation from Ethiopian suppression[15].

It is, however, doubtful if these disparities have completely disappeared within the independent State of Eritrea, as the ruling PFDJ claims. We have to ask why the internal level of violence has remained astonishingly low even in times of crisis like the one created by the war between Eritrea and Ethiopia from 1998-2000. In spite of rising political pressure on local communities, Eritrea so far shows very low levels of internal violence at the community level, and the tolerance of the multi-ethnic society in its daily interactions is impressing. Here we have to note that the process of demobilisation of ex-combatants, the return of about 140.000 former refugees from the Sudan and other countries of exile, the modernisation of agriculture (plantations), as well as the deportation of more than 70.000 Eritreans from Ethiopia and the displacement of hundreds of thousand people during the border conflict, led to rapid population movements. Traditional settlement areas of specific groups[16] have now

---

[13] Favali and Pateman 2003 provide a profound insight into the co-existence of traditional and modern law in Eritrea. Women and landless population groups were often excluded from decision-making though.

[14] The Unionist Party, dominated by Christian highlanders, opted for unification of Eritrea with Ethiopia during the time of the British administration (1941 – 1952). See Tekeste Negash 1997: Eritrea and Ethiopia. The Federal Experience. New Brunswick

[15] The liberation struggle was of course in itself a form of massive violence, but it was perceived by the population as a legitimate uprising against prolonged colonisation and supression.

[16] E.g. parts of the Western lowlands of Gash Setit, originally inhabited by the Kunama, Nara and Hedareb, where thousands of Tigrinya highlanders have now been settled, putting pressure on scarce land and water

become multi-ethnic spaces where a variety of groups have to find new modes of peaceful coexistence. This applies to rural and urban environments as well.

3   Patterns of violence and peace in Eritrea

The levels of violence and deviant behaviour are low in Eritrea. Private and common property is usually respected in spite of the general scarcity of resources and a high rate of poverty. Theft and robbery are generally seen as demeaning behaviour, and such incidents are usually reported to the police or, when victim and perpetrator are known to each other, to traditional mediators (Shemagelle) in order to get compensation for the victim. The frequency of murder is difficult to detect, as there is no free press reporting such cases and the government media conceal them. But the "rumour-mill" occasionally reports murders caused by family and jealousy dramas, just as they are common throughout the world. But they do not seem to be a widespread problem, certainly very different from areas like New York or Nairobi.

Sexual violence against women is a problem occurring especially in the military against young female conscripts[17]. All women have the duty to serve in the military, which is commonly known as a place where forced sexual relations with army commanders are not infrequent[18], but few women have the courage to speak out – they would face immediate reprisals by their army superiors. Generally speaking, sexual violence is a social taboo, and a young woman reporting it to the police will not only cause severe damage to her own reputation, but also to that of her family, and will find it difficult to get married.

The low rate of deviant behaviour in the country seems to be due to a combination of traditional norms and values as well as to those established by the former liberation movement, which now forms the government. The state makes use of its power of suppression combined with the traditional values of society as a tool to prevent criminality, but in a subtle way: Regular police wearing uniforms (apart from the traffic police) are rarely seen in the streets of Eritrean cities.

Traditional values and deviant behaviour: As the extended family still plays a major role in Eritrean every-day life (it provides social security, regulates marriage, access to land and other property, and is the base of social life), the pressure on the young generation to behave according to traditional demands is high. In the case of committing a crime, they would not only bring shame on themselves, but also on their extended family. Besides state-induced sanctions, they would face additional stigmatisation and exclusion. Not surprisingly, the pressure on female youths is even higher, as they are "representatives of the family's honour"[19]. Generally, the community as a whole keeps a careful eye on what is going on in the public sphere, establishing a mechanism of mutual control. If a conflict threatens to go out of control, spontaneous mediation will be almost certain. Only if this does not work, people would call the police.

---

resources. This led to a feeling of marginalization on the side of Kunama people and other minorities. Alexander Naty 2002

[17] See Asia Abdulkadir's contribution in this volume.

[18] See e.g. amnesty international, May 2004. Eritrea. AI Index AFR 64/003/2004, p.27

[19] One remarkable exception is the increase in prostitution in urba areas (which may also occur in the form of weekend prostitution to earn additional income) in the post-border war period, enforced by the arrival of UN-troops, which is silently ignored by many families who pretend not to know where the additional income of their daughters may come from.

The state's attitude towards criminality and deviant behaviour: The state promotes traditional values as it knows they help a great deal in stabilising the country. Even more, according to the government, "the Eritrean" is a person completely devoted to his/her duty towards the country, knowing only hard work and respect to their fellow Eritreans. As selfishness officially does not exist, crime is morally unthinkable and is seen as a violation of national pride. This ideology is enforced by practical measures to suppress criminal attitudes by intimidation: There are no clear rules as to what is going to happen to somebody involved in theft or violent assault. Often all suspects, even including the victims who turn to the police, are arrested.[20] Due to the lack of clear legal procedures (there is an uneasy co-existence between traditional and modern laws, see Favali/Pateman 2003) and trained judicial personnel, trials are often delayed for months and longer, meanwhile leaving the defendant in prison.

Both the existence of generally accepted traditional values of social solidarity and obedience to social rules and the picture of the "highly moral Eritrean" drawn by the government[21] can be seen as a base for low delinquency in the country. This is enforced by the rigid measures taken by both the government institutions and extended families against deviant behaviour. The Western concept of resocialisation, if applied, takes the form of "purifying" them through a life under military discipline. One might argue that a zone of peace is to some degree artificial and bound to collapse as long as it is based on coercion. But the traditional system goes far beyond coercion, as it also promises security, integration in social networks and a rich cultural life. Therefore, accepting lawful behaviour is not a process primarily based on repression, but there is also a deep-rooted internalisation of social norms and values which facilitate mutual respect.

4   Conflicts between different interest groups and their management: the case of a dispute over land between two ethnic groups

As Eritrea is an agrarian society where about 80 per cent of the population is living from the land, disputes over land ownership and usufructory rights were and are still among the most common conflicts between interest groups. Land property rights are established through descent, both in the pastoral and the sedentary segments of Eritrean rural society. Even the land reform of 1996[22], which declared all land as state property, could not significantly change the century-old customary laws. While conflicts within one single ethnic group can mostly be solved through traditional mediation mechanisms, there are unresolved conflicts between ethnic groups with a different perception of land property rights who claim the same territory for their subsistence needs. One such conflict is the dispute between Saho and Tigrinya ethnic

---

[20] This sometimes happens in case of brawls. All persons involved are arrested, beaten up once more by the police and left free the next day. In the case of other litigations, debtor and debitor might be arrested and put together in one prison cell, so that they might come to a solution without further 'bothering' police and judiciary.

[21] This is combined with an internalised or imposed feeling of obligation towards the Eritrean martyrs which incudes the duty to follow their example.

[22] Government of Eritrea, Land Commission, Systems of Land Tenure and Land Use Policy. Proclamation 58/1994

sub-groups in the highland of Eritrea in the regions of Seraye and Akele Guzay (today's Zoba Debub).

The Tigrinya are sedentary farmers whose land ownership system is based on descent (rist) or residence in a certain village (diessa). The Saho are pastoralists or agro-pastoralists who have a communal land ownership system without individual land property and they use many areas only seasonally for grazing and rain-fed agriculture. They live both in the Red Sea coastal areas and in the Southern highland. Over the past centuries, more and more Tigrinya groups settled in areas claimed by the Saho, which caused the marginalisation of the latter, as they lost many fertile pastoral and agricultural areas. This situation led to conflicts. Both groups have established systems of conflict resolution through their local leaders and elders, enabling them to mediate violent clashes. Both political leaders (the Redanto or Shum as clan leader of the Saho and the Chiqa Addi as the village head of the Tigrinya) and religious elders (Sheikhs and Keshis priests, respectively), were involved in this mediation process.

These mediation processes broke down during the time of the Federation with Ethiopia and the reign of Haile Selassie due to political reasons. The Muslim Saho favoured Eritrea's independence from Ethiopia, while the Christian Tigrinya opted for the unification with Ethiopia. Therefore, the Ethiopian government favoured the Tigrinya in the land disputes which were aggravated by the arrival of new settlers from the neighbouring Ethiopian Tigray Province, and armed the villagers against the Saho, who were forced to flee from their home areas to the western lowlands. During the independence struggle the conflicts continued, because most of the Saho supported the ELF, while the majority of the Tigrinya first favoured the Ethiopian government and later the EPLF. Land conflicts and political divisions remained intertwined, although both liberation movements tried to mediate in acute land disputes.

After independence, a long-standing conflict between T'aro'a and Tsenadegle (a Saho sub-clan and a group of the Tigrinya, respectively) could be resolved by the ruling PFDJ. Interestingly, it relied on the local elders to find a solution, using coercion to force the groups into negotiations: "The President of Eritrea gathered together the elders and leaders of both communities and told them the area was out of bounds for human and animal use until the communities came up with a satisfactory resolution to the conflict on their own. Troops were garrisoned to enforce the order" (Favali and Pateman 2003:162). Finally, after extensive discussions between the elders, a compromise was found. It should be noted here that the groups involved would probably not have come to any conclusion without government intervention. The case is generally lauded because the government did not impose its own solution, but used its power of coercion in order to bring the parties together, using mechanisms known from traditional mediation procedures.

On the other hand, there has been no solution so far for those Saho groups who had been forced out of the country during the liberation war. They were not enabled to resettle in their areas of origin in Seraye but had to settle in Gash-Barka (western Eritrea). In spite of a certain conflict potential with the local population in that area, Gash-Barka was chosen as the main resettlement area for returnees from Sudan, as it is a relatively vast area not densely settled as the highlands are. It is inhabited by various ethnic groups (Nara, Kunama, Beni Amer, Tigre, Maria and Saho who settled there during the 1950s), whose land rights are not as rigidly elaborated as those of the Tigrinya groups in the highlands. Therefore, we can speak of a strategy of conflict avoidance enforced by the government, as strong organised resistance against new settlers was less likely.

Generally it can be stated that the existence of conflicts between different interest groups in Eritrea is concealed by the government, as they do not fit into its "one people, one heart" ideology[23]. At the same time, it is well aware of the risk related to land disputes and seems to be anxious to apply preventive measures. In fact, very few violent clashes occurred after independence, but due to unresolved latent conflicts, a potential eruption of violence cannot be ruled out. The government depends on the traditional institutions of conflict resolution to keep them under control.

5   The absence of war-lordism and civil war in contemporary Eritrea

The phenomenon of war-lordism is not alien to the territory which now forms Eritrea. The so-called "shiftas" used to raid farmers and pastoralists as well as trade caravans throughout centuries up to the time of the British Military Administration. Nowadays, the state has established a strong monopoly of power which leaves no opportunity for raiding or modern forms of war-lordism like dealing with arms and precious materials extralegally. The last civil war in Eritrea was fought between the ELF and EPLF in 1981. Since then, the EPLF has established its monopoly of power. The liberation struggle created a feeling of unity among the people reaching beyond ethnic or parochial sentiments, and there are no indicators that any significant groups within the country have ambitions to start a civil war against a rivalling group or against the government. Up to the presence, there is a feeling that sabotage acts on army units, which occasionally occurred, and are usually attributed to opposition groups operating from Sudan, would kill army conscripts, who are seen as "innocent sons of the people".

6   Conflict mediation in Eritrean society today

In order to understand the mechanisms enabling Eritrean society to keep internal peace in spite of the growing scarcity of resources, it is necessary to analyse the conflict resolution strategies of the Eritrean population within a non-participative political environment. The analysis is based on participant observation and a survey conducted in Asmara and Sen'afe (Zoba Debub)) among 92[24] representatives of government institutions, representatives of traditional civil society, and different population groups in general. As a theoretical framework, we suggest the distinction between three systems of norms and values which exist simultaneously in the country:

1   Traditional norms and values dominating local strategies of mediation between competing local groups.

---

[23] The term "hade hzbi, hade lbi" (one people, one heart) is used by the government to symbolise the unity of the people, not only in relation to nationalism, but also to "political unity".

[24] Two seperate questionnaires were developed for the different target groups: one for government representatives (22 interviews), and one for the population in general (70 interviews).

2   The norm and value system developed and introduced by the former Liberation Movement.

3   "Modern" or "Western" norms and values partially introduced by the colonial administrations and forming a part of the nominal modern judicial system of the country. These modern values are further spread through the large Diaspora which has an impact at least on urban surroundings in Eritrea.

We can assume that during the independence struggle and the post-independence period, a hybrid system of norms composed of the three above-mentioned components emerged, and was helpful in avoiding the outbreak of internal violence under extreme external pressure, a restrictive political environment, and general scarcity of resources. While in many other societies under similar pressures of war and forced population movements, governments and civil society failed to avoid the outbreak of ethnically-motivated violence or the instrumentalization of ethnicity, Eritrea internally remained calm in spite of its ethnic, religious and economic varieties and latent potentials of conflict. Looking beyond the surface, it needs further elaboration whether it is the merit of the leading party's political culture, the merit of the traditional mechanisms of conflict resolution, or the impact of modern procedures that helps to avoid or solve local conflicts – or the specific interaction between these three. Our empirical study tries to explain which parts of the hybrid system contribute, and to which extent, to the success or failure of local conflict resolution.

6.1. Traditional civil society and its role in shaping political culture

Our interpretation of "traditional civil society" differs from the common concept of civil society to some extent. Most authors refer to it in relation to modern non-governmental organisations (NGOs) as institutions that can reflect grass-root needs and can act as mediators between local communities and governments. Eritrea lacks such a "modern" civil society. The National Unions of Women, Youth and Students and the Federation of Workers are not independent from the government. On the other hand, the government does not allow independent indigenous NGOs in the country, only very few foreign humanitarian NGOs are working under increasingly restrictive conditions – the majority having been expelled during the past years. At the same time, the ruling party, just like its predecessors, has to rely on traditional forms of local conflict regulation in the form of customary jurisdiction by local elders and mediators (Shemagelle). The traditional civil society reflects the interests of the communities they represent and who are still strongly attached to traditional norms and values. They are closely linked to their land and to their subsistence economy. This includes a strong focus on primary relationships and traditional culture. Elders and religious leaders play a strong role in strengthening and regulating the social interaction between members of the community. They act as representatives of the various customary laws in managing tensions and conflicts. Although there are differences between the customary laws of the respective ethnic and cultural groups and even within the laws of one single ethnic group, they follow one general objective: keeping the community stable and united by solving internal disagreements peacefully.

Although the PFDJ government accepts the traditional system of regulating social life and mediating conflicts in principle and is well aware of its contribution to internal stability

(Alemseged Tesfai 1996), it has tried to control this system by some reforms, namely the administrative reform (1994), and the land proclamation of 1996. The first one aims at weakening local decision-making procedures by village assemblies (the baytos) by reducing them to advisory status, the second one declared state ownership over all land, guaranteeing usufructory rights to the population. Problems like access to land of pastoral and agro-pastoral groups are not addressed by the Proclamation. The fact that the implementation of the land reform has shown very little progress so far points at the strength of traditional modes of land allocation and traditional local decision-making. The government is well aware that its land reform, once implemented, could be a "mine field" (Fullerton Joireman 1996) in some areas and would meet resistance, so it has been extremely reluctant to implement it especially in the highlands, where century-old land tenure systems exist. Only in the lowlands, where pastoralist and semi-pastoralist dwellers found it more difficult to defend their traditional usufruct rights over land, interventions in the settlement structure and agricultural schemes were more frequent.

The traditional mediation system in Eritrea, as confirmed by our empirical research in Asmara and Sen'afe, is highly valued by the population in both rural and urban communities. 76 out of 92 respondents confirmed that they consider the traditional mediation system most convenient in resolving tensions and conflicts between family members, neighbourhoods, and the local community in general. Especially the people living in Sen'afe expressed their preference of the traditional mediation system in conflicts over land issues. Even the 22 government employees confirmed the functionality of the traditional mediation system in both rural and urban areas. This shows a certain ambivalence between their role as government employees representing the modern administration and the modern court system and their attachment to traditional norms and values. When asked why they consider the traditional mediation system convenient, 71 out of 91 respondents stated that it is highly respected by the people and has practical advantages compared to the official administration: it is not time-consuming, inexpensive, has simple procedures compared to the modern administration and courts, and decisions are usually accepted by the conflicting parties because mediators are selected by both of them. The general acceptance of traditional mediation can be traced back to two different aspects: respect and acceptance by the majority of the population, as well as its practicality and efficiency.

6.2. The EPLF/PFDJ and its norms and values
There is no doubt that during the liberation struggle, the EPLF, apart from being a successful military organisation, developed useful strategies in mobilising human resources in the fields of production and social services under conditions of extreme scarcity. They were developed in the framework of Marxist ideology and the philosophy of self-reliance. After independence, self-reliant development and the mobilisation of all local resources were maintained as leading principles of nation-building. Self-sacrifice and postponement of personal interests were still expected from the "broad masses" of the population. During the times of the struggle, at first glance, there had been no open conflicts among the rank and file of the fighters: There was no individual property, and each combatant was tightly controlled by procedures of "criticism and self-criticism". There was high commitment to the common

cause, but once the political leadership of the Front felt threatened by internal opposition, it did not hesitate to use harsh measures (one example is the destruction of the leftist Menka' movement within the EPLF). After liberation, the common commitment to rebuilding the war-devastated nation was still seen as a base of peaceful coexistence. Under the motto "unity in diversity", balanced growth and equal rights for all segments of society was seen as a tool to avoid the outbreak of violence due to conflicting interests. At the same time, the militarised authoritarian environment of the pre-independence time remained a characteristic element of the new political structures. While this approach initially proved successful because of a wide-ranging consent among the civilian population and a general atmosphere of hope after decades of suppression, it is questionable if this system would provide valid mechanisms for an indefinite period of time and allow conflict resolution in the absence of political pluralisation.

The fact that up to now the government leaves conflict resolution in matters of civil right to the traditional mediators indicates a lack of such instruments from the side of the ruling party. Interestingly, out of the 22 government representatives we interviewed, seven said they have no knowledge of conflict resolution mechanisms developed by the EPLF. Six of the respondents considered it an advantage that the EPLF accepted traditional mediation procedures. Only four mentioned the "criticism/self-criticism" procedure as positive, while five respondents mentioned the imposing of decisions by power as a disadvantage of EPLF conflict resolution methods.

The past 16 years have shown that the positive part of the EPLF ideology, the strong dedication of Eritreans of all ranks for a common cause, has been overstrained by the government, and local divisions among communities might grow stronger sooner or later. Especially since the end of the war with Ethiopia, the military component of the political culture has been growing stronger. People are kept in the national service indefinitely and work for pocket money. This leads to increasing social inequality between families who lost their bread-winner to the "common cause" and those who somehow escaped this fate.

6.3. Liberal norms and values – globalisation as a new factor in the organisation of Eritrean society?

So far we can state that since independence a fragile co-existence between traditional and EPLF norms and values prevailed in the country. The impact of Western values on Eritrean society has remained limited. In 1987, the EPFL had declared a shift away from socialism to a partially liberal economy and planned the introduction of a multi-party system with some restrictions (no political organisation based on regional or religious grounds). A Constitutional Commission was installed to work out a constitution built partially on Western concepts, including the division between executive, legislative and judiciary. While the non-implementation since its approval by the Constitutional Assembly in 1997 can be attributed partially to the border conflict and internal power struggles of the PFDJ leadership, it is striking that the judiciary never experienced any significant impact of liberal Western values. On the contrary, in 2003 the government introduced community courts elected by local people, who are instructed to decide on the base of traditional customary law[25].

---

[25] Community Courts: Helping citizens settle disputes out of courts.
www.shaebia.org/artman/publish/article_4206.html, (official website of the PFDJ) retrieved on 08.01. 2006

In accordance with the three types of norms and values we elaborated (traditional, EPLF-specific, and modern), we find three levels of jurisdiction in Eritrea: *Customary laws* of the local communities which form the backbone of conflict mediation and resolution and are accepted by the government, relying on the ability of the traditional communities to manage and solve their conflicts and therefore even reflect a part of political authority. The PFDJ itself introduced its own courts in 1995, the so called *"Special Courts"* where high-ranking militaries perform the role of judges. These courts mainly deal with members of the Front in alleged cases of corruption. The court does not follow commonly accepted procedures; there is no possibility of defence by a lawyer and no possibility of appeal against the judgement. Ironically, in recent years the Special Courts turned out to be increasingly inactive. There are also *"modern" courts* in the country, which still operate with the Ethiopian Penal and Civil Codes of the 1950s with some small modifications. Civil cases are almost commonly in the hands of traditional jurisdiction. Even criminal cases are often delegated to traditional institutions of mediation by modern courts: While the defendant stays in prison, the families of the suspected criminal and the victim are asked to find a mode of compensation with the help of Shemagelles.

The responses given in our survey confirm the mistrust of the population against the modern court system: Out of 70 persons interviewed, 22 stated that the modern court system does not work satisfactorily in solving conflicts, 17 said it should be involved only in some cases, e.g. severe crimes like murder. The shortcomings of the modern court system were identified as corruption, inefficiency, long and unclear procedures, high costs, lack of sovereignty and lack of justice. Thus, we can conclude that the modern system of jurisdiction plays a relatively marginal role in Eritrea.

7   Conclusion: *A zone of peace under threat - Eritrea's hybrid system of conflict resolution – guarantor of stability or precarious balance between conflicting norms?*

Eritrea is and will remain a society characterised by cultural diversity, different languages, religions and modes of production (e.g. sedentarised agriculture and pastoralism). Thus stability in times of extreme scarcity of resources can only be maintained by mutual tolerance and decision-making processes accepted by the affected population groups. Continuous suppression of certain group's interests might easily lead to rising tensions and even violence among groups struggling for survival.

To some degree, the EPLF's "code of conduct" developed during the independence struggle remains internalised by large segments of society and leads them to refrain from extreme greediness and to value nationalism higher than local dissent. The problem is that the PFDJ leadership itself is moving away further and further from their roots. In a sort of George Orwell's "Animal Farm"- effect, officials and high-ranking militaries drink whiskey in fancy bars and drive cars with a government label in their leisure time, while common people work for 140 –500 Nacfa a month in the national service (7 to 25 €).[26] Regular salaries are devalued by inflation and the rural people struggle for survival. At present, the customary

---

[26] See also: Treiber, Magnus 2005: Der Traum vom guten Leben. Die eritreische "warsay"-Generation im Asmara der zweiten Nachkriegszeit. Münster

laws of local groups enable the people at grass-root level to solve conflicts, distribute scarce resources and guarantee their survival, thus maintaining an informal zone of peace. Empirical research clearly confirms this suggestion: The overwhelming majority of our respondents (83%) see traditional mediation as the most important factor contributing to the social cohesion of Eritrean society.

So far, there has been no political instrumentalization of ethnicity which caused a sudden outbreak of violence in other societies (such as in Rwanda or former Yugoslavia). In Eritrea, the instrumentalization of ethnicity is also contrary to the leading group's ideology[27]. On the other hand, in an environment without any possibility of legal expression of political dissatisfaction, the easiest and traditionally best-established way of organising oneself is related to ethnic or religious affiliation. As people are still very well aware of their origin, political polarisation along ethnic lines might become the last resort when alienation from the state rises further.

While so far no concrete indicators for such developments can be observed, there are some possible political and economic scenarios which may challenge internal peace in the country:

a. A possible new round of war with Ethiopia would lead to a further destabilisation of the country.

b. On the other hand, the implementation of the EEBC[28] boundary decision, ending the "no war, no peace" situation between Eritrea and Ethiopia may shake the system as well.[29] This would deprive the government of the justification given for holding large segments of the youth in the army/national service, of delaying the implementation of the constitution and withholding elections, as well as keeping prominent PFDJ-dissidents in prison. Many Eritreans still blame the Ethiopian refusal to establish lasting peace for the deteriorating situation in their own country (especially those living in the Diaspora). Thus, in peace-times, feelings of frustration might explode.

c. Internal power struggles within the military, which doubtlessly exist, could get out of control.

d. The deteriorating economic situation might lead to a collapse of the system in case of further aggravation. As the government tries to control each and every economic activity, the further deterioration of the situation is almost certain. This leads to growing dissatisfaction, which might finally lead to violence if other destabilising events will occur.

Although the liberation struggle has created a strong nationalism and feeling of Eritreanness among the people, this feeling is gradually losing the sentiments of pride, hope, and

---

[27] See Alemseged Tesfai: "Diversity, Identity and Unity in Eritrea", in: epd-Entwicklungspolitik 6/2000, p 31-34

[28] Eritrean-Ethiopian Boundary Commission. This arbitration commission based at The Hague decided in 2003 that most of the land claimed by Ethiopia during the war, especially the highly symbolic village of Badme, belongs rightfully to Eritrea. The Ethiopian government has since denied to accept and implement the decision.

[29] So far, there has been no move towards ending this situation – the border is now delineated on maps by the EEBC, but the actual threat of war has not diminished. Although the Eritrean President has recently stressed that the border issue has been settled by the delimination of the border line, Ethiopia occupies territory which belongs to Eritrea as indicated on the map, while Ethiopia shows no willingness to accept the decision and act accordingly. The hostility between both governments is unchanged and armed clashes occured along the border in late 2007. Thus, the Eritrean government can continue to justify its policy of militarisation.

belongingness attached to it during the past years because of the negative developments since the end of the Eritrea-Ethiopian war. Although people feel growing disillusion about the future of their country, they are still afraid to lose their hard-won independence and fear even worse developments in the future in case of a change of government. Another reason for the absence of resistance is the lack of a convincing alternative to the present system. Many of the numerous Eritrean opposition parties operating in the Diaspora are based on regional or ethnic sentiments rather than on clear political programs. There is no opposition party which clearly and decisively promotes a political system based on political pluralism. In the future, this may lead to growing regionalism and challenge the unifying role of nationalism and the traditional civil society as an established integrative force in Eritrea. As the latter has survived for centuries, it is most probably the most stable factor within the hybrid system of norms and values which could so far maintain internal peace. This internal peace nevertheless is not without a bitter taste, as the patience of the society is not rewarded by the government. The missing link to bring about political change is a modern civil society striving for reform, a concept alien to traditional values. But the government is well aware that a modern civil society might challenge their absolute control and thus simply declared the party and its former mass organisations as the only modern representatives of society. Under these circumstances, uneasy stability remains more probable than fundamental changes.

Bibliography

Abbink, Jon 1995: 'Transformations of violence in twentieth-century Ethiopia: cultural roots, political conjunctures'. In: *Focaal* 25, pp. 57-77

_____ 2001: 'Creating Borders: exploring the impact of the Ethio-Eritrean war on the local population'. In: *Africa* 56, Roma, pp. 447-458

Abdulkader Saleh Mohammad 1984: *Die Afar-Saho Nomaden in Nordost-Afrika. Die sozio-ökonomischen und politischen Bedingungen des Nomadentums und der Versuch einer Sesshaftmachung der Nomaden am Beispiel der Afar-Saho in Nordost-Afrika.* Münster: Lit-Verlag

_____ 2003: *Challenges to an Ethnic Identity: The Case of the Saho in Eritrea.* Paper presented at the 15th International Conference on Ethiopian Studies, Hamburg

Alemseged Abbay 1998: *Identity Jilted or Re-Imagining Identity?* Lawrenceville: Red Sea Press

Alemseged Tesfai 1996: Governance: Issues and the Eritrean Context., in: WSP Eritrea Country Project. The Challenges of Reconstruction. An overview note. Asmara

Alexander Naty 2002: 'Environment, Society and the State in Western Eritrea'. In: *Africa. Journal of the International African Institute*, Vol. 72 (4), pp 569 - 597

Bruchhaus, Eva-Maria (ed.) 2003: *Hot Spot Horn of Africa. Between Integration and Disintegration.* Münster: Lit-Verlag

Christmann, Stefanie 1996: *Die Freiheit haben wir nicht von den Männern. Frauen in Eritrea.* Unkel/Rhein, Bad Honnef: Horlemann

Clapham, Christopher 1996: 'The Horn of Africa: A Conflict Zone'. In: Oliver Furley (ed.): *Conflict in Africa.* London – New York

Connell, Dan 1997: *Against All Odds. A Chronicle of the Eritrean Revolution.* Lawrenceville, Asmara: Red Sea Press

Doornbos, Martin with Alemseged Tesfai 1999: *Post-Conflict Eritrea: Prospects for Reconstruction and Development.* Lawrenceville, Asmara: Red Sea Press

Elwert, Georg 1997: 'Gewaltmärkte: Beobachtungen zur Zweckrationalität der Gewalt'. In: Trutz von Trotha (ed.): *Soziologie der Gewalt* (Kölner Zeitschrift für Soziologie und Sozialpsychologie, Sonderheft 37), Köln, S. 86-101

Favali, Lyda and Pateman, Roy 2003: *Blood, Land and Sex. Legal and Political Pluralism in Eritrea.* Bloomington

Fullerton Joireman, Sandra 1996: 'The Minefield of Land Reform: Comments on the Eritrean Land Proclamation'. In: *African Affairs* 95, pp. 269-285

Giday Degefu Koraro 2000: *Traditional Mechanisms of Conflict Resolution in Ethiopia.* Addis Ababa (Ethiopian International Institute for Peace and Development)

Hirt, Nicole 2001: *Eritrea zwischen Krieg und Frieden. Die Entwicklung seit der Unabhängigkeit.* Hamburg: Institut für Afrika-Kunde

Kemink, Friederike 1991: *Die Tegrenna-Frauen in Eritrea. Eine Untersuchung der Kodizes des Gewohnheitsrechts 1890-1941.* Stuttgart

Matthies, Volker 1998: 'Kriegerische Konflikte und friedliche Konfliktbearbeitung in Afrika'. In: Ferdowsi, Mir A. (ed.): *Afrika zwischen Agonie und Aufbruch.* München

Markakis, John 1987: *National and Class Conflict in the Horn of Africa.* Cambridge

Pateman, Roy 1990: *Eritrea. Even the Stones are Burning.* Trenton

Ruth Iyob 1995: *The Eritrean Struggle for Independence.* Cambridge

Schlee, Günther (ed.), 2002: *Imagined Differences. Hatred and the Construction of Identity.* Münster, Hamburg, London

Smidt, Wolbert 2000: 'Äthiopisch-eritreische Kriegsführung in den Medien'. In: *S + F, Vierteljahresschrift für Sicherheit und Frieden,* Jg. 18, Heft 3, pp. 233-238

Tetzlaff, Rainer 2001: 'Ist der postkoloniale Leviathan in Afrika entbehrlich? Fragmentierte Gesellschaften zwischen Staatszerfall und sozialer Anomie, Kriegsherrentum und privater Organisation von Überlebenssicherheit'. In: Laurence Marfaing und Brigitte Reinwald (eds): *Afrikanische Beziehungen, Netzwerke und Räume,* pp 201-228. Hamburg.

—— 2003a: 'Politisierte Ethnizität als Kehrseite von politischer Partizipation in unsicheren Zeiten. Erfahrungen aus Afrika'. In: *WeltTrends* 1/2003

—— 2003b: 'Afrika als Teil der Vierten Welt, der Welt der erodierenden Staatlichkeit – abgeschaltet von der Globalisierung? Ursachen und Hintergründe von Staatsverfall und Ent-Menschlichung (zivilisatorische Regression)'. In: Hans Küng (ed.), *Weltethos: Ein neues Paradigma internationaler Beziehungen?* München

Tronvoll, Kjetil 1998: *Mai Weini, A Highland Village in Eritrea, A Study of the People, Their Livelihood, and Land Tenure During Times of Turbulence.* Lawrenceville, Asmara: Red Sea Press

—— 1998: 'The process of Nation-Building in post-war Eritrea: Created from below or directed from above?' In: *The Journal of Modern African Studies,* Vol. 36, No 3, pp. 461-482

von Trotha, Trutz (ed.) 1997: *Soziologie der Gewalt*. In: Kölner Zeitschrift für Soziologie und Sozialpsychologie Sonderheft 37. Opladen/Wiesbaden

Step by Step – Migration from Eritrea

Magnus Treiber, Lea Tesfaye

Leaving Asmara

„Eritrea? A catastrophe...", an Eritrean taxi-driver in Frankfurt in October 2007 comments the country's development during the last few years.[1] Disappointment and incomprehension inside and outside the country have superseded the early 1990s' enthusiasm and sympathy, when the former Italian colony at the Horn of Africa, postponed by three decades of Ethiopian occupation, finally became independent. Dreams and hopes have been far-reaching and ambitious, turning the victory over 'foreign' oppression into a national development project with the participation of all nationals and the help of roughly a million migrants and former refugees overseas. These in fact contributed decisively to make Eritrea's case internationally known and to win the support of Western and Arab politicians and political activists, unionists and journalists. The historical and economic success of Asia's 'Tiger'-states was presented as a model to reach European life-standard in the foreseeable future, surpassing the 1980s disillusioning and impoverishing effect in an already independent Africa. The notion of self-reliance, referring less to Julius Nyerere's political philosophy,[2] but to the military success of the liberation struggle, became metaphoric for post-war Eritrea.

The sudden outbreak of the intensive and devastating war with neighbouring Ethiopia in May 1998 and the following internal political oppression in September 2001 invited Eritreans and international observers to reflect, if the policy of Eritrea's leadership, emerging from the Eritrean People's Liberation Front (EPLF), could have been anticipated (Gilkes, Plaut 1999; Negash, Tronvoll 2000, Iyob 2000). Warning signs were numerous – e.g. the offending treatment of Jehova's witnesses and other minority religions (Tronvoll 1996),[3] the authoritarian implementation of a compulsory national service, the early imprisonment of journalists[4] and last but not least the increasing concentration of power in the hands of the EPLF's secretary-general and today's national president Isayas Afeworki (Pool 2001: 172).

Today the Eritrean ruling clique – power distribution cuts across different political institutions such as government, party and military[5] – has consequently lost all its moral

---

[1]   In summer 2002 first ethnographic raw material from Asmara was presented at a VAD-workshop in Hamburg, organized by Eva-Maria Bruchhaus. Since then the political and economic situation in Eritrea decreased considerably, most of the young urbanites who contributed as informants to the book "Der Traum vom guten Leben" (Treiber 2005) meanwhile opted for emigration. Visits in the USA in April 2007 and – together with Lea Tesfaye – in Addis Ababa and Shimelba refugee camp in Ethiopia in August and September 2007 enabled us to meet old friends as well as to get into contact with numerous Eritreans between 19 to 65 years, all hoping to lead a more promising life one day (Tesfaye 2007). When possible we hold contact by letter, e-mail or phone. Our stay as visiting volunteers in Shimelba refugee was kindly been made possible by the World Food Programme, Ethiopia. Without the committed collaboration of field informants, ethnographic research can not be realised – to them and the courageous deserters of Eritrea's brutal military regime in general this article shall be dedicated.

[2]   Nyerere, Julius: Freedom and Socialism. Dar Es Salaam et al. 1972

[3]   Tronvoll, Kjeti[l]: The Eritrean Referendum. Peasant Voices. In: Eritrean Studies Review. 1/1. 1996: 23-67

[4]   Committee to Protect Journalist (CPJ): International Press Freedom Awards 1998: Ruth Simon. www.cpj.org/awards98/frameset.html

[5]   Awate: The Accused. Isaias & His Clique. 01.09.2007 (www.awate.com)

credit, with the exception of some loyal diaspora communities, who bitterly try to defend Eritrea's policy as an important pillar of their own diaspora-identity. Thousands are in jail because of desertion from the compulsory and de-facto open-ended national service (including parents unable to pay compensation for their deserted children),[6] political or journalistic activities or religious practice of evangelical – and therefore foreign – faith (Donham 1999: 143).[7] People in urban as well as in rural areas suffer from poverty, lack of (formerly imported) supplies and commodities, as well as from steadily increasing prices. Mistrust, suspicion, rivalry on resources and denunciation in order to get additional food supplies have lead the country into a state of silent resignation and agony. Just as the Ethiopian government – evolving from the EPLF's Ethiopian junior partner, the Tigray People's Liberation Front (TPLF), ally as well as rival during the guerrilla war against Mengistu Haile Mariam's *Derg* regime – the Eritrean leadership carefully adds fuel to the pending conflict with the neighbouring state, to preserve the precarious situation of 'no war, no peace', which legitimates both countries' repressive interior policy. With the end of the sudden and intense border war, uniting the nation in (guided) hatred and contempt towards the enemy, recruits of the Eritrean Defence Forces were hoping to be able to concentrate on their own individual life projects in a more promising post-war situation. But normalisation did not take place as hoped for. In the national military training camp in Sawa in the Western lowlands a spontaneous rebellion of armed recruits, demanding their own demobilisation, was downed in bloodshed, the surviving ringleaders were executed on the spot – unnoticed by the public.[8]

Considering the successive generation as 'inheritors' of the EPLF's struggle for national liberation, the national service recruits are thus called *warsay* in the locally dominant language Tigrinya. Strongly reminding of Foucault's idea of biopolitics, official propaganda leaves no doubt that individual needs and wishes have to be put aside for the benefit of the nation, its collective development, prosperity and defence (Foucault 1976). Especially in Eritrea's cities and towns there are, however, only few people left who still believe in promises of the liberation struggle. In 2002, then 29 year-old Hussein reported from Sawa military training centre that the *yikealo*, the former EPLF's 'all-powerful' liberation fighters, behaved as if they owned the country and its people they claim to have freed. It must be added that a lot of educated people and intellectuals have been EPLF members during the liberation struggle. However, they returned to civil life, are in exile or in prison today, while the remaining ones who enjoy high positions in the militarised state administration have

---

[6] Reacting to increasing desertion – today whole units flee together – the Eritrean regime introduced different measures to control warsay-recruits in the last few years. The Eritrean school system was reformed, centralising the 11th grade education at Sawa military training centre in order to restrict the students' movement. Students have to enlist together with their fathers, a photograph of both assures, that the father can be held responsible should daughter or son disappear. Accused and imprisoned parents, however, are given the chance to buy themselves out. In Zeberga's case the so-called compensation fine was 3000 USD. In this manner even desertion serves the financial alimentation of the Eritrean regime which is notoriously in need of foreign currency.

[7] Amnesty International: Report 2007. The State of the World's Human Rights. London. 2007: 112-113; Amnesty International: Eritrea, 'You have no right to ask', Government resists scrutiny on human rights. AFR 64/003/2004. 05. See also Connection e.V.; Eritreische Antimilitaristische Initiative: Eritrea. Kriegsdienstverweigerung und Desertion. 2. Aufl. Offenbach 2004

[8] My informant Hussein learned about the 2001s upheaval, when reassigned to the military service in July 2002 after leaving university and serving several months in the capital's administration.

basically learned to kill during the guerrilla war and – in many cases - lack formal education. Abraham, a *yikealo* himself, remembers that he – as a university student – was always mobbed by the EPLF's cadres and leaders. Professional brutality, the lacking esteem for individual human life and anti-intellectualism survived the transition 'from guerrilla to government', as David Pool puts it (2001). During her training phase in Sawa Jersilem, a then 18 years old, wrote on the wall next to her bed, "The stupid will not end to increase their stupidity". As she was never questioned or punished for this, she understood it as a clear prove that she was right.

The professional work of administrative *warsay* includes school teaching besides all kind of office work, is shaped by the symbolic pay of 500 or 1000 Nakfa (depending on the respective cohort and assignment), strict subordination under office hierarchy. The younger generation responds with go-slow-strategies, is unmotivated and without career perspective (cf. Scott 1990). As a consequence most *warsay* are unable to afford their own apartment before marriage, which is often delayed due to financial constraints and can rarely be realised without family subsidiaries. Accordingly, scarce living space has to be shared with parents, siblings and further relatives, who demand respect and mutual consideration. Since the end of the war young urbanites, who either enjoy the privilege to serve as *warsay* in Asmara's national administration or have deserted their assignment, have developed strategies of how to cope with precarious daily life under Eritrea's military dictatorship. To compensate these restrictions they use public places like bars and cafés for recreation after office hours, to meet like-minded friends, with whom they stage a preferred life-style (Hannerz 2004: 34-69), create and confirm a specific cultural milieu, depending on differing notions of society and an appropriate life career within. While some prefer to meet in dark and ill-reputed, but integrative pubs, others present themselves as chic and mundane urbanites in exclusive bars or stroll Asmara's main boulevard up and down as urban 'flâneurs', frequenting one of Liberty Avenue's numerous cafés.[9] Different individual and collective forms of saving and spending money are crucial for all these vespertine activities of course (cf. Whyte 1993: 104-106). Another milieu which has become very popular despite an official ban and subsequent persecution, emerged from the evangelical faith in its numerous different sects, providing social solidarity and hope, since the collective dream of a prosperous nation has failed. While few informants thought of emigration shortly after the war in early 2001 – the Eritrean government did not yet react to criticism and public debates – there was literally no one left in 2005, who did not at least dream of leaving Asmara.

In his presentation at the 2006 conference of the African Studies Association (ASA-UK) at SOAS in London, the British-Eritrean scholar Gaim Kibreab, an expert in the field of migration studies (Kibreab 2004, 1999), guessed that 80,000 Eritreans have fled their country since the official end of the two-year long Ethio-Eritrean border war in 2000. Existing figures of the UNHCR suggest tens of thousands of refugees at least, but the total, including unreported cases, remains unclear. Even the Eritrean government is no longer able to hide this mass phenomenon and has pragmatically changed its policy. Deserters will be imprisoned in holes in the ground, in metal shipping containers, in the ruins of the old Italian colonial prison

---

[9] Benjamin, Walter: Moskau [1927]. In: Benjamin, Walter: Kleine Prosa, Baudelaire-Übertragungen. Gesammelte Schriften. Bd. IV 1-2. Frankfurt/M. 1972: 316-348; see also Denison Edward; Ren, Guang-Yu; Gebremedhin, Naigzy: Asmara, Africa's Secret Modernist City. London, New York 2003

on Nokra island in the Red Sea – or will be shot on the spot. If you have, however, successfully managed to get to Sudan, the Eritrean embassy in Khartoum will issue a passport for about $100 within days – since the Ethiopian embassy started to do so. Despite the two countries' rivalling propaganda, emigrants to the first world mean future cash influx and have to be considered as a governmental investment, which sounds quite paradox of course.

Most of Eritrea's second generation of refugees, succeeding the 1980s refugees of Eritrea's independence struggle as well as the civil war between the rivalling liberation movements, are young and educated urbanites. They either originate from urban middle class or came from rural areas to Asmara for academic education. Their affiliation with urban life and education is far more decisive for their decision to migrate than ethnic or religious identity. Moreover, migration from Eritrea has clear gender-specific characteristics. The country's new migrants may be predominantly male, but women catch up. As migrants are often demobilised in their twenties, educated women have better chances to get an official Eritrean exit visa through marriage with an Eritrean living abroad or with an academic scholarship. In consequence, a considerable portion of Eritrean women leave the country illegally to Ethiopia or Sudan. Zeberga, who thanks to a regular student visa made it from the world's periphery to a global centre of political power, Washington D.C., remembers in an interview in April 2007:

> „I wouldn't hesitate to do it again. It was time for a change. Being denied my rights, what do you expect me to do, sit there? Government is keeping everyone there crippled. There was 50% risk, 50% chance, I could be in a concentration camp or might be killed now, but without taking such risk, things do not change. It was a risk for my family and myself, but I would always live with my guilt if I would have staid, inside something pushes you. [...] My family was on my side, they advised me: leave!"

While migration studies often concentrate on certain migration periods or on arrival and integration into a 'host-society' – mostly due to pragmatic reasons – research that takes the wider process of migration into consideration, starting from an initial situation and departure, is rare (cf. Riccio 2001, Schiffauer 1991). We assume that the phenomena of migration can be better understood when the migrants' respective views, reflections and comments during different stages of migration from leaving to (provisional) arriving are shown. Itineraries, strategies and biographical trajectories, transforming notions of migration, home and the First World, constant (and constantly changing) communication back and ahead as well as reflexive processes of identity-formation have to be examined through selected contextualisation and comparative analysis (cf. Glick-Schiller et al. 1992), focussing on local conditions of temporary survival and further migration planning on the one hand as well as repression and exclusion of arriving refugees on the other (Treiber 2007).[10] In this context we want to discuss the idea of agency in refugees' migration trajectories, showing migrants in an earlier and a later stage of migration and commenting on their perception of space and time in their respective situations.

---

[10] For the field construction in anthropological research see also Amit, Vered: Introduction. Constructing the field. In: Amit, Vered (ed.): Constructing the field. Ethnographic Fieldwork in the Contemporary World. London, New York. 2000: 1-18 and Marcus, George: Ethnography in/of the World System: the Emergence of Multi-sited Ethnography. In: Annual Review of Anthropology. 24. 1995: 95-117

The dynamic lifeworld of Eritrean refugees, trying to reach the European Union via Libya, Malta or Italy, Turkey, Russia or Israel, or even to get to North America, broadly perceived as the ideal option, consists of rapid and hopeful change as well as long and disillusioning periods of monotonous waiting in an unfriendly environment, sometimes quite similar to the one they left.[11] Strategic decisions on what to do next depend on available capital, information and contacts and have to be taken carefully (Collyer 2005, Schuster 2005, Kastner 2007). Biniam, who recently arrived in Khartoum, leaving two little children with their grandparents in Asmara, writes in an e-mail in November 2007:

> „[M]ost of my time I prefer stay home than going out and hearing a lot of r[umour], like 500 people they caught and return[ed] home, 100 people [-] they [have] been shot down by Egypt mil[itary] police and so on...“[12]

Lacking reliable news, informal rumours on US visa opportunities, quickly increasing prices for specific routes to Israel via Cairo or to Turkey, language classes in Russia or asylum in Sweden or the UK, shape the refugees' boring day as much as constant danger of being denunciated, harassed, robbed, imprisoned and deported, leading to a strategy of maximal invisibility (Kibreab 1999: 393). This situation is not a new phenomenon. In 1940's Marseille European refugees fleeing Nazi-Germany's invasion eagerly struggled for visa documents and transit permits to far and unknown countries, as described in Anna Seghers' novel „Transit".[13]

Hoping for official 'resettlement' in a better place – offers range from Burkina Faso to the USA – around 9,000 Eritrean refugees currently live in Shimelba refugee camp, in Ethiopia's northern Tigray province.

„We miss Asmara so much!"– Shimelba refugee camp, Tigray/Ethiopia

In May 2000 the redrawing Ethiopian forces were accompanied by a large group of Kunama- and a few Tigrinya farmers, who started builing up provisional houses in Wa'ala Nihibi, a hamlet in the formerly embattled border area on the road between Sheraro and Badme. For 'security reasons' the refugee camp, growing larger and larger, was moved some kilometres further inland to Shimelba in 2004.[14] Today's camp is situated in a dry valley at the bottom of a hill from which various governmental and international agencies overlook the area, among them the official Ethiopian 'Administration for Refugee and Returnees Affairs' (ARRA) and its health centre, an UNHCR-office and some NGOs, commissioned with different administrative assignments. While these representatives of state force and international resources cooperate formally on camp level, they seem to work widely independently from each other in practice, most visibly restricting themselves to their separately fenced compounds with guarded gates. In terms of spatial semantics the hierarchical opposition

---

[11] For the aspect of waiting in the life of refugees see e.g. Vöckler, Kai: The Waiting Room. On Refugees and Space in Berlin. In: Bittner, Regina; Hackenbroich, Wilfried; Vöckler, Kai (eds): Transnational Spaces. Transnationale Räume. Berlin 2007: 36-45
[12] Cf. Gedab News: Secret Meetings, Defections, Refoulement & Expulsions. 20.11. 2007 (www.awate.com)
[13] Seghers, Anna: Transit. Roman. [1944/48] Berlin 2007
[14] Obviously these security reasons concern less the protection of refugees, but their spatial isolation from the nearby border and the possible influx of arms, spies and insurgents, hard to control.

between top and bottom is as obvious as the administrative contradictions among them.[15] The refugee camp itself is divided into several zones, but two different living areas can be identified on the spot. The neighbourhood of the Kunama families is shaped by small maize gardens – at least during the rainy season – and traditional, mostly circular huts with straw roof, *tukhul*, reminding of the Eritrean countryside, the other neighbourhood shelters mostly young urbanites, predominantly male, speaking Tigrinya or Amharic[16], and consists of rectangular mud houses, canopied with UNHCR plastic sheets. In the latter shops, cinemas, bars and cafés are numerous and provide an urban atmosphere (Tesfaye 2007, Agier 2002, cf. Bourdieu 1997), offering satisfaction to the respective needs the refugees brought along with their urban life-style. Even a brothel house can be found. The cafés' and bars' names remember of Asmara and Massawa and are called 'The Mask Pastry', 'Diana Entertainment', 'Hollywood', 'Dolphin Café' or 'Sunshine'. Interior design is carefully constructed with or carved into mud bricks, allowing to imitate and rebuild the beloved city one left behind, with the simple means available. Loud music is omnipresent, indicating the absence of family structure and local youth dominance. Here even nightlife is offered, few light bulbs provide some illumination at least, while daily life in the Kunama neighbourhood quickly fades away after 6 p.m. Perpetuating urban migration from one generation to the next, some urban refugees have successfully contacted relatives within the Eritrean diaspora in the West or in Arab countries. It is this financial support from abroad which allowed to open up *dukwan*-shops, pool houses and restaurants – while a lot of Tigrinya- and almost all Kunama-speakers, rural as well as urban, usually lack any external support and fully depend on their ration allotted by the international agencies and distributed by the Ethiopian government in large store tents on the hill plateau.

The camp as a whole lies in the former Tigray People's Liberation Front's area of retreat during the 1980s guerrilla war against the Mengistu-regime (cf. Hammond 2002). Thus the local population treats the refugees from Eritrea in a hostile way, defending 'its' land against the refugees, while eagerly selling natural resources instead of sharing them. Obviously the local population is supposed to assist as loyal and efficient watchdog in the spatial control of the refugees – besides the formal prohibition to leave the camp without permit. Even though the camp is not fenced, there is an imaginary line, separating the camp inhabitants from their surrounding. A nearby checkpoint controls the in- and efflux rigorously to prevent refugees from submerging in Addis Ababa. Local, semi-official militia men patrol through the camp. „It is a highly political camp" says one of the humanitarian workers, comparing Shimelba to other refugee camps in Ethiopia. The concerned Ethiopian security agencies fear the infiltration of their Eritrean counterparts.

---

[15]   It has to be stated that basic security measures for agencies' staff like fences and guards are usual measures of protection of staff working in refugee camps and a standard requirement for all UN-agencies operating in UN-security phase III areas.

[16] A considerable amount of the urbanites are so-called AMCE (pronounce amitshe), children of Eritrean immigrants in Ethiopia, who grew up in urban Ethiopia, mostly Addis Ababa, but have been deported to Eritrea during the border war 1998-2000. They name themselves after the Automotive Company of Ethiopia, a bus and lorry manufactory in Gerji/Addis Ababa, assembling imported spare parts, alluding to their descent tending to result in exclusion from both countries' societies. Ironically these young AMCE, who have been among the first to flee, have now returned as refugees in the country in which they grew up and from which they have been forcibly deported.

Alula calls his stay in Shimelba a „physical and mental imprisonment" in which 'individual freedom' has no space. He is a former Eritrean liberation fighter and musician, who carefully expressed critique in some of his songs performed in Asmara – and therefore left three years ago, fearing persecution and arrest. Since then he claims to be an artist solely and to refrain from political activities. These days Alula is anxiously waiting to be listed for resettlement. While some signs from the camp administration back his hope on some days, he feels lost and desperate on others. In his song „Individual Freedom", which he performed on a concert in the camp, he expresses future hopes and current problems:

> „Thanks country for asylum
> and thanks UNHCR
> for sheltering my life.
> But I am not living enough,
> still thinking to resettle my life
> to forget suffering.
> The future will be fine,
> please UNHCR save my golden time
> for what I need: individual freedom
> to solve my tangled problem,
> to jar [sic!] in my artistic frame.
> So I['m] begging again and again
> to those capable to fulfil my vision."

Alula's song describes the refugees' indefinite waiting and persistent hope for progress in their slow resettlement processes and sudden realisation of their anticipated life, postponed into a fictional future and only dreamed of in the present. His song hints at the specific role of time and space in camp life and construction of the refugees' role as a dependent recipient of humanitarian assistance and donations (cf. Malkki 1995; Kibreab 1999). According to Michel Agier their classification as victims...

> „[...] makes them, from a humanitarian standpoint, *nameless*, in the sense that no identity referent is supposed to affect the support provided to the physical maintenance of the victims (security, health, food); this care is aimed at persons belonging indifferent[ly] to factions, regions or states which may be friendly or hostile. Thus the humanitarian system induces the social and political non-existence of the recipients of its aid. Recognizing in principle only 'victims', refugee camps are spaces that produce a *problématique* of identity[...]" (Agier 2002: 322).

Despite bureaucratic victimisation refugees remain acting subjects, who perform their agency even within their limited scope, still constructing their own biographies (cf. Appadurai 2005). The plea to the international organisation, to „save my golden time" shows the refugees' dilemma as a dilemma of time. In a 'dual perception of time' a present life full of privation is tolerated in favour of a promising future (Schiffauer 1999: 172). In this manner one hopes to realise an appropriate life in future, perceiving the refugee-status as only temporary on the one hand, while waiting in a transitory and provisional state, which can only be tolerated if one makes the best of it, on the other.

Still there are opportunities to create some life-quality at least, but money is rare. Jobs outside the camp are not accessible, so most of the camp inhabitants, who do not get regular support from relatives abroad, remain without income, but have plenty of time to hang around and use the camp's remarkable infrastructure – as much as they can afford it. During the rainy season some backyard gardening is possible, but practiced by rural migrants mainly, as the urbanites lack the necessary knowledge and motivation. Some 150 educated young men and women have been employed as social or community health workers by one of the camp's administrative agencies and thus can decisively contribute to the monthly budget of the commonly set-up self-help groups, formed by the single urban refugees. Few non-educated men are temporarily assigned with construction and maintenance works. While they get 10 Birr a day, one kilogram of tomatoes is 6-7 Birr, one kilogram of chickpea-made shiro-powder is 8-15 Birr.

So people, mostly men, usually sit around and smoke, drink tea, chew *khat* and listen to loud Ethiopian or Eritrean pop music. „Everything you want is available" says a writing on the wall in Texas Bar. In principle beer or soft drinks are available, but financially out of reach. The Abyssinian coffee ceremony, in 'regular' life usually performed on weekends, has become nearly a daily luxury (1 kg is 25 Birr). Filmon, a 40 year old engineer, comments: „That's what we do to kill time here". Kunama men, who used to plough their land and to herd their cattle, nowadays meet in front of their huts to play cards. Waiting drives you crazy, people say.

Affluent waiting time bears both, chance and curse. Isayas' story has become famous in the camp. He, now a man in his thirties, was among the unlucky group of refugees who managed to get to Malta, but have been deported to Eritrea in autumn 2002.[17] The Eritrean security forces imprisoned the deportees first on the Red Sea island Nokra in the ruins of an ancient Italian colonial prison and later on at Adi Abeito, near Asmara. Somehow he managed to get to Shimelba. Today he is hardly responsive. He sleeps on the bench of a tea house, as a 'madman' he is socially avoided and isolated. After a medical treatment did not bring any change, he was sent back into the camp to eke out his miserable existence.

At the other extreme Tesfai, the owner of a *dukwan*-shop, appreciates the time he has *nolens volens*. As a *warsay* in Eritrea, Tesfai tells us, he would have never had the chance to see his little son grow up. The child's grandparents in Asmara – contacted via siblings in the USA, who also enabled Tesfai and his wife to open up a little shop in Shimelba – can hardly believe, how one could get a child in a refugee camp, but Tesfai did not want to waste the years until their resettlement. 'Life is going on', he says, and compared to others it could be worse. Thanks to financial support and their small shop, he counts his little family to the camp's 'upper class'.

A wedding we had the privilege to visit, obviously a very rare event, can equally be understood in the context of the migrants' dilemma of when to live. To fetch the bride from

---

[17]The deportation from Malta became publicly known, when some of the deportees managed to flee Eritrea a second time. One of the deportees, a young man called Robel, was shot during one of several escape attempts from Adi Abeito. Asmarino.com: Robel is presumed dead. Was it necessary to suffer like that? An open letter to the people of Malta. 21.01.2004 (news.asmarino.com); EHRAG: Testimony of Eritreans Deported From Malta, Jailed in Dahlak. Provided by Elsa Chyrum. Translation by Awate.com. 22.07.2005 (www.awate.com).

her house the bridegroom's best men were able to organise one of the UNHCR's white off-road vehicles. Making the best of the means available – while being well aware of the improvised character – allowed at least temporary realisation of an appropriate life-quality. To this end a lot of people had contributed to the wedding. As the parents could not be present, close friends symbolically took over their roles. Besides the usual meat dishes even a wedding cake had been prepared. The music finally attracted neighbours from all sides and soon people were sweating from frolic dance in the midday sun. Distraction from monotonous daily life is most welcome, but additionally the wedding was considered to be 'real life' in the common make-shift existence, as one of the numerous guest commented.

Haimanot and Ariam, two 19 year old girls from Asmara and staunch members of Jehova's witnesses, have found own strategies to feel a bit more at home. In front of their little mud house they planted red and yellow flowers, colourful batik draperies embellish the neat interior. Mikael decorated the living and sleeping room, where he and his girl-friend live, with wall sculptures, chairs, a broad bed and even a faked fireplace in decent colours. Just the dried mud's uncomfortable stoniness remembers of the disguised provisionary arrangements. The other reality, however, is always there. „Here I am only living physically", Alula tells us in an interview. Indeed Shimelba offers its own reality „'hors-lieux', outside of places and outside of the time of a common, ordinary, predictable world, which itself tends to shrink as the spaces and the situations that deny it expand" (Agier 2002: 323). The refugee as a protagonist, makes her/his living in this setting. „We miss Asmara so much", say Haimanot and Ariam before we leave, asking to send 'Nutella', shampoo and green tea, unavailable in the camp's shops. Seemingly this means a bit of life-quality and 'home', converting the exile into a refugium.

Scarce supply with 'non-food items', like dinner set, plastic sheets and soap, and distribution of a standardised food ration do not even fulfil basic needs. Of the 16 kg of unground grain, people have to sell a third or even half to be at least able to buy firewood or charcoal to prepare a meal. Additional vegetables, oil, salt, sugar and coffee have to be purchased in one of the shops.[18] While cooking the common lentil dish *shiro*, Yonathan, a 30 year old young worker from Asmara, stated, he usually does not use the distributed food ration, but buys the Abyssinian flatbread *injera* for one Birr. As other young men, he did not yet learn to bake it himself.

As a consequence the ration does not last for the full month. Kunama mothers allow themselves two or even three meals a day in the beginning, but then have to add water to the sauce and strategically omit meals in the month's second half. Women's work, traditionally concentrating on house and garden, however, has not decreased. Firewood has to be fetched from the surroundings, always fearing physical attacks by the locals, and water has to be carried from the next public pump – for which one has to wait in long queues during the dry season. „All we then can do", Dehab, comments on their weak condition, often still worsened by endemic malaria and poor water quality, „is sleeping like the dogs".

---

[18]UNHCR and WFP support the refugees with basic materials. While UNHCR provides certain non-food items, WFP distributes food rations on a monthly basis. These include 16 kg unground grain, 1.5 kg fortified blended cereals, 0.9 kg oil, 0.15 kg salt, 1.5 kg lentils, and 0.45 kg sugar. In total the food ration follows the official WHO minimum standard in emergencies of 2,100 kcal per person per day, plus compensation for milling costs in the form of 20% additional cereal grains. Due to the need to sell grain in order to buy vegetables and firewood the WHO-standard remains an abstract figure.

Seemingly not everyone gets the chance to step beyond the camp. Ruta, a young and non-educated mother of two, became a widow, when her husband, who left the camp overnight and desperately tried to get to Europe by himself, drowned in the Mediterranean Sea. Afterwards one of her husband's brothers, living in the same house in Shimelba, tried to rape her, accusing her of his brother's death. While trying to defend herself, she does not seem to be in the position to raise sufficient interest for her case. Education and language skills, access to the camp administration, its formal and informal information and communication channels and a certain ruthlessness help to push one's 'case' – a resource largely controlled by informal political pressure groups, agitating in the camp. When we asked 65year old Abo Arafaini for an interview, he happily agrees. In the past seven years it is the first time for him to be asked about his situation.

The Kunama-speaking farmers were incrementally expropriated by the Eritrean regime, thus are now considered a culturally oppressed minority and granted with humanitarian 'group resettlement' to the United States – a doubtful fate, by the way. Arafaini, however, who refused to hunt young deserters of the Eritrean Defence Forces and therefore joined the Kunama-exodus in May 2000 as a Tigrinya-speaking individual, seems to be just far too old to be an attractive immigrant to the First World.

Reaching the First World

„Still I wake up in the morning and say to myself, wow, I am in the US" (Ariam, Zeberga's fiancée, April 2007, Washington D.C.).

„Everything was tough in that last few months that I have been [here. M]y brother got imprisoned and we didn't know where he was, my business [was] falling apart, I thought of going back but at this moment it looked too risky. As you know that repressive government is really killing the country and I was lucky to get out" (E-Mail Mussa, June 2007, Los Angeles).

While crossing countries and continents, hope to reach the First World is the crucial motivation: just tolerate any hardship, try to survive and get on until you arrive at your imagined final destination. Individual experiences and numerous narrations circulating among refugees state and confirm that there is nothing to expect and obtain from any other place than the First World, neither from African and Arab countries nor from Southern or Eastern Europe, including Russia. On arrival exhaustion and disillusion of one's expectations culminate with the need to speed up life in order to regain the past years lost „on the road" (Kastner 2007: 270).

„First of all, I was not having *big* expectations, I mean, there is always difficulties, problems everywhere, if it is 1st world or 3rd world. I was not expecting 'this heaven thing', but I was expecting that life will be better, that I can work and think independent from pressure from government 'back home', I mean you have freedom. I thought getting papers will be hard, but it was more complicated than hard" (Halima, April 2007, Minneapolis).

Halima arrived by plane in autumn 2002 with an official Eritrean exit visa, representing her country in an international youth meeting. Husband and daughter in Eritrea were considered to guarantee her return. Halima stayed. Finally making a far-reaching decision she chose to build up a new existence and bring in her husband Hussein and her daughter as soon as possible. She started to work as geriatric nurse, assembly line worker packing electronic calculators, as cashier in an electronics supermarket, gas station attendant, shuttle-bus driver at an international airport and as bank employee. Finally she got a job in a housing bank in another city, being recommended by an Eritrean friend. Accordingly she has finally been integrated into a large local network of Eritreans, Ethiopians and Somalis who to a large extent form the housing bank's lower staff (cf. Hannerz 1974). After being robbed in a hold-up – a welcome, that also Zeberga came to receive – Halima „stopped doing nice things as people sometimes take advantage of it" and withdrew from public life, where possible:

> „[...] if you interact with people you can make the circle bigger, I was making the circle smaller. It is really hard to trust people in that country. I don't take risks [...]" (April 2007).[19]

Soon after successful arrival migrants inevitably experience their transformation from refugees to potential supporters of those left behind 'back home' or in earlier and still distant stages of migration. In our informants' perception the best integration into US-American society is to build up one's existence as quickly as possible. Eager to find a job, to save money and pay back accumulated debts, to pursue further education and/or to finally set up a family – briefly, to get productive in as many fields as possible – newly arrived migrants suffer from formal restrictions and less formal rejection as well as from social pressure to succeed and to assist others.

> „First I have to assure myself that I am not deported, second try to find any job. [...] Feeling lonely is not a priority. Don't think of loneliness... so what, move your ass" (Zeberga, April 2007, Washington D.C.).

Zeberga, a young man in his late twenties, can be considered a lucky migrant. Still in Asmara he won a full scholarship to complete his Masters degree in Munich. With the help and support of his family he was able to pay $ 1,500 (today already $ 2000) for being smuggled to Khartoum via Tessenei and Kassala – a nowadays well-established service. While Eritrea does not issue exit visa to its *warsay*, Germany accepts visa holders to fly in from Khartoum. In his transitory one-year stay in Munich Zeberga got used to living alone in a Western country and to pursue a personal and professional life career in a foreign and not always friendly environment. Before being able to miss Munich, Zeberga had to learn to like it. At first he was even shocked:

> „The first thing I experienced was when you got to the U-Bahn you see people, they don't laugh they don't speak. Strange to me..., if you go to Bus No. 1, Bus No. 2 in Asmara and you see all these [people] talking loud, laughing, making jokes, even insulting, you enjoy that kind of atmosphere. But in Munich I felt like 'What is this? Why are people so sad?'" (April 2007)

His master-studies opened up the way to further studies in the USA. His successful application did not only lead to one of the best reputed universities in the United States, but also to a legal way of immigration and a happy reunion with his financée. Ariam belongs to the group of young women, who have been released from the national service in their mid-twenties. These enjoy – in the absence of men – the relative freedom to work in professions

---

[19]On the interdependency of ethnicity and social interaction see Abner Cohen 1974.

such as computer technology and internet administration and are able to apply for an exit visa. Ariam studied in the United States and is a greencard holder today.

Disillusion after arrival often emerges from administrative problems due to strict immigration laws, xenophobia, closed labour markets in the migrants professions, refusal by the local diaspora because of differing political ideals and perceptions and/or feared material stress. In Zeberga's case the United States did not offer a utopian paradise, too. Unforeseeable problems evolved: Being robbed in his first days made Zeberga deeply mistrust his new environment and home. This time his scholarship did not cover his daily living expenses. While being a student at an élite-university among co-students from the American and international upper classes on the one hand, he is an African immigrant on the other, living in a dark, very simple and still quite expensive basement, even if the landlord, an Eritrean taxi driver, offers a considerable rent reduction. Service jobs consume as much of his time as studying for exams. „They even stole my Sunday here," he says. While he enjoys meeting his fiancée once a week, he does not feel very content to be financially dependent on her. The knowledge to be privileged and to live a dream, that thousands of his age-mates in Eritrea do not even dare to dream, creates social pressure and stress. Zeberga's illegal emigration has soon been discovered by the authorities „back home" (as Eritrea is called here). Therefore his father – a former *yikealo* – was arrested until a friend of the family declared himself ready to pay a fine of $ 3,000, doubling the sum Zeberga already needs to pay back. And finally his legal status is connected to his studies. To stay in the United States he had to apply for political asylum, a Catholic Charity offered an experienced lawyer – for another $ 750. „Of course I would do everything again," he states, „if you want to change things you have to take the risk."

In September 2007 Zeberga asked us to visit his four under-age cousins with their mother, currently illegal in Addis Ababa after a long and difficult migration from Eritrea via Sudan, Uganda and Kenia. A young Saho in Shimelba-refugee camp turns out to be a cousin of Halima. Her sister's husband is expected, but at that time still in a screening and transfer centre. We promise to establish contact and to pass her telephone number to her relatives. A few weeks later, her telephone number – enabling direct contact to someone who made it successfully and perhaps may not dare to say no – seems to have become an attractive ray of hope for more than just her cousin. Waiting migrants clutch at a straw and ignore that she has to care for her baby in the USA as well as for her mother and a daughter still back in Eritrea, while still mourning for her husband, who tragically died in a traffic accident.

> „I just wanna know for how many people u gave my phone? Am gettin a lot of calls from ethio and malta??? I don't even know those who are callin" (Halima, November 2007).

How to grasp the refugees' agency?

The idea that human beings choose, decide and act and therefore are principally able to initiate change is not a new one.[20] Nevertheless individual action is subject to structural conditions beyond total control. Bourdieu's 'habitus'-concept tries to mediate between individual action and structure, describing human practice as the dialectical meeting point of *opus operatum* and *modus operandi* (Bourdieu 1987: 98), embedding individual perceptions, choices and decisions in a social history of self-produced orientations and boundaries. According to Bourdieu a habitus, perpetuating past experiences into the future, tends to become stolid, harmonising and self-assuring unless unforeseeable experiences do no longer fit into the already experienced or expected schemes of everyday-life.

In contemporary urban Eritrea young people are forced to reflect decisions in daily life, as the society in which they have grown up experiences – after Haile Selassie and Mengistu Haile Mariam – the third dictatorship in five decades. Successful life careers can just be imagined (Treiber 2005, cf. Appadurai 2005, Schiffauer 1991: 101-106). The parents' and grandparents' generation, whose life careers usually provide orientation ‚blueprints'[21], did also not live their lives under peaceful conditions. Every day in Asmara as well as in the countryside can – again – be one's last, if surprised by a military police patrol. Migration, risk as well as chance, becomes an increasingly chosen option, often supported by the parents' generation. Migration trajectories often turn into year-long projects leading from one stage to another, differing in time and place. As most individual Eritrean migrants enjoyed secondary school or even academic education and often have an urban middle class background, a common habitus can certainly be stated. Also it seems plausible to assume that these Eritrean migrants will develop a specific kind of habitus after reaching the First World, integrating their individual as well as collective migration experiences. It is however debatable whether the migration's different steps and stages offer enough stability to make a certain habitus apparent. While being restricted to a provisionary position in space-time, imagination is already ahead in time and geographically deterritorialised. Information and communication networks are spun around the globe. Far from a reified essential and victimising 'refugee experience' as criticized by Liisa Malkki (1995: 509-511), migrants strategically construct their route towards an imagined better world, preferably aiming for Northern Europe and North America. Their individual agency and range of available opportunities is widely restricted, but also subject to their own *bricolage*[22] (Agier 2002: 333, cf. Anderson 1975). Trust or mistrust are strategic decisions that mirror informal collective knowledge as well as individual experiences. The unsettled, constantly disappointing and transforming life-world during actual migration might thus be better explained referring to a concept of agency as proposed by Goffmann (1969:3) or Giddens (1990), stressing strategic decision-making within a certain spectrum of dispositions. Asif Agha calls agency „a capacity whereby social

---

[20] Luxemburg, Rosa: Einführung in die Nationalökonomie [1925]. 572-573. In: Luxemburg, Rosa: Gesammelte Werke. Bd. 5. Ökonomische Schriften. Berlin 1990: 524-778; Marx, Karl: Theses on Feuerbach [1888]. 28. In: Marx, Karl; Engels, Friedrich: Selected Works. Moscow 1986: 28-30

[21] Beck Ulrich: Individualisierung. In: Endruweit, G.; Trommsdorff, G.: Wörterbuch der Soziologie. 2. Aufl. Stuttgart 2002: 227-229

[22] Lévi-Strauss, Claude (1968): Das wilde Denken. [La pensée sauvage. Paris 1962] Frankfurt/M. 1968: 30

actors (whether individual or institutional ones) effectively transform a context of action and thereby enlarge the sphere of their enablements" (Agha 2007: 388).[23]

While the question of how migrants' agency is produced, conditioned and transformed would certainly need a lot more empirical research as well as more fundamental theoretical consideration, at least some vertices and paradoxical extremes, that Eritrean refugees face, can be given here: Spatial restrictions by legal documents, hostile surroundings and criminality contrast the refugees' global communication and mobility (Schuster 2005), boredom and temporary lack of perspectives alter with periods of rapid change and lead to a speedy ‚normalisation' of the anticipated life career. Individual trajectories are necessarily shaped by rivalry and selfish competition – use the opportunity before anyone else does! – but never detached from continuously changing social networks, mutual self-help relationships and reliable bonds of kinship and friendship – back and forth in terms of geographic distance as well as time and status (Schuster 2005, Collyer 2005).

> „I found someone who take[s] me to Cairo, it takes three days by 1000 USD, if I find 5 or 6 people he promised me, he will discount by half, I am looking for those g[u]ys, currently I am just doing brokerage [...]" (Biniam, December 2007, Khartoum).

References

Agier, Michel, 2002, 'Between war and city. Towards an urban anthropology of refugee camps.' In: *Ethnography*, Vol. 3 (3), pp. 317-341.

Anderson, Nels, 1975, *The American Hobo. The Sociology of the Homeless Man,* [1923] Leiden: Brill.

Appadurai, Arjun, 2005, 'The Power of Imagination.' In: Eryılmaz Aytaç et al. (Hrsg.), *Projekt Migration*, Köln: Dumont, pp. 50-61.

Bourdieu, Pierre, 1997, 'Ortseffekte.' In: Bourdieu, Pierre et al., *Das Elend der Welt. Zeugnisse und Diagnosen alltäglichen Leidens an der Gesellschaft*, Konstanz: UVK, pp. 159-167

Bourdieu, Pierre, 1987, *Sozialer Sinn. Kritik der theoretischen Vernunft,* [1980] Frankfurt/M.: Suhrkamp.

Cohen, Abner, 1974, 'Introduction. The Lesson of Ethnicity.' In: Cohen, Abner (ed.), *Urban Ethnicity*, London, New York: Tavistock, pp. ix-xxiv.

Collyer, Michael, 2005, 'When Do Social Networks Fail to Explain Migration? Accounting for the Movement of Algerian Asylum-Seekers to the UK.' In: *Journal of Ethnic and Migration Studies*, Vol. 31 (4), pp. 699-718

Donham, Donald L., 1999, *Marxist Modern. An Ethnographic History of the Ethiopian Revolution,* Berkeley, Los Angeles, Oxford: University of California Press.

Foucault, Michel, 1976, *Überwachen und Strafen. Die Geburt des Gefängnisses,* Frankfurt: Suhrkamp.

Giddens, Anthony, 1990, *Die Konstitution der Gesellschaft. Grundzüge einer Theorie der Strukturierung,* [1984] 2. Aufl. Frankfurt/M., New York: Campus.

---

[23] Agha, Asif: Comment on Paul Kockelmann: Agency. The Relation between Meaning, Power and Knowledge. 388. In: Current Anthropology. 48/3. 06. 2007: 387-388

Gilkes, Patrick; Plaut, Martin 1999, *War in the Horn. The Conflict between Eritrea and Ethiopia*, London: Royal Institute of International Affairs.

Glick-Schiller, Nina; Basch, Linda; Blanc-Szanton, Cristina, 1992, 'Transnationalism: A New Analytic Framework for Understanding Migration.' In: Glick-Schiller, Nina et al. (eds): *Towards a Transnational Perspective on Migration. Race, Class, Ethnicity, and Nationalism Reconsidered*, New York: New York Academy of Sciences, pp. 1-24.

Goffman, Erving, 1969, *Wir alle spielen Theater. Die Selbstdarstellung im Alltag* [1959]. Frankfurt/M.: Piper.

Hammond, Jenny, 2002, 'Garrison Towns and the Control of Space in Revolutionary Tigray.' In: James, Wendy; Donham, Donald L.; Kurimoto Esei; Triulzi, Alessandro (eds): *Remapping Ethiopia. Socialism and after*, Oxford et al.: James Currey, pp. 90-115.

Hannerz, Ulf,1974, 'Ethnicity and Opportunity in Urban America.' In: Abner, Cohen (ed.): *Urban Ethnicity*. London, New York: Tavistock, pp. 37-76.

Hannerz, Ulf, 2004, *Soulside. Inquiries into ghetto culture and community*, Chicago, London [1969]: University of Chicago Press.

Iyob, Ruth, 2000, 'The Ethiopian-Eritrean conflict. Diasporic vs. Hegemonic States in the Horn of Africa, 1991-2000.' In: *The Journal of Modern African Studies*, Vol. 38 (4), pp. 659-682.

Kastner, Kristin, 2007, ',My baby is my paper!' Familiäre Bindungen nigerianischer Migrantinnen auf dem Weg nach Europa.' In: *Afrika Spectrum*, Vol. 42 (2), pp. 251-273.

Kibreab, Gaim, 1999, 'Revisiting the Debate on People, Place, Identity and Displacement.' In: *Journal of Refugee Studies*, Vol. 12 (4), pp. 384-410.

Kibreab, Gaim, 2004, 'Pulling the Wool over the Eyes of the Strangers: Refugee Deceit and Trickery in Institutionalized Settings.' In: *Journal of Refugee Studies*, Vol. 17 (1), pp. 1-26.

Malkki, Liisa H., 1995, 'Refugees and Exile. From „Refugee Studies" to the National Order of Things.' In: *Annual Review of Anthropology*, Vol. 24, pp. 495-523.

Negash, Tekeste; Tronvoll, Kjetil, 2000, *Brothers at War. Making Sense of the Eritrean-Ethiopian War*, Oxford: James Currey.

Pool, David, 2001, *From Guerrilla to Government. The Eritrean People's Liberation Front*, Oxford: James Currey.

Riccio, Bruno, 2001, 'From ,ethnic group' to ,transnational community'? Senegalese migrants' ambivalent experiences and multiple trajectories.' In: *Journal of Ethnic and Migration Studies*, Vol. 27 (4), pp. 583-599.

Schiffauer, Werner, 1991, *Die Migranten von Subay. Türken in Deutschland, Eine Ethnographie*, Stuttgart: Klett-Cotta.

Scott, James, 1990, *Domination and the Art of Resistance. Hidden Transcripts*, Yale: Yale University Press.

Schuster, Liza, 2005, 'The Continuing Mobility of Migrants in Italy. Shifting between Places and Statuses.' In: *Journal of Ethnic and Migration Studies*, Vol. 31 (4), pp. 757-774.

Tesfaye, Lea, 2007, ,Rebuilding Asmara. Nutella, Grüner Tee, Shampoo und die Verwirklichung von Lebensqualität im Flüchtlingslager Shimelba.' In: *Hinterland*, Vol. 6, pp. 36-41.

Treiber, Magnus, 2007, 'Dreaming of a good life – Young urban refugees from Eritrea between refusal of politics and political asylum.' In: Hahn, Hans; Klute Georg (eds): *Cultures of Migration. African Perspectives,* Berlin: LIT.

Treiber, Magnus, 2005, *Der Traum vom guten Leben, Die eritreische warsay-Generation im Asmara der zweiten Nachkriegszeit,* Münster: LIT.

Notes on Contributors

Abdulkader Saleh Mohammad: holds an M.A. and a PhD degree in Sociology from the University of Münster. After lecturing in Sebha, Libya, for several years, he returned to his home country Eritrea in 1992. He participated in the institutional development process of the University of Asmara, where he was Professor of Sociology and head of the Department of Sociology and Social Work.

Abdulkadir, Asia: PhD des., is educational scientist and sociologist specialized on gender issues and violence against women particularly in crisis regions. In 2007, she completed her doctoral thesis on "The perception of Violence against Women in the Eritrean Military" which was supported with a scholarship of the Heinrich-Böll-Foundation. Currently, she is working as a consultant with local and international NGOs in the Horn of Africa.
Contact: asia_abdulkadir@hotmail.com

Dereje Feyissa: PhD in Anthropology, his dissertation was titled 'Ethnic groups and Conflict: The case of Anywaa-Nuer relations'. He is Research Fellow at Max Planck Institute for Social Anthropology, Halle/S, Germany. Main areas of research are ethnic conflicts in their inter-linkages within the regional and international arena. Contact: dereje_dfd@yahoo.com

Girke, Felix: is PhD candidate at the Max Planck Institute for Social Anthropology in Halle/Saale. He has done field research in Southern Ethiopia since 2003, and is affiliated with the South Omo Museum and Research Center (SORC) in Jinka, southern Ethiopia. He has also worked on rhetoric culture theory with Prof. Ivo Strecker and Dr. Christian Meyer.
Contact: girke@eth.mpg.de

Hirt, Nicole: Nicole Hirt holds an M.A. degree in Political Science and Sociology from the University of Tübingen and a PhD degree from the University of Hamburg. She conducted several field studies in Eritrea and taught as Assistant Professor at the Department of Political Science, University of Asmara, from 2001 – 2003. She is research fellow at the University of Hamburg and Institute of African Affairs/German Institute of Global and Areal Studies, Hamburg. Contact: nicolehi2001@yahoo.de

Johannsen, Anna Lena: (born Schmidt) holds a M.A. degree in Cultural Anthropology from the Uppsala University and post-graduated at the University of Maastricht and Padua with the degree of E.M.A. in Human Rights and Democratisation. Field studies on the topic of ethnical belonging and identity as well as on human rights of street children in Ethiopia. Contact: al@aljohannsen.de

Meckelburg, Alexander: has received his MA in Ethiopian Studies and Political Sciences at the University of Hamburg. He worked and undertook field research in Ethiopia: in Tigray, Addis Ababa and Gambella in the years 2001, 2002, 2005 and 2006. Main interests include conflict, social and population movements in the Horn of Africa with a special focus on Ethiopia. Contact: alexandermeckelburg@gmx.de

Medhane Tadesse: M.A., Director, Center for Policy Research and Dialogue (CPRD), external lecturer at the Department of Political Science and International Relations, Addis Ababa University, Ethiopia. Research interest in peace and security issues, specifically in Eastern Africa. Contact: cprd@ethionet.et

Merera Gudina: received his PhD in Development Studies from the Institute of Social
Studies, The Hague. Currently he is Assistant Professor of Political Science & International
Relations, Addis Ababa University and serves as Chairman for the Department. He is a
leading figure in the Ethiopian Opposition and Member of Parliament. Contact:
merera@psir.aau.edu.et

Mohammed Hassan Ibrahim: is the lead researcher at the Academy for Peace and
Development (APD), Hargeisa/Somaliland. He has worked with APD since 1999 and has
published extensively on governance, democratisation and the economy of Somaliland. Some
of his publications are available at http://www.apd-somaliland.org

Rosendahl, Christina: At the beginning of 2007 the author was a fellow at the Academy for
Peace and Development (APD) in Hargeisa, Somaliland. Today she is a participant of the
German Development Institute's (GDI) post-graduate programme for development
cooperation in Bonn, Germany. Contact: christina.rosendahl@hotmail.de

Seifert, Matthias: Matthias Seifert has completed his studies of Political Science and English
at the University of Freiburg in May 2007 and lives in Munich. Main areas of interest are
failed/failing states and Nation-Building as well as questions of (Good) Governance. He is
especially interested in alternatives to the classical Western model of democratic development
and in the diverging theoretical discourses of Governance as developed in the OECD-
countries and the development-oriented discourse. Contact: matzeseifert@gmx.de

Smidt, Wolbert: M.A., doctoral dissertation in social science, researcher at the Ethiopian
Studies Unit, Asien-Africa-Institut and Political Science Department, Hamburg, guest lecturer
at Mekelle University and at the École des Hautes Études en Sciences Sociales, Paris.
Contact: wolbert_gc@hotmail.com

Sommer, Monika Maria: M.A., lawyer (bar-exam), doctoral candidate at the Department of
Political Science, University of Hamburg, is currently research associate at the Department of
Political Science and International Relations at the Addis Ababa University (AAU). She
earned her European Masters in Mediation (E.M.A.) at the Institut Universitaire Kurt Bösch
in Sion, Switzerland. Her research interest is on conflict transformation and the inclusion of
local capacity and potential into processes of peace-making. Contact: monika@msommer.de

Terlinden, Ulf: is a political scientist specialized on governance and conflict issues in the
Horn of Africa Region. He pursues his PhD on Governance in Somaliland, supported with a
scholarship of the Heinrich-Böll-Foundation. Previously, he undertook field research in
Somaliland as part of the project on "State Failure and Local Governance in Afghanistan and
Somaliland", funded by the German Foundation for Peace Research. His publications are
available at http://www.ulf-terlinden.de

Tesfaye, Lea: is a student of social anthropology, law and sociology at Munich University.
She is especially interested in the region Horn of Africa, in the work of international relief
organisations as well as in the field of refugee and migration studies. She recently published
"Rebuilding Asmara. Nutella, Grüner Tee, Shampoo und die Verwirklichung von
Lebensqualität im Flüchtlingslager Shimelba" (Hinterland, Vol. 6, 2007: 36-41).
Lea_corvo@hotmail.com

Tetzlaff, Rainer: Prof. em., Dr., Institute of Political Science in Hamburg, member of the
Centrum für Globalisierung und Governance (CGG), currently serves as lecturer at the

prestigious Jacobs University Bremen. He looks back to a rich academic career in his fields of research on Africa and issues of development. Contact: prof@rainertetzlaff.de

Treiber, Magnus: Magnus Treiber is currently teaching at the Institute of Social Anthropology and African Studies, University of Munich. His work focuses on Asmara's youth milieus and the current Eritrean migration to neighbouring countries, Europe and the United States. His doctorate has been published under the title "Der Traum vom guten Leben. Die eritreische warsay-Generation im Asmara der zweiten Nachkriegszeit" (Münster 2005). Contact: griasna@hotmail.com

Venkatamaran, M: M.A., M.Phil., Ph.D, earned his Doctoral Degree from the University of Madras in South India with specialization on China and Southeast Asia. Later he branched out to teach and research on the Horn of Africa and published several related research papers. He served as Assistant Professor of Political Science at the University of Asmara between 1999 and 2004, followed by his current assignment as Associate Professor of Political Science and International Relations at the Addis Ababa University. Moreover, he was visiting professor at the Universidad de las Americas, Puebla, Mexico in 2005. Contact: venks44@yahoo.com

Weber, Annette: PhD des., currently researcher at the German Institute for International and Security Affairs (SWP), Research Division Middle East and Africa. Her current research interests are focused on conflict in Somalia, Darfur and Sudan, interconnectedness of conflicts and regional stability in the Horn of Africa. Contact: Annette.Weber@swp-berlin.org

Afrikanische Studien

Manfred O. Hinz, F. Thomas Gatter (Eds.)

Global Responsibility – Local Agenda

The legitimacy of modern self-determination and
African traditional authority

LIT

Fred Krüger; Georgia Rakelmann;
Petra Schierholz (Hg.)
Botswana – Alltagswelten im Umbruch
Facettes of a Changing Society
Bd. 14, 2000, 224 S., 15,90 €, br., ISBN 3-8258-4671-7

Deutsch-Madagassische Gesellschaft e. V.
(Hg.)
**Madagascar: Perspectives de Développe-
ment**
Croissance de la Population et Croissance
Economique contre Sauvegarde de la Nature
Bd. 15, 2000, 344 S., 20,90 €, br., ISBN 3-8258-4807-8

Joe L. P. Lugalla; Colleta G. Kibassa
Urban Life and Street Children's Health
Children's Accounts of Urban Hardships and
Violence in Tanzania
Bd. 16, 2003, 176 S., 20,90 €, br., ISBN 3-8258-6690-4

Christoph Haferburg;
Jürgen Oßenbrügge (Eds.)
**Ambiguous Restructurings of Post-
Apartheid Cape Town**
The Spatial Form of Socio-Political Change
Bd. 17, 2003, 200 S., 20,90 €, br., ISBN 3-8258-6699-8

Manfred O. Hinz; F. Thomas Gatter (Eds.)
Global Responsibility – Local Agenda
The legitimacy of modern self-determination
and African traditional authority
In various African countries, governments are forced to accept and/or establish decentral structures
in order to facilitate ways in which the poor sections of their population might gain influence on
and access to development resources. Yet, there is
confusion about the role and functioning of such
decentral structures as well as about sustainable
political approaches to the top down transfer of
government power in the context of local agendas. The book highlights major aspects of the legitimacy of local power as presented by modern
self-government structures as well as traditional
communal authorities. Although the main focus is
placed on Southern Africa (Namibia, South Africa,
Botswana), examples from other regions (Ghana,
Democratic Republic of the Congo) are also put into perspective.Contributors: B. Benzing, Th. Gatter,
G. Hilliges, M. O. Hinz, H. Kammerer-Grothaus,
B. Katjaerua, E. Okupa, N. Olivier, B. Oomen,
H. Patemann, D. Quintern, D. Schefold, G. Stuby,
G. Tötemeyer, Ö. Ülgen, M. Wulfmeyer.
Bd. 18, 2006, 288 S., 25,90 €, br., ISBN 3-8258-6782-x

Eva-Maria Bruchhaus (Ed.)
Hot Spot Horn of Africa
Between Integration and Disintegration
Bd. 19, 2003, 208 S., 19,90 €, br., ISBN 3-8258-6835-4

Michael M. Cernea ;Kai Schmidt-Soltau
(Eds.)
**Biodiversity Conservation versus Resettle-
ment in Rainforests**
Balancing Environmental and Social Su-
stainability
Bd. 20, Frühjahr 2008, ca. 104 S., ca. 9,90 €, br.,
ISBN 3-8258-7030-8

LIT Verlag Berlin – Hamburg – London – Münster – Wien – Zürich
Fresnostr. 2 48159 Münster
Tel.: 0251 / 620 32 22 – Fax: 0251 / 922 60 99
e-Mail: vertrieb@lit-verlag.de – http://www.lit-verlag.de

Ludwig Gerhardt, Heiko Möhle, Jürgen Oßenbrügge,
Wolfram Weiße (Hg.)

Umbrüche in afrikanischen Gesellschaften und ihre Bewältigung

Beiträge aus dem Sonderforschungsbereich
520 der Universität Hamburg

LIT

Ludwig Gerhardt; Heiko Möhle;
Jürgen Oßenbrügge, Wolfram Weisse (Hg.)
**Umbrüche in afrikanischen Gesellschaften
und ihre Bewältigung**
Beiträge aus dem Sonderforschungsbereich
520 der Universität Hamburg
Hamburger WissenschaftlerInnen aus elf Fachrich-
tungen schlossen sich in den Jahren 1999 bis 2003
zu einem neuartigen Vorhaben interdisziplinärer
Afrikaforschung zusammen: Der vorliegende Band
bilanziert wichtige Ergebnisse des Hamburger Son-
derforschungsbereichs „Umbrüche in afrikanischen
Gesellschaften und ihre Bewältigung". Die Beiträge
beschäftigen sich unter anderem mit afrikanischen
Staatsbildungsprozessen in Geschichte und Gegenwart, mit der Rolle christlicher Kirchen und isla-
mischer Gemeinschaften im Übergang Südafrikas
zum Postapartheidsstaat sowie mit der Ausbildung
transnationaler Sozialräume in Urbanisierungs- und
Migrationsprozessen zwischen Afrika und Deutschland. Die Autorinnen spannen einen weiten Bogen,
der vom mittelalterlichen Äthiopien bis in die Gegenwart der zentralafrikanischen Konfliktregionen
und der postkolonialen Metropolen Europas reicht.
Bd. 22, 2006, 320 S., 19,90 €, br., ISBN 3-8258-7518-0

Anne Schröder
Crossing Borders
Interdisciplinary Approaches to Africa
Bd. 23, 2004, 240 S., 19,90 €, br., ISBN 3-8258-7787-6

Erik Bähre; Baz Lecocq (Eds.)
The Drama of African Development
The state, conflict, and modernization in the
20th century
Bd. 24, Frühjahr 2008, ca. 288 S., ca. 29,90 €, br.,
ISBN 3-8258-7790-6

Verena Böll; Steven Kaplan; Andreu Martínez
d'Alòs-Moner; Evgenia Sokolinskaia (Eds.)
Ethiopia and the Missions
Historical and Anthropological Insights
Bd. 25, 2006, 272 S., 29,90 €, br., ISBN 3-8258-7792-2

Jürgen Oßenbrügge; Mechthild Reh (Eds.)
Social Spaces of African Societies
Applications and Critique of Concepts about
"Transnational Social Spaces"
Bd. 27, 2004, 256 S., 24,90 €, br., ISBN 3-8258-7850-3

Paula Viterbo; Kalala Ngalamulume (Eds.)
Medicine and Health in Africa
Multidisciplinary Perspectives
In the last two decades, the implosion of African
economies under the burden of debt, the negative
repercussions of the structural adjustment programs, the crisis of legitimacy, civil wars, and the
collapse of some states resulted in a serious health
crisis across the continent. Newly emerging diseases, such as Ebola virus and HIV/AIDS, killed and
disabled millions. Some „old diseases", such as yellow fever, tuberculosis, and polio, have reappeared.
Malaria, cholera, and meningitis continue to kill
thousands. In many countries, the medical infrastructure has collapsed, while an increasing number
of physicians and nurses have migrated to more
hospitable places. Stigmatization of the affected
people has compounded on previous social and ra-
cial discrimination, and has affected the implementation of national and international public health
programs. The complexity of the situation requires
an interdisciplinary approach. Including contributions by historians, sociologists, anthropologists,
and biologists, this essay collection emphasizes the
social and cultural contexts of African health, paying particular attention to the history of the colonial
public health system and its legacy.
Bd. 28, Frühjahr 2008, ca. 304 S., ca. 29,90 €, br.,
ISBN 3-8258-9226-3

LIT Verlag Berlin – Hamburg – London – Münster – Wien – Zürich
Fresnostr. 2 48159 Münster
Tel.: 0251 / 620 32 22 – Fax: 0251 / 922 60 99
e-Mail: vertrieb@lit-verlag.de – http://www.lit-verlag.de

Manfred O. Hinz (Ed.) in collaboration with Helgard K. Patemann
The Shade of New Leaves
Governance in Traditional Authority. A Southern African Perspective
Omudile muua ohapo; epangelo liua ohamba. Freely translated, this proverb of the Ovakwanyama of
northern Namibia means: New leaves produce a good shade; the laws of a king are always as good as
new. The proverb paints a picture of wisdom to express the dialectical relationship between continuity
and change in customary law. Since royal orders are supposed not to change from one king to the next,
they are always as good as new, reads the explanatory note to the proverb by the anthropologist Loeb,
who recorded the proverb. Traditional authority is like a tree standing on its roots, rooted in the tradition
created by the ancestors of the ruler and the community. These roots remain firm, stable and unchanged,
not so the concrete manifestation of authority that changes and responds to changes of the environment.
This makes that new leaves are produced by the rooted tree. The new leaves are new and old. They are old,
because in structure, colour and their capacity to protect by giving shade, they are more or less like the
leaves of last year and the year before; they are new because they react to the challenge of seasons. The
Shade of New Leaves emerged out of an international conference on the living reality of customary law
and traditional governance held in Windhoek in 2004.

Bd. 29, 2006, 512 S., 39,90 €, br., ISBN 3-8258-9283-2

LIT Verlag Berlin – Hamburg – London – Münster – Wien – Zürich
Fresnostr. 2 48159 Münster
Tel.: 0251 / 620 32 22 – Fax: 0251 / 922 60 99
e-Mail: vertrieb@lit-verlag.de – http://www.lit-verlag.de

Michael Bröning, Holger Weiss (Hg.)

Politischer Islam in Westafrika

Eine Bestandsaufnahme

LIT

Michael Bröning; Holger Weiss (Hg.)
Politischer Islam in Westafrika
Eine Bestandsaufnahme
In der öffentlichen Debatte wird nur selten beachtet, dass „der" Islam nicht nur den Nahen- und Mittleren-Osten, sondern auch Afrika südlich der Sahara entscheidend prägt. Insbesondere in Westafrika ist der Islam eine bedeutende gesellschaftliche Kraft – mit ganz eigenen Ausprägungen. Doch welche Rolle spielt der Politische Islam heute in Westafrika? Wer sind die relevanten Akteure und welche Bedeutung haben Formen des „radikalen" Islam?Antworten auf diese Fragen liefert der vorliegende Sammelband mit Beiträgen von renommierten Autoren aus Großbritannien, den USA, Finnland, Mali und Deutschland.
Bd. 30, 2006, 224 S., 14,90 €, br., ISBN 3-8258-9349-9

LIT Verlag Berlin – Hamburg – London – Münster – Wien – Zürich
Fresnostr. 2 48159 Münster
Tel.: 0251 / 620 32 22 – Fax: 0251 / 922 60 99
e-Mail: vertrieb@lit-verlag.de – http://www.lit-verlag.de

Wolbert G. C. Smidt, Kinfe Abraham (Eds.)

Discussing Conflict in Ethiopia

Conflict Management and Resolution

LIT

Wolbert G. C. Smidt; Kinfe Abraham (Eds.)
Discussing Conflict
Proceedings of the Ethio-German Conference
on Conflict Management and Resolution,
Addis Abada 11 to 12 November 2005
This volume contains the papers presented at the
Conference 'Ethiopian and German Contributions to Conflict Management and Resolution' of
November 2005, Addis Ababa. The aim of this conference was to bring researchers and those working
in the practical field of conflict resolution together,
before the background of renewed internal and international conflict. Research in conflict resolution
mechanisms is one of the most hopeful fields in
modern social sciences. Local conflicts can have
devastating effects on the state and even involve the
international level. In turn, international conflict
can also destabilize society and create new local
conflicts. However, local conflict resolution mechanisms could be of a great importance even within
the international scene. This volumes examines the
experiences in Ethiopia and the impact the acquired
knowledge could have for future conflict resolution
and management.
Bd. 32, 2007, 296 S., 29,90 €, br.,
ISBN 978-3-8258-9795-6

Werner Zips (Hg.)
To BEE or not to be?
Black Economic Empowerment im neuen
Südafrika am Beispiel der Weinindustrie
Wie kaum ein anderer Wirtschaftszweig Südafri-
kas war der Weinbau bereits seit den Anfängen
Mitte des 17. Jahrhunderts durch krasse soziale Un-
terschiede geprägt, lange bevor das Konzept der
Apartheid erfunden und institutionalisiert wurde.
Darauf nimmt der Titel des Buches „Aparte Weine"
Bezug. Er soll mit seiner Doppelbedeutung auf die
historischen Disparitäten, Abhängigkeits- und Aus-
beutungsverhältnisse verweisen, zugleich aber auch
die bisherigen Errungenschaften der sozialen Transformation in der Post-Apartheid Ära ansprechen.
Diese sozialen Veränderungen sind zweifellos mit
dafür verantwortlich, dass südafrikanische Weine
auf den internationalen Märkten immer attrakti-
ver und erfolgreicher werden. Befreit von dem
ethischen Stigma der „aparten" (getrennten) ge-
sellschaftlichen Entwicklung und dem Wegfall der
Handelsschranken erhält das Wort „apart" zuneh-
mend den im Weinbau gebräuchlichen Sinn eines
angenehm schmeckenden Erzeugnisses.
Bd. 31, Frühjahr 2008, ca. 320 S., ca. 29,90 €,
br., ISBN-DE 978-3-8258-9819-9,
ISBN-AT 978-3-7000-0520-9

Didier Péclard; Caroline Jeannerat;
Eric Morier-Genoud
**Swiss Churches, Apartheid and South Afri-
ca**
The Case of the Swiss Mission in South Afri-
ca
vol. 33, Frühjahr 2008, ca. 344 pp., ca. 29,90 €, br.,
ISBN-DE 3-8258-9796-6, ISBN-CH 3-03735-009-1

Daniel Branch; Nic Cheeseman (eds.)
Our turn to Eat
Politics in Kenya Since 1950
Bd. 34, Frühjahr 2008, ca. 208 S., ca. 29,90 €, br.,
ISBN 978-3-8258-9805-2

LIT Verlag Berlin – Hamburg – London – Münster – Wien – Zürich
Fresnostr. 2 48159 Münster
Tel.: 0251 / 620 32 22 – Fax: 0251 / 922 60 99
e-Mail: vertrieb@lit-verlag.de – http://www.lit-verlag.de

Johannes Müller, Michael Reder (Eds.)

Africa and Europe

Co-operation in a Globalized World

Conference of Scribani – European Jesuit Network

LIT

Johannes Müller; Michael Reder (Eds.)
Africa and Europe
Co-operation in a Globalized World. Conference of Scribani – European Jesuit Network 2006
In Europe, Africa is often called the forgotten continent. The collapse of states, violent conflicts and natural disasters shape the public perception of Africa in Europe, while the political perspectives tend to
be grossly neglected. This book wants to challenge this image in the eyes of many people through a profound analysis of main aspects of African-European relations (e.g. economics, migration, HIV / AIDS). In
particular, it will be discussed what can be done to improve the relations between both continents and to
develop a constructive and genuine cooperation. The book is based on the presentations and discussions of
a congress of the Jesuit Scribani Network.
Bd. 35, 2007, 232 S., 29,90 €, br., ISBN 978-3-8258-0518-0

LIT Verlag Berlin – Hamburg – London – Münster – Wien – Zürich
Fresnostr. 2 48159 Münster
Tel.: 0251 / 620 32 22 – Fax: 0251 / 922 60 99
e-Mail: vertrieb@lit-verlag.de – http://www.lit-verlag.de